PENGUIN BOOKS

THE BATTLE OF LONG TAN

David W. Cameron received his PhD in biological anthropology in 1995 at the Australian National University and is a former Australian Research Council QEII Fellow at the Department of Anatomy & Histology, University of Sydney. He has conducted fieldwork in Australia, Europe, the Middle East and Asia. He is the author of several books on Australian military history and primate evolutionary biology and has published over 60 papers in internationally peer reviewed journals. He lives in Canberra.

T0359157

ALSO BY DAVID W. CAMERON

Bones, Stones and Molecules: 'Out of Africa' and human origins
(with Colin Groves)

Hominid Adaptations and Extinctions

25 April 1915: The Day the Anzac Legend was Born

'Sorry, lads, but the order is to go':
The August Offensive, Gallipoli 1915

Gallipoli: The Final Battles and Evacuation of Anzac

The August Offensive: At Anzac, 1915

The Battle for Lone Pine:
Four Days of Hell at the Heart of Gallipoli

Shadows of Anzac: An Intimate History of Gallipoli

Our Friend the Enemy: A Detailed
Account of Anzac From Both Sides of the Wire

The Charge: The Australian Light Horse victory at Beersheba

David W. Cameron

THE
BATTLE
OF
LONG
TAN

Australia's Four Hours of
Hell in Vietnam

PENGUIN BOOKS

PENGUIN BOOKS

UK | USA | Canada | Ireland | Australia
India | New Zealand | South Africa | China

Penguin Books is part of the Penguin Random House group of companies
whose addresses can be found at global.penguinrandomhouse.com.

Penguin
Random House
Australia

First published by Penguin Random House Australia Pty Ltd, 2016
This edition published by Penguin Random House Australia Pty Ltd, 2017

10 9 8 7 6 5 4 3 2 1

Cover and text design by Adam Laszczuk © Penguin Random House Australia Pty Ltd
Cover photograph © Australian War Memorial [ID number: FOR/66/0676/VN]
Typeset in Adobe Garamond Pro by Samantha Jayaweera,
Penguin Random House Australia Pty Ltd
Colour separation by Splitting Image Colour Studio, Clayton, Victoria
Printed and bound in Australia by Griffin Press, an accredited
ISO AS/NZS 14001 Environmental Management Systems printer.

National Library of Australia
Cataloguing-in-Publication data:

Cameron, David Wayne, 1961– author.
The battle of Long Tan / David W. Cameron.
9780143786399 (paperback)

Subjects: Long Tan, Battle of, Vietnam, 1966.
Long Tan, Battle of, Vietnam, 1966 – Anniversaries, etc.
Vietnam War, 1961–1975 – Participation, Australian.
Vietnam War, 1961–1975 – Campaigns.

penguin.com.au

CONTENTS

MAPS

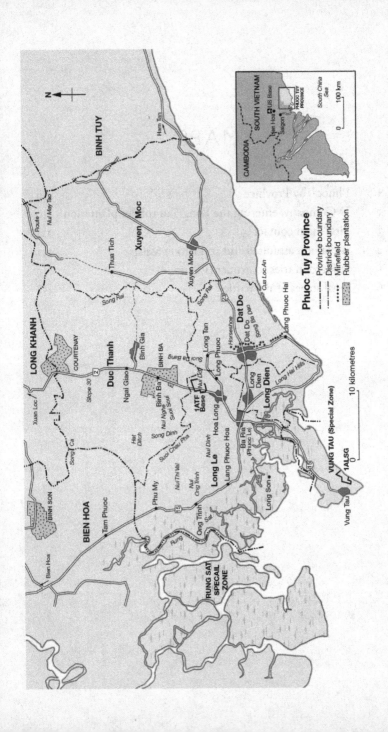

Phuoc Tuy Province

- ·—··—··— Province boundary
- — — — District boundary
- ·•••••• Minefield
- Rubber plantation

0   10 kilometres

N↑

Inset map

CAMBODIA

SOUTH VIETNAM

Xuan Loc
Ben Hoa · US Base
Saigon ·
PHUOC TUY PROVINCE

South China Sea

0   100 km

Place names on main map

BINH TUY

Ham Tan

Route 1
Nui May Tao

XUYEN MOC

Thua Tich

Xuyen Moc

LONG KHANH

COURTENAY

Binh Gia

DUC THANH

Song Rai

Song Rai

Cua Loc An

Lang Phuoc Hai

DAT DO

Long Tan
Long Phuoc
Dat Do
Song Ba Dao
Horseshoe

Nui Dat

1ATF Base

Long Dien

LONG DIEN

Long Hai Hills

Ngai Giao
Shine 30
Nui Nghe
Suoi Soi
BINH BA
BINH BA
Suoi Chau Pha
Nui Dinh
Song Dinh
Hat Ditch

Song Ca

Xuan Loc

BIEN HOA

BINH SON

Bien Hoa

Tam Phuoc

Phu My

Nui Thi Vai
Nui Ong Trinh

Ong Trinh
Sat
Rung

15

RUNG SAT
SPECIAL
ZONE

Long Le

Nui Dat

Hoa Long
Lang Phuoc Hoa

Ba Ria
(Phuoc Le)

Long Son

VUNG TAU (Special Zone)

15

1ALSG

Vung Tau

0

Part One
THE WAR

For you, intervention in . . . [Vietnam] will be an entanglement without end . . . The ideology that you invoke will not change anything. Even more, the masses will confuse it with your will to exert power. This is why the more you commit yourself there against Communism, the more the Communists will appear to be champions of national independence, the more they will receive help and first of all, that which comes from desperation. We French have experienced this . . . I predict to you that you will, step by step, become sucked into a bottomless military and political quagmire despite the losses and expenditure that you may squander.

President Charles de Gaulle to President John F. Kennedy, 1961

1

'. . . the grass needed cutting'

At 2.43 a.m., 17 August 1966, the 1 Australian Task Force (1 ATF) base at Nui Dat, 80 kilometres south-east of Saigon in South Vietnam, was shelled by Viet Cong mortar, artillery and recoilless rifle fire; the shelling ceased at 3.05 a.m.

The commander of D Company, 6th Battalion, Royal Australian Regiment (6 RAR), Major Harry Smith, was lying in his cot after sharing a few beers with some visiting US fighter pilots at what went for the officers' club when he heard the 'pop, pop, pop, pop' of mortars – 30 seconds later, the mortar bombs and shells came in. 'All hell broke loose as officers, NCOs [non-commissioned officers] and soldiers shouted orders to take cover and prepare for attack. I rushed out of my tent, boots on the wrong feet. Cursing, I ran 50 metres across to the company headquarters command post, standing the company to their weapons pits and awaiting further action and orders.'[1]

One of Smith's officers, Lieutenant David Sabben, commanding 12 Platoon, was with his men out in the forward defence line when the bombs and shells exploded some distance from his position; he, like many others, took compass bearings of the enemy firing positions and provided them to company headquarters, who relayed them to the battalion. One of his NCOs, Corporal Kevin Miller, who commanded 8 Section, had been manning an M60 machine gun close to the perimeter. He had moments earlier woken his relief and put him on the gun. He recalled it was soaking wet because of the rain 'and I just wrapped up in a cot and wet blanket and thought I'd try and get some sleep and I heard the popping in the distance over towards Long Tan and then I heard the shells coming in over the top of us . . . and then hitting the Task Force . . . and one dropped short, not that far from us . . . I started to wake up my blokes, because some of them were still asleep . . . it was pitch black and they were bumping into rubber trees and I told them to get into their slit trenches . . . we jumped into the trenches [which were] half full of water.'[2]

Another of Sabben's men, Private Terry Burstall, recalled how 'inside the rubber . . . it was quite dark and in vain we strained our eyes to see . . . we could hear the mortars letting go – a PUMPH, PUMPH sound'.[3] Close by, Private John Heslewood, also of Smith's company, recalled hearing the standard 'Bang, bang, bang' of what he believed to be their own artillery, but this time it was followed by a 'thump, thump, thump' as the enemy shells and bombs came in exploding some distance away from A Company's lines.[4] Also in the forward location, out beyond the wire and just south of Nui Dat, was a New Zealand standing patrol under the command of Sergeant Richard Wilson of 161 Battery; with him was signaller Patrick Duggan, who recalled the first shells and bombs that came in sounding 'not unlike . . . an express train approaching . . . and after a short pause which gave you time to ponder where it might fall, you'd hear that oncoming-train whoosh and the thud of the burst'.[5]

Corporal Robin Jones of B Company, 6 RAR had just finished sentry duty in his weapons pit; he was taking off his boots when he heard the sound of mortar bombs popping to the east of the base, quickly followed by explosions to the south-west of his location in and around Nui Dat hill, which was the location for the Special Air Service (SAS). He left in one hell of a hurry, minus his boots, yelling out to those around him that they were being mortared and to get under cover.[6] Now Australian mortar fire begun to illuminate the base's 10-kilometre perimeter. Jones recalled that the 'light cast eerie shadows, moving through the rubber trees. Our eyes looked everywhere at once. Seeking out shapes or movement. We were certainly "on our toes".'[7] To the relief of those who could look into the momentary light defining no-man's land, there was no sign of any enemy movement – but they also noted that the grass was thick and high. Just outside of the base perimeter at a listening post, Corporal Ross McDonald and a few of his men from D Company, 6 RAR had a perfect view of the incoming and outgoing shells and mortar bombs. He recalled that 'with the mortars coming in and the artillery going out, it was quite an experience'.[8]

Most others in the base were also rushing from their tents carrying their gear, heading for the flooded weapons pits, while the officers took up their positions at the command posts. As the first shells and bombs came in, Captain George Bindley of 103 Field Battery recalled that they arrived 'with a roar like flying kerosene tins filled with loose stones'.[9] As he rushed from his tent to his battery, another round came in and he turned to see the tent 'shrouded in smoke rolling down from the tree bursts'.[10] Private David Buckwalter and his mate Private Peter Ericson were attached to the 1st Reinforcement Unit and remembered hearing Buckwalter's NCO yelling just before the first round exploded: 'Incoming mortar fire! Into the pits!' Within seconds, mortar bombs were exploding all around them.[11]

Major Brian McFarlane, commanding C Company, 6 RAR, recalled how his company command post was at this stage just a 3-metre-square hole in the ground, 2 metres deep, with three levels – more by 'accident than design. The lowest had become a drainage sump which was full of water. The main bottom was slushy, and there was a higher part on which you could stand to see out over the countryside. On that bit we saw by the starlight the extraordinary sight of Sergeant [Paul] "Blue" Pearce, stark bollocky naked except for a steel helmet, talking on his radio to his platoon of six mortars located near battalion headquarters.'[12]

Those sick and injured at the regimental aid post were helped into the weapons pits to take cover. One of these was Private Mick Levin of A Company, who was suffering from a severe case of pyrexia and was more concerned about getting to the latrine. During the shelling and bombing he turned to a medic and said, '"Listen, mate, if I don't get out of this pit, I'm going to shit myself right here". Reluctantly, the medic let me go to the thunderbox. After that, I was too tired and crook to care about mortars or anything else. I just staggered back to bed.'[13] Similarly, Private Ken Tronc, of D Company, recalled making his way down to the perimeter and coming across Sergeant James 'Paddy' Todd. The private asked what he should do and was told to go back to bed. 'So I went back, put on my steel helmet, and went back to sleep.'[14]

Some of those from the signals squadron were not overly concerned, as recalled by signaller Neil Tonkin: 'When we were first mortared at Task Force headquarters we were all so "green" that no one got into their personal weapon pit except for Alex Fracas. Some members even ran to the diggers' canteen to get a beer to keep them occupied. At the time we thought Alex was a bit stupid, but looking back he was the only sensible one.'[15]

Not all, however, recognised the shelling for what it was. Recently arrived 23-year-old US Army Lieutenant Gordon Steinbrook of the attached US 35th Artillery was in his tent and recalled that 'the night was stormy, with wind blowing and rain falling heavily. About 3.00 a.m., my tent mate and I awakened to what we thought was extremely violent thunder and lightning. We got up off our cots, walked around a little, noticed bright flashes outside that we took for lightning, and then went back to bed. The next morning we awoke to discover that the entire Task Force base camp had been mortared and had taken recoilless rifle fire as well. Not far from our own area several 82mm Chicom [Communist China] mortar shells had hit.'[16]

Similarly, an exhausted Private Alan Parr of 12 Platoon, D Company, 6 RAR had fallen asleep hours earlier and slept through the whole thing. He later wrote that nearly every night at Nui Dat there were Anzac artillery rounds and mortar bombs being fired at 'different grid positions at different intervals throughout the night so, unless you were in the Company or Platoon CPs [command posts] with a radio that night or they landed very close to your area and you were in the FDL [forward defensive location], you wouldn't take much notice (and especially if you were a sound sleeper)' – like Private Parr.[17]

Even before the mortaring of the base, 1 Field Regiment, Royal Australian Artillery had been conducting a routine harassment and interdiction mission. They weren't aiming at a specific Viet Cong target but were shelling to keep the enemy on edge and make sure anyone out there kept moving through. Within minutes the officers and gunners abandoned their fire plan and conducted counter-battery fire using compass bearings supplied by New Zealand officer Major Harry Honnor and other reports that were coming in. Sergeant Graeme Smailes of 103 Battery recalled how they managed to get off a few rounds as the enemy mortar bombs continued to explode close to their position. No one had given it much thought and they continued to fire, but the gunners kept their heads down a bit further than was the norm, as some of the bombs were now exploding 'too close for comfort'.[18]

Major Smith reckoned that an artillery piece was firing three times in between the mortar fire – he would later be proven right as shells from a Japanese World War II vintage small mountain gun were found. Normally, radar from the detachment of the Australian

131 Divisional Locating Battery, commanded by Captain Barry Campton, would zero in on the enemy positions, but the dispersed pattern of firing and its intensity made it difficult to gauge the accuracy of the pinpointed position. Firing was coming in from at least three directions, each with multiple weapons – not to mention the Anzac batteries firing missions from 1 ATF.[19] However, Captain Campton had previously produced a counter-battery fire plan harking back to the basics developed during World War I, which proved to be very accurate.[20]

The Australian and New Zealand gunners did not cease firing until 4.10 a.m. In all they fired 480 shells. Captain Bindley recalled that the rest of the night passed quickly and all were relieved to see the dawn. The morning was bright, with 'clear blue skies vividly highlighting the green vegetation and still-wet laterite'.[21] Perhaps of even greater relief to him and others was that there was no sign of any further enemy activity. He recalled the Task Force commander, Brigadier David Jackson, making an appearance at 103 Battery; he was 'clearly delighted by our effort and said so', although 1 Field Regiment commanding officer Lieutenant Colonel Richmond Cubis could not help but notice his 'gun position was untidy and the grass needed cutting'![22]

Earlier, A Company – who were about 4 kilometres east of Nui Dat – had an uneasy night in the field, having spent two days and nights out on patrol. Hearing the mortar attack, at first they thought they were being targeted. Captain Charles Mollison had replaced Major Peter Smeaton a few weeks earlier as company commander when the major was wounded during Operation Hobart. Mollison later wrote that when the first bombs were fired, his heart sank. He cursed his decision not to dig in for the night and waited for the bombs to start exploding around him and his men. He recalled: 'Ten seconds, 20 seconds – then the explosions! But the bombs were not landing on us. I grabbed the handset of the battalion radio. "What the hell is going on?" I called. "It sounds like a regiment of mortars firing." Captain Les Peters, our mortar-platoon commander, was on duty in the battalion HQ command post. "Give us a bearing quickly," he yelled. "They are coming down on us!". . . I hurriedly took a compass bearing on the sound of the mortars and passed this information to Les.'[23] Mollison's position was almost at right angles to the line of fire, which enabled Captain Peters to better direct the fire of his mortars and artillery against the enemy firing positions.

Within minutes the response from the Anzac gunners became of concern to Captain Mollison and his men, as their shells were falling close by. Corporal Ross Smith, commanding 8 Section, 3 Platoon, recalled that as the Anzac artillery shells and mortar bombs started firing back at the enemy, the explosions seemed way too close for comfort. He and the others 'clung to the ground and hoped they knew where we were. We also prayed for no "drop shorts". We had already lost four wounded from a New Zealand Artillery drop short on the previous operation.'[24] Just before dawn, Corporal Smith and his men heard the sound of movement to their front, not knowing if it was friend, foe or animal; his section held their fire. At first light Smith went forward and saw 'Ho Chi Minh sandal' footprints (from footwear made from tire treads), representing a small party of five to ten individuals, possibly one of the mortar teams. Captain Mollison and the men of A Company were now ordered by the Task Force commander to retrace their steps to the hills north-west of their present position, close to the elongated hill called Nui Dat 2.[25]

Meanwhile, 7 Platoon, C Company, 6 RAR, under the command of Lieutenant Mike Gillespie, had spent the night in a harbour position south of Nui Dat. At first light, they were to conduct search operations to the south before returning to base, while 9 Platoon, C Company, 6 RAR, commanded by Lieutenant Stewart Penny, would conduct search operations mounted in armoured personnel carriers (APCs) to investigate other suspected mortar firing positions south-west of the base. The men of B Company, 6 RAR, were to conduct a patrol east of the base in and around the Long Tan rubber plantation to try to locate the enemy mortar teams or at least their firing positions.[26] The men of D Company, 6 RAR, who had the day before conducted a patrol of the Long Tan plantation, would remain at the base to help defend it – they were apparently the lucky ones.

2

'We have come to reclaim our inheritance'

Decolonisation – or the lack of it on the part of the French after World War II – set in motion what would result in the Second Indochina War, more commonly known as the Vietnam War.

France had begun to incorporate present-day Vietnam, Laos and Cambodia aggressively into its colonial empire in 1853, finally conquering the region in 1893 and establishing French Indochina. The region was governed solely for the benefit of Paris, with the local market flooded with French goods, and colonial administrators forcing villagers off their land to work in large plantations and mines while at the same time making them pay exorbitant taxes and high rents. The French turned the village culture into a class system with themselves at the top and the Vietnamese at the bottom. The traditional Confucian way, where education was paramount and dictated a person's social status and position, was replaced by a class system based on economics and race. The French tried to deny the Vietnamese their identity further by imposing the French language, culture and religion (Catholicism), and suppressing indigenous political movements.[1]

Even so, a number of clandestine political parties were

established, including the Indochina Communist Party (ICP), which was formed in 1930 by the charismatic Vietnamese revolutionary Ho Chi Minh. During this period Ho was based in either China or Russia, and often eliminated his perceived political rivals within Vietnam by slipping their names to the French authorities. The main aims of the ICP were national independence and social equality. In the 1930s the party remained insignificant, with just a few hundred members scattered throughout the region. During this period a directive from Moscow to the ICP stated that the communists in Indochina were to downplay their nationalist anti-colonial campaign – and went as far as to place the ICP under the French Communist Party! This was designed to shift the emphasis from 'anti-colonialism to the proletariat's struggle against capitalism'.[2] Not surprisingly, the directive was ignored by the ICP. World War II and the defeat of Japan would provide an important stepping stone for Ho and his anti-colonial stance.

The Japanese took advantage of France's surrender to Germany in 1940 by helping to establish a Vichy French colonial government in Indochina that did Japan's bidding. The Japanese were keen to stop the British and Americans (who were then not at war with Japan) from supplying Nationalist China with war material via Burma and northern Indochina. Unlike the French administrators, Ho Chi Minh became a leading opponent of the Japanese during the war, forming in 1941 the Viet Minh (Front for the Independence of Vietnam). The goals of the Viet Minh were the removal of the Japanese and their Vichy French 'lackeys', and the formation of a free and independent Vietnam. Many who joined the Viet Minh were not communists but Vietnamese nationalists – indeed, the term 'Viet Minh' became synonymous with 'patriotism'.[3] During the war, Ho focused on recruitment and organisation rather than conducting major military confrontations against the Japanese and French. Towards the end of the war, however, Japan was forced to invade Indochina after the liberation of Paris in 1944.

The Viet Minh's main area of operations during this period was the northern mountainous provinces of Tonkin, close to the Chinese border. Ho's revolutionary teaching had taught him that there were three distinct phases in a successful insurgency operation: the passive phase, the active phase and the counteroffensive phase. He was at that time in the passive phase, building and husbanding his forces and focusing on firmly establishing the Viet Minh organisationally at the village and township level, while minor military operations were undertaken against the Japanese with some assistance from the US. Ho's main operational tactics were based around propaganda and assassinations.[4]

With the defeat of Japan in 1945, Ho Chi Minh swung into action. Viet Minh agents took control of the villages and townships in the region of Tonkin, while in Hanoi, ICP officials occupied the vacated government buildings. On 2 September, Ho declared the creation of the Democratic Republic of Vietnam (DRV). He tried to downplay the communist character of his regime and movement by disbanding the ICP – to be replaced in 1951 by the Lao Dong Party (Vietnamese Workers' Party). While he had no mandate from the Vietnamese people to take control of the country, his opposition to the Japanese and French meant that many within Vietnam and beyond supported his declaration, including some in Washington.[5]

Earlier, as World War II was coming to a close, the Potsdam Conference of 1945 agreed that British-led Indian troops would temporarily occupy the southern parts of Vietnam to disarm the Japanese, while the nationalist Chinese would do the same in the north. This provided Ho Chi Minh with valuable propaganda material as he paraded himself as the sole representative of the Vietnamese people, sandwiched between the British and Chinese invaders. Meanwhile, with the end of the war the French had dispatched an expeditionary force to re-establish their colonial authority. French general Philippe Leclerc arrived in Saigon on 23 September 1945 and arrogantly announced: 'We have come to reclaim our inheritance.'[6]

The French soon made an agreement with Nationalist China, and within months the Chinese troops were leaving Hanoi and the north. While the French initially managed to extend some authority over south and central Vietnam, the north was another matter. The Viet Minh, with a steady stream of recruits, helped to bolster Ho Chi Minh's 'mandate'. With the French having returned, Ho returned to establishing independence by revolutionary means, invoking the 'active' phase. This dictated an intensification of insurgency actions, with the establishment of areas of operations and bases; the organisation of larger guerrilla units and a corresponding increase in the targeting of government and military infrastructure; and preparing the Viet Minh as a credible alternative government.[7]

The French came back to Indochina to conduct conventional military operations against the Viet Minh that equated to capturing and retaining territory, and killing as many of the enemy as possible. However, Ho and the Viet Minh were conducting a political insurgency that did not require capturing and holding territory but 'winning the hearts and minds' of the people – winning the war by sapping the will of the French to continue the fight, forcing them to acknowledge that the cost was just too great. To the Viet Minh, political values were crucial – not military operations. Borrowing from the Chinese communist leader Mao Tse-tung, Ho Chi Minh understood that 'to gain territory is no cause for joy, and to lose territory is no cause for sorrow'.[8] Also, relying on a war of attrition meant that for every Viet Minh killed in the struggle, two or three others would take his or her place. While in traditional military terms the French had some victories, the insurgents were able to conduct successful hit-and-run operations, disappearing into the safety of their jungle and mountain strongholds and more often than not leaving the French to lick their wounds.

The French had earlier appealed to the US to support their operations in Indochina, but American politicians and military strategists found themselves in a bind. While they were keen to support a European ally, particularly with the escalation of the Cold War in the late 1940s, most US policy-makers were opposed to the re-establishment of colonialism. Before the outbreak of the Korean War and the entrenched mindset of the 'domino theory', the conflict in Vietnam was seen as a small Asian nation striving for independence from its French masters. Indeed just years earlier, in 1943, President Fraklin D. Roosevelt had written to his secretary of war that he had seen the British ambassador to Washington and told him that 'it was perfectly true that I had for over a year expressed the opinion that Indochina should not go back to France . . . [which] has had the country . . . for nearly one hundred years, and the people are worse off than they were in the beginning'.[9]

However, all this changed when in 1950 the newly established communist regime in China and the Soviet Union both recognised the existence of the DRV, which Ho Chi Minh had proclaimed in 1945. While the western powers, including the US and Australia, recognised the independent states of Vietnam, Cambodia and Laos, they did not recognise the DRV as a legitimate government and feared a communist international alliance out for world domination.

By the early 1950s the counteroffensive phase of Ho's insurgency had begun, with overt attempts to topple the French colonial administration, including conventional warfare. During this time, General Vo Nguyen Giap emerged as the pre-eminent leader of Viet Minh forces. He soon had the French on the back foot, not only in terms of insurgency operations but with large-scale conventional military operations, finally resulting in the battle of Dien Bien Phu.

While peace talks were taking place in Geneva to settle the First Indochina War in late 1953, the French sought to bolster their bargaining position and foolishly sent paratroopers deep into Viet Minh territory, close to the Laotian border, at Dien Bien Phu. Completely underestimating the Viet Minh, the French knowingly occupied an isolated position in a valley, which enabled the Viet Minh to surround their position and occupy the high ground. The only way the French could be reinforced and resupplied was via a small airfield. They had wanted to bring on a decisive battle to bleed the Viet Minh white, but General Giap knowingly took the French 'bait' for what it was: a gift. He later wrote: 'The landing by the enemy of his airborne troops on Dien Bien Phu was advantageous to us. It laid bare the contradiction of the enemy between occupation of territory and concentration of forces.'[10] In essence the French had established an Asian Stalingrad, where they willingly played the role of the doomed German 6th Army. Giap did not attack immediately but prepared his positions and brought up sufficient heavy weapons, ammunition, supplies and reinforcements to help assure victory.

The battle for Dien Bien Phu commenced on 12 March 1954. It was not long before the Viet Minh artillery batteries (supplied by Communist China) made the French airfield inoperable; the garrison could be resupplied only by airdrops into an ever-shrinking French perimeter. It was now, with a likely communist victory about to occur, that the US considered a possible intervention on the behalf of the French. American policy had recently shifted back towards the French, with the creation of Communist China in 1949 and its involvement in the Korean War. However, any military intervention would require a coalition including Britain, Australia and New Zealand.[11] President Dwight Eisenhower's secretary of state, John Dulles, towards the end of the Dien Bien Phu crisis failed in a last-ditch effort to arrange air strikes against Giap's forces. He went so far as to declare the operation would extend into China if the US intervened on the behalf of the Viet Minh. Not surprisingly, the US allies baulked at this. Two weeks later, France suffered a humiliating defeat at the hands of General Giap. On 7 May the French surrendered the garrison, with over 12 000 French troops taken prisoner.[12] Ho Chi Minh ensured that the surrender was captured on film, with the sight of thousands of French prisoners marching into captivity being flashed onto cinema screens around the world.

The day after the French defeat at Dien Bien Phu, peace talks between France and the Viet Minh in Geneva took on a new urgency. The First Indochina War was coming to a close. The Geneva Accords of July 1954 merely represented an armistice and importantly did not approve a political or territorial boundary – there was no agreement for elections. However, while elections were listed as an addendum to the document, along with a military demarcation line designated at the 17th parallel, no party signed the addendum.[13] Even so, Vietnam was 'partitioned' along the 17th parallel. With the formation of the two 'nations', it was estimated that over a million people relocated north or south; the majority were Catholic Vietnamese, who fled south.[14] As stated in the Pentagon Papers, the actions of the Viet Minh were 'widely and genuinely feared, and many refugees took flight in understandable terror. The refugees were the most convincing support . . . that free elections were impossible in the DRV.'[15] The day after the Geneva Accords were signed in Paris, Dulles announced: 'the remaining free areas of Indochina must be built up if the dike against Communism is to be held'.[16]

3

'. . . whose heads they nailed to the nearest bridge'

While the north was now firmly under the control of Ho Chi Minh, the south was governed by the strident Catholic prime minister, Ngo Dinh Diem, who was seen by many as a proxy for the West. While the Viet Minh had established some legitimacy in coming to power by fighting the French and Japanese occupiers, the government in the south had been established by the French just before they left, using the Vietnamese emperor, Bao Dai (living in Paris), to appoint Diem, with the support of the US. It was not long before Prime Minister Diem removed the absent emperor and appointed himself president. The battlelines were drawn, as the US did not want to risk the desolation of South Vietnam (officially known as the Republic of Vietnam, or RVN) by an election that Diem would almost certainly lose. President Eisenhower was aware of the likely result, writing: 'I have never talked or corresponded with a person knowledgeable in Indochina affairs who did not agree that had elections been held . . . possibly 80 per cent of the population would have voted for the communist Ho Chi Minh.'[1]

The US had escaped the dilemma of trying to stop communism without serving the stench of French colonialism in Vietnam –

indeed, the French had been a surrogate army for US ambitions to stop the spread of communism in South-East Asia. The US now set a policy course of financial and military assistance to the increasingly corrupt, inefficient and brutal Diem regime that would ultimately lead to the Vietnam War. At first, Diem succeeded in smashing the armed gangs that had been raised by the French and were masquerading as military units, and managed to bring some parts of the south together as a more unified force, but soon he began to believe in his own infallibility and ignored his advisers, relying solely on his brother Nhu and Nhu's wife, who was known for good reason as the 'Dragon Lady'. The US increasingly needed to help legitimise the government of South Vietnam and its subsequent actions, supporting the inept and corrupt regime in the eyes of the domestic and international communities.[2]

In September 1954, the US was largely responsible for establishing the Southeast Asia Treaty Organization (SEATO), which comprised itself, Britain, France, Australia, New Zealand, Pakistan, Thailand and the Philippines. SEATO was viewed as a collective defence organisation in South-East Asia, a southern version of the North Atlantic Treaty Organization (NATO). The Geneva Accords, however, meant that South Vietnam, Laos and Cambodia were not eligible to be signatories. The US made it clear that the role of SEATO was to stem the growing tide of international communism in South-East Asia, which was aimed directly at China and North Vietnam. Indeed, it was during this period that Viet Minh insurgents in the south become known by the derogatory name 'Viet Cong' – meaning 'communist traitors to Vietnam'. Unlike NATO, SEATO was not overly significant in military terms: important states such as Indonesia and Malaya did not sign up; Pakistan was using SEATO against India with no real interest in supporting the organisation's aims; while France was a signatory, there was no way it would become embroiled in another war in South-East Asia; and, critically, it did not tie the US down to any joint military planning or operations.³ The real achievement of SEATO was that it provided the US with an international coalition that was calling for a stop to communist infiltration into South-East Asia – the Americans were seen not to be standing alone on this issue.⁴

Meanwhile, Diem's government was seemingly going out of its way to isolate large segments of the population and the international community. By January 1956, the south was effectively a police state, directing brutal measures against anyone who disagreed with the prevailing edicts of the president and forcing all opposition into 'the agonizing choice of self-imposed exile (if rich), total silence (if less fortunate and thus forced to remain in Viet-Nam), or armed resistance'.⁵

The regime also reinstated some of the most hated policies of the French. Truong Nhu Tang, who would later become the minister of justice in the Provisional Revolutionary Government in the south, recalled how in the countryside Diem 'destroyed at a blow the dignity and livelihood of several hundred thousand peasants by cancelling the land-distribution arrangements instituted by the Vietminh in areas they controlled prior to 1954 . . . Farmers who had been working land they considered theirs, often for years, now faced demands for back rent and exorbitant new rates. It was an economic disaster for them.'⁶ The growing stench from Diem's government, with its nepotism, incompetence and corruption, managed to isolate large segments of the population; only a small number of Catholic elites benefited from his power.

However, things were no better in the north – indeed, they were arguably far worse. Ho Chi Minh continued to summarily eradicate anyone who held different political views from his own. This included land 'reforms' that were based on the intimidation and suppression of landholders, which resulted in major crop failures. Land was confiscated, and peasants who owned just small parcels of land were branded 'landlords' – which was often a death sentence. After the unification of the country, the Vietnamese government would admit that about 172 000 people in the north were executed during this period.[7] General Giap said:

> We attacked the landowning families indiscriminately, according no consideration to those who had served the Revolution and to the families with sons in the [northern] army. We showed no indulgence towards landlords who participated in the Resistance, treating their children in the same way as we treated the children of other landlords. We made too many deviations and executed too many honest people. We attacked on too large a front and, seeing enemies everywhere, resorted to terror, which became far too widespread . . . Worse still, torture came to be regarded as a normal practice during party reorganization.[8]

As succinctly put by historian Mark Dapin, 'Ho was like Stalin's own Vietnamese Jesus, walking over lakes of blood to demonstrate his divinity. He cultivated an air of sanctity, and an almost holy asceticism, but he was less a socialist saint than a Comintern King Herod, a slaughterer of innocents.'[9] Even so, in the south, Diem's government had made it relatively easy for Ho to penetrate the provinces with propaganda and insurgents, supplying his growing cadres (local leaders) who were eagerly recruiting and invoking the action phase of his insurgency program.

The communists claimed to be liberating the people from the worst of the Diem regime. Many of the cadres were those who had earlier fled north with the partition of Vietnam; they were now trained and actively encouraged to go back to the south to conduct insurgency operations. They set about selectively targeting local government officials for assassination, killing schoolteachers, village leaders, police officers and members of the military, often in gruesome fashion. Assassination and intimidation continued to be the mainstay of those refusing to bend to the Viet Cong doctrine and often such killings were conducted in the presence of a whole village. Spectacular assassinations took place in and around the provinces of An Giang and Phong Dinh (Mekong Delta region). In the village of Thanh My Tay, 'armed men appeared in the dead of night, wakened the inhabitants, read a death sentence, and beheaded four young men, whose heads they nailed to the nearest bridge'.[10] The security question in the provinces had to be given top priority, but the regime would never come to terms with this issue, as the hinterland outside the heavily urbanised areas of Saigon and some other larger urban areas would mostly remain the domain of the Viet Cong cadres and their growing number of insurgents.

By 1959 the time was ripe for the counteroffensive phase of Ho's insurgency. As such, the North Vietnamese Central Committee of the Lao Dong Party authorised the use of protracted armed struggle to overthrow Diem and to stop US assistance from propping up his regime. The Viet Cong now set about building what would become known as the Ho Chi Minh trail, which cut through the eastern borders of Laos and Cambodia, allowing ready movement and infiltration of insurgents and supplies, north and south.[11]

In 1960, the Lao Dong Party established the National Front for the Liberation of South Vietnam (NLF) to coordinate the struggle against the RVN. The central committee announced that the NLF had been established to 'unite closely various classes of South Vietnamese patriotic population in the struggle against the Americans and Diem in accordance with the wishes of the South Vietnamese. This [move] securely guarantees that the Revolution in South Vietnam will quickly and successfully restore peace and carry out the unification of our fatherland.'[12] The communists of Ho Chi Minh in North Vietnam who formed the NLF were keen to ensure it was not seen for what it was – a communist insurgency organisation. Its prime purpose was to establish a single organisation around which the anti-Diem activity could cluster. It developed three main forces: self-defence teams and village guerrillas; province and district armed teams; and full-time troop units at the regional level.[13]

Reasons why individuals joined the NLF were many and varied – far from all of the members were communists. A broad spectrum of the population joined, representing various religious organisations, nationalists, political representatives, individuals from the professional and academic class, and urban and rural workers concerned with regional and local issues. That said, the NLF was certainly a proxy used by the Lao Dong Party to infiltrate non-communist groups that attached themselves to the nationalist ideals of the NLF, and to play one group off against another. The fundamental objective of the communists in the north in creating the NLF was to achieve political control of the area below the 17th parallel.[14]

Truong Nhu Tang, who had by now become a founding member of the NLF, recalled how President Diem and the RVN considered the veterans who had resisted the French and Japanese as 'rivals for power who had to be crushed. Labeling them all communists or procommunist, he was using the secret police and the blue-shirted Republican Youth to hunt down these people – people who were considered by almost everyone else as freedom fighters. It was a disastrous tactic . . . Diem was irrevocably alienating himself from the emotional nationalism which had been the most potent force in Vietnam for a decade.'[15] By contrast, the southern insurgents of the NLF, while far from being universally supported, were often part of the social fabric of rural communities through ties of family, friendship and common interests. Soon the Lao Dong Party, in order to covertly differentiate itself from the NLF, declared that the communists in the south would unite under the banner of the People's Revolutionary Party. Both, however, were placed under the overall command of the Central Office for South Vietnam (COSVN), which was responsible for organising and supporting the insurgency.[16]

Within 18 months NLF guerrilla activity was widespread throughout the RVN, which resulted in a US-backed military coup and the assassination of President Diem in November 1963. By 1964 the position in the south was such that one coup quickly followed another. Buddhist protests, a Montagnard revolt (the Degar or Montagnard are the indigenous peoples of the Central Highlands of Vietnam) and large-scale civil unrest were all evidence of leadership failure – the south was in real danger of fragmenting. Among the most enduring images captured on film during this period were those of Buddhist monks dousing themselves with petrol and becoming 'human torches' in protest at the government's actions.[17]

The north was now sending well-trained conventional forces of the People's Army of Vietnam (also called the North Vietnamese Army, or NVA) to confront the weak and demoralised forces of the south. In mid-1963 generals from Hanoi had arrived in the highlands of the south to act as advisers to or commanders of Viet Cong forces against the RVN.[18] Very soon it became increasingly obvious that the insurgency was escalating into a covert invasion of the south by northern forces. It wasn't long before the situation there became untenable, with any movement beyond Saigon requiring a large military escort. At the same time the US set about increasing its aid to the south, not only in financial terms but in direct military assistance. By 1963 there were 16 000 US advisers and trainers in South Vietnam (Australia also sent a small team initially), while the north was fielding regimental-sized units to the south, showing the impotency of the Republic in defending its own borders and territory beyond Saigon. When the conventional military forces of the south confronted these forces, they invariably suffered badly. The south in 1963 alone was losing on average around 1000 personnel per month to insurgent operations against them, and in

September 1964 it suffered 3240 casualties at the hands of the Viet Cong. However, by 1965 desertions were far greater, estimated at around 9000 per month.[19]

By early 1965 the US had only two options: direct military intervention, or allow the north to reunify Vietnam under a communist banner. If the US was going to intervene it had to do so now, as Saigon was about to fall. Earlier, in August 1964, President Lyndon Johnson alleged that American warships in the Gulf of Tonkin had been attacked by North Vietnamese patrol boats in international waters, and he ordered American planes to bomb DRV shore installations for the first time. While the north accepted responsibility for the attack on USS *Maddox*, the subsequent claim by the US of an attack by North Vietnam against USS *C. Turner Joy* would prove false.[20] On 13 February 1965 President Johnson authorised Operation Rolling Thunder, a 30-day bombing campaign against North Vietnam, and a month later US marine and army combat troops were deployed to South Vietnam. Within two months, Australian combat troops would also be on the ground.

4

'. . . find, fix and finish'

The conscription Act that sent young Australians to Vietnam was originally invoked in late 1964 to boost military numbers for a likely confrontation with Indonesia over the recent independence of Malaysia. At the time, Australian troops from 2 RAR and 3 RAR were involved in an undeclared war with Indonesia in Malaysian northern Borneo; the government and military were gravely concerned that this might degenerate into open warfare.

An earlier review of the Australian Army had resulted in a reduction of the infantry battalion to 841 personnel across all ranks; each battalion was commanded by a lieutenant colonel. The battalion consisted of four infantry companies: Alpha (A), Bravo (B), Charlie (C) and Delta (D), each with 120 men led by a major. Each company had three platoons with 33 men per platoon, led by a lieutenant with a sergeant second in command. Each platoon consisted of three sections of ten men, each commanded by a corporal. In addition, each battalion had a support company (consisting of signallers, mortar crew and assault pioneers) and an administration company. The training and equipping of the battalion was centred on counterinsurgency operations.[1]

Throughout the early 1960s the army was losing personnel at an alarming rate, while Australia's military commitments were growing. Jobs were abundant, and even though the government increased army wages by 30 per cent, jobs that offered plenty of overtime meant the army could not compete. In mid-1965 the army numbered just 22 750 regulars; it needed to be increased to 37 500 to maintain a nine-battalion regiment.[2] National conscription – for a two-year period – was brought in to increase the numbers, and unlike previous national-service schemes, this one would enable the soldiers to be sent overseas to serve with the regular army. Conscription meant that the army could now take the pick of the litter. Indeed, a relatively large number of potential conscripts were rejected – 4421 alone in the first ballot – for various reasons.[3]

Those accepted were to be fully integrated into the army, with no distinction being made between regulars and 'nashos' (national service personnel). However, Private Grant Collins of 5 RAR, a judo champion from South Australia, recalled that their NCOs 'weren't really allowed to swear at us [nashos], so they'd yell out "Cons, get your arms up or you'll be sexually intercoursed!"' That's not quite how then-private John Robbins, 6 RAR, remembered his first day at Kapooka. His instructors barked out to one and all of the bewildered recruits: 'Get over there, you dickhead; not there, you stupid arsehole. What are you, a fuckwit or something? Answer me, you penis-with-ears, and call me sir or I'll come down on you so fucking hard you won't get up for a month. Stop laughing, you stupid shit-for-brains. What's your name, you dopey prick?'[4]

Within 12 months, members of the Australian regular army, along with those conscripted into the military under the National Service Scheme, would find themselves in South Vietnam. Most of the national servicemen would be allocated to the infantry as riflemen, which was one of the most dangerous jobs in Vietnam. The rifleman was the most likely to die in Vietnam (along with the sapper), and this would have significant implications in terms of casualties. While they would make up about 33 per cent of the Task Force in Vietnam, 70 per cent of national servicemen ended up in rifle companies as opposed to other arms of service. Even so, the distribution of regulars and nashos *within* rifle companies remained at about 50 per cent each.[5] Bruce Davies, who conducted three one-year tours with 1 RAR and the AATTV (Australian Army Training Team Vietnam), and would go on to write the definitive account of Australia's involvement in the Vietnam War, provides a more telling comparison. The number of those killed in action (KIA) in the army during the Vietnam War – not including those who died from wounds or other causes – amounted to 172 regular-army recruits and 143 national service personnel. Subtracting the number of those KIA in units in which national servicemen did not usually serve, including in the AATTV and 1 RAR first tour, gives a total of 63 KIA. Subtracting this from the 172 who were KIA provides a total of 109 regular army versus 143 national service personnel, which puts a stark emphasis on the difference between the two enlistment categories.[6] Using this data national service personnel accounted for 57 per cent of those infantry KIA. The reasons for this remain unclear.

Australian defence policy since the conclusion of World War II had been based on a fear of instability in South-East Asia. Many Australians were concerned that communism would take hold, and with the emergence of Communist China in 1949, these fears appeared to be realised: the small nation-states in South-East Asia were in danger of becoming a giant satellite region controlled by Beijing (and Moscow). To help counter this, Australian defence policy was tied to maintaining a formal coalition with either Britain or the US – preferably both. Australia as a middle power would never have the resources to have any meaningful military presence in the region; it needed strong allies to help in its own defence and particularly in the case when 'push came to shove' in the region. With the original threat from Japan in World War II (1941–45), and with the Korean War (1950–53), Australia was looking towards the US as its principal ally. While the Australian prime minister, Robert Menzies, still believed the British Commonwealth was the cornerstone of Australian defence policy, the secretary of the defence department, Frederick Shedden, acknowledged at the outbreak of the Korean War that the 'political considerations of Australian–American relations are very weighty and . . . we must keep with the Americans, short of imperilling the development of our military potential. Briefly, while steering a set course of British Commonwealth co-operation, we may have to do some tacking to keep with the Americans even though the tacking might have the appearance of veering away from the set course.'[7]

It was Australia's and New Zealand's participation in the Korean War that enabled them to successfully lobby the US for the formation of a military alliance. In return, the US required Australia and New Zealand to recognise Japan as a legitimate power in its own right – America needed Japan to help to fight the war in Korea, and a strong Japan was also seen as vital to help counter the growing power of Communist China. In 1951 the Australia, New Zealand, United States Security Treaty (ANZUS) was signed, coming into effect in 1952. It was viewed very much by the junior partners as an insurance policy against communist aggression.[8] John Buckley, an assistant secretary in the Australian department of defence, wrote to Shedden just after the signing of the treaty that it was the most 'important development in Australian defence in the post-war years . . . [and] he [Buckley] used every means to ensure that the US understood very clearly the extent to which Australia had placed her trust and reliance on the formally agreed terms and applications of the ANZUS Pact.'[9]

The Korean War and the active involvement of Communist China in supporting North Korea's aggression further fuelled the concept of the domino theory. What had formerly been seen by many as a political struggle for self-determination by the Vietnamese from French colonialism in Indochina had by the early 1950s morphed into an international communist threat directed from Beijing and Moscow. The communist north was viewed firmly through the prism of international communism – today North Vietnam, tomorrow the south, followed by Laos, Cambodia, Thailand, Burma, Malaya and Indonesia. Indeed, in June 1954, at the time of the Geneva Conference, the Australian government was so concerned about keeping the US interested in the region that a Cabinet minute stated that the ministers did 'not underestimate the importance of events in Indochina to Australia . . . [our] . . . destiny in the Pacific is so wrapped up with the US that we should support them even if we believe that the course of action proposed by them is wrong'.[10]

By the mid-1960s, Prime Minister Robert Menzies was firm in his belief in the domino theory. Communist aggression against South Vietnam had to be stopped and Australia needed to be seen as directly supporting its American ally. Australia needed the US actively engaged in South-East Asia – Australia (and New Zealand) would have to pay a price for the ANZUS Treaty.[11]

On 29 April 1965, Menzies announced in Parliament that he had received a formal request from the government of South Vietnam to provide military assistance to help protect the country from North Vietnamese communist aggression. In fact, the Menzies Government, with the support of the US, had petitioned the South Vietnamese government to request Australia's assistance in the escalating conflict. Menzies stated that Australia would join the US in sending troops to Vietnam. Three years earlier, the first of the AATTV had been sent to the RVN; now Australia would be increasing its commitment to supplying combat troops and logistical support to help defend South Vietnam against North Vietnamese aggression.[12]

The Viet Cong veterans were confident that the same principles and tactics they had used to defeat the French and undermine security in the RVN would work against the US and her allies. Like the French, the Americans sought a military solution to the communist insurgency – no clear distinction was made between conducting a conventional war and conducting counterinsurgency operations.

In 1965 US general William Westmoreland was placed in command of all forces in South Vietnam – excluding South Vietnamese forces – and tasked with defeating the communist insurgents as quickly as possible. He would focus on capturing territory, defining battle zones, and establishing lines of communication, bases of operation and rest areas. The control of territory and the killing of Viet Cong defined his tactical operations – crude and brutal tactics of killing the enemy at a greater rate than he could kill you, and a war of attrition, which would later devolve into victory based on body counts. Westmoreland planned to clear South Vietnam of insurgents province by province. The term 'find, fix and finish' (search and destroy) was invoked to describe his style of operation.[13] Above all else, he would rely on firepower and advanced technology to defeat the insurgency.

While this style of warfare played to the strength of his forces, it meant that it was the wrong army, in the wrong country, fighting the wrong war. Westmoreland's tactics would play directly to the strengths of the fluid strategy and tactics of the Viet Cong. His failure would be in applying the same tactics employed during the battles of Europe in World War II to the insurgency in Vietnam. With the arrival of the US, the communist insurgents reverted to small-scale attacks and skirmishes in the jungles and mountains. Counterinsurgency operations require light infantry formations, firepower restraint, and the resolution of political and social problems – which were well beyond the remit or experience of the senior US military commanders on the ground.[14]

The long-term development of the Viet Minh and, later, the

Viet Cong political and military cadres in the south, placed the Americans and their allies at a serious disadvantage and ensured that the conventional military approach was doomed. The cadres consisted of local leaders who knew the area, knew the people and had established their own cells of supporters, operatives and fighters. They were responsible not only for conducting local insurgent operations against the military and government targets, which included assassination and intimidation, but also improving local logistics; gathering intelligence; conducting propaganda and education campaigns particularly aimed at the young; and increasing agriculture production, which benefited the people and the cause. All of this was in line with the principle of 'winning the hearts and minds' of the people. Only an effective cadre could hope to achieve this.

While the US military would also set about trying to win hearts and minds, the inherent contradictions in running a conventional military campaign with defined battle zones, bases of operation and lines of communication meant that this was an impossibility, as the people continually got in the way of military operations that took precedence over political considerations.[15] As succinctly put by Bruce Davies, it was all well and good for staff officers and others to dictate how the war should be fought and for them to write about the 'political war back in Canberra or Washington or Saigon without putting their arse on the line in a lonely hamlet while attempting to "guide" the Vietnamese in the ideals of western democracy'.[16]

Unlike the Americans, the Australians had a relatively successful record of counterinsurgency operations in South-East Asia. Much of this collective experience came from members of the regular army who had conducted such operations in Malaysian Borneo, many of whom were veterans of the communist Malayan Emergency, the Korean War, and fighting the Japanese in the jungles of South-East Asia during World War II.[17] Lessons learnt were published in a number of army manuals, such as *Ambush and Counter Ambush*; *Patrolling and Tracking*; and *The Division in Battle: Counter Revolutionary Warfare*.[18] Indeed, in Malaya the Australians had become known as leaders in the art of jungle warfare, tactics and training. Many of these lessons were being passed on to the next generation of Australian soldiers at the Jungle Training Centre at Canungra in Queensland, which focused on physical fitness and instinctive shooting and had the men living in similar conditions to those they would experience in Vietnam. Large numbers of national servicemen who would make up substantial parts of 5 RAR (formed in New South Wales) and 6 RAR (formed in Queensland) were being trained by veterans of counterinsurgency operations, and their experience was priceless. By the time the announcement was made that Australian combat troops would be sent to Vietnam, soldiers of these battalions either had direct experience in counterinsurgency operations or had been trained to conduct such operations. Even so, they had little experience of working with helicopters and armoured personnel carriers (APCs), and lacked training in attacking enemy troops entrenched in bunker and tunnel complexes.[19]

While Australian troops had gained a wealth of experience fighting against the insurgents in what was still then Malaya, Vietnam was different. The insurgency in Malaya had been relatively small and was principally generated by local Chinese insurgents, who were not well equipped, could readily be identified and were small in number. Just as crucially, they had little local support. Also, home-grown food was relatively scarce in Malaya and almost unobtainable in the jungle; thus, the control of logistical supply was crucial, and once insurgent supply 'routes' had been identified they could be dealt with effectively and the insurgents would 'wither on the vine'. The Viet Cong, however, were well trained and experienced; had a vast cadre network that might include mothers, fathers, siblings, uncles, aunts and village friends; and could not be readily identified. Also, they usually had ready access to food and were not greatly hampered by logistical supply routes – they could live off the land, and frequently did. Even so, the NVA and Viet Cong at times faced serious logistical challenges and there were confrontations between the southern Viet Cong and the northern NVA in terms of 'who got what'. During those periods when they were forced to live off the land for extended periods, morale and health deteriorated. Malaria was one of the greatest medical problems and sometimes reduced units to ineffectual levels.[20]

Unlike the Americans, the Australian force would not be relying on overwhelming firepower and an abundance of 'high tech'. The Australian troops going to Vietnam were well trained, disciplined and professional, but very much a traditional infantry force that used tactics based on patrolling and ambushing – tactics they had perfected since World War II. In many ways, the Australian force was better suited to deal with the Viet Cong than the Americans. The American forces at first would be frustrated with the Australian tactics – the Americans were tasked with getting in, clearing out the enemy and getting out of Vietnam as quickly as possible. The Australians, however, knew there would be no 'quick fix'. They knew from experience that you had to fight an insurgency with like tactics – upfront and personal. The Australians would focus on having boots in the jungle on patrol, conducting anti-logistics operations, trying to keep a light footprint in the area and, wherever possible, conducting civil action projects to help garner political support. This would not always be possible, as the Australians were trying to walk a line between their own tactical priorities and those of the Americans. Like the Americans, they set up bases of operations, which required at least some focus on territorial security at the expense of the local population.

The starkness in contrast between the American and Australian approaches to the war in Vietnam is perhaps best summed up by an observation made by Australian brigadier Stuart Graham when he was serving as the Task Force commander and attending a senior

US briefing. The opening remark was that the key objective of winning the war was to 'kill VC'. Graham's objectives were much more nuanced: his task was to help ensure the 'security of the main areas of population and resources of Phuoc Tuy [a province assigned to the Australians] and so enable the Government to restore law and order and get on with the job of developing the social, economical, and political life of the province'.[21]

5

'Keep those bloody choppers away from us'

In early June 1965, Australian combat troops arrived in South Vietnam to fight the communist insurgents. Australia's commitment at this stage consisted of an infantry battalion under the command of Lieutenant Colonel Ivan Brumfield. The battalion group was built around 1 RAR; Australians of 2 RAR, 3 RAR and, more recently, 4 RAR were being rotated through the conflict in Malaysian Borneo.[1] In addition, New Zealand deployed a field battery that served alongside 1 RAR – the Anzac connection was re-established. At this point the battalion was staffed by regular personnel only, as the first intake of conscripts were then being trained in Australia. Command of the force was assigned to Brigadier David Jackson of Australian Army Force Vietnam (AAFV), based in Saigon to facilitate communications with US forces. The chief of the general staff in Australia, Lieutenant General John Wilton, directed Jackson to place the AAFV under the operational command of General Westmoreland, who assigned 1 RAR to the 173rd Airborne Brigade based at the American air base at Bien Hoa.[2] Members of the AATTV, which had first arrived in South Vietnam in 1962, were still working in small dispersed units throughout the south, assisting US forces to bring the Army of the Republic of Viet Nam (ARVN) up to scratch. An ARVN battalion had an advisory group, usually of three US advisers and one Australian adviser. AATTV members were also assigned to operational units, including ARVN battalions, Special Forces units and some activities controlled by the Central Intelligence Agency.[3]

Jackson's initial orders from Wilton were that his force was not to venture beyond the Bien Hoa area unless ordered to do so by Army headquarters in Canberra. As such, Westmoreland assigned the Anzac contingent to defend the air base, but this was an inappropriate use of a well-trained battalion. Restricting the soldiers to garrison duty meant they did not suffer the same risk as the Americans, which minimised Australia's role in the war and negated one of the government's prime reasons for the deployment: that Australia needed to be seen to be pulling its weight.[4] By September 1965, Wilton and Westmoreland agreed that 1 RAR's area of operation would include the entire tactical zone assigned to the American III Corps, which included the provinces around Saigon. While Westmoreland remained in operational control, Jackson had the right to veto his forces' involvement in any operations that violated Australian national interests.

1 RAR was involved in a number of significant actions working with American forces. It continually outmanoeuvred and outfought the Viet Cong, culminating in a major success in early 1966 when, as part of Operation Crimp (8–14 January 1966), 1 RAR assaulted a large Viet Cong headquarters complex in the Ho Bo Woods that was found to contain a mass of tunnels. Soon Australian infantry and engineers of 'small stature' were assigned to descend into the tunnels; they became famous as the much-admired 'tunnel rats'. Among those selected for this dangerous and fearful task was Corporal Lex McAulay, one of two linguists in the battalion. He later wrote a detailed, fascinating account of Operation Crimp:

By the end of the day [day two of Operation Crimp] it was
obvious to all concerned that the tunnels posed a complex
problem, about which there was no background of experience,
lessons learned, or published policies. The narrowness of the
tunnels, the small size of the trap doors, the twists and turns,
the different levels, the lack of airflow, the darkness, dead ends,
and the strong possibility of enemy in the form of armed people
or booby traps, combined to present an operational problem
outside any previous experience of the Australian forces, or
their allies. The tunnels would have to be attacked with what
was available close by, and by men who would literally crawl
down into the darkness and into the unknown, equipped only
with an electronic torch and a pistol. The qualifying factor was
size – only slim agile men could enter.[5]

Another qualifying factor was guts. Corporal Bruce Davies of
1 RAR, who also took part in Operation Crimp, recalled that after
smoke and/or tear gas was pumped into the tunnels, the tunnel rats
of 3 Field Troop, Royal Australian Engineers, 'went down inside the
labyrinth in search of the hiding enemy, a terrifying task given that
their only weapons were a 9mm Browning pistol and a torch. The
tunnels were just over half a metre each wide and high . . . Some of
the troop passed out from the lack of oxygen.'[6] During Operation
Crimp, Corporal Bob Bowtell came across a small trapdoor and in
'his usual way of leading from the front went first. Apparently the
tunnel became a dead-end – there was no airflow, and what air was in
the small enclosed space had become foul.'[7] Despite urgent attempts
to get him out, Bowtell died in the narrow, dark tunnel. Corporal
Trevor Hagan of 1 Platoon recalled: 'We heard that Corporal Bob
Bowtell had been killed in a gas trap at the bottom of a tunnel.
This was a shock to me, as I had put Bob through [recruit training
at] Kapooka in 1963. It was a waste of a very good soldier.'[8] The

Australian tunnel rats in Vietnam were in a class all of their own, undoubtedly tasked with one of the most stressful and dangerous jobs in the whole war.

The Americans hailed Operation Crimp and the capture of this headquarters with its tonnes of military supplies and thousands of documents as their first strategic intelligence victory of the Vietnam War. The Australians spent several days discovering more supplies and documents while they destroyed an extensive three-level tunnel system.[9] Indeed, although it was unknown at the time, this tunnel system was then the largest in South Vietnam. Casualties also occurred above ground, with B and D companies of 1 RAR sustaining the heaviest casualties – many caused by grenades rigged as anti-personnel mines with trip-wires strung among trees from ankle to head height. Not only this, but steel punji sticks were buried in concrete blocks.[10]

By the time 5 RAR and 6 RAR arrived in Vietnam in May and early June 1966, the men of 1 RAR had been on continuous active frontline service for almost 12 months. They returned to Australia a month later, but 18 young Australians of the battalion were not with them. The battalion would provide the core of combat-hardened officers, NCOs and soldiers who would train the next intake of men to be sent to Vietnam.[11] Indeed, many of these veterans not only made sure 'their protégés knew what was ahead of them, but also commanded and supported them during their tours of duty' in the war zone.[12]

American and Australian troops got on well overall, but one major difference between them was the cockiness of many US soldiers. The American forces were overconfident, with a gung-ho attitude that they backed up with a scale of weaponry beyond anything the Australians had seen.[13] The US was keen to bring its military might to the fore, believing it would quickly clear the south of communist insurgents. However, with the Viet Cong refocusing on 'hit and run' tactics, such firepower became less critical in terms of defeating the insurgency. It was the disruption of the cadres and political organisations that needed to be confronted, not the conventional warfare doctrine using large-scale forces against the fluid Viet Cong in order to temporarily occupy a province.

American troops patrolled in an aggressive and obvious manner, 'like a noisy hunting party – eagerly seeking battle'.[14] They set about trying to clear vast areas using overt military presence and according to predetermined timetables drawn up by staff officers, patrolling along tracks, smoking and talking, wearing flashy bright and colourful unit patches, firing their weapons into suspicious areas and making sure that the whole province knew they were there, looking for a fight. They actively encouraged the Viet Cong to 'take them on', which the VC often did in set hit-and-run operations and ambushes, disappearing before the Americans could bring their firepower to bear. Many Americans seemed to have a complete disregard for their enemy's fighting abilities. Once a US force had 'cleared out' an area and moved on, the Viet Cong invariably moved back in.[15]

By contrast, the Australian force, by training and necessity, was far more cautious and much leaner. Australian commanders were just not prepared to pay the price the US commanders seemingly were for inflicting casualties against the enemy – they would examine likely tactical success before committing their men. Sometimes this planning and assessment resulted in lost opportunities to inflict casualties against the Viet Cong; however, this was preferable to suffering casualties. Australians had the patience to wait for another opportunity. One soldier remarked about having to patrol with the US paratroopers: 'It was a bit too bloody dangerous. They talk and smoke and generally set themselves up as pretty good targets. The Americans are good blokes but not when they are on patrol.'[16]

Australians were not only about patrolling a province but also about controlling it. They avoided tracks and moved with stealth, patrolling slowly and silently, fanning out in sections, keen not to give away their position. Indeed, while the Americans regularly used helicopters in support, the Australians avoided using them when on patrol. One Australian observer declared: 'Keep those bloody choppers away from us – they give away our position'.[17] Australian patrols were also not dictated by a timetable but were fluid, taking into account local and unforeseen circumstances. Australian troops wore just one set of their drab green clothes during an operation: those they went out in. They wore army greens, a bush hat, a sweat scarf, socks and boots. Unlike US troops they did not wear flak jackets or helmets; both were uncomfortable, were considered almost useless and hindered movement, and the helmet made it difficult to hear.[18]

The enemy often found it difficult to ambush Australian patrols successfully because of their unpredictability, usually having no idea where the Australians were until it was too late. The Vietnamese themselves described the Australian soldiers as 'very experienced mercenaries having fought a counter-guerrilla war in Malaya . . . Different to the Americans, the Australian troops were very proficient in ambush tactics, small-scale raids, operating dispersed in half-section and section groups, and striking deep into our bases. They acclimatised to the weather and adapted to the tropical jungle terrain. They could cut through the thick, thorny jungle and would hide in the swamps and marshes – lying in ambush for many days at a time.'[19]

It was not long before the Americans recognised the Australians as masters of patrol and ambush, as recalled by US Lieutenant Colonel George Dexter, commander of the 2/503rd Battalion:

> When we found something, we shot at it. We did not wait and establish the patterns, looking for opportunities after out-thinking the local Viet Cong commander. We were just not patient enough – there was too much to do in too little time. We did not use reconnaissance enough. Our

ambushes were for security, not to kill. Australians were quiet hunters – patient, thorough, trying to out-think the Viet Cong. I would not have liked to operate at night and know there was a chance of ending up in an Aussie ambush.[20]

Even so, going out on patrol was nerve-racking. With every operation there was a real chance of death or serious wounding – not just from engaging the enemy directly, but from suffering casualties from deadly booby traps. No one enjoyed going out on patrol. Despite the courageous work of sappers in trying to clear these deadly obstacles, from June 1966 to May 1970, 87 Australians were killed and 481 were wounded, many severely, by mines and booby traps.[21]

The different approach that US and Australian soldiers took in combating the enemy can be seen in the strict rules-of-engagement regulations that the Australians enforced, even when in villages and hamlets known to be well infiltrated with Viet Cong. Operation Sydney 2 was one such operation. The village of Duc My was a known hub of Viet Cong activity and on 19–20 July 1966, the men of 5 RAR and supporting units conducted a successful cordon-and-search mission. Before the operation began, Lieutenant Colonel John Warr (who had been seriously wounded in Korea) provided strict rules of engagement. It must be stressed that Duc My was no 'sleepy village' but a known facilitation hub of Viet Cong activity.

Rules of Engagement
(a) Fire only:
   (i) When fired at.
   (ii) When a suspect is about to commit a hostile act.
   (iii) If a suspect attempts to run through a cordon and
      fails to halt after challenge.

(b) <u>If in doubt don't shoot.</u> [author underline]

(c) Don't fire into the cordon area unless the fire is controlled and the target can be clearly seen.

(d) If fired on from a house:

    (i) Take cover.

    (ii) Call interpreter forward.

    (iii) Get loud hailers.

    (iv) Have interpreters advise occupants to surrender.

    (v) If no success, call for the village chief and have him speak to the house-holder.

    (vi) If the occupants still refuse to surrender, burn the house.

(e) These are the only circumstances under which houses are to be burnt.

(f) All males of military age are to be taken to the Bn cage [in order to identify likely Viet Cong].

(g) Don't harass women and children; and

(h) Soldiers will not be used to search women.[22]

'If in doubt don't shoot.' During this mission, Lieutenant John Carruthers, commander of 4 Platoon, saw two Viet Cong moving on a track into the centre of the village. He did not open fire as the cordon was not completely in position and any noise would alert the enemy and give them an opportunity to escape. A few minutes later, three Viet Cong moved towards him and in the semi-darkness Carruthers personally and silently captured them and disarmed them. He would later (on 24 February 1967) die from wounds sustained during Operation Renmark.[23]

Once the Viet Cong became alerted to the presence of the Australians by Vietnamese translators using loudhailers ordering them to surrender, one Viet Cong with an ammunition belt wrapped around his waist was seen to dive into a nearby tunnel. A tear-gas grenade was thrown into the entrance but the man did not come out. Sounds of distress were heard, but instead of throwing in a high-explosive grenade to collapse the tunnel, an unnamed sapper from Lieutenant Dennis Rainer's platoon donned a gas mask and at great personal risk went in after the enemy combatant. The Australian dragged him out; the combatant had been overcome by the gas and was unconscious. The battalion medical officer, Captain Tony White, was summoned and the man was revived with mouth-to-mouth resuscitation and then handed over for interrogation. Captain Robert O'Neill of B Company recalled that word of the incident was soon doing the rounds 'among the villages and by the end of the day our soldiers were getting along very amicably with many inhabitants of the former Viet Cong village'.[24]

General Wilton increasingly recognised that with his troops now operating beyond Bien Hoa, the Australian force should be increased to a task force so that they would have greater national recognition. More importantly, however, it was recognised that the Australian and US forces had very different approaches to fighting the war.[25] Increasing Australia's involvement to a task force would enable the Australians to use their own tactics.

Wilton was also concerned to hear that the Americans planned to use 1 RAR in operations close to the Cambodian border, but Brigadier Jackson objected and 1 RAR was withdrawn. Wilton approved of Jackson's decision, later writing to Edwin Hicks, secretary of the defence department, that this was the 'first occasion on which it has been necessary for Brigadier Jackson to exercise his responsibility, laid down in his Directive for the safety and well-being of AAFV'.[26] Wilton had also become aware of the 'gung-ho' reputation of the US 173rd Airborne Brigade, to which 1 RAR was attached, and his own experiences in the Korean War made it clear to him that the US was prepared to sustain greater casualties than the Australian government would tolerate or could afford.[27] He was right to be concerned, as Brigadier General Ellis Williamson, who commanded the 173rd, stated that his job 'was not to pussyfoot around the jungle hoping to bump into the Viet Cong. Our job was to get in there and bring him to battle – to keep him off balance.'[28]

In early March 1966, the new Australian prime minister, Harold Holt, confirmed an increased commitment to Vietnam with the creation of 1 Australian Task Force (1 ATF). Holt considered this the upper limit of the Army's capacity in the conflict.[29] A Cabinet paper from the time stated: 'the prime consideration for Australia is the continued commitment of the United States to the defence of South East Asia, and thus [for Australia] to play what the United States will recognise as a full part in the defence of South Vietnam'.[30] This would be the largest overseas commitment of Australian defence force personnel since World War II. General Wilton, who now replaced Air Chief Marshal Frederick Scherger as chairman of the chiefs of staff committee in Canberra, was adamant that neither the committee nor the politicians should interfere in the operational matters of 1 ATF. He emphasised:

> having set down the policy and the tasks which could be done the local man on the spot should be allowed to get on with it. It's not the kind of war which you can run even at battalion level let alone company level from Canberra. This is ridiculous, you would get nowhere. It's quite contrary to all military practice to try and run the war from Canberra, you just can't do it . . . And remember we have . . . three lots of judgment there: an experienced COMAFV [Commander Australian Force Vietnam], . . . experienced brigadiers [Task Force commanders], [and] . . . good battalion commanders and good company commanders.[31]

The Task Force would consist of an APC squadron, 1 Field Regiment (consisting of the Australian 103 and 105 field batteries and the New Zealand 161 Field Battery), 1 Field Squadron, 21 Engineer Support Group, 103 Signals Squadron, two infantry battalions (5 RAR and 6 RAR), 3 Special Air Service (SAS) Squadron, 1 Australian Logistics Support Group (which included medical personnel of the Royal Australian Army Medical Corps), 161 (Independent) Recce Flight, and a detachment from 1 Division Intelligence Unit. To help facilitate communication with the Americans, signallers and liaison officers were linked to US headquarters in Saigon and elsewhere. New Zealand would subsequently expand its commitment to two infantry companies and a unit from its SAS squadron.[32]

Because 1 ATF did not have any heavy artillery, the Americans provided a battery of six 155mm self-propelled howitzers from A Battery 2nd Battalion 35th Artillery (US 2/35th). One of the two forward observation officers attached to this unit, Lieutenant Gordon Steinbrook from Nebraska, was on board a troopship just off the coast of Vietnam when he was told that his battery would be assigned to supporting the Australians and New Zealanders. That night he wrote to his wife of just eight months, Frances, telling her of the news:

All of us are happy about joining the Australians rather than the Vietnamese div. At least we'll know who our friends are. Not only that, but the Australians are an elite group especially trained and sent to Vietnam for this type of war. Rumor has it that they are tremendous fighters and actually better soldiers man for man than the American soldier in Vietnam. I just can't say how pleased I am to be going to such an elite group of men. Of course this will be quite an experience for us. We'll have to get used to their rough and tough methods of doing things. From what I understand, they are truly professional hard-core type people, and because of this we'll have to work our butts off to keep up with them.[33]

6

'. . . started swimming for home, clutching a bottle of gin'

With the expansion to 1 ATF, the Australians were now granted a semblance of independence from the US forces. Although 1 ATF remained under the operational control of American HQ II Field Force Vietnam at Long Binh, the Australian commander could veto the inclusion of Australians in any US-led operation. Brigadier Jackson, who had been based in Saigon commanding AAFV, was now assigned to command 1 ATF, while Major General Ken Mackay arrived in Saigon as commander of Australian Force Vietnam (AFV), which replaced the AAFV – Australia's commitment had grown to include Australian air-force and naval personnel and was no longer just an Army operation.[1]

1 ATF was given responsibility for Phuoc Tuy Province (meaning, in Vietnamese, 'prosperous and peaceful'), which was a known Viet Cong stronghold just south-east of Saigon. It may have been prosperous, but it was anything but peaceful. Even so, the majority of people in the district were neutral in that their allegiance was dictated more by pragmatism than ideology. Overall, they favoured the side that could best provide the conditions that would enable them to get on with their life without harassment or disruption.

The main role of 1 ATF was to win the allegiance of, or at least acceptance by, the locals – to try to neutralise the ongoing violence of the Viet Cong, which would enable the RVN government to reassert some authority within the province and improve its social and economic circumstances. Given all of the competing priorities, this was a big ask.[2]

Operationally, Phuoc Tuy fulfilled Wilton's criteria as it was an area of significant enemy activity and Australia would be seen as pulling its weight. The importance of Phuoc Tuy was its dominating position in relation to the city of Vung Tau and Route 15, the highway connection between the port and Saigon. As the Saigon docks became increasingly congested, Vung Tau grew in strategic importance as a site of commerce and a means of entry for military supplies. However, the enemy controlled the province, except for the capital, Ba Ria, and the narrow strip connecting it to the Vung Tau Peninsula. The region was critical for the South Vietnamese government not only for the security of the province itself, but because while it remained in enemy hands it contributed to the isolation of Saigon. The terrain and vegetation suited the Australian operating method of patrolling and ambush; it also favoured the separation of enemy forces from the population and their sources of replenishment – a basic element in Australian counter-revolutionary warfare.[3]

Of crucial importance to the Australians was that the province did not border Cambodia or Laos; they did not want to get involved in cross-border conflicts. It also provided ready access via air and sea. Wilton and Westmoreland agreed that the main task for 1 ATF was to secure and dominate the 'tactical area of responsibility' (TAOR), extended out 4 kilometres from the base (maximum enemy mortar range), which defined Line Alpha; it would later be increased to 9 km (maximum enemy artillery range), which defined Line Bravo. 1 ATF would conduct operations to keep Route 15 open, conduct operations within the province as needed, and be prepared to

conduct operations within III Corps Tactical Zone, and potentially in Binh Thuan, which lay in II Corps Tactical Zone, further
north.[4] Westmoreland and Wilton discussed the area of operations
for the Australians: Westmoreland's emphasis was on keeping open
Route 15 and the Rung Sat Zone (which included Long Tau River,
the main shipping channel from Saigon to Vung Tau). However, Air
Chief Marshal Scherger, before stepping down as the chairman of
the chiefs of staff committee in Canberra, directed Major General
Mackay to take over Phuoc Tuy Province and not just protect Route
15 and the Rung Sat Zone.[5]

An Australian regular, Private Terry Burstall, who had originally been
a late replacement for 1 RAR and was later assigned to D Company,
6 RAR, recalled his first memory of hearing about Phuoc Tuy. It
was far from reassuring. He and others from 1 RAR had heard
stories from US troops that the Viet Cong were strong in Phuoc
Tuy – some troops from 1 RAR had been on operations there with
the US 173rd Airborne Brigade. The word was that the Viet Cong
force in the area was extremely well equipped, well trained and
disciplined, and that the 173rd had suffered heavy casualties there.[6]

Indeed, Phuoc Tuy Province was no easy assignment. Virtually
all of its 100 000 inhabitants had lived under communist control,
and the forces of South Vietnam had kept clear of the area, knowing
it had a strong insurgent presence. Indeed, Viet Cong cadres had
established a strong operational and political presence there since
the time of the French. Australian sergeant Bob Buick recalled how
he heard that the 'Viet Minh had done the French over so many
times in this province during the Indo-China War that the French
only occupied the towns. We were going to an area which the Viet
Cong controlled and where they were now conducting large-scale
and successful military actions against the government forces supported by the USA.'[7]

Indeed, any movement along Route 15 was extremely hazardous, requiring a strong escort, and going off the main route was even more dangerous, if that were possible. The borders of the province were defined by mountains and jungle, which provided bases of operation for the Viet Cong. Within the province itself mountains and hilly areas abounded, including the Long Hai Hills in the south, the May Tao Mountains in the north-east, the Nui Dinh and Nui Thi Vai hills overlooking Route 15, and the Hat Dich area along its north-western borders. All of these provided additional bases for Viet Cong operations. Overall, the province was defined by deciduous rainforest with patches of primary jungle and lightly wooded undulating areas, with numerous areas providing for rice, banana and rubber cultivation.[8]

At first, 1 ATF set up base at Vung Tau and most were pleased, as recalled by a first-intake national serviceman, Private Harry Esler, D Company, 6 RAR. 'We landed on a beach and I thought, "This is it. This is going to be great. A nice little beach at Vung Tau".'[9] Not all were pleased, however, as recalled by Private Robin 'Pom' Rencher, D Company, 6 RAR, an Englishman who had enlisted in the Australian Army. He thought Vung Tau was hot and humid and a lousy place to be stationed. He clearly wasn't the only one, remembering that one of his mates in his company, Private Ian 'Tubby' Campbell, had enough and 'started swimming for home, clutching a bottle of gin. He was eventually shepherded back to shore by a passing helicopter.'[10]

The Australian commanders had other plans about staying in Vung Tau: 1 ATF would soon be relocated to an abandoned rubber plantation, smack bang in the middle of the province. This was designed to disrupt Viet Cong operations. The main geological feature of what would define 1 ATF base was a 70-metre-high volcanic vent called Nui Dat (which can be translated as 'bald hill'). Two small streams originated on the slopes of Nui Dat, one flowing south-east and the other west. Seventy per cent of the area was rubber plantation and the remainder either banana plantation or covered in waist-to-chest-high grass.[11] The surrounding ground was typical red basaltic soil with laterite of varying quality, which would result in the characteristic red dust and mud that all Australians and New Zealanders based there would become familiar with. Private Douglas Bishop, C Company, 5 RAR wrote home: 'The soil in our area is Red Mud, RED-BLOODY-MUD. It drives me mad. I put on clean greens. 2 minutes later I'm wearing RED greens . . . It's the only place in the world where you can be bogged down in mud up to your neck and get dust in your eyes.'[12]

Another consideration for the selection of Nui Dat was communications, as recalled by the appropriately named Major Peter Mudd. The decision was 'based on a wide variety of factors. One of these was the requirement for a position which would allow communications coverage of the area of operations . . . so we were forced towards [Nui Dat hill]'.[13] Indeed, in the commander's log books (now housed in the Australian War Memorial), many pages are marked and smudged with the red mud of Nui Dat.

Nui Dat would be occupied in three phases as part of Operation Hardihood. First, the province's leaders were required to resettle all locals within a 4000-metre radius of Nui Dat. This would be followed by the US 173rd Brigade, 1 RAR and advance elements of 5 RAR securing the base area. Finally, the main body of the Task Force would move forward from Vung Tau. The clearance of the inhabitants around the base was done to provide a protective zone in which close patrols could operate freely without fear of causing civilian casualties. Also, it would deny the Viet Cong the ability to use one of their favourite tactics – deploying mortars within inhabited areas and thus preventing retaliatory fire for fear of civilian casualties. The perimeter of this cleared zone was called Line Alpha.[14]

The Australians were well aware that establishing their base of operations at Nui Dat would not sit well with the Viet Cong, and this was one of the reasons they chose it. The enemy needed to maintain control of the people, food supplies, intelligence-gathering capabilities, recruitment, clothing, medicine, labour, money, and whatever else was required or demanded of them.[15] The location of Nui Dat also enabled the nearby 'friendly' provincial capital, Ba Ria, to be protected, and facilitated communications with local Vietnamese authorities, thereby further isolating the enemy. Indeed, Viet Cong Commander Chau, the leader of *D445's Reconnaissance Platoon,* later stated that they were angry at the Australians as the base was located precisely on the route the platoon used when going from the 'western part of the province, past Nui Dat, to visit Long Tan and Long Phuoc villages'.[16] Years later the commander of this battalion, Major Nguyen Van Kiem (a local), who would command the battalion after the Battle of Long Tan and was not present during the battle itself, stated that 'establishing . . . the Australian Task Force base at Nui Dat and the evacuation of the nearby "revolutionary villages" of Long Tan and Long Phuoc had threatened to separate the guerrilla forces from the local people'.[17] He admitted it was precisely the action he would have taken in the Australians' place.[18]

From May to June 1966, 1 RAR, with 5 RAR and two battalions of the US 173rd Airborne Brigade, as part of Operation Hardihood had the mission of clearing the Viet Cong strongholds of Long Tan and Long Phuoc villages, which lay within Line Alpha of Nui Dat. The initial phase of removing the populations from these villages, which had been assigned to the provincial authorities, soon devolved to the US brigade, as the local South Vietnamese did not have the resources to accomplish it. However, events had already overtaken the initial phase of Operation Hardihood, as a month earlier, as part of Operation Abilene, three brigades of the 1st US Infantry Division (the famous 'Big Red 1'), 1 RAR and elements of the South Vietnamese Army had been assigned to locate and destroy

Viet Cong *274* and *275 regiments* operating in the province. As part of this operation, South Vietnamese troops entered the village of Long Tan and found it to be honeycombed with tunnels and bunkers; weapons and equipment were recovered and destroyed. The villagers had already been relocated by South Vietnamese troops to the villages of Dat Do, Long Dien, and Hoa Long 2.[19]

While the principal objective of finding and destroying the enemy regiments was not achieved, there was one significant contact with *D800 Battalion* of *274 VC Regiment*; around 40 enemy troops were reportedly killed. The operation signified to the Viet Cong and the population within and beyond Phuoc Tuy that the province was no longer 'owned' by the Viet Cong. Substantial intelligence had been obtained and large amounts of weapons, equipment and food caches were located and destroyed. It was a significant propaganda win for the US and the South Vietnamese and a psychological shock to the local Viet Cong forces.[20]

Meanwhile, 5 RAR had just arrived in Vietnam and taken up a position at Vung Tau and was acclimatising. Within the week it was scheduled to join the US 173rd Airborne's 1/503rd and 2/503rd battalions, who on 17 May had landed at Nui Dat by helicopter to clear the immediate area of enemy troops. The enemy were waiting. One company of 1/503rd Battalion alone suffered 12 killed and 35 wounded within hours of landing; around 20 enemy troops were killed. Two days later, operations to relocate the 3000 villagers from the nearby Long Phuoc village commenced. The immediate and swift aggressive action by the local Viet Cong forces did not bode well for a smooth operation.[21] Indeed, the mission to relocate the villagers resulted in a battle between at least two companies of *the D445 VC Battalion* and the US 1/503rd Battalion, elements of the South Vietnamese Army, and Australians from 1 APC Troop commanded by Lieutenant Adrian Roberts and 3 APC Troop commanded by Captain Bob Hill. The Viet Cong used to great effect the tunnels, bunkers and trenches that made up its defences.

Long Phuoc village was not 'captured', and the South Vietnamese relocated, until 24 May. During Operation Hardihood, the US paratroopers alone suffered 23 killed and 160 wounded. Only then could the task of locating tunnels, weapons, equipment and food caches get underway. It was then that 5 RAR arrived at Nui Dat, along with about 50 members from 1 RAR who had volunteered to help out with securing the base; 5 RAR was tasked with seeking out and destroying any enemy force within 6000 metres east and north-east of the base. In doing so, among the five Australians killed as part of Operation Hardihood was 21-year-old Errol Noack from 5 RAR, the first national serviceman killed in Vietnam. He had been 'in-country' for less than two weeks and died from wounds received in action on 24 May 1966.[22]

1 ATF base occupied 3 square kilometres that were originally divided into seven main occupation areas; these comprised five perimeter positions occupied by 5 RAR in the north and 6 RAR to the north-east and east, with a broad gap of about 700 metres to the engineers' area, which covered the south-east and south flank. The field artillery held the southern side, while the cavalry regiment with their APCs and the reinforcement unit held part of the western flank, astride Route 2. There was another gap on the western side to the north, which was dominated by Nui Dat. The two central areas were taken up with task-force headquarters, with signals, SAS and Task Force service units.[23]

The men inherited the tents formerly used by 1 RAR, which were in a very bad state of disrepair. Living conditions during this early period were primitive: the construction of the first huts (supplied with electricity) would not begin until October that year. Private Esler, who had been happy with his 'little beach' at Vung Tau, recalled being 'whipped . . . up to Nui Dat into the middle of a rubber plantation. When we got there it was all mud. There was no machinery to help us, we had to [build the base] all by hand, using entrenching tools.'[24] Private John Heslewood remembered that there were 'absolutely no defences, no barbed wire, no pits, nothing. From the minute you got there, you were putting up barbed wire and digging pits, and we also had to start patrolling straight away, to make sure that the area around the place was clear. When you weren't patrolling or doing ambushes at night-time, you were in camp digging holes in the ground or putting up barbed wire . . . All your gear got wet every day. It got dry the next day, then got wet again . . .'[25]

With the completion of a small airfield in December 1966, the men and aircraft of 161 Recce Flight were moved forward to Nui Dat. However, the helicopters of Royal Australian Air Force (RAAF) No. 9 Squadron, under the command of Wing Commander Ray Scott and designated to support 1 ATF at Nui Dat, remained at the air base that had been established at nearby Vung Tau, where infrastructure was already available in terms of fuelling and maintenance. Also based there was 1 Australian Logistics Support Group.[26]

1 ATF officially occupied Nui Dat on 5 June 1966 with the arrival of the Task Force headquarters. Brigadier Jackson now initiated Operation Enoggera, which was to destroy the already 'cleared' Long Phuoc village (within Line Alpha). It was found to still contain a large number of tunnels and food caches and was being continually used by the Viet Cong as a major logistics hub. It was also assessed as being used by the local *D445 VC Battalion* as a base for rest and observation against Nui Dat.

While it was a successful operation, the men of 6 RAR who were assigned the task did not like it, as recalled by the battalion commander and Korean War veteran Lieutenant Colonel Colin Townsend: 'It was obviously a rich village in the days when that part of the country was at peace . . . The buildings were well constructed and sound, filled with furniture, the place just reeked of a pretty rich productive area. Not a dirty hamlet with shacks falling down or anything like that. We knew we had to do it and we bloody well did it quite successfully, but we did not like it.'[27]

In all, 537 houses were destroyed, about 500 escape tunnels and air-raid shelters were collapsed, and over 1000 metres of tunnel were searched and destroyed. Large amounts of food (including 42 tonnes of rice) and medical and dental supplies were found, most of which were redistributed, while small arms, ammunition and land mines were found and destroyed.[28] Undoubtedly, the destruction of the village added to the local people's resentment of the presence of the Australians in the province and increased their allegiance to the Viet Cong, but importantly it also forced *D445 VC Battalion* deeper into the jungle, away from Nui Dat.[29]

Unlike many US bases, the Australian base at Nui Dat was under strict military control. Few members of the ARVN or civilians were allowed anywhere near it. The only Vietnamese to walk through the gates at Nui Dat were ARVN liaison officers and interpreters, prisoners and detainees.[30] Lights were out at 7.30 p.m. and men were placed on picket duty throughout the night. Australian commanders were adamant that there would be no advance warning each time an Australian force moved out.

In contrast, US bases routinely employed local Vietnamese to perform tasks such as laundry and garbage disposal, and to work as waiters, kitchenhands, barbers, canteen staff, and so on. Lights remained on all night, lighting up the camps like Christmas trees. US bases were also usually set up close to a major township. This was a godsend to Viet Cong intelligence gathering, as operatives literally fell over each other collecting identity cards, base details, details of troop movements and particularly medical supplies, facilitating attacks against the bases themselves.

7

'... aware of the threat to their stomach and nervous system'

Earlier, in February 1965, the communist COSVN had established a two-battalion regiment to operate in and around Phuoc Tuy Province – the People's Liberation Armed Forces (PLAF) *4th Infantry Regiment* (*Dong Nai Regiment*). Its presence was soon identified by US forces, who gave it the name *274 Viet Cong Regiment*.[1] The regiment was based in Hat Dich, which was to the north-west of the province, and consisted of *D800* and *D308 battalions*.[2] It first saw significant action on 12 March 1966, when it conducted an attack on Route 15 and the US and ARVN base at Vung Tau. A month later it mounted an attack at Nui Le, north of Binh Gia, on the US 1st Infantry Division,[3] and a few months after that it conducted an attack on the ARVN, successfully ambushing a convoy on Route 15 in Long Khanh Province, north of Phuoc Tuy. This was soon followed by a joint operation by *274 VC Regiment* and the *240th Company* of Long Khanh Province attacking a military training centre and capturing a large cache of arms and ammunition, including two 81mm mortars. Another attack against a convoy quickly followed, resulting in the capture of a large quantity of ammunition. This force focused its attention on attacking convoys along Routes 1, 2, 13, 14, 15 and 20.[4]

By September 1965, *274 VC Regiment* was reinforced with *D265 Battalion*, making it a three-battalion regiment. Orders soon reached the commanders of *274 VC Regiment* and the local *D445 VC Provincial Battalion* that they were to defend the Long Phuoc, Long Tan and Hat Dich base areas of Phuoc Tuy Province. Over the next six months they confronted the ARVN.[5] There has been much confusion regarding the presence of *D440 VC Battalion* and *D806* and *D860 VC battalions* within the area and their participation in the Battle of Long Tan. Research by Ernest Chamberlain has shown that *D440 VC Battalion* did not exist until mid-1967 and that *D806* and *D860* were actually code names used by the Viet Cong for *D445 VC Battalion*.[6]

It wasn't long before another force, the recently raised PLAF *5th Infantry Regiment*, consisting mostly of personnel from the Mekong Delta region, was identified in the province; it was designated *275 Viet Cong Regiment* by the US military.[7] This regiment was initially in the May Tao Mountains to the north-east of the province. It was commanded by Senior Captain Nguyen Thoi Bung and consisted of about 900 individuals in three battalions.[8] These troops did not fare well, as recalled later by an officer of the *5th VC Division*: most were 'unfamiliar with the climate, life was difficult and the unit had to urgently build bases and organize training, while at the same time, finalize the re-organisation and pay attention to the health of the cadre and soldiers, which was declining'.[9] The great bulk of the men in this regiment suffered from malaria while trying to organise, study and train. Due to casualties sustained during fighting in Binh Tuy Province and sickness, *275 VC Regiment's 2nd* and *3rd battalions* were combined to make up the *2nd Battalion*; the regiment would soon be reinforced with the NVA (*D605 Battalion*), which would be assigned as the regiment's *3rd Battalion*, making it a three-battalion regiment.[10]

There has also been much confusion regarding the presence of an NVA regiment during the battle of Long Tan – NVA *45 Regiment*.

The day after the battle, a 6 RAR situation report noted recovering 'ID cards issued in North Vietnam. Enemy units involved in battle identified as *014 Company, D3 Battalion, Q5 Regiment; D605* and incorrectly the *45 NVA Regiment*'.[11] Only one member of *445 VC Battalion* was captured at Long Tan, while two members of *275 VC Regiment* were captured – the latter declared that they were members of '*Doan 45*', a cover designator for the *3rd Battalion* of *275 VC Regiment*. Later that day, 1 ATF incorrectly reported that the two 'Northern' prisoners were members of NVA *45 Regiment* while the other was a member of *D445 VC Battalion*. However, in reality, *Doan 45, D605 Battalion* and *C14/D3/Q5 Regiment* were all designators for the *3rd Battalion* of *275 VC Regiment*, which alone consisted of NVA regulars.[12]

Both Viet Cong regiments were essentially staffed by southern-born Viet Cong, albeit with some northern political cadres.[13] These units making up *the 5th VC Division* had a strength of about 3500 and were equipped with a number of 75mm recoilless rifles, 81 and 82mm medium mortars, 12.7mm anti-aircraft guns, rocket-propelled grenades (RPGs), light and heavy machine guns and an assortment of small arms, including AK-47 assault rifles. Each regiment consisted of three battalions of varying strength, with each battalion having three service companies, combined artillery, recoilless rifles and light mortars, as well as signals (with three radio sets) and a reconnaissance unit.

Lieutenant Colonel Chuyen, who defected to the south in early 1966, provided an assessment of the abilities of the two regiments of the division. The *1st* and *3rd battalions* of the *274 VC Regiment* he considered battle-hardened and extremely reliable, but the *2nd Battalion* he considered very poor. His assessment of the *275 VC Regiment* indicated that its *1st* and *2nd battalions* lacked combat experience and were not ready for offensive operations in any strength. Many remained sick with malaria (in June 1966, 10 per cent of *274 VC Regiment* suffered from malaria, while those in *275 VC Regiment* suffered much worse at around 30 per cent and some operations had to be cancelled due to sickness) and most of its recruits were still very young – some just 16 years old. Its *3rd Battalion*, however, was judged to consist of recruits from the north (formerly NVA *D605 Battalion*) and assessed to be more aggressive.[14]

On 23 October 1965, the *VC 274* and *275 regiments* were combined with *22 Mountain Artillery Battalion*, *12 Anti-Aircraft Company*, *95 Reconnaissance Company*, *23 Mortar Company*, *25 Engineer Company*, *605 Communications Company* and *96 Medical Company* to form the PLAF *5th VC Infantry Division*, under the command of Colonel Nguyen The Truyen, a patient and intelligent man who maintained his headquarters in the May Tao Mountains.[15] With the expansion of his force, the division was assigned a greater area of operation that included not only Phuoc Tuy Province but also Bien Hoa Province and parts of Long Khanh Province, which were collectively known as Ba-Bien. During the first half of 1966 the *5th VC Infantry Division* conducted a number of operations in Ba-Bien, but with the arrival of the Australian Task Force in Phuoc Tuy in mid-1966, COSVN reassigned the *5th VC Infantry Division* the task of defending the province from the incursion by the newly arrived enemy force.[16]

In early July 1966, *275 VC Regiment* was located just south-east of Phu Mountain, near the boundary of Binh Tuy and Long Khanh provinces, north-east of Phuoc Tuy, while *274 VC Regiment* and other units of the division, including its headquarters (which consisted mostly of North Vietnamese staff), were located in Xuyen Moc District in the eastern part of Phuoc Tuy. In all, the total Viet Cong strength allocated to operations within Phuoc Tuy Province amounted to around 4500 troops.[17]

The Viet Cong set about trying to come up with a strategy to force the Australians out of Phuoc Tuy and hopefully, in the process, out of South Vietnam. Nguyen Thanh Hong, an operational officer of the *5th VC Infantry Division*, recalled that when the Australians began to construct their base at Nui Dat in 1966, they assessed that their role was to be an independent mobile strike force that would focus on destroying *D445 VC Battalion*, which in 1966 could field just 380 troops consisting of three rifle companies, *C1* to *C3*, and *C4*, which was a heavy-weapons unit.[18]

While small in size, these local insurgents, commanded by the experienced major Bui Quang Chanh, had conducted successful operations against the US and ARVN forces before the Australians arrived, and their morale was high. In addition, there were about 400 local guerrillas operating in groups of various sizes from five to 60 out of local villages and hamlets.[19] That said, the Viet Cong were 'well aware of the threat to their stomach and nervous system' that 1 ATF presented in this location.[20] While the commanders of the *5th VC Infantry Division* were concerned about Australian commando tactics, they were confident that in any conventional confrontation the Australians would come off second best.[21]

In August 1966, a group led by the deputy commander of the *5th VC Infantry Division*, Lieutenant Colonel Tran Minh Tam, met with the commander of the Ba Ria unit, Dang Huu Thuan, who had responsibility for military operations within Phuoc Tuy Province. They discussed a mobile ambush operation 2–3 kilometres in length against the Australian troops in the rubber plantation of Long Tan. The *2nd Battalion* of *275 VC Regiment*, along with a company of the local *D445 VC Battalion* with RPGs and a 57mm recoilless rifle, would be located along the eastern edge of the plantation to block the forward elements of the Australians, while the *3rd Battalion* of the same regiment (the former NVA *D605 Battalion*) would be located 800 metres south-west – it was this battalion that would attack the main Australian force. Meanwhile, the *1st*

Battalion, reinforced with the remaining two companies from *D445 VC Battalion*, would be responsible for blocking the retreat of the Australians and was to assist in the attack led by the *3rd Battalion*.[22]

This planned large-scale mobile ambush was not just a military priority: it was also seen as a political necessity to help garner further local support. It would be seen as revenging the evacuation of Long Tan village and the destruction of Long Phuoc. (Indeed, after the Battle of Long Tan, a considerable cache of food, ammunition and explosives was found in Long Tan village, perhaps representing early preparations for the intended Viet Cong ambush.) However, events would overtake this operation, as the Battle of Long Tan commenced before the planned ambush could be put into effect.[23]

While most histories to date, including the Australian official history, state that *274 VC Regiment* was to be involved in the mobile ambush of an Australian unit in the Long Tan rubber plantation by acting as a blocking force against any US forces coming down from the north, the captured notebook of the second-in-command of *274 VC Regiment* (Nguyen Nam Hung) reveals this was not the case. Elements of *274 VC Regiment* were spread over a number of base camps in north-eastern Phuoc Tuy at the time and had no plans for any involvement in operations supporting a battle to take place in Long Tan rubber plantation (or the Task Force base, as some have suggested) during August 1966. This was also later confirmed by contemporary signals intelligence.[24] Captain Trevor Richards, commanding 547 Signal Troop, advised the 1 ATF commander on 18 August of the location of *274 VC Regiment* and commented that it did not appear to be preparing for combat: it 'seemed to be on R&R [rest and recreation]'.[25]

There has also been much ink spilled regarding the Viet Cong forces making an attempt to attack the Task Force base itself. The base at Nui Dat has been described as far from secure, with normally just two infantry companies (around 200 frontline troops) thinly spread around a long perimeter, itself defined by minimal wire and few if any minefields.[26] Even though the base would seem to have been a realistic tactical option, the history of the *5th VC Infantry Division* makes no mention of it being attacked; nor is there any suggestion that *274 VC Regiment* would be involved in any operations, including as a blocking force north of the base or elsewhere.[27] All available evidence indicates that the intent of the Vietnamese force was to conduct a mobile ambush against an Australian force in the Long Tan plantation. A common tactic of the Viet Cong was to also set up an accompanying ambush for any relief force. This could result in the destruction of two Australian companies at least, if not a whole battalion. Indeed, Nguyen Nam Hung has stated that their intent was to draw out an Australian patrol in force so that it could be ambushed and annihilated in the Long Tan plantation.[28]

However, before this ambush could be set up, the Viet Cong forces would collide with an Australian rifle company numbering 108 men in the Long Tan plantation on 18 August 1966. The Viet Cong force consisted of troops from *275 VC Regiment* and *D445 VC Battalion*, amounting to around 2000 'rifles' (including at least one heavy-weapons company) – impossible odds at 20:1.

8

'. . . it was the one grain of gold amongst all the crap'

Since mid-June, 5 RAR and 6 RAR had been conducting ongoing day and night patrol and ambush operations in Phuoc Tuy. The first serious encounter with the Viet Cong by the Task Force was during Operation Hobart in late July, in a five-day 'search and destroy' operation that was to be conducted north-east of Nui Dat. In what can best be considered a foretaste of the Battle of Long Tan – which would be fought less than a month later – 6 RAR with three platoons from 5 RAR took on a strong force of Viet Cong from *D445 VC Battalion*, unexpectedly colliding close to Long Tan village. An intense firefight developed and Australian and New Zealand artillery support was called in, with the enemy replying with mortar fire. The sound of bugles could be heard close by as the Viet Cong units tried to signal each other. This sent a chill into the heart of every Australian – the Viet Cong were obviously out there in numbers.[1]

One shell exploded in the centre of B Company, 6 Platoon's position. As reported by Australian journalist Patrick Burgess at the time:

One Australian machine-gun changed hands four times during the action as soldiers took over from their dying and badly wounded mates. On an M60 machine-gun [Private] Bob Vikukus, 20, of Townsville, took a bullet through the shoulder. His No.2 on the gun, 19-year-old [Private] Johnny Stevens, of Melbourne, began putting field dressings on his mate. Blond, happy-go-lucky Lance Corporal Col Jacket, of Brisbane, ran in and took over the gun; then he gave it back to Stevens and begun firing his own weapon. Stevens was hit in the legs and Jacket sprang back onto the gun. Then [Private] John Burns of East Perth moved in, too. Although the fire was intense, the soldiers, even those badly wounded, joked aloud. Bob Vikukus said when he was hit the first time: 'It's true, you know, you don't feel the bullet that hits you.' Then he was hit with a grenade.[2]

The engagement lasted for over an hour, with 6 RAR suffering its first killed: a national serviceman, a 21-year-old bulldozer driver from Mansfield in Victoria, Private Anthony Purcell, and an army regular, 26-year-old from Cairns in Queensland, Corporal John Norris. Fourteen others were wounded, among them two New Zealand forward artillery observers, including a forward observation officer (FOO) for B Company, 6 RAR, Captain Pat Murphy. One of the Australian wounded, 21-year-old sapper Leslie Prowse from Goomeri, Queensland, with 1 Field Squadron, Royal Australian Engineers, would die from his wounds on 27 July 1966. Corporal Boyd Rutherford, B Company, 6 RAR, was later awarded the Military Medal for disregarding his safety in rallying his men, who were heavily outnumbered, and continuing to distribute ammunition and move about attending the wounded while under fire.[3]

Major Noel Ford, commanding B Company, was impressed with the abilities of the enemy, commenting that 'the VC force encountered was very quick in reacting and deployed when the contact was made. Their fire and movement were good and the soldiers brave and determined. Their fire power was impressive and virtually every man appeared to have an automatic weapon of some kind. Their 60-mm mortars were accurate and searched the company position thoroughly.'[4]

Lieutenant Colonel Colin Townsend, commander of 6 RAR, had good reason to be proud of his men: they had only been in country for two months; this was their first serious, prolonged engagement with a major enemy force; and they acquitted themselves well. In his after-action report he wrote that the company 'conducted itself well during this action and commanders at all levels handled the situation competently and calmly. The enemy force was *C1/D445 Battalion* and it fought well [its political officer, To Dung, was killed in the engagement.[5]] It is to B Coy's credit that it was successful in this action, the first in which it had ever been involved, against an experienced and well-trained battle-wise enemy.'[6]

Operation Hobart was the introduction to the Australian way of doing things for US Lieutenant Steinbrook and his battery of 155mm guns assigned to 1 ATF. They arrived at Nui Dat just as the battle started and could hear the action from there. He wrote that day to Frances: 'Not too far away a big battle is raging, and it keeps us jumping. Believe me, this area is not quite as secure as Bien Hoa.'[7] A few days later he wrote to his parents: 'as a whole so far, the Australian and New Zealand officers seem much better than ours. They're all so darn professional. They really impress us.'[8]

Lieutenant Colonel John Warr recalled that by August, 'we were just pushed to the limit to both defend the base area and to carry out the patrolling that we were required [to do] to clear the province'.[9] He and his men were exhausted. When platoons and companies returned to base, they were assigned to work details – there was no choice, as preparing the base for defence was a top priority. However, given that 1 ATF was already below strength, rotating the men through leave added greater stress on those left behind who had to perform increased duties, which further reduced capabilities. The only solution was more men, but that was not going to happen in a hurry, if at all. Even so, ongoing patrolling and intelligence collection throughout August had indicated that there was no credible information of any enemy force in strength being close to the Task Force base. While some low-grade human intelligence alleged that enemy activity was taking place to the east, including within the vicinity of Long Tan, vigorous patrolling within supporting artillery range of Nui Dat by 6 RAR indicated that this was not the case.

That said, there was some signals intelligence that indicated 'increasing enemy interest to the EAST of the Task Force base area which resulted in our attention being directed towards this area in order to locate any sizeable enemy force'.[10] Given the sensitivity of this source information, it was only made available to Major Richard Hannigan (operations officer); the two intelligence officers at Task Force headquarters, Captain Bob Keep and Major John Rowe; and Brigadier David Jackson.[11] While battalion commanders could be told of the content of the intelligence, they were not told its source, making it difficult to assess its overall credibility and/or significance. Clearly the battalion and company commanders at the very least should have been informed of the source of information supplied so they could make a meaningful assessment when planning operations; however, the policy from Canberra was clear – only indoctrinated officers were to have access to signals intelligence. That said, as noted by Major Harry Smith years later, 'one would think Jackson would have whispered it into our CO's ear, and suggest we be very careful'.[12]

While 6 RAR had boots on the ground patrolling the area, the battalion commanders were not informed of the ongoing signals radio direction-finding intelligence that indicated increased enemy activity to the east of 1 ATF base. Signals intelligence from the Australian 547 Signal Troop – which at the time was reliant on US Air Force C-47 aircraft for direction-finding fixes on VC radio transmissions – indicated that an enemy detachment had begun to move towards Nui Dat.[13] The signallers of this small unit, commanded by Captain Richards, had become so adept at differentiating between Viet Cong radio sets that they had fixed the sets belonging to *274 VC Regiment* just north-west of its sister unit, the *275 VC Regiment* east of the Song Rai River, just north of Xuyen Moc, 22 kilometres east of Nui Dat.

In July both Viet Cong regiments were assessed to be resting and conducting training, but it was noted in August that signals activity of *275 VC Regiment* had increased in traffic and duration. Additional intelligence indicated that this regiment was receiving reinforcements from North Vietnam.[14] As noted earlier, in May 1966 following the heavy casualties that were inflicted on the regiment during the second battle of Vo Xu (Binh Tuy Province), *275 VC Regiment's 2nd* and *3rd battalions* were forced to combine to make up the *2nd Battalion*, and soon troops from the NVA (*D605 Battalion*) would arrive in the province and be assigned to *275 VC Regiment* as its *3rd Battalion*.[15]

With this increased activity, Richards was concerned that something was brewing and passed the information on to intelligence officer Captain Keep, who was subordinate to the chief of intelligence, Major Rowe. Neither Rowe nor Brigadier Jackson appeared to have much confidence in the radio-direction abilities and seemed to dismiss it. Indeed, Major Rowe is reported as telling Richards to 'disappear into 103 Sig Sqn and keep out of the way as he – the intelligence major – knew what he was doing and we (547) were not part of it'. Richards was also not invited to participate in Task Force operations or intelligence briefings.[16] However, Keep was aware of its potential significance and went behind Rowe's back to provide the latest information to Jackson – at the same time not providing it to his own superior, Rowe.[17]

Both Richards and Keep tried to assess the importance of the intelligence, not just from signals but from a number of other sources, not all of which were credible. They set about trying to sort the 'wheat from the chaff'. Even so, Richards knew that his men had provided 'hard' intelligence that should be given priority. He knew his signallers could identify and locate enemy radios. Keep later stated: 'You knew . . . it wasn't a ten-man foot patrol and it had to be – the least it could be – regimental if it was North Vietnamese. If it was Viet Cong . . . it was something equivalent or perhaps a bit less but certainly it wasn't a ten-man foot patrol and you'd better take notice of it.'[18] They became even more concerned when the signals intelligence indicated that a radio set associated with *275 VC Regiment* began to move slowly west (around 1 kilometre a day) towards Nui Dat. Richards kept passing the information to Captain Keep, who in turn passed it on to Jackson – bypassing Hannigan and Rowe.

Rowe and Hannigan became aware of Keep's disloyalty when Jackson called a conference to discuss the latest signals intelligence. Neither major had any idea of the intelligence being discussed. After the meeting Rowe 'gave a rocket' to Keep and reprimanded him 'in the strongest terms for not having kept Hannigan and myself informed of these SIGINT [signals intelligence] developments, which were of the utmost importance'.[19] Even so, the problem now for Rowe was that he was reviewing not only the radio direction-finding intelligence, but a mass of human source information, captured documents, US and South Vietnamese intelligence, and enemy radio traffic intercepted by other non-Australian signal units. Unfortunately the signals intelligence from 547 unit got 'lost' within the mass of intelligence being collected – regardless, Rowe did not put much faith in Richards' radio-fixing intelligence anyway.[20]

The Australian historian of the Signal Corps later wrote: 'It was thought that the enemy force was much smaller than it actually turned out to be. The problem was that the enemy regiment's headquarters travelled with a battalion as protection and therefore did not need radio communications with them and the second battalion was close enough to have the use of a runner. The third battalion in the regiment was the only radio link discovered and as a result no network could be pieced together from the radio intercept. Jackson thought that it was only a part of the third battalion but [Richards informed] him that it was in fact a regiment.'[21]

However, on 13 August, 1 ATF notified the AFV based in Saigon that signals and recent human intelligence indicated that an enemy force, probably at company strength, was active in the area to the east of the base, close to Nui Dat 2 and the Long Tan rubber plantation. The next day, Captain Richards informed Brigadier Jackson and Australian liaison officer Major Alex Piper at US II Field Force Vietnam that his signallers had also identified enemy radio traffic from *275 VC Regiment* just 5 kilometres east of the base. He made it clear he was merely tracking the position of the radio and was unable to provide any context to the messages being sent or received. While he acknowledged that he could provide only the position of one of *275 VC Regiment*'s radios and that it could be a ploy of the Viet Cong, he argued that 'it was the one grain of gold amongst all the crap' and strongly indicated the presence of the regiment, or at the very least an advance party, in the vicinity of the Long Tan plantation.[22]

Major Rowe, who had previously served as a liaison intelligence officer with the US 173rd Airborne, had learnt to be suspicious of radio fixes as he'd had numerous experiences of enemy regimental radio sets being located close by but rarely if ever resulting in an attack.[23] Rowe knew that boots on the ground were required to assess the significance of any intelligence gathered by radio tracking. This was a time for Jackson to insert an SAS patrol a few kilometres east of the Long Tan plantation to provide an update of potential enemy

movements, but for whatever reason, and through no fault of the
SAS, no such patrol was conducted.

Even so, Jackson recalled that by mid-August 'it had become pretty
obvious – there were certainly growing real indications – that the
5th VC Infantry Division intended, as we had always expected, to try
and destroy the Australian force at Nui Dat. There was every indication that we could look forward to a major attack from the East
against the base.'[24] Jackson now increased patrols, with the specific
intention of seeking out *275 VC Regiment* to the east. Accepting
that a large enemy force might be approaching their tactical area
of responsibility, a 'company was the minimum sized patrol that
could safely take on this sort of task – even though we had enormous artillery support of course and enormous air support with
it. So we went out looking for *275 Regiment* somewhere to our East
or North East.'[25]

On 15 August – two days before the mortar attack – D Company,
6 RAR, which within days would find itself fighting for its very
existence against overwhelming enemy forces in the plantation at
Long Tan, was sent out to the hilly area just north of Long Tan
plantation known as Nui Dat 2. From there they were to sweep
back through Long Tan plantation to the Task Force base. They
did so and came across nothing of significance.

The following day, A Company, 6 RAR, under the command
of Captain Charles Mollison, was sent out on a three-day patrol in
the area of Nui Dat 2 and along the ridge to the north-west. The
company was to send out a number of patrols, each of which was
to be at least a platoon in strength. Any sizeable enemy force in
the area should be picked up. The first day of the patrol was largely
uneventful until 3.20 p.m., when machine-gun fire from Mollison's
3 Platoon broke the silence. They had spotted a small group of enemy
troops in army greens, not the typical 'black pyjamas' of the Viet

Cong – indicating that these Vietnamese might belong to members of the regular NVA. The enemy returned fire, then disappeared.[26]

Just as Mollison finished his report to 1 ATF via radio, additional fire broke out from 1 Platoon on another enemy party. Lieutenant Trevor Gardiner, commanding the platoon, and his men were preparing to move out after a brief rest when the section facing south alerted them with a hand signal: 'Enemy!'

> We hit the deck and there soon appeared two soldiers wearing green uniforms. My first reaction, since we had not expected contact with any enemy regular forces up to that stage, was almost to stand up and say 'Bloody 3 Platoon, lost again'. But the next figure to appear was dressed in black pyjamas. This was an enemy patrol that had walked into our position. The Section opened fire . . . The enemy reacted quickly with automatic fire and grenades to cover their withdrawal south. I conducted a sweep with one Section but we only located one enemy wounded and a blood trail. I reported two enemy wounded one of whom had been captured. I also reported that the enemy were wearing green uniforms and that they had withdrawn south.[27]

Soon another small enemy party arrived and, while most escaped, platoon marksman Private Johnny Needs shot and captured what turned out to be an officer; on searching his pockets the men found a notebook. With the help of their Vietnamese interpreter, the platoon determined that the notes were about the positioning and firing of mortars. Lieutenant Gardiner tried to interrogate the captured prisoner without success, and the prisoner died from his wounds an hour later. The young lieutenant reported all of this, again stating that the enemy were in army greens, indicating the Australians had possibly encountered troops from a main force and not just local Viet Cong insurgents from *D445 Battalion*.

Just before dusk, Mollison and a small reconnaissance party made their way onto the northernmost knoll of Nui Dat 2 and soon heard someone moving around close by, even though the thick undergrowth muffled much of the sound. The small party stood motionless, as the captain recalled, 'the whole of our being straining to hear, straining to see; our mud-stained uniforms blending with the scrub. Only our eyes moved – staring out from blackened faces. Now that we had stopped, I could feel the blood trickling down my leg from the leeches dispatched earlier when I had detected their blood-sucking presence. The sounds came again – closer this time. And there! A branch cracking . . . THUMP! . . . All around us! Monkeys! A bloody great family of monkeys! They bounded off, chattering and screeching into the undergrowth.'[28]

Meanwhile, back at the Task Force base, intelligence officer Captain Keep and his superior officer, Major Rowe, had each been evacuated suffering medical ailments – by 16 or 17 August, 1 ATF had lost its intelligence officers. Given that the active patrolling had revealed no evidence of any sizeable force within the Nui Dat 2 or Long Tan plantation area, when the mortar attack occurred on 17 August it was assessed to be a hit-and-run exercise, with no evidence of intent by the Viet Cong to begin operations against the base itself:

> The accepted explanation was that D445 VC Battalion mounted the attack on orders from the Viet Cong provincial headquarters possibly in retaliation for the recent search for the headquarters by 5 RAR [Binh Ba]. Alternatively it could have been in response to A Company patrols engaging three small parties of enemy in the general area of the Nui Dat 2 feature on the afternoon of 16 August. A Viet Cong ground attack on the Task Force was thought to be unlikely.[29]

Intelligence to date had indicated that the local *D445 VC Battalion* was active in the area and it was possible that a North Vietnamese battalion – possibly from *275 VC Regiment* – was also present within or adjacent to 1 ATF's tactical area of responsibility. However, the constant patrolling by 6 RAR of the area to the east and north-east of the base, with no sign of any significant enemy activity (besides the hit-and-run mortar attack), suggested that there was no imminent threat coming from that direction.[30] That said, it was known that the enemy regiments could assemble quickly and relocate at short notice anywhere in the province within just 48 hours. [31]

9

'We then proceeded to brief the diggers'

The mortar attack against Nui Dat during the early hours of 17 August resulted in 23 Australians and one New Zealander being wounded – two seriously. One of these was a 21-year-old postman from Granville, NSW, gunner Philip Norris of 103 Battery. He had been hit in the head with shrapnel and was later listed as having died from his wounds.* Lieutenant Colin Browne of the Royal Australian Engineers was later awarded the Member of the British Empire for his actions in assisting the wounded, ten of whom were from the Engineers.[1] Casualties were such that the shelling (combined with the casualties from the Battle of Long Tan, to be fought the next day) had a serious impact on the stocks of medical supplies.[2] The enemy barrage had targeted the south and south-east perimeter of the base, where 103 Field Battery, 1 Field Squadron of the Royal Australian Engineers, 3 SAS Squadron and 1 Australian Reinforcement Unit were positioned.

That morning, as Brigadier Jackson was inspecting the damage

---

* In a remarkable story it was not until 2005 that his army mates learnt that Philip had survived his injuries and had been living in a number of repatriation hospitals since his wounding in 1966. He was later reunited with his daughter, and died in August 2010 (see *Missing presumed dead*, www.103fieldbatteryraa.net).

to the base, Captain James Townley of 103 Battery came out of a crater with a piece of a mortar fin. He told the Task Force CO that it had come from an 81mm Chicom mortar or perhaps one made in the Soviet Union. Jackson immediately dismissed his assessment, stating that it was clearly from a 60mm mortar, as only the NVA would have such long-range equipment. Townley did not push the point, but many who saw the evidence before them knew that it was from an 81mm mortar round. Lieutenant David Harris of the Armoured Corps, an aide to Brigadier Jackson, later recalled that the brigadier wanted to believe they had only been attacked by local Viet Cong elements.[3]

Jackson was not in a position to respond in force to the mortar attack, as one of his two battalions, 5 RAR under the command of Lieutenant Colonel Warr, was still conducting operations in and around Binh Ba, about 7 kilometres to the north, while A Company of 6 RAR was still out on a three-day patrol near Nui Dat 2. This left just three infantry companies to hold and defend the base.[4] While 1 ATF was adequately supported with artillery and machine guns for base defence, it was relatively weak in infantry, which impacted significantly on the force's offensive capabilities. As such, Jackson ordered 5 RAR to complete operations around Binh Ba as soon as possible and return to base.

Indeed, the clearing and reclamation of Binh Ba had been one of the first priorities for 1 ATF on taking over Phuoc Tuy Province just two months before: it was the most important village under the control of the Viet Cong, located on Route 2 leading north to Long Khanh Province. The men had been involved in Operation Holsworthy (8–18 August) to clear the village of enemy concentrations within and around Binh Ba.

Operation Holsworthy not only successfully cleared the Viet Cong from the immediate area but opened up Route 2 for the locals, including those further north at the Catholic village of Binh Gia, who up until then had been isolated from other villages. The ability to renew contact with other townships greatly improved the economic and social fabric of these villages and the surrounding hinterland. Major Bruce McQualter, who would die on 5 March 1967 from wounds suffered during Operation Renmark, wrote in his after-action report how the soldiers were soon playing soccer with the local kids and volunteered to join the villagers in their religious services. He also wrote that when the Australians tried to pay for bananas the villagers refused to sell them – rather, they gave them away for nothing. Many Australians found themselves being invited into homes for 'tea and, in some cases, whisky'.[5]

The battalion medical officer, Captain Tony White, was also happy that he could set about doing some humanitarian work treating the locals, who suffered from a great variety of ailments. Around 1200 patients were treated in just nine days, with malnutrition being the main concern; this was soon remedied with the opening-up of Route 2, which allowed increased quantities and varying food types to be delivered to the villages from nearby townships. Indeed, Lieutenant Colonel Warr remarked that the effect of opening Route 2 'on the morale of the villagers was "remarkable". . . In the first two days 500 people travelling on Lambrettas, ox carts, bicycles, tractors and army transport moved south to Ba Ria'.[6] Captain Robert O'Neill recalled that 'one felt that the environment was growing more friendly towards us. Certainly we no longer sensed the presence of immediate hostility moving about amongst the rubber and banana trees.'[7] Even so, when any intelligence report suggested an attack against the base was likely, it was sufficient merely to pass the word that the 'Binh Ba Ten Thousand is on tonight'.[8]

Meanwhile, back at Nui Dat, Brigadier Jackson was still keen to consolidate his force in case of an attack against the base, and anxiously awaited the arrival of 5 RAR. He needed intelligence of possible locations of any nearby enemy force. A few hours after the mortar attack, at 4.50 a.m., Lieutenant Colonel Colin Townsend, commander of 6 RAR, instructed Major Noel Ford, commanding B Company, to prepare to take his company out on patrol. In all he had a strength of 80 men, including the forward artillery observers. They were to pinpoint the enemy firing positions to the east, somewhere close to the cleared and now deserted village of Long Tan and not far from the elongated hill of Nui Dat 2.[9] After finding the enemy firing positions, which were likely already evacuated, Ford was to establish which routes the Viet Cong had taken to escape.

Lance Corporal Phil Buttigieg recalled his OC as a rather cool and aloof character who wore his pistol more like a 'badge of office rather than as a weapon'.[10] The next day, while in battle, Ford was found to have no ammunition for it. 'Fordie', as his men called him (but not to his face), was well respected because a few weeks earlier he had calmly led the 'repulse of numerous company attacks against our company just east of the Long Tan rubber [plantation] where we experienced the terror of bugle attacks and witnessed the close-up devastating effect of our own artillery for the first time'.[11]

Corporal Robin Jones, also of B Company, recalled being issued with his orders for the patrol. Dress was to be basic webbing, with first-line ammo of 60 rounds per man and 200 rounds per machine gun. They were to take a meal and enough for a brew as they were scheduled to be back sometime after midday, or mid-afternoon at the latest. He and the other NCOs went about briefing their men and completing preparations for the day patrol.[12] The men of B Company departed from the base for Long Tan plantation at 6.30 a.m. Corporal Jones recalled:

> As first light broke we left silently into the grey shadows and undergrowth. The going was slow and even at that early hour it was hot and humid, and the chance of running into Viet

Cong even close to the wire was a real possibility in those days. We didn't use any tracks in the area, and scrub bashed, so that by mid morning in the heavy scrub we had only covered about 1,500 metres. We were also slowed down by having to stop frequently and send out recce parties to try to find any enemy sign, or any sign of use on any of the known tracks in the area.[13]

Within two hours of leaving the base they came across a mortar-base plate, east of the Suoi Da Bang stream, approximately halfway between the base and Long Tan plantation. It was relayed back to base at 8.10 a.m. that 'we are checking area to try to establish the number of people involved. A heavy track leading NE [north-east] from the area. Base plate mark seems [to] confirm 81mm Mor[tar] used.'[14] As they checked the area, they found another six base-plate positions, each represented by holes lined with rocks at the bottom to support the mortars. The positions had apparently been quickly abandoned, as small personal items, including a tobacco pouch and rice, had been left behind. It was estimated that around 25 Viet Cong had occupied the positions during the mortar attack.[15]

After reporting the information, B Company was ordered to break into three platoon patrols and push on further towards the western edge of Long Tan plantation. One of these patrols came across some Vietnamese women picking fruit; each had an iden-tification card, and the troops moved on. For the rest of the day they swept the area following a number of tracks, but found noth-ing to indicate any other significant enemy activity. It was deter-mined by 1 ATF command that they would spend the night out beyond the perimeter and set up a harbour position on a fresh track heading south. The men of Lieutenant Eric Andrews, 8 Platoon, C Company, 6 RAR were sent out to provide the men of B Company with rations for their unintended overnight stay in the bush, and the next morning the men of B Company were to continue their sweep of the area.[16]

About two-thirds of B Company had been due for leave the next day in Vung Tau, and it was agreed that at first light these men would make their way back to the Task Force base. The men of 5 RAR and 6 RAR were utterly exhausted – physically and mentally – after two months of constant patrolling day and night with no rest from base-defence duties. They were operating in platoons and companies that were under strength due to casualties and sickness, and despite the combat circumstance, it was imperative that they be given leave to recover. As recalled by Corporal John Robbins, 'You're working all day in that heat, plus patrolling, and at night you had to have all-night ambushes. They'd tell you to sleep, because you're going out on an all-night ambush. Well you couldn't bloody sleep. You can't sleep during the day, in that sort of heat, particularly if artillery are putting rounds off all the time. It was bloody hard. And the morale was probably at a low point, because of the rain and the mud. The mud was bloody awful.'[17]

The remaining composite platoon, B Company, numbering 32 men and made up of a section from each platoon from men who had already had leave, were the next morning to carry on the search under the command of national service officer Lieutenant John O'Halloran, who commanded 5 Platoon, and Sergeant Harry Keen. Major Ford would stay behind to command the operation. They took up a harbour position for the night about halfway between Task Force base at Nui Dat and the main track leading into Long Tan plantation from Route 52.[18]

Earlier, A Company, north of B Company, under the command of Captain Charles Mollison, was patrolling the area north, north-east and west of the Task Force base. They radioed in that they had come across a track that had been used recently, probably within the last 48 hours. Just after 2 p.m., A Company made contact with a single Viet Cong fighter who quickly disappeared. They too were slated to return to base by mid-afternoon the next day.[19]

Back at Nui Dat, the men of D Company, 6 RAR were apparently the lucky ones of the battalion – it was their day off. They were assigned to maintain base security and like everyone at 1 ATF were anxiously awaiting the arrival of Little Pattie (Patricia Amphlett) and Col Joye, who were to play a number of concerts for the troops the next day (18 August) – the first such event to be staged at the 'sharp end' of the combat area of Nui Dat. That night, C and D companies split up to cover their own forward defence positions, along with those of A and B companies, who had with darkness taken up harbour positions well beyond the Task Force perimeter.[20]

While 1 ATF base was being shelled during the early hours of 17 August, a number of Australian SAS field operations were being conducted within the province. In Vietnam the men of the Australian SAS had become recognised as masters of stealth and battle-hardened warriors. Their main job was to provide intelligence, which required ongoing patrols deep within enemy territory. They built a fearsome reputation with Australian soldiers, who called them 'super grunts', and with the Viet Cong, who placed a price on the head of any SAS 'phantom of the jungle' who was brought in.[21]

One of the SAS patrols being conducted that day was about 16 kilometres east of Nui Dat, along the Song Rai River. These men had been flown in by Flight Lieutenant Bob Grandin during the late afternoon of 16 August.[22] Sergeant Ashley Urquhart, who commanded the patrol, noted signs of recent enemy activity and assessed that the Viet Cong, up to a company strong, had become aware of their presence in the area and were out looking for them. This information was not reported until after they had been extracted by helicopter on 19 August, a day after the Battle of Long Tan, due to radio interference and a faulty set. Regardless, there was no indication that a strong enemy force was within the area, and nothing to suggest that any attack against the Task Force was in the offing – although they would have been too far east to identify the presence of *275 VC Regiment* and *D445 Battalion*, which by then were likely just a few kilometres east of the rubber plantation.[23]

Meanwhile, on the same day, another SAS patrol, under the command of Sergeant Max Aitkin, had been inserted about 16 kilometres north of the Task Force base, beyond the township of Binh Gia. The patrol identified four individuals dressed in army greens speedily heading south. Like Urquhart's, Aitkin's radio was out of action but this sighting alone did not indicate anything of significance. Another SAS patrol just east of Aitkin's, commanded by Sergeant Alan Kirwan, identified ten Viet Cong heading west of Binh Gia, and later identified another group moving east, quickly followed by a third group he could hear moving east; he radioed this information back to the Task Force.

This area was known to be populated with Viet Cong and there was nothing to indicate that the enemy was massing for an attack.[24] Indeed, a number of SAS patrols had been conducted since mid-July in Phuoc Tuy Province; their key objective as described by Brigadier Jackson was to 'search for [the] VC main forces and give early warning of any major enemy movement through areas where the infantry battalions were not operating'.[25] Like the infantry patrols, those of the SAS came across no evidence of any significant enemy activity near or approaching 1 ATF base.

A few days before the mortar attack against the Task Force base, a number of Australians from 12 Platoon, D Company, 6 RAR were in the make-do canteen having a drink when the mail arrived.

Among them was Private David Beahan from Armidale, NSW. He recalled: 'We were all reading our mail, and the next minute this bloke yelled, "You beauty – she's accepted!" We all looked at him. "She's agreed to marry me," he said. "She's agreed to marry me!"'

The men carried on reading their mail, and soon after Private Beahan got a pat on the shoulder and Private Paul Large asked if he could see him for a minute. 'He said, "Mate, I want you to be my best man at the wedding." I said, "Don't be bloody silly, Paul. You've got your school friends and your mates from Coolah." And he said, "No, no, read this paragraph here of the letter" and it said, "Paul, please pick an army friend for your best man, rather than a school friend or a Coolah boy".' Beahan said they had known each other for less than 12 months, but even so had become great mates, and Private Large said, '"I want you to be best man" and that was it.'[26]

In the early morning of 18 August, Private Mick Levin of A Company had recovered from his case of pyrexia and had returned to his tent. There he found an old mate from D Company, 6 RAR, a 21-year-old army regular from Bendigo, Private David J. Thomas, who had been staffing A Company's base area while the company was out on patrol. Private Levin recalled that when he got back to his tent he came across Private Thomas, who was sleeping there. Both had been in the same platoon at the training camp in Ingleburn, NSW. They sat on the cots and 'chewed the fat' and before leaving to go back to D Company, Thomas left two cans of Swan Lager for his mate. Thomas would be killed in action that afternoon.[27]

Sergeant Bob Buick had a similar experience. He recalled the previous afternoon picking up two reinforcements for D Company: privates Colin Whiston and Frank Topp. He was not to know that within 24 hours both would be killed in action.[28]

Part Two
THE BATTLE

D Company, Sixth Battalion, Royal Australian Regiment, distinguished itself by extraordinary heroism while engaged in military operations against an opposing armed force in Vietnam on 18 August 1966 . . . As the battle developed, it became apparent that the men of D Company were facing a numerically superior force. The platoon of D Company were surrounded and attacked on all sides by an estimated reinforced enemy battalion using automatic weapons, small arms, and mortars. Fighting courageously against a well armed and determined foe, the men of D Company maintained their formation in a common perimeter defence and inflicted heavy casualties upon the Viet Cong . . . The conspicuous gallantry, intrepidity and indomitable courage of D Company were in the highest tradition of military valor and reflect great credit upon D Company, Sixth Battalion, The Royal Australian Regiment and The Australian Army.

United States presidential unit citation presented to D Company, 6th Battalion, Royal Australian Regiment on the second anniversary of the Battle of Long Tan

10

'I'm staying in and doing my time'

Thirty-three-year-old Major Harry 'The Rat' Smith, commanding Delta Company, 6 RAR, got his nickname during the Malayan Emergency, when he finally tracked down a bunch of noisy gamblers who had been keeping everyone awake for a few nights with their antics. Smith recalled years later that 'after many successive but unsuccessful investigative incursions into the barracks area, I walked into the offending hut some nights later to discover a group of well-oiled soldiers noisily playing poker and two-up. I announced something like "At last – got you – you rats." From then on, my nickname followed me everywhere.'[1]

He had joined the army in 1952, served in Malaya from 1955 to 1957 and was promoted to major in 1965. Smith was a hard taskmaster and made sure his men were prepared for anything; he would keep them (and himself) going until it hurt and then push on further. The men were justifiably proud of their company. When battalion commander Lieutenant Colonel Colin Townsend specified a 10 km march, D Company did 12 km; when 15 kg packs were to be carried, D Company put on 20 kg; when an exercise specified sandshoes, Smith ordered boots.[2] They were undoubtedly the fittest company in the battalion and had adopted as their theme song the Nancy Sinatra hit 'These Boots Are Made for Walking'. Sergeant Bob Buick recalled: 'We didn't walk anywhere – we fucking ran.'[3]

When Smith first took command of D Company he earned the wrath of the well-liked and respected Townsend, recalling how his CO* did not approve of the way Smith was training his company, which seemed more akin to commando training with 8 km runs every morning. The major was accused of trying to elevate his company above the standards required for an Australian infantry company.[4] Smith had qualified for the commando green beret, but Townsend insisted he wear the infantry officers' peaked cap. His CO was also distinctly unhappy that the young major would lead his junior officers astray by teaching them to do 'parachute rolls' out of the top-floor mess windows. This had already resulted in at least one broken ankle. However, Townsend agreed that the battalion was training for what would largely be company patrols and company-level engagements with the enemy, and as such each company commander had the right to train his men the best way he saw fit.[5]

One of Smith's men, first-intake national serviceman Private Harry Esler, described his commander as a 'very good soldier, in that everybody respected him . . . He was a bloke you trusted with your life. Nothing seemed too hard for him. He seemed calm at all times and gave a feeling of confidence. Don't get me wrong – he could be a very hard man. The look he'd give you if you were playing up was enough to drill a hole in you.'[6] Private Robin 'Pom' Rencher for his previous unknown sins was allocated as Smith's batman and signaller. One of his first tasks as the OC batman was to cook the major's dinner; he wasn't happy about this until he looked around to tell the major his meal was ready and found him nearby, stripped to the waist, doing his share of digging a weapons pit with his men. Private Rencher later admitted that Smith was

---

* CO (Commanding Officer) refers to battalion commander, rank of Lieutenant Colonel and above; OC (Officer Commanding) refers to the rank of major, captain and lieutenant.

one of only two men he would follow to hell and back, stating: 'Harry was a soldiers' soldier, whose professionalism rubbed off on the whole company.'[7] Smith's strict training regime and discipline would pay huge dividends in the hours to come.

Major Smith was grateful to have as his company sergeant major an experienced, exceptional and dependable 31-year-old Korean War and Malayan Emergency veteran, Warrant Officer 'Big' Jack Kirby. Sergeant Major Kirby was a bear of a man who was not as fit as he used to be and feeling his age compared to the young soldiers in his charge. Even so, he accompanied the men in all their runs during training and, while not being able to keep up with them, always finished. He had recently been an instructor at the British jungle training centre in Malaya and was up to date on all the current teaching and techniques. Kirby was a welcome addition to the company and, like his OC, insisted that everyone give 110 per cent. He was known as a fair and just disciplinarian:[8] all knew his bark was far worse than his bite. He was very much the rock of the company, and his actions during the Battle of Long Tan would only deepen and broaden the men's appreciation for his steadiness, bravery and humour under enormous pressure. It was principally due to the efforts of Smith and Kirby that D Company became the crack rifle company it became.[9]

The company consisted of three platoons. A 25-year-old regular, Lieutenant Geoff Kendall from the Officer Cadet School at Portsea, commanded 10 Platoon. He had been a professional rugby league player and coach in western Queensland, but with the season finished was working as a roustabout on a station when he saw an advertisement that read 'Would you like to be an officer in the Australian Army?' and recalled thinking to himself, 'Boy, it's gotta be better than this!'[10] He reckoned he could handle a year at a holiday resort called Portsea, with sport, a hectic social life and eventual graduation as a dashing young lieutenant; that was quickly drummed out of him when he was dropped off by bus at the officers' training school. On hearing that he had been accepted, his father, who was a World War II veteran, remarked that there was nothing wrong with the army: 'It's the bastards who are in it that'll give you a problem!'[11]

After completing training as a lieutenant and on hearing that he was to be appointed to D Company, Kendall's immediate reaction was horror that he would have to help train the influx of national servicemen. That attitude changed, certainly after the Battle of Long Tan. Early on, however, he remembered one occasion when a national serviceman in uniform passed him in the classic 'thumb in bum, mind in neutral' mode. The young lieutenant let the soldier get about 5 metres past and then roared, 'Don't you salute officers?' The startled soldier turned around and saluted, replying, 'Oh, Jesus – sorry, mate!'[12] Private Tony Stepney of the young lieutenant's 3 Section recalled: 'Geoff Kendall was a fantastic platoon commander – he was easygoing and spoke to you nicely, and he'd get the respect.'[13]

Sergeant Neil Rankin, a veteran of Malaya from 1961 to 1963, was the recently installed sergeant of 10 Platoon. The quiet, fatherly figure and respected NCO had recently been transferred from 11 Platoon. He joined the army in 1960 and was posted to 6 RAR as a corporal, but was soon promoted to sergeant with the first national servicemen intake. His primary concern was always the wellbeing of the men under his command. Like the company OC, he led by example and was often seen working with his men, doing his share. The men of 11 Platoon, his previous assignment, were sorry to see him go: while he could and did invoke his stripes, he did so judiciously.

Twenty-one-year-old lieutenant Gordon Sharp, who would command 11 Platoon, was a national serviceman who had been a television cameraman on the popular *Mavis Bramston Show* before being drafted and sent to the Officer Training Unit at Scheyville, near Richmond, New South Wales. While there he suffered concussion and broke both his forearms when training on the scramble nets; each was covered in plaster, but even so he pushed on and completed his training. His cousin Don Sharp told him: '"There's your way out, if you don't want to go on." He said, "No, I'm staying in and doing my time."'[14] This would be highly commendable at any time, but especially so when he had previously admitted that he would lose a lot of experience as a cameraman while away, and would not have volunteered for overseas service but went anyway.[15] His fellow officer cadets obviously held him in high regard. It speaks volumes that the young trainee lieutenant with both arms covered in plaster could not graduate without his uniform and equipment all being in order (pressed and polished to perfection) – his fellow classmates, no doubt led by Gordon's boyhood friend and fellow trainee officer John O'Halloran, ensured that all was correct and accounted for.[16] Both Gordon and John would graduate and be posted to command an infantry platoon of 6 RAR.

Lieutenant Sharp liked playing cards and would often be found with his men, cards in hand. Just before leaving for Vietnam, the young lieutenant in his sports car was with one of his men, the then Private John Robbins, in Melbourne when Gordon spotted a sign that said 'Delta Company Construction'. The later-to-be-corporal Robbins recalled: 'Sharpie says, "I've gotta have that sign." So he swings around, pulls into the curb, walks onto the road, stops a passing truck, tells the driver the story, gets up on top of the truck and acquires the sign. He converted it to Delta Company *De*struction and that sign went with us to Vietnam, along with a nude photo in a frame from a hotel in George Street.'[17]

Another member of Sharp's platoon, Queensland bank clerk Private John Heslewood, remembered: 'He mixed with the diggers as much as the officers. He come down with the diggers when we're having a beer, but he never drank in his life . . . but you'd go out with him and you'd think he was as drunk as you were . . . He just had that natural personality to enjoy company . . . [but] if he had to be hard, he could be as hard as anyone – a real leader. As I said, he enjoyed the company, but if he had to put his foot down . . .'[18]

During the 70 minutes or so that would define the young lieutenant's battle command of his platoon, from the first contact during the afternoon of 18 August 1966, he indeed showed himself to be a leader, taking command of his men and the situation and exposing himself to concentrated enemy fire to call in artillery fire to protect them. He would be killed in action.

Sharp's second-in-command was South African–born 26-year-old sergeant Bob Buick. He had joined the Australian Army in 1959 and served until 1965. Within months of being honourably discharged he re-enlisted and was posted to the newly formed 6 RAR as a private, but was soon promoted to corporal and then sergeant. Buick was a no-nonsense disciplinarian, and when he gave an order he expected it to be obeyed without question.[19] He would take command of the 11 Platoon after Lieutenant Sharp's death during the battle.

Twenty-one-year-old lieutenant David Sabben, a layout artist based in Sydney, had been called up by the ballot but was told he would not be going in this round of intakes. He recalled many years later he was determined to be a part of the first National Service contingent and packed his bags and presented himself first thing at Victoria Barracks. He argued with the authorities there, who eventually gave up and put him on a train for Kapooka. His determination to join resulted in him becoming the subject of newspaper articles, and even a cartoon. He too was a graduate of Scheyville and commanded 12 Platoon, D Company. Like Gordon Sharp, he was a likeable character and would prove his leadership value in combat.[20]

Sabben's second-in-command was the extremely popular and experienced Korean War and Malaya Emergency veteran Irishman Sergeant James 'Paddy' Todd. The oldest man in the company, he had completed two tours in Malaya with the same battalion as Jack Kirby, and they were great mates. In demeanour he was similar to Kirby and took great care of his men, often providing sound advice and always playing the peacekeeper. When one of his men was charged for accidental discharge of his rifle despite claiming the safety had malfunctioned, Todd advised the young soldier to insist on a court martial, which he did; predictably, the matter was dropped.[21] After arriving in Nui Dat, the war-experienced sergeant was having a few beers with his OC, Major Smith, and remarked, 'There's something wrong with all this. It might not be us, but one of these days one of our companies is going to run into something.'[22]

11

'I noticed everyone else had done the same . . .'

It was 6.30 a.m., 18 August 1966 – the day after the mortar attack against the base. Lieutenant Colonel Colin Townsend, commanding 6 RAR, radioed to A Company, who had taken up a harbour position west of the Suoi Da Bang stream, that they were to 'search area SOUTH and EAST of present location but NOT EAST of the creek line which was searched previously. Providing nothing untoward happens you will return as planned this afternoon.'[1] Captain Charles Mollison replied that they were preparing to move out and would commence platoon searches; they moved out at 6.42 a.m.

Townsend then radioed Major Noel Ford of B Company at 6.35 a.m.: 'D Coy will take over approx 1200hrs. Continue search to EAST and NORTH. No farther EAST than track 473660 [the main track running into Long Tan Plantation from Route 52]. Can you get your R&C [rest and convalescence] people back early? – 48 pers., will return by approx 0830. Aim for B Coy is to determine whether en [enemy] withdrew to EAST.'[2]

At 8 a.m., Captain Mollison of A Company, patrolling about 2 kilometres north of B Company, radioed to Townsend that they had come across a track showing strong indications that several people had recently used it. A platoon was sent south to follow it for a short distance; they were soon back with nothing to report.[3] Even so, Mollison sent out a number of platoon-strength patrols to cover the immediate area. With one of these was Private David Hede, who was patrolling through the numerous paddy fields that were then in flood. Each man kept to the bunds (embankments) to keep dry. Even so, someone – Private Hede believes it was Private Gordon Best – tripped and fell into the paddy field head first. The men of the patrol couldn't help laughing, even though they knew the fertiliser used included human excrement. There is no comment regarding Private Best's reaction, but it probably involved a few expletives at their expense![4]

Back in Nui Dat, Major Harry Smith and his men were looking forward to the concert that was due to start around midday – there would be three concerts in all. At 8 a.m., Smith got word he was required at battalion headquarters and on arriving was informed by the battalion CO that he and his men would be missing the concert. His orders were to relieve the depleted B Company at around noon and continue the search for the enemy mortar crews that had shelled the Task Force the day before; these crews were expected to amount to no more than 40 Viet Cong from the local *D445 VC Battalion*.

Smith's CO asked him what he thought he had out there. Smith replied that B Company had found what appeared to be the heavy-weapons platoon base plates of *D445 VC Battalion*, who had fired the mortars and rockets into the Task Force base the night before and who by now were probably long gone. Colonel Townsend told him to go out and find the Viet Cong heavy-weapons team.[5]

Lieutenant Geoff Kendall, commanding 10 Platoon, recalled being warned to prepare for a three-day company patrol; their objective was to locate and destroy Viet Cong mortar and recoilless-rifle units that had fired on the Task Force base. However, at no stage of the briefing or later was he, or anyone else, told there might be an enemy regiment somewhere near Long Tan. Given the ongoing 'shoot and scoot' tactics used by the enemy to that date, Kendall and his men believed that the enemy were by now many kilometres east of the plantation, heading back to one of their jungle bases.[6]

Attached to D Company for this operation was the 35-year-old quiet, experienced and competent New Zealander and Duntroon graduate Captain Maurice 'Morrie' Stanley, from 161 Field Battery, Royal New Zealand Artillery. He would act as the artillery FOO. Accompanying him were Lance Corporal William Walker and Bombardier Murray Broomhall of the battery. In all, Smith's command would total 108 men.[7]

At 8.20 a.m., a much-depleted B Company with just 32 men radioed Townsend that they were located at position 467670 – indicating that they had crossed the eastern branch of the Suoi Da Bang and were heading in a north-easterly direction about a kilometre from the western edge of Long Tan Plantation. Those who were due for R&C were already heading back to Nui Dat. Two hours later, at 10.20 a.m., Major Ford and B Company radioed their position as 47256740, at the very western edge of Long Tan Plantation. There they found freshly dug enemy defensive pits, dug after the last rain – each large enough to hold two people.[8] Corporal Robin Jones remembered entering the plantation. It had been 'pretty nerve-racking stuff in the open, but eventually we entered the rubber plantation and felt immediate relief from the heat and from the threat of enemy ambush. But just under the second row of trees we located many hastily prepared but freshly dug enemy fighting pits.'[9]

The enemy seemed to have cleared out in a hurry, leaving behind 16 'metal ammo containers of Chinese origin' likely used for recoilless-rifle rounds; a track leading south-west was noted to have recently been used to carry a heavy load.[10] Soon additional ammunition containers were found nearby, totalling 22 in all. Major Ford assessed that the track had likely been used by one of the mortar crews. Additional tracks were identified leading to the north-east and south, suggesting that the area had been used as a rendezvous point for the recoilless-rifle teams moving south. Ford sent out two sub-section patrols, one along each track.[11]

The first patrol was under Sergeant Harry Keen, who, along with three of his men, moved into the heart of the plantation. They came across the familiar small rubber-tapper's hut about 1000 metres east of the main track that originates from Route 52. They searched the hut and found no signs of any enemy activity; close by they found plenty of fresh tracks but did not see anyone. It was obvious to all of them that the enemy had been there, and might still be around.[12] With Sergeant Keen was recent reinforcement to the company Private David A. Thomas (not to be confused with Private David J. Thomas of D Company), who saw a nearby well that had recently been used, as there were signs that water had recently slopped on the ground. He also noticed some ammunition boxes and Ho Chi Minh sandals. He then experienced 'a very creepy feeling. The plantation was too quiet. No birds. No insects. I slid down the tree I was standing next to and took up a prone position. I noticed everyone else had done the same without any orders or signals.'[13] He recalled feeling that something sinister was present – they could all feel it, but whatever it was, it was not going to declare itself. He had never been a superstitious person by nature, but from that day onwards he developed certain habits as the section scout that he practised for the rest of his time in Vietnam.[14] They moved back to Ford and reported what they had found.

The other patrol was conducted by Corporal Jones, who, along with machine gunner Brian Bodley, rifleman Michael Nicholas and signaller Geoff Schifcofske, had a similar nagging suspicion that all was not as it seemed. They headed down the track leading south – they were to go no further than 1000 metres and return. Jones recalled that the plantation with its overhead canopy was silent and eerie. They soon came across fresh oxcart tracks, and a little further on they identified bloodstains on the track and on the lower parts of the tree trunks.[15] Several times Jones believed he saw movement up on the slight rise to the east as they moved forward, but he couldn't be sure. Soon after that, the patrol came across enemy recoilless-rifle pits.[16] Jones radioed in his position as 469668. The area contained three weapons pits, each with eight 75mm shell cases; it was the position used by three recoilless-rifle teams. He also noted that the area had been hit by Anzac counter-battery fire from Nui Dat: along with shell holes they found discarded clothing with bloodstains, indicating at least two casualties.[17] The corporal and everyone else knew it was unusual for the Viet Cong to leave anything behind – they recycled everything, even worn-out tyre treads to make sandals.

At this stage he and the others had the distinct feeling they were not alone and were under observation from the east. While none of them could see any signs of enemy activity, each had a nagging feeling that something was wrong. It was about noon. Jones advised Ford by radio of their findings, and soon the major approached to check it out for himself.[18] Arriving with him was Lieutenant John O'Halloran. Three or four large rubber trees had been cut down, indicating to them that the recoilless rifles (RCLs) had been deployed there during daylight and the trees had been used for cover. During the night the trees had been cut down to provide a clear field of fire. However, the destruction in front of them indicated that the Anzac counter-battery fire during the early hours of 17 August had been effective. There were some body parts and bloodstained clothing, with empty shell cases strewn around that would normally not be left behind. Clearly at least one shell had hit the oxcart and those manning the position, and the enemy had left in a hurry.[19] Jones told Ford he thought he had seen enemy movement out to the east, but his OC did not seem to believe him, which 'pissed off' Jones a bit. Ford checked the position and they quickly headed back to the north-east corner of the plantation, all feeling relieved to leave the area.[20]

At Nui Dat, two RAAF Iroquois helicopters from 9 Squadron, assigned to transport the Col Joye and Little Pattie group of entertainers to Nui Dat, had arrived. Captaining A2-1020 was Flight Lieutenant Frank Riley, with Flight Lieutenant Bob Grandin, Leading Aircraftsmen (LAC) Dave 'Blue' Collins, and George Stirling. A2-1022 was captained by Flight Lieutenant Cliff Dohle, with Flight Lieutenant Bruce Lane, Corporal William (Bill) Harrington, and LAC Brian Hill.[21]

Grandin remembered as a 25-year-old being excited about being assigned to transport the Australian celebrities. As the concert party arrived to be transported to Nui Dat, the flight crews were lined up waiting for them. The atmosphere was light-hearted and everyone, including the entertainers, was pretty excited about the day's planned events. Jokes were flying around and there was much talking and laughing as they flew to Nui Dat. However, as soon as they landed, the army moved in and that was the last they saw of Col Joye, Little Pattie and the band. With nothing else to do, crew members stayed on the helicopter pad and set about going through their usual boring routine. As far as they knew, in a couple of hours the three planned concerts would be over, the entertainers and their gear would be packed on board the choppers, and they would be on their way back to Vung Tau. It would turn out to be anything but. Like the men of D Company, 6 RAR, they would soon be in the thick of the action.[22]

Meanwhile, Major Brian McFarlane, commanding C Company, 6 RAR, was doing his rounds checking on his men and decided to visit the makeshift concert stage that was located to the rear of 6 RAR's position. He witnessed the band warming up and wondered what the Viet Cong would think when they heard the music blaring out of the loudspeakers and whether they would think the base was 'trying to lure them to surrender to the wiles of the siren songs of Little Pattie'.[23] He saw that a number of units had already parked trucks in 'advantageous positions to act as viewing platforms, taking the place of private boxes in more civilized circumstances'.[24] As he moved among the men he noticed a strange sense of relief had descended as they started to gather. He felt compelled to linger and chat with men from other units. All were happy to escape the tedium and constraints of army life, if only for a few hours. A small sense of normality prevailed.[25] He later recalled that 'for Col Joye and the Joy Boys, Little Pattie, and friends, it was going to be a day (and a night) to remember, but not for the concert, although that was a great success and tumultuously received by the audience'.[26]

Indeed, Little Pattie (Patricia Amphlett) recalled being surprised at how large the base was. It was 'really quite exciting. And it was exciting because probably for the first time we'd have very big audiences, and, as performers, the more people that are enjoying the performance obviously the better. We'd experienced before quite a few Australian audiences in Vietnam, and they were just the best, they were terrific. So this was a good day, and it promised to be a great day for us. And for the fellas there as well.'[27]

Meanwhile, Major Smith could not help but notice how disappointed the men were at having to miss the concert and conduct a three-day patrol that had little prospect of achieving anything. Company No. 2 signaller Private William (Bill) Akell, attached to company headquarters (CHQ), recalled being 'disappointed when being told "No concert – you have to go out to B Company"... we were all looking forward to attending the concert.'[28] Some of Smith's men could not help but think (incorrectly) that it was because of the strained relationship between Smith and the battalion CO that they ended up getting all of the 'dirty jobs'. Smith gave their patrol the operational codename 'Vendetta' in revenge for the VC mortar attack of the day before. All of his platoons were below strength due to illness, R&C, odd attachments to other units, and involvement in language training: 10 Platoon numbered 32, 11 Platoon 28 and

12 Platoon 29, with CHQ at 19, including the three New Zealanders of the battery.[29]

Just after 11 a.m., Smith and D Company left the base, making their way east to link up with B Company. The average age of the men under Smith's command was just 21. Private Alan Parr of 12 Platoon recalled as they left the base passing 'through the wire in front of D Company's position. We could hear the concert in full swing.'[30] Lieutenant Geoff Kendall recalled: 'We were moving out, just as we were walking up. We were all pretty cranky – it was just going to be a waste of time . . . we were going to miss the concert [for nothing] . . . we certainly didn't expect to run into a huge [enemy] force.'[31] Sergeant Bob Buick was in a similar mood, recalling as he left Nui Dat that the patrol would just be another hard slog through the scrub, with nothing of significance to show for it.[32] Corporal John Robbins remembered most of the men, including himself, being 'pissed off' at having to miss the concert – everyone pretty much had 'the shits'. It was the first entertainment to arrive at the base, and at the last minute they're ordered to head out on a three-day patrol.[33]

At 11.25 a.m., Smith radioed in their position as 455674, about 2.5 kilometres west of B Company. There was no way they would be relieving them at midday, as planned. Smith opted for single file, with Lieutenant David Sabben's 12 Platoon out in front; Sabben was good with a map. Smith told the young officer: 'OK, Sabben, we want to get there. Go for it.'[34] This formation would increase its speed through the already-searched low scrub, swamp and paddy fields between the Task Force base and B Company's position. Sabben remembered that pushing quickly through the undergrowth, the heat and the machete work required to get through the 2-metre standing grass meant it was crucial that the lead section be relieved every 15 minutes – it was becoming a real slog. They had to cut their own path through the grass towards the plantation for about half the total distance. He recalled that it was 'stiflingly hot down in the long grass, with no breeze to carry the chaff and insects away. Add to this, there was the pressure of the OC to get to the rendezvous as soon as possible, as the Bravo group needed to return to base before nightfall. Behind us, the rest of the company enjoyed a slower pace and reported hearing the deep throb of the bass and drums plus the distant strains of music as the Task Force's first concert got underway back at base.'[35]

About an hour after leaving Nui Dat, the regimental signaller, Corporal Graham Smith, who had the critical role of maintaining communications between the company and the Task Force base, recalled passing the two platoons of B Company heading in the opposite direction making their way back to the base and Vung Tau for R&C. He said 'G'day' to a couple of friends as they passed by.[36] Likewise, Private Parr recalled passing the men from B Company as they were returning to the base. The men from D Company pushed on, with the sounds of the concert blurting out behind them, heading for B Company, which was now represented by just one composite platoon.[37]

Meanwhile, A Company, which was close to completing its three-day patrol, radioed its position as 474683, placing it about a kilometre north of B Company. Captain Mollison stated that they had come across a very old cache of rice and salt. At 11.31 a.m., he radioed in his new position as 461681, indicating that he had crossed the western branch of Suoi Da Bang. He reported hearing 'voices to his SOUTH – investigating'.[38] Fifteen minutes later, Mollison radioed in that Lieutenant Peter Dinham's platoon had detained a woman and two children with no identification cards who were acting suspiciously. They were ordered not to move further south and to sweep back to base and bring in the Vietnamese. This last order was not appreciated, as it meant some of the men from Dinham's platoon would now be burdened with carrying not only their own gear but also the heavy bunches of bananas the Vietnamese were collecting. Regardless, these men could begin thinking about the imminent prospects of a shower, clean clothes and a cold beer.[39]

Mollison was satisfied with the results: they had made contact with an enemy force; killed two and wounded three Viet Cong; and captured two weapons, much ammunition, clothing and equipment, and a quantity of very valuable documents, with no casualties to A Company.[40] He radioed through to his company quartermaster sergeant (CQMS), Staff Sergeant Ron Morritt, to arrange for a hot meal for his men on their return. Unbeknown to him, however, the company cooks were already preparing a feast to congratulate the men on their successful patrol.

Just before midday, Major Smith radioed in D Company's position as 458672 – still west of the Suoi Da Bang, about 1.5 kilometres from the edge of the plantation. They had suffered their first case of heat exhaustion.[41] In the distance the men could hear the 'beat of the drums and the occasional strains of song pushed out by loud-speakers as the patrol moved further from Nui Dat'.[42] The hot, stifling and humid weather, combined with the company moving at a fast pace, added to the men's foul mood. Private Terry Burst all of 12 Platoon was pushing through the scrub with sweat oozing from every pore. The terrain was flat, but the bush was thick and a lot of low areas were very wet. He and others tripped over tangled roots with mud clinging to their boots, which sucked hard with every step. Several times on the way out they were 'drenched by sharp sudden storms. At times we could hear the concert music beating through the fetid air – it seemed to come in quick smashing blasts of sound that stopped suddenly with hardly an echo.'[43]

The men from A Company, heading back to base, could also hear the band; some of the more musical among them mimicked the performers, using their rifles as mock guitars. However, those carrying the increasingly heavy bananas were in no mood for any tomfoolery, and likely let the other blokes know it.[44]

Going in the opposite direction, the men from D Company soon came up to the Suoi Da Bang. The stream was flowing pretty rapidly and it was difficult to get across with their packs and weapons. Even so, the crossing was made relatively quickly and safely, with every-one wringing wet. They took it in their stride – just another wet, muddy patrol – but even so, were acutely aware of the dangers, and their fingers remained on their trigger guards. The rubber plantation was becoming visible from the stream, so they knew they were close to making contact with the remainder of B Company. The men of 12 Platoon were still at point and headed for the plantation, push-ing through the thick long grass until they came to the edge of the plantation.[45] Lieutenant Sabben recalled being relieved to reach the relatively cool shade at the edge of the rubber and meeting up with their brother company.[46] Having led the way, the men of 12 Platoon were thankful that their time at point was over. When moving out again, they would be placed as the reserve platoon so they could recover from their gruelling and nerve-racking time at point.

Sometime after 2 p.m., D Company reached the small group of B Company, now represented by a composite platoon, on the edge of the Long Tan rubber plantation, about 4 kilometres from Nui Dat.* The men of D Company took up their defensive posi-tion while majors Smith and Ford discussed the situation. The men could hear the distant concert, now well and truly under-way, while they brewed up their meagre combat-ration packs of

---

* While just about all narratives to date regarding the Battle of Long Tan (including the Official History) state that B and D companies joined up at around 1 p.m., the signals provided in 6 RAR commander's diary indicate that D Company was still moving towards the plantation at 1257hrs (12.57 p.m.) and 1332 hrs (1.32 p.m.). It is not until 1430 hrs (2.30 p.m.) that the log indicates that both B and D companies are located at 473674 – the position of the weapons pits found by B Company that morning.

tinned meat and biscuits. Captain Stanley came across his fellow New Zealand FOO for B Company, Captain Pat Murphy, and they compared notes, with Murphy informing him of the tracks they had found and suggesting some possible directions for further patrolling.[47]

Ford briefed Smith on what they had found and showed him the weapons pits. Smith recalled years later looking at the Viet Cong position and seeing that it was obvious that the Anzac artillery had hit something there. The Ho Chi Minh sandals and bits of equipment distributed randomly about indicated to him and others that there had been some casualties and that the survivors had fled in a hurry towards the north-east. Smith gave quick orders to his platoon commanders that they would soon be heading out towards the north-east in a one-up formation.[48] He recalled Ford summarising the situation as being 'quiet'. They had reconnoitred the area up to the tapper's hut about 1000 metres to the east and agreed that the Viet Cong mortar and RCL squads had done the usual shoot-and-scoot operation, fleeing in small groups.[49] Indeed, D Company had patrolled the plantation a few days before (on 15 August); A Company had been patrolling the area just north of their position over the last three days with some contacts but nothing indicating enemy presence in any strength; and B Company had nothing of significance to report.

Most of the men eating their rations and boiling up a brew had come to the same conclusion: that the enemy had 'pissed off' as per usual. Private Brian Reilly, D Company, 12 Platoon, had come across some mates from B Company who told him, 'There's nothing out here.' He went to take a look around, not overly impressed at having missed the concert for nothing: 'it was fairly mundane . . . we had a look around at the mortar base plates, and that was it'.[50] Corporal Robbins took the opportunity to have lunch with a newly arrived private, Frank Topp, who had joined his section the night before. Robbins recalled: 'I knew everyone else but I didn't know Frank, so I had lunch with him and got to know him a bit. I put him at ease as it was his first time out.'[51]

Meanwhile, Lieutenant O'Halloran of B Company recalled sharing his lunch with his friend Lieutenant Gordon Sharp. They had grown up together in Armidale, NSW and had played rugby and hockey together in the same school team; their parents had been married on the same day and hence shared their wedding anniversaries; they were called up together in the first intake and graduated from the Officer Training Unit at Scheyville; and both were assigned to command infantry platoons in 6 RAR.[52] It would be the last meal the boyhood friends would share. O'Halloran recalled sadly: 'Delta Company arrived sometime after 1330 hours and shared their rations with us. During lunch, which I had with . . . Gordon . . . we could occasionally hear the guitars of the Col Joye show playing in the base. As we departed Gordon's last words to me were "It's all right for you to be going back to listen to the music while we have to stay out here and face the music."'[53]

Another who would lose a good friend that day was Private David A. Thomas of B Company, who was assigned to carry an enemy artillery cleaning rod and brush that had been found in the area. He remembered as he was leaving how his mate Private Topp (they had completed basic training together) laughed at him as he headed back to Nui Dat, telling him, 'You're a warrie [stories of glory and valour] bastard, Thommo.'" Thomas replied, 'If they get hold of you out there, you will be too.' 'Poor Frank was killed later that same afternoon.'[54]

Back at 1 ATF base the Anzacs were being entertained. It was only a few months ago that these young men had left Australia and New Zealand, but that seemed a lifetime ago. As they relaxed, 6 RAR intelligence officer Bryan Wickens was arranging for a 161 Recce Flight using an Australian Army Sioux observation helicopter, commonly called a 'bubble' because of its cockpit appearance, to conduct reconnaissance over the area to the east of 1 ATF. It would be piloted by Lieutenant Rob Rich. Wickens was keen to identify trails or any other signs that would show the likely escape route taken by the Viet Cong weapons team.

At the eastern edge of the Long Tan rubber plantation, a small command and staff unit belonging to the *5th VC Infantry Division*, led by Lieutenant Colonel Tran Minh Tam, along with the three battalions of the *275 VC Regiment*, commanded by Senior Captain Nguyen Thoi Bung, were entering the plantation. Not far from them were Major Bui Quang Chanh and his troops of the local *D445 VC Battalion*, located in and around Long Tan village to the south. Also present was a reconnaissance element from the division, likely commanded by Le Huu Nghia.[55] Other elements, including mortar teams, were taking up positions close to Nui Dat 2 and further south. Small reconnaissance patrols had been sent out earlier; all indications were that the Australians had left the plantation, and most of the Vietnamese were relatively relaxed. They would set about preparing for an ambush that would hopefully, in the next few days, destroy in detail an Australian patrol. Local intelligence indicated that the Australians were now sending out company-sized patrols, and the Viet Cong estimated that an ambush consisting of the *275 VC Regiment* and *D445 VC Battalion* could pick off such a patrol with little risk to themselves; certainly they would need a larger force if they hoped to take on the Task Force base with any real prospect of success. The intended ambush was more of a political necessity as the COSVN Military Affairs Committee was keen to propagate a victory against the Australians – a major ally of the US.

Sometime during the mid-afternoon a helicopter from RAAF 9 Squadron piloted by Flight Lieutenant Max Hayes was on a leaflet mission. He flew over the supposedly deserted village of Long Tan and saw a number of people in and around the small hamlet. No one fired at the helicopter, and he dropped a bunch of leaflets that urged the Viet Cong to join the South Vietnamese Army, with promises of land as soon as they changed sides. Those in the village were almost certainly elements of the *D445 VC Battalion* who likely took little if any notice of the pamphlets other than using them to roll cigarettes. The Australian chopper banked away to find other places to conduct its propaganda war.[56]

12

'I was surprised when he introduced himself as Frank'

1500–1540 hours

It was 3 p.m. when D Company moved out on rising ground away to the east across the shallow basin of the Suoi Da Bang valley. Lieutenant David Sabben recalled that there was a heavily used bullock-cart track that led directly into the heart of the plantation. It was defined by deep ruts in the mud, so they knew that the carts were 'heavily loaded and we assumed, therefore, that they were loaded with all the weapons that had bombarded us. It was now thirty-six hours after the shelling, so the people on foot would've been long, long, gone.'[1] Major Harry Smith ordered the company to move out in one-up formation (arrowhead configuration), following the bullock track. Lieutenant Geoff Kendall and his men of 10 Platoon were in the lead. Directly behind by about 100 metres was CHQ, while the other two platoons fanned out either side of CHQ to cover each side of the track, with Sabben's 12 Platoon on the left and Lieutenant Gordon Sharp's 11 Platoon on the right.[2] It was the duty of each man to scan his arc of responsibility, with his weapon sweeping slowly from side to side in line with his vision as the company penetrated deeper into the plantation.[3]

Given that its objective was to track down the Viet Cong mortar teams, the patrol was conducted in a more fluid manner than was normal. The soldiers were not assigned to a specific sector, which enabled those back at base to coordinate other operations around them, including predetermined artillery harassment and interdiction (H&I) fire plans. The current operation, as recalled by Sabben, required them to advise the Task Force base of their position and direction so that battalion headquarters (BH) could reroute other patrols and change H&I fire plans to take into account their patrol movements. As such, it was entirely up to the commander on the ground to decide where he would go.[4] For this reason it was also critical that Captain Maurice Stanley, as FOO, stay in contact with Major Smith at all times. It was his job to provide advice regarding artillery support to the company commander as required. He also needed to be sure of the company's location, including the three platoons, and how far away they were from CHQ. These were crucial concerns for any FOO, and for the gunners back at the Task force base, who might be called upon to provide fire support to friendly troops in the immediate area of any contact.[5]

As they pushed their way through the outlying areas of the plantation, old and disused trees with undergrowth gave rise to new plantation trees and a more orderly landscape of avenues of trees, providing long views in one direction but reducing visibility in others – maximum visibility was about 250 metres.[6] Sabben remembered moving into the cool of the plantation. Though it was still dry, clouds were gathering above, a little heavier and darker than usual; the men were anticipating heavy rain later in the afternoon.[7] Kendall radioed back to Smith that they were about 150 metres into the plantation and had come up to a point where the 'track separated in a Y – the left-hand track stuck with the edge of the rubber which was [mostly scrub] and the main track continued into the centre of the rubber'.[8]

Smith advanced up to 10 Platoon and saw a smaller track break off, going for a short distance in a north-east direction before turning in a south-east direction running generally parallel with the main track, straight through the plantation towards its distant eastern edge; each track now running roughly parallel was separated by about 300 metres. The plantation here was still about 2000 metres deep to the east, and just visible through the lines of rubber trees to the north-east lay the jungle-covered Nui Dat 2; to the south-west and north-west lay an impenetrable forest of bamboo, leading back to the stream.[9] Smith reported to the battalion commander, Lieutenant Colonel Colin Townsend, seeing signs of scattered clothing and odd bits apparently dropped in a hurry. Townsend asked Smith which way he thought the Viet Cong had retreated, and Smith informed his superior that he would toss a coin, then jokingly said, 'Go west, young man, but in this case I'll go east.'[10]

Smith renewed the advance but now in two-up formation, bringing forward 11 Platoon. Kendall and 10 Platoon followed the northern branch, while Sharp and 11 Platoon followed the southern branch, which was on slightly higher ground; both were heading into the heart of the plantation. Each platoon was now itself in two-up formation with two sections forward and one section back.[11] Behind was CHQ and not far behind that was Sabben with 12 Platoon. Company frontage and depth were about 400 metres. At this point all platoons and CHQ were in visual contact.[12]

The men of B Company were in a hurry to get back to base. Lieutenant John O'Halloran recalled how their pace quickened the closer they got – they were keen to see the last concert of the day and then take R&C leave to Vung Tau.[13] Corporal Robin Jones remembered that the platoon set off, 'happy to be on our way, thinking about something to eat as it had been mid-morning the previous day since we had eaten anything substantial. Leaving the

rubber we crossed the Suoi Da Bang stream and made our way past
the area of an enemy mortar base-plate position.'[14]

Back in the plantation, the forward sections of 11 Platoon had come
up to another sunken bullock track, this one running north–south
and cutting across their path. The left forward section of 11 Platoon
was commanded by Corporal John Robbins (6 Section), while
the right forward section was commanded by Corporal William
Moore (5 Section). Corporal Jeff Duroux (4 Section) was behind
with platoon headquarters. Sergeant Bob Buick recalled moving
slowly. Robbins' section had crossed the north–south track, which
was relatively straight and wide enough for a bullock-cart to pass
through the plantation. There was a two-strand barbed-wire fence
on the western side of the track about half a metre high. Tracks
and fences are obstacles that impede progress and require caution
when trying to negotiate them. At this point the terrain sloped
slightly downhill to the north, to the left of 11 Platoon, and the
hill crested about 75 metres to the right. It was a gentle slope, but
even so, when the men were on the track it limited their visibility
to the south and any Viet Cong would have experienced the same
problem when moving north along the trail towards 11 Platoon.
By now Lieutenant Sharp had got 6 Section across the track and
was advancing 5 Section to secure the other side. The platoon commander and his radio operator, Private Vic Grice, now crossed
the track, with Private Barry Meller and Sergeant Buick some 20
metres behind them.[15]

Lance Corporal Barry Magnussen, 2IC (second-in-command)
of 5 Section, recalled being in the lead with two scouts, privates
Allen May and Doug Fabian. They, like the command group, had
just crossed the track when to their right moving along the track
they saw a small group of Viet Cong. Magnussen was with Private
Ian Munro, his section machine gunner. Neither could fire at the

D Company, entering the Long Tan rubber plantation

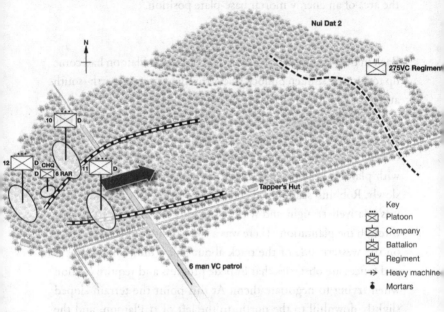

3.35 p.m.: D Company begins crossing the main bullock track, while a Viet Cong Patrol from the south moves towards them unaware.

Viet Cong as the platoon scouts were in their field of fire.[16] The Viet Cong had literally walked into the middle of D Company as it was crossing the same track. Private May recalled seeing what he thought was a 'bunch of kids . . . then I realised that these kids had weapons . . . Doug Fabian and myself both opened up on these people'.[17] Buick, who was about to cross the track, recalled vividly many years later looking up and seeing all of a sudden on his right about six Viet Cong dressed in greens almost among them. He recalled that they 'were going along quite nonchalant. They weren't bloody interested at all and I thought, "Hang on, these guys are walking straight into the middle of the company!"'[18]

The fire from May and Fabian, which was quickly followed by fire from Buick, wounded one Viet Cong and forced the others to take cover 'out of sight in the light rubber and tall grass that was about half a metre high in the "dirty rubber"'.[19] The enemy patrol, almost certainly from *275 VC Regiment*, had walked between the last man of the right of 6 Section (leading section) and the leading man of 5 Section just coming up, with a gap of about 50 metres. They were soon retreating, having picked up their wounded comrade, and heading east off the track; the wounded Vietnamese soldier was later found dead close by. Buick remembered that the Viet Cong never returned fire but just took off, running past the right side of 6 Section towards the small tapper's hut used as the collection point for the latex tapped from the rubber trees. This hut would figure prominently in the battle that soon broke out all around.

First contact – it was 3.40 p.m. Just north and to the rear of 11 Platoon, Kendall and his men of 10 Platoon heard the firing break out a few hundred metres to their right. He moved the platoon away from the track and listened as the 11 Platoon contact moved from patrol contact to section attack to platoon attack.[20]

It was not only the Australians who were surprised by the sound of small-arms fire. The North Vietnamese commander, Lieutenant Colonel Tran Minh Tam, chief of staff of the *5th VC Infantry Division* and deputy divisional commander, was based at Nui Dat 2, while his second-in-command, Nguyen Thanh Hong, a staff officer of the division, was located in the small deserted hamlet of Ap Phuoc Hung about 2 km north-east of Long Tan village and 3 km east of the battlefield.[21] The commanders had earlier assessed that there were no enemy troops within kilometres of the plantation or the village of Long Tan. Surprise, which was their greatest ally for the successful large-scale mobile ambush planned for the following days, had dissipated within a matter of seconds.

Back at Nui Dat, A Company was finally entering the base after its gruelling but successful three-day patrol. Waiting for the men were a number of replacements for the battalion, including two for A Company, 2 Platoon, privates Phil Murray and Laurie Bodey. When the company returned, recalled Private Bodey, they reported to the platoon sergeant and were surprised when he 'introduced himself as Frank [almost certainly Sergeant Frank Alcorta] (not as sergeant this or that). However, I didn't have time to dwell on it because he quickly introduced me to my new section commander, Corporal [Louie] Stephens. The corporal told me to take over "that camp stretcher in that tent" as he sprinted off to the showers, nude except for a towel around his waist and an OMC [Owen machine carbine] over his shoulder.'[22] Another reinforcement for A Company, Private Mick Greenwood, was luckier than his mate Private Col Whiston. Both had spent about six weeks together in Vung Tau doing general duties, waiting to be assigned. On 16 August, Private Whiston was moved up the line to Nui Dat and assigned to D Company, 11 Platoon; he arrived just in time to go out on his first and last patrol. Private Greenwood arrived on 18 August, just in time to be thrown into the battle to help relieve D Company.[23]

Not far away was US lieutenant Gordon Steinbrook, who with his battery had recently arrived at Nui Dat to provide heavy artillery support to 1 ATF with six 155mm howitzers. He had been allocated to 6 RAR as an FOO and was having a few beers with some recently made mates from the battalion at what went for the officers' bar. He had earlier recalled how the US and Australian military viewed quite differently the status of FOOs:

> All the [Australian and New Zealand] FOOs were captains or senior first lieutenants, the most experienced and capable officers of their batteries. Not only that, the FOO assignment was sought after as 'the job to have'. In contrast, FOOs in the American artillery were usually junior lieutenants, and the job

itself was regarded as the most dangerous and least desirable
of any. As I moved in with the infantry, therefore, it came as
quite a shock to find that the Aussies and Kiwis assumed I
must be the 'chosen one' from the battery to have gotten such
a coveted assignment. Mistaken as they were, moving in with
the Aussies and working for a New Zealand artillery battery
proved interesting and unforgettable.[24]

As he chatted with his mates, the first of the New Zealand battery
fire missions was about to fire against the small group of fleeing
Viet Cong. It would not be long before a runner from battalion
headquarters would come looking for them to tell them that
D Company had run into something big – but for now he and the
others enjoyed their beers, unaware of the battle that was about to
break out just 5 kilometres east of the base.

13

'. . . then all hell broke loose'

1540–1610 hours

Everyone behind 11 Platoon heard the scattered firing. At CHQ, Private Bill Akell recalled on hearing the first shots that 'we all went to ground of course, the standard thing to do on contact'. He and likely almost everyone one else thought, 'Well, we've made contact with a couple of enemy, they're going to nick off, and we're just going to move on and continue the patrol. That seemed to be the standard way the Viet Cong operated at that time . . . fleeting contact with the enemy.'[1]

Private Terry Burstall of 12 Platoon was bringing up the rear and recalled covering about 200 metres into the plantation when he heard fire from the first contact. He and the others went to ground, as they were trained to do in such circumstances, but he wasn't overly concerned and turned to look at Private Harley Webb, a new reinforcement who had joined the company a day or two before, saying, 'That's a good start on your first patrol.'[2] Webb just looked at him with a forced grin. Another of Lieutenant David Sabben's platoon, Private Alan Parr, recalled: 'We heard the contact out to our right front. Then everything fell silent again . . . If we'd been carrying the signal set for Lt Sabben we might have had some idea what was going on as 11 Pt would have called Coy HQ about the contact.'[3]

Indeed, Lieutenant Gordon Sharp had radioed back to CHQ, telling Major Harry Smith that he had made contact with enemy troops who were not in black pyjamas but in khaki – this usually meant members of a main force. Sharp asked permission to pursue them, and Smith agreed. Smith at 3.40 p.m. relayed to battalion headquarters to inform Lieutenant Colonel Colin Townsend: 'Contact with 6 to 8 enemy dressed in greens at YS478873 possibly wounding one. Enemy fled east.'[4]

Sharp's platoon now changed into line formation, with 6 Section commanded by Corporal John Robbins to the left, 4 Section and Corporal Jeff Duroux in the centre, and 5 Section with Corporal Bill Moore on the right; the platoon headquarters was about 15 metres behind 4 Section. With 11 Platoon now in an extended line, they swept forward to catch up with the retreating enemy if possible, the platoon front stretched out to about 250 metres. Smith radioed 10 Platoon to maintain its direction and rate of advance and for 12 Platoon to its rear to close up with CHQ. FOO Captain Morrie Stanley conferred with Smith and confirmed the position of the dispersed company on his map. At 3.42 p.m., Stanley called in an artillery strike from his New Zealand battery against position 482668, about 500 metres east of first contact; this would hopefully disrupt the enemy's line of retreat.[5]

Just as the New Zealand battery opened fire against the fleeing Viet Cong, the tired and weary men of A Company, with their three Vietnamese detainees, were finally putting down their gear and 'their' bananas. No one paid much attention to the rounds being fired as they were likely just another routine fire mission. However, the Australian entertainers, who were playing their second concert of the day, were affected by the sudden sound of anger, with some giving a tentative laugh and others jumping with fright.[6]

Meanwhile, Lieutenant Adrian Roberts, whose 3 APC Troop would soon be in action, was having a shower and didn't take any notice, thinking that the fire was of no significance to him. Captain Ian Darlington, in the Fire Support Coordination Centre (FSCC), had just minutes before left the concert as he was to take over command of the FSCC at 4 p.m. He was chatting with Major Peter Tedder of 105 Battery about developments when Captain Alan Hutchinson, one of Tedder's FOOs, came in looking for a place to bunker down for a few days. He had just returned to base with 5 RAR and within days was to fly back to Australia, having completed his first tour of duty.[7]

Not far away, Captain George Bindley of 103 Field Battery, whose tent had gone up in flames during the early-morning attack against the base the day before, did take notice, as the day had been relatively quiet and he wasn't aware of any plans to fire the battery at this time. Even so, it was still not that unusual, and he enjoyed his hot shower from the standard army canvas bucket, taking in the view across the gun position to the hills in the south and west, where a tropical storm was developing. It would soon be upon them.[8]

Back in the plantation, each soldier had released his safety catch and had his fingers on the trigger guard, eyes focused on identifying any sign of movement up ahead through the rubber trees. It was not long before a Chinese-made AK-47 was picked up by Lieutenant Sharp, who radioed in his find to Smith, who contacted battalion headquarters at 3.55 p.m. stating: 'Recovered one AK-47 carbine at scene of contact.'[9] The fact that the enemy were dressed in khaki trousers and shirts resulted in some discussion, as the men of *D445 VC Battalion* usually wore black and mostly carried bolt-action rifles or carbines, even though some from this battalion had been seen carrying AK-47s previously. Indeed, an AK-47 had been taken weeks earlier from a killed member of *D445 VC Battalion*; the fact that an enemy soldier was carrying an AK-47 was not in itself significant.[10] Even so, Lieutenant Sabben of 12 Platoon recalled that it occurred to him at the time that something was amiss, as they were not expecting to encounter uniformed troops carrying AK-47s. However, Sabben also knew they were searching for a Viet Cong heavy-weapons platoon consisting of mortars and recoilless rifles, and he didn't really know what equipment these blokes normally carried – maybe this equipment was the norm.

Smith radioed back to base at 3.50 p.m. that the enemy was 'probably local', but also that they were wearing khaki; five minutes later he radioed in that they had found the AK-47. Smith believed, not unreasonably, that the soldiers were likely from *D445 VC Battalion*. Unknown to Smith, however, at this point *D445 VC Battalion* was still in and around Long Tan village to the south, preparing for their part in the planned ambush operation and having not yet entered the plantation. Smith later admitted in relation to the enemy's dress and equipment that the penny didn't drop that they might represent a North Vietnamese main-force unit. In reality, however, the penny didn't drop at battalion headquarters at Nui Dat either, as Townsend was notified of the contact, including the enemy in uniform and the AK-47, and failed to make any connection. In reality, it was not an NVA main-force unit. Rather, it was a PLAF (VC) main force, with one recently integrated *NVA battalion – D605 Battalion*, now representing the *3rd Battalion* of *275 VC Regiment*.[11]

At Nui Dat, Lieutenant David Harris (aide to Brigadier David Jackson), was at the Task Force operational centre when the messages from D Company started coming in. He was the most junior officer attached to headquarters. Harris had been privy to some of the intelligence (unlike Lieutenant Colonel Townsend or Major Smith) that indictated the possible westward movement towards Nui Dat by *275 VC Regiment*. He had been impressed with Captain Bob Keep's assessment. He had heard on a spare radio in the operations centre the discussion between Smith and Townsend of the contact just made, and recognised the possible significance of the uniforms and AK-47. He believed that D Company may have come into contact with advanced elements of *275 VC Regiment*, as opposed to the local *D445 VC Battalion*. It was 4.07 p.m. when Task Force command was first officially made aware of the contact by Townsend, but by then Harris had already alerted Jackson, who at the time was preparing to conduct his usual afternoon briefing. Jackson quickly made an appearance at the operational centre. Harris also called Major Bob Hagerty, commander of 1 APC Squadron, unofficially warning him to stand-by one of his troops, as they may be needed.[12]

Major Hagerty was no doubt grateful for the early heads-up. The APCs of 1 Squadron were M113s and more than a little worse for wear and tear. Many had operated with 1 RAR during their 12-month tour and were in urgent need of an overhaul, but the ongoing demands placed upon them and their crews made that impossible. To make matters worse, a number of these tracked vehicles did not have a mounted gun shield around their .50-calibre machine gun, which left the gunner – and APC commander – completely exposed to enemy fire. Worse still, some had no intercom system, which made verbal communications impossible within the noisy APCs. To help rectify this, a string was attached to the left and right epaulets of the driver so the commander could provide steering directions. Also, in some APCs the pivot steering used during stream crossings was worn out, which added to the problems of getting across the often-flooded Suoi Da Bang.[13]

Sergeant Bob Buick, back in the plantation, recalled: 'Moving very quickly and with all three sections now in a battle assault formation – that is, in extended line – we spread out in a single-line frontage some 250 to 300 metres wide.'[14] Sharp's forward movement in trying to follow up on the retreating Viet Cong had further widened the gap that had developed between the two forward platoons – 11 Platoon was now about 300 metres forward of 10 Platoon, with 12 Platoon bringing up the rear with CHQ. The forward position of 11 Platoon and its rapid advance in line formation meant that the inner flanks of 10 and 11 platoons had lost sight of each other. The space between the two forward platoons was now greater than the maximum combat opening range for either the rifle or machine gun: about 300 metres.[15] Private John Heslewood recalled that at the time 'no one really expected anything much to happen after that [first contact]'.[16]

The company moved on another 250 metres or so. At 3.59 p.m., Sharp radioed Smith they had reached the small tapper's hut – the same hut that had been searched earlier that day by Sergeant Harry Keen of B Company – and he reckoned there were voices coming from inside. He said he would check it out and search the immediate area. A few hundred metres to the rear and north of Sharp was Lieutenant Geoff Kendall of 10 Platoon, who remembered thinking at the time: '"Sharp, you lucky so-and-so!" It was every platoon commander's dream: a platoon attack, bowling over an enemy section or squad – and picking up an MC [Military Cross] on the way through.'[17] Sabben, commanding 12 Platoon, was thinking along the same lines: 'When the firing broke out with 11 Platoon I really thought that Gordon Sharp had had the contact that we were out looking for. He had had the fire-fight. In military terms he had won, he had got the contact. It was his battle. We didn't expect more than a half a dozen or so [contacts] for our whole tour. The radio news came back, "Yes, I've contacted half a dozen or so." Once this fire-fight was over, that was all. He would perhaps get a Military Cross for Christmas.'[18]

After a few minutes, Sharp reported in at 4.02 p.m., having found nothing in the hut or in the immediate area other than a few hand grenades.[19] Private Jim Richmond of 6 Section recalled that after they moved out from the hut they moved out again into extended line and a fair way into the rubber to the east. Sharp and his men continued their advance eastward with the three sections abreast – 6 Section on the left, 4 in the centre and 5 on the right.[20] As recalled by Buick, they were all keen to catch up to the retreating enemy with the three sections strung out in a single line – except for the platoon headquarters, which remained behind and to the centre to help with communications.

Each soldier was spaced about 8 to 10 metres apart and with the front line numbering about 20 or so, it provided a frontage of around 200 to 250 metres.[21] As such, the platoon had no depth. The most efficient way of catching up to the fleeing enemy was to shake out into extended line. As they pushed on Buick was thinking, 'Oh well, these blokes have shot through again. You know, this has been the story of every contact we've had for weeks and really, I suppose, I was like everyone else, you know. "Where have these bastards gone, can't we get into a decent fight?"'[22] Be careful what you wish for.

Undoubtedly the contact would have been heard by the officers and soldiers of 275 VC Regiment, just east of D Company. As Sharp and his men pushed further into the young rubber trees, they approached a clearing with a green wall of scrub beyond. The young lieutenant was still carrying the captured AK-47. They now came across a strand of wire running through the trees and, as Private John Heslewood recalled, 'Then the shit hit the fan – this huge, huge amount of bloody fire, automatic and single fire, and we were ordered to hit the ground.'[23] Buick recalled that the enemy opened fire from the north-east at the base of Nui Dat 2.[24] Lance Corporal Barry Magnussen remembered going to 'ground in a long line . . . I raised myself up so I could see . . . I yelled for them to get back, then all hell broke loose. The incoming fire was unbelievable. [Private] Jim Houston was dead. A couple of others wounded.'[25]

First main contact

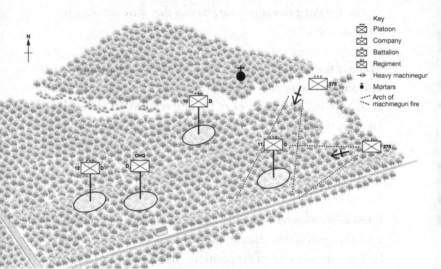

4.08 p.m.: 11 Platoon takes concentrated Viet Cong machinegun enfilade just north of their position from Nui Dat 2, quickly followed by fire to their front.

The bulk of the original enemy fire focused on Robbins' 6 Section on the left. The immediate volume, concentration and intensity of fire was unbelievable. It was not only that: as the men hit the ground to return fire, they saw the Vietnamese advancing straight towards them. Robbins recalled how well dressed they were and believed them to be North Vietnamese; they were likely members of *275 VC Regiment's 3 Battalion*, consisting mostly of NVA:

> The thing that surprised me was that they were attacking and we weren't expecting to run into any well-trained soldiers. We thought we were following Viet Cong in the black pyjamas and when they started to attack . . . they were pretty well

> trained, this group . . . It was pretty much a surprise to me
> that they were coming towards us . . . The first time I saw
> them was 200 metres [away] and there was a lot of them, they
> were forming up and moving forward [from the left] – that
> was the thing that struck me was that they were attacking us.
> I saw them.[26]

Those a few hundred metres behind in the other platoons of
D Company were also shocked by the sudden avalanche of fire
breaking out. Private Parr of 12 Platoon recalled: 'It just exploded
into this frightening roar that lasted for the rest of the day. When
we heard the battle start I can't properly explain in words how we
felt. But I know I'll be haunted by it for the rest of my life.'[27]

A few minutes earlier, the Vietnamese company that had sent out
a six-man patrol was reacting to the firefight that had apparently
broken out just west of its position. The survivors of the patrol
likely made their way back to the company just as the enemy shelling exploded close by. Clearly, the Australians would have radioed
through to their base at Nui Dat of the contact, and the Vietnamese
knew they could expect to be targeted by enemy artillery. Even so,
they assessed that the Australians were only in platoon strength and
could be easily overrun given their own overwhelming superiority
in numbers.

A number of platoons took up a position within low-lying scrub
that blocked the Australians' advance. They didn't need to wait
long before they saw a line of Australian soldiers advancing straight
towards them, but before they could react, a heavy-weapons unit
to their north opened fire, tearing into the open left (north) flank
of the Australians' extended line. The mobile ambush was now
prematurely underway, 24 hours ahead of schedule. The company
engaging the Australians' front would act as the blocking force,

while other elements of the *275 VC Regiment* would be organised to move around and locate the Australian flanks and attack them from there. Meanwhile, the *D445 VC Battalion* located around Long Tan village south of the Australian force, when they got the word, would move west of the Australians' position to attack it from the rear, sealing off any chance of escape. Even though they had been surprised and were not entirely prepared, they could still crush the unexpected Australian force now fighting against them in Long Tan Plantation.

Sharp ordered 5 Section on the right to sweep across the front of the platoon to offer some protection to 6 Section. No sooner had the men begun to move out in a 45-degree arc to the front of the rest of 11 Platoon than the Viet Cong who had taken up a position in the scrub to their front opened up with intense fire on a broad front from several directions.[28] Private Peter Ainslie saw 'a million little lights seem[ing] to come out of the rubber, from knee height to above our heads, and a helluva noise'.[29] The men had no choice but to try to return to their former position; most made it back as others provided covering fire. Private Heslewood of 5 Section recalled that by now '4 Section was inside us and literally for the first few minutes, there wasn't panic – you just didn't know what was going on. And then the training kicked in, and the orders [came] in telling people to go here, there and everywhere.'[30]

Private Brian Halls from the same section recalled being forced to the ground. It was a 'natural reaction bred into us before going to Vietnam . . . I remember being left out forward by myself, and Johnny Heslewood from Brisbane was next to me. There was a VC coming up on my right . . . [Johnny] yelled out, "Can you see him?" I said, "No!" "Well, keep your bloody head down" and he fired across the top of my head and got this bloke, then said, "You're right now – you can pull back." And we did, into a single line.'[31]

Buick knew they were in an extremely serious firefight: the air was full of bullets and tracers.* He recalled that the tracers were like fireflies and were coming into their position from everywhere. So much ordnance was being fired that his head was full of a buzzing sound, and it was impossible to move. If you 'moved you became a target. Once you became a target, you were dead.'[32]

It was 4.08 p.m. when Sharp radioed Major Smith that 6 Section on the left was being hit by 'fairly heavy fire'[33] and he was taking fire from what appeared to be at least a platoon to his front. Close by, Kendall (10 Platoon) and Sabben (12 Platoon) were listening and noticed the strain in Sharp's voice – it was obvious to everyone in the company that 11 Platoon had run into a sizeable enemy force just a few hundred metres to their front. Indeed, the men of 11 Platoon had run into forward elements of *275 VC Regiment*. Kendall later recalled that the fire was increasing and getting very heavy and Sharp came on the radio and said, '"It's too big for me – I think they're about to attack us" – not in fear, just surprise in his voice'.[34] Robbins was commanding 6 Section on the left, which took the brunt of the fire. He knew instinctively that his section had suffered casualties. All around men were calling out that the Viet Cong were in the trees and on the ground. The fire was getting heavier, and Sharp was calling out to Robbins to bring his men closer to the platoon headquarters position to his right. However, Robbins was having difficulty getting the message to his men to his extreme left, and wasn't about to abandon them. He got up and ran across to them to order them back towards Sharp's position and only then realised just how serious his losses were. He immediately came across a couple of his men who were already dead, which staggered him.[35]

Buick recalled that two enemy machine guns were firing to his left front among the scrub and the creek line at the base of

---

* Tracers are bullets with a small pyrotechnic charge in their base, so the shooter can see what/where they are hitting.

Nui Dat 2. He assessed that the fire from these machine guns had cut down nearly all those in 6 Section, who were about 75 metres from this enemy position. The other three sections, including the platoon headquarters section, immediately went to ground as the enemy fire swept the area with machine-gun and rifle fire. They were now pinned down as a storm of fire cut a swathe through their position.[36]

14

'I could tell by his voice that the platoon was in trouble'

1610–1620 hours

At 4.10 p.m., Major Smith radioed to Lieutenant Colonel Townsend back at the 1 ATF base: '11 Pl under heavy fire from approx 485669'. This confirmed that the bulk of the initial fire was enfilade from the area just forward of Nui Dat 2, which was joined by additional fire originating from the scrub to their front.[1]

At first, Sergeant Buick believed another two heavy machine guns were firing from the scrub in front, as he saw their green tracers. While Australians generally had red tracers, the Vietnamese usually used green, helping to further identify friend from foe. He reckoned that the return fire from his men had hit about half a dozen Viet Cong, but it was of great concern that the platoon was being engaged from the left flank and its front 'by at least an enemy company using small arms and RPGs which I thought were heavy machine-guns with explosive rounds because the rubber trees were being blown apart'.[2]

Close by, Private Jim Richmond, who would be one of just two survivors from 6 Section, remembered the first tracers coming in.

'We couldn't return fire straightaway as there was nothing to be seen, from my angle anyway. The air was thick with fire, and bullets were taking chunks out of the rubber trees all around me. It was about then I noticed the tracers coming out of the trees, so myself and someone else fired into them and two or three Viet Cong fell out of them.'[3] Private John Heslewood of 5 Section, on the other end of the line, also remembered lots of 'heavy-weapons fire coming in, and a fair bit of tracer. I remember particularly some smoke rising from a fallen tree and I called to the blokes near me to try to fire into that, as I thought it was a heavy machine gun. We fired into it – I don't know whether we achieved anything or not – but I think it was the weapon that did a fair bit of [initial] damage to our platoon.'[4] Another member of 5 Section, Private Allen May, was 'shocked and amazed when I saw the tracer . . . and a bloke stepped out from behind a rubber tree and opened up on us with an automatic weapon. I was so amazed that I said to [Corporal William] "Bluey" Moore, "That bloke's trying to kill me," and Bluey said, "Well, get the bastard first." Next time he popped up I let him have it, and I hit him with a tracer in the chest, and he stood up screaming like a banshee and tearing at his chest, and did a backflip and I reckon he died.'[5]

Meanwhile, at the FSCC at Nui Dat, Major Peter Tedder, who had already spent 11 months in Vietnam, was still talking to Captain Ian Darlington as the messages began to come in. He knew that something big was developing – the Viet Cong were attacking and preparing to fight it out. He said so to Darlington, who looked at him, not completely appreciating the gravity of the situation. Tedder soon left for 105 Battery, convinced a major battle was brewing.[6]

By now 6 Section, on the left flank, was out of action: most were either dead or fatally wounded. Commanding this section, Corporal

Robbins was still trying to come to terms with the fact that his section had been shattered by enemy fire. The attack against his men continued to develop; it was initially led by a platoon-size unit that could be seen rushing out of the foliage. He recalled starting to say the Lord's Prayer but 'only got halfway through it and something else'd start and I'd have to start again. I couldn't remember where I was, at the end of it or the beginning. I was just saying it in my mind. I thought, *Christ, I don't think we're gonna get out of this*. It was just bloody ferocious, the rattling of machine guns, the mortars, the explosions.'[7]

Close by, Private Jim Richmond saw some Viet Cong jumping up and down and waving their arms about, yelling above the sound of battle. He thought they were shouting orders, but because they were drawing so much attention to themselves, they didn't last long. Others were darting from tree to tree, while still others started bellying along the ground towards Richmond's position. He had no cover, and quickly pulled his pack off and put it in front to provide some protection from the hail of fire that was tearing into 6 Section's position from the left.[8]

Sergeant Buick was surprised as he had never considered that they would be attacked. The general feeling was that the Australians would be the aggressors – the Viet Cong up until now had tended to shoot and scoot. Buick had seen no movement or any fire coming from 6 Section, and feared the worst. Then the monsoon broke: rain poured down and blanketed the area, reducing visibility to just 50 metres and turning the ground into red mud. All around trees were being shattered by RPG fire, leaves and branches were falling among the men and streams of latex sap seeped down the shattered tree trunks onto the ground. While it was still broad daylight, the monsoon and surviving canopy significantly reduced the available light.[9]

Robbins and his few survivors of 6 Section tried to hang on as best they could, firing into the oncoming enemy troops. The young corporal recalled that as he fired into the enemy and some went down, he was never really sure if they had been hit. He said it wasn't like shooting a kangaroo, which only went down when it was hit; with the Viet Cong you were never really sure that a man was even hit, let alone killed. It was extremely intense and it was about then that the rain came. The corporal was aware that his section had just about had it.[10]

Close by, Private Jim Richmond heard his mates, privates Douglas Salveron and David J. Thomas, yelling out, 'wanting to know who was on our left, so I yelled out up the line, and got a return answer that there were no friendly troops in that area . . . the fire coming in from there was really horrendous'.[11] Thomas shouted that he had been hit, but he continued to return fire at the advancing enemy troops to his front. Richmond then yelled out to Salveron, but Thomas shouted back that the 20-year-old student and national serviceman was dead. In the next moment Thomas, aged 21 and from the regular army, was himself killed with a burst of automatic fire.[12] It was also then that their machine gunner was killed, and 21-year-old clerk and national serviceman Private Warren Mitchell, 2IC on the gun, took over. Robbins crawled over to Mitchell to keep feeding the ammunition belt into the gun, but had no sooner taken up the position than he was wounded and Mitchell was killed. Robbins was shot in the right arm and lay there thinking, '*I don't know what I'm gonna do here.* There was no one around. I couldn't use my right arm.'[13]

Meanwhile, a few hundred metres north and to the rear, Lieutenant Geoff Kendall, commander of 10 Platoon, had ordered his men to dump their packs and 'shake out into a loose assault formation. Knowing Smithy, my immediate thought was that if there was an [enemy] platoon there we'd be doing a quick company attack, and I was certainly in a perfect position to hit from the left, so I assumed I would get the job of being assault platoon while Sharpie supplied fire support.'[14] Smith confirmed Kendall's request to advance towards 11 Platoon, but just as the platoon begun to wheel around, two-up in extended line towards the sound of battle, the increasing fire made it obvious that there were more than just a couple of enemy platoons out there. Nonetheless, they pushed forward, very determined and steady despite the sound of the bugles that blew intermittently. Kendall recalled that just then it began to rain: 'And when I say rain . . . it rained like it rains in Vietnam in the afternoon. It absolutely started to pour monsoonal rain.'[15]

Lieutenant Gordon Sharp radioed Smith requesting artillery support, telling his OC of the increasing attacks along his front and flanks. He yelled into the radio above the hail of fire, 'It's bigger than I thought it was. They're going to attack us!'[16] At 4.15 p.m., Smith radioed battalion headquarters that other enemy troops, estimated at platoon strength, were now also firing from position 487674 – the southern slopes of Nui Dat 2; Smith requested artillery support against the position. The company commander ordered 11 Platoon to fall back towards the rest of the company, but this was impossible.[17] Smith told Sharp to withdraw towards his position, but Sharp was not prepared to do this, as it would mean leaving wounded behind at the mercy of the enemy. Instead, he asked for more artillery fire.[18]

Meanwhile, Major Noel Ford, commanding B Company, on first hearing the fire coming from the plantation halted his platoon and reported his position to battalion headquarters as 458665, expecting to get orders to return. Smith recalled radioing Townsend asking for urgent reinforcements and moments later making radio contact with Ford, about 2 km west of his position, and asking him to return to the plantation to support his company.[19] However, Townsend ordered Ford to hold his current position and await further orders.[20] For the next hour or so, Ford and his men were apparently forgotten about. B Company section commander Lance Corporal Phil Buttigieg recalled hearing a 'massive volume of fire. The radios told us D Company had chased a fleeing standing patrol, but now it sounded like they had been sucked into an ambush . . . We smoked and listened to the battle develop, anticipating a return to D Company to help. In fact the volume of fire was so massive I could not understand why we were not already on our way.'[21]

All in B Company could hear the battle. Private David A. Thomas recalled hearing a 'crescendo of rifle fire. We turned around and went back to another position where we were standing in a banana patch.'[22] Lieutenant John O'Halloran was listening to D Company radio traffic: 'I heard my mate Gordon Sharp say, "They are going to attack us!" I could tell by his voice that the platoon was in trouble.'[23] He and his men stood around waiting for the order to head back to the plantation, listening to the firing and the traffic on the radio net. They could not understand why they had not been ordered back to assist D Company.[24]

At 1 ATF base, Sergeant Jim King of 105 Field Artillery Battery had just finished replenishing the front-line ammunition as a result of the previous night's firing missions. As he started to relax, he heard the gunners of 161 New Zealand Artillery Battery open fire towards targets somewhere east of the Task Force. 'We guessed from the rate of fire they were on to something and then, when "Fire Mission Regiment"* came over the tannoy system we knew it was bigger than normal.'[25] This mass of firepower alerted those in the base that somewhere just beyond them someone was in real trouble.

Lieutenant Adrian Roberts of 3 APC Troop was in his tent putting on a clean uniform after his shower when a soldier arrived

---

* 'Fire Mission Regiment' is the call for all 18 guns of the three batteries of the regiment to fire.

looking for him. He was to report immediately to his senior officer, Major Bob Hagerty, and bring his maps. He hurriedly dressed and ran over to squadron headquarters.[26] Close by, Little Pattie was still on stage. She recalled that things were heating up: officers were being whisked away and the former relaxed and laid-back atmosphere had changed. She and the other entertainers realised that they were, indeed, in the middle of a war. She recalled: 'Suddenly things were changing, quite suddenly actually, during that second show. And I could hear more artillery in the background. And in an increasing way.'[27]

Meanwhile, Brigadier David Jackson had moved from the operational centre to the FSCC, which had better signals equipment and provided better conditions for conducting and coordinating operations.[28] He found that RAAF Group Captain Peter Raw was also there. They discussed the situation and Raw assured Jackson that air-force support could be called for if necessary. Indeed, at Nui Dat there were already the two RAAF Hueys commanded by flight lieutenants Dohle and Riley, who had earlier transported the concert party to the Task Force base. In the operation room at 9 Squadron at Vung Tau, Flight Lieutenant Phil Cooke was the duty pilot. At that point all he knew was that an Australian Army group was in contact with the enemy in the Long Tan rubber plantation. Soon word started to reach him that it was becoming increasingly precarious and the Australians had come across a much larger enemy force than expected.[29]

Located between 1 ATF base and Vung Tau was Australian captain Mike Wells, the adviser to the South Vietnamese Army based at Baria. The people there could clearly hear the barrage of booming shells being fired from Nui Dat and knew that something big was up – this volume of battery fire had never been heard before. Wells soon became aware of nervous looks being sent in his direction: if the Australians were in trouble, they were likely to be next. Wells flicked the frequency of his radio to the Task Force and listened as the battle unfolded, piecing together items of information using his knowledge of Australian Army lingo to help read between the lines, while trying to look unconcerned and show no alarm. The more he heard, the more concerned he became, but he kept it very much to himself.[30]

15

'. . . give me every gun they have'

1620–1640 hours

The rain continued to pour down and the enemy continued to push their advantage in numbers. At 4.22 p.m., Captain Morrie Stanley called in corrections for the artillery: they were to fire a moving barrage of high explosives back and forth over a 200-metre area at position 487669. Stanley recalled that the initial salvos had to be directed some distance from 11 Platoon's known position, walking the fire to around 200–300 metres of its position.

However, Stanley was out of visual contact with 11 Platoon and was completely reliant on Lieutenant Sharp using the radio to provide him with up-to-date information of where the shells were falling relative to their position. Stanley would then use his waterproof map to provide updated firing orders to the batteries, while wiping away the splashing mud and rain from it. He was calling on every ounce of his experience and training to ensure accuracy in the turmoil of battle; his M16 rifle was lying next to him in the accumulating puddles of water despite the repeated reminders by his radio operator, Lance Corporal William Walker, to keep it in his hand.

The other member of his team, Bombardier Murray Broomhall, recalled that if you lay on the ground the enemy could not see you; however, conversely you could not see the enemy. He stood up to help direct artillery fire to Stanley and a few seconds later some of the branches above him started to disappear, so he quickly gave up that idea and lay down next to his officer.[1]

Major Smith's signaller, Private Robin 'Pom' Rencher, was responsible for the critical and stressful role of passing information from all platoons to Smith and Stanley. He recalled that as the noise of battle and the rain made communication difficult, many times he had to ask 'Say again, over' because he couldn't hear the grid references easily – and one wrong numeral could result in disaster. He started to get worked up and began shouting into the handset. 'I remember,' recalled Rencher, 'starting to get panicky, until a quiet voice came over the net and said, "Calm down, Pom". The near-hysteria burst like a pricked balloon and I carried on with the war. I have searched memory and heart, and can say it was caused by frustration and fear of letting the platoons down, rather than fear for myself.' He looked around and saw his OC like a 'rock, always cool and collected; but the calmest man in CHQ was Maurice "Morrie" Stanley, calmly working out fire orders as if he was on exercise back home'.[2]

The men of D Company heard the distinctive 'pop' of enemy mortars from the south followed closely by the exploding bombs. Smith ordered CHQ and 10 and 12 platoons to move further north to avoid the fire, which pushed them further away from 11 Platoon – as recalled by regimental signaller Corporal Graham Smith: 'As company headquarters and 12 and 10 platoons were following up [to 11 Platoon] there were some 60mm mortars fired which were coming very close to us, so we picked up our pace and detoured slightly to avoid those.'[3] Private Terry Burstall of 12 Platoon recalled moving up a small slope with the firing quickly escalating. They did not know what was going on but kept going, and when they crossed a road

running north–south they came under mortar fire to their right.[4]
The first bomb exploded about 50 metres from Burstall, quickly followed by half a dozen other rounds. The platoon moved to the left,
but as they ran through the rows of rubber trees, the mortar bombs
continued to explode around them. Sergeant James Todd recalled
that they had hardly moved 12 Platoon 'when the greatest firepower
you've ever heard went . . . Mortars started falling.'[5] Corporal Kevin
Miller, commanding 8 Section of 12 Platoon, recalled Lieutenant
Sabben telling his platoon to 'run to the left [north]; the mortars
were walking right on to us. We ran over to the left and they went
right by us, and then I think our artillery must have knocked them
out because they stopped.'[6]

Indeed, Stanley conferred with Smith and confirmed the revised
positions of the dispersed company on his map. At 4.26 p.m., Smith
radioed to Lieutenant Colonel Townsend that they were being mortared. Stanley and Smith's mortar fire controller, Sergeant Don
Thompson, took a compass bearing of the mortar location, and
Smith requested that all available artillery be brought to bear against
it.[7] Smith informed his CO that he wanted 'the whole [artillery] regiment – give me every gun they have'. Townsend, however, replied:
'Leave the artillery fire to the gunners.' Even so, within minutes
Stanley informed Smith: 'We've got the guns of the whole regiment.'[8]

Back at the Task Force base, in FSCC, Captain Ian Darlington, on
receiving Stanley's coordinates for the location of the enemy mortars, plotted the position on his map and immediately recognised
it as a place he had previously identified as a good position for the
enemy to place mortars, defined by a thick cluster of trees near
the road junction at Long Tan. The coordinates were immediately
relayed to Captain Glen Eure's US battery of 155mm guns, assigned
to the Task Force. They quickly fired into the position, using overwhelming firepower, and the mortaring from this position at least

ceased.[9] Still at the FSCC was FOO Captain Alan Hutchinson, who sat listening to the excited transmissions coming from the radios on the various nets (including those being managed by 'Pom' Rencher and Graham Smith in the thick of battle) while the tropical monsoon storm raged all around. An endless stream of fire orders were coming across the artillery net, while the frantic transmissions on the infantry net were listened to by all.[10]

Moments earlier, a runner from Townsend's headquarters had arrived at the officers' bar, where Lieutenant Gordon Steinbrook and his mates were still enjoying their beer. They were informed that D Company had 'just made a really big contact in the rubber to the east of us,' recalled Steinbrook. 'All of us to a man scrambled out of there and ran to our assigned areas for future orders. I tagged along to the TOC [Tactical Operations Centre] with the 6 RAR commander and my boss, the 161 Battery commander. Inside the TOC everyone was working at fever pitch. They were in radio contact with D Company, the sounds of the battle faintly audible as they transmitted to one another.'[11]

Meanwhile, Lieutenant Rob Rich was waiting at the helicopter pad when intelligence officer Captain Bryan Wickens came rushing towards him with his maps. Within minutes they were airborne, sweeping their way towards the east of the base. Wickens pointed towards Nui Dat 2, indicating that it was their destination. 'So away I went,' recalled Rich. '[The officer was still] organising his radios and maps. I was orbiting this hill and became aware of a tremendous amount of enemy ground fire. In a helicopter, this is quite noisy. These tracer bullets were coming up past the helicopter, and I tapped him on the shoulder, and said, "Are you sure this is the right place?" He then looked out and saw all this stuff coming up, and said, "No, no, no, that's *them*, that's *them* [Viet Cong]. We're over there somewhere." So we flew away from that hill.'[12]

Earlier, army chaplain Les Thompson had been visiting the men of C Company, 6 RAR in their area of the base when the intense counter-battery fire alerted him and battalion medical officer Captain Vic Bampton that something big was on. Both rushed to Townsend's headquarters and stood aside, trying to stay out of the way. They and others listened as the sound of battle and the urgent requests being made by Smith and Stanley were brought to them via the crackling airwaves of D Company's CHQ radio. All knew that 'Harry the Rat' and D Company were in serious trouble. Undoubtedly the chaplain would have been praying for the safety of the men.[13] Also present was Private Ken Tronc, D Company, 11 Platoon. He had been forced to stay behind that morning due to an injury to his foot. At the time he hadn't expected to be missing out on much – just another hard slog through the scrub. Now he was listening in distress as his mates of 11 Platoon were taking casualties: 'I think for the first time since I went to Vietnam I cried my eyes out. I prayed for mates I had, as I didn't know who had been killed and who wounded. But I prayed. I've never prayed so much in my life.'[14]

New Zealand 161 Field Battery had been assigned to and affiliated with 6 RAR since arriving at Nui Dat. Major Harry Honnor of the battery and Townsend had known each since their days at Duntroon. Now the major was located with Townsend at his HQ and controlling the fire of the three Anzac batteries with coordination from Townsend. Honnor was relying on the dependable Stanley to provide him with coordinates and a brief of what was happening in the plantation. From this, Honnor selected areas and ordered the fire. The overall commander of the artillery regiment, Lieutenant Colonel Richmond Cubis, was based with Brigadier David Jackson and kept him informed of all developments well before they would reach him through infantry channels.[15]

Captain George Bindley of 105 Battery had earlier cut short his shower on hearing all 18 guns of the regiment, along with the six US howitzers, thundering with deadly intent to the east. He rushed to the Battery Command Post to find out what the hell was going on, but knew soon enough as he listened to the radio traffic. He headed for his battery. When he got there he found all his men had left the concert and were pouring fire into the enemy positions as defined by Stanley back in Long Tan Plantation. Bindley recalled a series of 'missions followed with quite unprecedented calls for ten rounds fire for effect, plus repeats. It quickly became clear that if fire was to be sustained at this rate, ammunition was going to be a big problem.'[16] As he later admitted, he needn't have worried, as the sergeant major and section commanders had that in hand, making sure the rounds kept coming as needed. All Bindley had to do was monitor ammunition handling – which was no small job in itself, especially given the urgency of the situation.

Typically each gun would have 100 rounds on hand with another 300 in reserve in the battery dump. The physical 'effort involved in moving 105mm ammunition rounds should not be underestimated,' recalled Bindley. 'A box containing two 105mm rounds weighs just under 100 pounds [45 kg], and unpacking poses special problems. It is crated and packed to withstand rough handling and does not fall apart when needed.'[17] Ammunition boxes were braced with steel rods that had to be removed using butterfly nuts, which in the tropical climate of Vietnam could (and did) become corroded and bent. Sometimes it took brute force to get a box open. When the shells were removed and laid out they had to be inspected by the senior ammunition member of the gun crew, and then, after each shell was fused it was loaded, requiring strength, stamina and skill. Any lapse of concentration could result in injuries including broken bones and fingers cut off by the breech block – and worse.

The seven-man crews were reacting instinctively to the demands, with all their training and experience coming together. The rhythm had been set: shells were unboxed, inspected, fused, loaded, fired, firing positions adjusted as required, and the fast accumulation of empty shell casings from the batteries removed. The gunners were now firing between five and ten rounds per minute, with each shrapnel shell having a killing zone of 30–50 metres.[18] Stanley kept calling in his requests, and the rain kept pouring.[19]

Meanwhile, Captain Barry Crompton and his men of Australian 131 Divisional Locating Battery were frustrated by the amount of ordnance flying around, which made it impossible for them to pinpoint the exact position of the enemy mortars. There were 'so many rounds in the air that you couldn't pick up what was incoming and what was outgoing. It just completely flooded the radar. There was no positive information, mainly because of the heat of the battle.'[20]

Also concerned was Lieutenant Trevor Gardiner of A Company, 1 Platoon, who had earlier returned from their three-day patrol. He had been assigned the role of battalion paying officer and after a quick shower made his way to battalion headquarters to collect the payroll. While he was there, things began to heat up, with 'sustained artillery missions being fired. I called in to the Battalion HQ Command Post to ask what was going on and was promptly chucked out.'[21]

Back in the plantation, Major Smith informed his CO that the enemy force they were facing was at least a company, but more likely a Viet Cong battalion from *275 VC Regiment*. Even with Anzac counter-battery fire, the enemy mortaring continued. At 4.36 p.m., Smith requested battalion headquarters to send out armed Chinook helicopters or to call in an airstrike to suppress the enemy mortar fire that was now originating from the north at 488672 – Nui Dat 2. He also stated that his wounded would need to be evacuated by helicopter and requested that the choppers stand by.[22]

Forward of Smith's position, Sharp was still trying to bring the men of 6 Section back into the centre of the line. Sergeant Buick recalled that the young officer was reporting back to company headquarters by radio.[23] Private Peter Ainslie was wondering how 'any of us could have survived. Two fellows were killed . . . The platoon fell back and attempted to get into all-round defence.'[24] However, they were pinned down and any movement meant almost certain death. It was now that a large enemy formation – about a company in strength – begun to advance upon 11 Platoon to their front. These troops were in an extended line, 2 metres apart, and moved forward at a steady, purposeful pace firing from the hip. Sharp's men poured fire into the line and the Viet Cong went to ground, taking heavy casualties. There was no way that 11 Platoon, even if they left their dead behind, could extract themselves from their position.[25]

Sharp was attempting to push back another ferocious enemy attack along his front, with increasing pressure also being brought to bear on his right. The fire was intense and the young officer must have known that they had come up against at least a battalion of enemy troops. Buick believed that 6 Section to his left had been virtually wiped out except for one or two soldiers, leaving just 4 Section in the centre, platoon HQ section just behind it, and 5 Section covering the right – all had taken casualties.[26] Private John Heslewood recalled that he and his mates could see down the lines of trees, and the enemy troops were forming up and moving forward:

They had green pith helmets on and that's when we woke up that these weren't ordinary bloody Viet Cong [the NVA veterans from *3rd Battalion, 275 VC Regiment*]. They were probably forming up to 200 metres away, maybe a little bit longer. You could clearly see then coming together getting their orders and they started rolling forward. Then we got our artillery . . . the artillery kept coming down in front of us and it was spot on . . . it was bloody great . . . They seemed to be attacking all along the line and they weren't running, they were walking at a fast pace with a rifle in their hand. They were sort of – we were talking about it and you'd say these blokes are likely bloody zombies the way they were moving in. They didn't run and didn't duck or dive, just kept walking in at a fast pace.[27]

The front line of the enemy had now gone to ground just 75 metres from 11 Platoon, making it difficult for the Australians to provide accurate return fire – not only because of the cover the enemy had taken, but also because the rain continued to pour down, making it difficult to see and hear clearly. Australians and Vietnamese, however, each tried to gain the upper hand, as recalled by Buick, as the Viet Cong attacked using fire and movement while they now numbered only about 20 effective rifles. Each of his men was hugging the ground and defending his position, all waiting for the remainder of D Company, somewhere behind them, to come up in support.[28]

It was now that the conscientious Sharp, the young National Service officer who had commanded his men from the front, was killed instantly with a bullet to the throat as he exposed himself to call in artillery fire against Nui Dat 2. He was on his knees trying to observe the position of the enemy and where the Anzac shells were falling when he was hit. Lance Corporal Robbins remembered seeing 'Gordon Sharp, who seemed to be controlling things pretty well with the radio at that time, stand up . . . that was when he went'.[29] Regimental signaller Graham Smith, part of CHQ, recalled how 'Sharp was trying to keep things together . . . and he was to his credit kneeling up and trying to ascertain exactly where to have his artillery put and he got shot'.[30] Lieutenant Gordon Sharp was the first National Service officer to be killed in Vietnam.

Not far away, between Nui Dat and Long Tan, Lieutenant John O'Halloran of B Company recalled listening to the radio net and being stunned to hear the voice of Sharp cut short and then Buick yelling into the radio. He instantly knew that that his boyhood friend was dead.[31]

For the men of 6 Section, 11 Platoon, the battle was over. Almost all had been killed in the first ten minutes of combat. Clinging on desperately were the wounded Corporal Robbins and Private Richmond. The Viet Cong kept coming on and were now within metres of the two men; both believed their time was up. Robbins recalled: 'They came right to us . . . Because at that stage I was shot, and I was playing dead, I could hear them – they were just behind some bushes and the rubber was coming down with the artillery. I could hear them and see them . . . We were spread out a fair bit. There was a gap between us probably 5 to 8 metres . . . and the noise was unbelievable.'[32]

Somewhere close by, Richmond saw movement out of the corner of his eye. He turned and found himself looking straight down the barrel of a rifle – but just as the enemy soldier fired, Richmond dropped his head behind his pack and the bullet slammed into it, missing him by centimetres. He had no idea what to do, but instinctively grabbed a grenade from his pack. Just as he pulled the pin, an enemy mortar bomb exploded and he took a piece of shrapnel in the left side of his back, but the fire killed the enemy soldier outright. He lay there feeling like someone had hit him in the back with a sledgehammer. He didn't have any pain at this point – that would come later – but was extremely worried as he had no feeling from his torso down. He was too afraid to look back, fearing what he might see. However, within minutes he got feeling back in his legs, which gave him some relief. He was still holding the primed grenade in his hand, with no way of safely getting rid of it. He was worried that if he threw it, it might hit a rubber tree and bounce back on him or any of his mates who were still alive. Then he remembered having a rubber band around one of his trouser legs: he reached down and managed to remove it and wrap it around the lever of the grenade. He lay there among his dead mates and the exploding barrage, the only thing stopping the grenade from going off a flimsy rubber band. It was about then that he passed out.[33]

16

'. . . tell the boss that the radio's gone'

1640–1650 hours

Sergeant Bob Buick at this point reckoned he was about to die. More than a third of the men under his command were either dead or wounded. At 4.43 p.m., battalion headquarters radioed Major Smith: 'Have dust-off [medical evacuation by helicopter] standing by, details later.'[1] Even if word was passed back to Buick, it probably meant nothing to him as there was no way the wounded could reach the helicopters for evacuation. They were on their own. Private John Heslewood recalled:

> 5 Section [had] moulded in with 4 Section – I knew all the blokes and we were all settled on the ground in our position . . . There was myself and Brian Halls (he was from 5 Section), and there was Allen May, Barry Mags [Magnussen] and Doug Fabian from 5 Section, and we were firing from four rubber trees and I know our machine gunner had gone to the right – they'd gone forward on the right and Kenny Gant was the gunner . . . Ron Eglinton was the other bloke on the

gun . . . how far right they went I'm not sure. When we were
training the word was for the machine gun to go to the high
ground or to the right, so when the firing started they'd gone
to the right and how far forward they went or whether we
pulled back a little bit when the firing started I'm not too sure.[2]

Anzac and US artillery fire continued to explode against the
reported mortar position on Nui Dat 2. However, Buick and his
men probably did not notice it with the intense enemy small-arms,
RPG and mortar fire now targeting their position, not to mention the monsoonal downpour. The enemy began to move around
11 Platoon's exposed southern (right) flank, past Corporal William
Moore's 5 Section. Private Ron Eglinton, with the machine gun of
the section, was positioned a bit forward of the line. At this point,
he couldn't see any Viet Cong from his position as he was placed
along the extreme right flank. Private Kenny Gant, who was his
section's 2IC, kept screaming out to him 'Can you see them?', but
he couldn't as they were coming in diagonally across on his left
out of sight. It wasn't long before the Viet Cong started moving
around towards the right and Eglinton saw them. He recalled that
their firepower was increasing with every minute and reckoned
a number of his mates had been killed early on from the intense
fire. The enemy seemed to be probing their position, unsure of the
Australians' strength and exact location.[3]

It was then that 21-year-old butcher and national serviceman
Private Kenny Gant was killed. Eglinton needed someone to help feed
the rounds into the machine gun – he was in real trouble. Meanwhile,
the Viet Cong human wave pushed ever closer. Eglinton managed to
keep up a stream of fire against the approaching enemy but recalled
that 'it didn't seem to perturb the Viet Cong . . . they just kept coming and coming. Most of the other blokes around me had been
killed, certainly Kenny Gant and Jim Houston.'[4] Buick saw Eglinton's
initial fire cut a deadly swathe through the enemy ranks, inflicting

heavy casualties. Eglinton continued to fire at the oncoming waves of enemy troops even though mud in the ammunition belt clogged the feeding mechanism of his M60 machine gun. Buick recalled how Eglinton overcame 'stoppages, and at times only firing one round at a time, he kept the VC under fire. Ron, a national serviceman, was later awarded the Military Medal for his actions at Long Tan. It was his efforts that prevented the Viet Cong from assaulting and overrunning the platoon from the south, and although wounded he maintained his tenuous position and kept his machine gun firing.'[5]

With every passing minute the fire against 11 Platoon – originating from many positions, some less than 50 metres away – became more intense. It was not only small-arms fire that continued to tear into the platoon's position. Their perimeter was defined by 70 square metres of rain-sodden mud and sentinel-like rubber trees, some of which were now just shattered trunks from the RPG and mortar fire. The noise made communications near impossible: the sound of battle was deafening in such a small, deadly space. Buick had to yell into the radio and repeat his messages numerous times before he could be understood, and the Vietnamese were trying to jam their radio frequencies. The sound of battle was a battle in itself. Men just 5 metres away had to shout at the top of their voices to be heard and understood, and hearing beyond that distance was hopeless.[6]

Buick ordered Corporal Jeff Duroux, commanding 4 Section, to try to make contact with 6 Section. Duroux's section was forward of the platoon headquarters by some 15 metres. Buick recalled that only about 12 of the platoon were capable of firing and there seemed to be no one alive in 6 Section; 4 Section had by now suffered, as best as he could make out, two dead and a number of wounded, and he had no idea how 5 Section was coping on the right. The situation was extremely grim and he recalled that the Anzac artillery fire was still not close enough.[7] Buick radioed Captain Morrie Stanley, who was effectively calling in the artillery. The conscientious New Zealand officer was the crucial link for all indirect fire support from the artillery of the regiment. Buick recalled that it was Stanley's efforts in calling in the artillery and adjusting the fire of the guns, along with the skills of the 105mm gun crews back in Nui Dat, that allowed them to stay in the fight.[8] Corporal John Robbins also recalled that 'Bob Buick did a great job with calling in the artillery. He called it in more or less pretty on top of us – he had to, because that's where they were . . . he excelled there, I thought.'[9] Indeed, Smith stated that if it hadn't been for Buick's ability to call in and direct the artillery fire, 11 Platoon would have been overrun, followed by the rest of the company.[10]

At 4.46 p.m., Stanley called in another artillery strike against 487669 and 'walked the destruction back and forth, and to the right, over a 200-metre area'.[11] The avalanche of exploding shells provided air bursts forward of the Australian position, causing terrible destruction to the Viet Cong in the open, including those few who had climbed the trees to better snipe from as well as observe.[12] John Heslewood recalled: 'There were odd tree bursts – one might explode in the tree on the way down, but none of the blokes I was with got hurt by any of it. It just landed spot-on all the time. You'd see all these 50 or 60 blokes coming at you and all of a sudden they're blown away. The blokes would start cheering, "Have a look at that!". . . The artillery was just spot on, that's all I can say.'[13] Even so, it still looked hopeless as the Viet Cong were pushing their advantage in overwhelming numbers and their main attacking force was now within 50 metres of the scattered and dispersed Australian firing line, with others even closer.

The renewed Anzac barrage was now falling behind the front line of the enemy while the US howitzers conducted counter-battery fire against Nui Dat 2. While the Anzac shelling was undoubtedly causing many casualties to the Vietnamese to the rear, the immediate threat were those to their front who could be seen advancing towards them. This was a typical Viet Cong tactic when fighting an enemy with artillery support: 'holding the belt with one hand and punching with the other'. It required close contact with the enemy to deny them artillery support from the fear of killing their own men. As stated by Nguyen Thanh Hong, 'If we were to confront the Americans in a conventional manner over a protracted period, we would be wiped out by their firepower. To be victorious over the Americans, we would have to exploit surprise and attack aggressively. By close combat – "grabbing them by their belts" – we would be able to make their firepower ineffective.'[14] Buick later recalled: 'Looking back, this was when I really became frightened, not for myself but I could see 11 Platoon being overrun and thereby opening the gate and the possibility of the whole company being wiped out.'[15]

The survivors of 11 Platoon recalled how some rubber trees were continually hit with a thud while others exploded from RPG fire. Red mud was splashing around as bullets tore into the ground around the men, some finding their mark. Buick described how the fire from the men of 11 Platoon was stopping the enemy in their tracks, but mates on either side were being killed or wounded. Even so, everyone was sticking by their 'mates and defending their patch of dirt to the death'.[16]

Buick again contacted Stanley asking him for more artillery support, yelling into the radio above the sound of battle and pouring rain that they were almost surrounded, were suffering heavy casualties and could not extract themselves, and were just about out of ammunition.[17] Then the radio went dead, its antenna shot away. Smith feared the worst, having lost contact – that the platoon had been overrun.[18] While the radio operator of 11 Platoon, Private Vic Grice, was replacing the antenna with a spare, he saw a large group of Viet Cong moving around their left flank about 100 metres north of their position. With the radio again operating, an artillery-fire mission was called on to this enemy force. A few minutes later, to the relief of the survivors of 11 Platoon, the artillery shattered the Viet Cong's attempted flanking movement.[19]

Meanwhile, back at Nui Dat, the final concert was being called off – not just because of the noise of the guns, but also because of the torrential downpour. However, Little Pattie recalled that 'the Joy Boys were playing, and the officer in charge of us said "You've got to finish – cut the show short, cut the show short. We're getting out earlier!" And it was a troubled voice that told me that. And I thought, "No, this isn't right. Something's going on that's bigger than we know". . . Once again people were whisked away from the audience, and once again, even more noise now, from the artillery.' While the show went on for a little while longer, it was finally shut down unceremoniously by an officer who yelled at the entertainers still on stage to 'Get off, get off, get off!'

Not long after, Little Pattie was being driven around the base by Lieutenant Ian Savage, who was using his OC's APC. He got an urgent message to bring the APC back to the unit, so he unceremoniously dropped the Australian entertainer off at the helicopter pad and bolted back to his unit. It had been decided to fly the entertainers back to Vung Tau and out of harm's way. Earlier, before the battle had commenced, Col Joye had been 'kidnapped' by a sergeant who had driven him away to drink with the men – by all accounts, Joye happily obliged. The helicopter with Little Pattie on board took off, minus Joye, and she looked back as it thrashed its way south to see the continuing flash of the Anzac and US artillery. 'I looked down and I could see lots of orange and red fire, and lots and lots of it. I knew [there] was a big battle happening. And for the very first time then the penny dropped to me that, you know, Australians are in the middle of a war. This is fair dinkum; this isn't just doing concerts and having a good time. This is really war.'[20]

Back in the heart of the plantation, Lieutenant David Sabben's 12 Platoon had made their way to CHQ. He recalled that while they were moving up, the torrential downpour 'pelted through the rubber-tree canopy and beat into the bare red earth below. Within minutes, the earth had become sticky red mud, staining the greens we wore. As the rain formed puddles on the ground, the force of the heaviest squalls raised a mist of muddy spray almost up to our knees. It was like walking through a thin red mist. When we went to ground, we were lying in it, with only our heads raised above it.'[21]

Meanwhile, 10 Platoon, north of 11 Platoon, was still moving through the mist, mud and rain in a south-east direction towards their stranded mates, who were desperately fighting for their lives against an overwhelming enemy force. Lieutenant Geoff Kendall recalled advancing with his men about 150 metres; they had yet to receive any fire directed against them, although the sound of firing in front was enormous.[22] Private Len Vine of Kendall's 2 Section recalled: 'We moved up to support 11 Platoon and the firing . . . it was unbelievable . . . and it was raining. It was very difficult to see, and it was starting to get misty as well.'[23] As they pushed towards 11 Platoon, Private Kevin Branch recalled going 'down and up a bit of a dip, and onto level ground, and came across all these VC . . . with their backs to us! There was a bit of a hump on the ground, and there were thirty to fifty VC, I think.'[24] Vine recalled: 'At first we were very cautious because we were concerned about firing on our own men of 11 Platoon . . . there was so much confusion because of the rain, it just kept pouring down, pouring down.'[25] However, it soon became clear from the weapons that the men in front were carrying, and some of the hats they wore, that these were enemy troops.

Kendall estimated that the enemy force just to his left represented a large platoon of about 30–40 Viet Cong. They were assaulting using the same tactics used by the Australians, walking forward, well spaced. They hadn't seen his platoon as they had gone slightly past them.[26] Branch now heard his platoon commander telling them, 'This is it. Keep going, keep going.' Branch was thinking, 'Christ, he's mad! We'll be able to shake hands with 'em soon!' He recalled: 'We kept going, and with all the commotion going on they didn't know we were there.'[27] The closest Viet Cong to Kendall was just '20 yards [18 metres] away and the ones on my left were even closer, and it was bucketing down rain, very hard to see, and it wasn't until I saw one guy wearing one of those bamboo-type hats that I was sure it was the enemy. We didn't want to start firing on one of Gordon's sections. They were wearing similar things to what we were wearing – some had raggy hats, some had bamboo ones, pith helmet type things.'[28]

Lieutenant Colonel Tran Minh Tam and his staff still believed they were fighting a lone Australian platoon that had strolled into their ambush preparations. He had earlier made the fateful decision to withdraw his forward observation posts, which enabled D Company to arrive unnoticed in the heart of the plantation.[29] Some Vietnamese commanders were sending out runners to help with communications, while others were using bugles to provide orders. Soon an order arrived, likely from Tran, at the headquarters of 275 VC Regiment just north of the battle, close to Nui Dat 2. Senior Captain Nguyen Thoi Bung was to advance with a force behind the enemy platoon, to ensure all lines of retreat were cut off. The senior captain immediately sent out a force to come up behind the left flank (north) of the enemy.[30] However, this force was taken by surprise by Kendall and his men of 10 Platoon, along with the artillery strike called in moments earlier by Stanley against the enemy force, radioed in by Buick as moving around his northern flank.

Kendall ordered his men to fire. Private Kevin Branch blasted away from the hip with his Armalite, but after ten rounds or so he said to himself, 'This is no good, I'm wasting them.' He knelt down and took aim and managed to hit a couple of Viet Cong. 'They were really surprised,' he recalled. 'I think we cleared up about 20 in a few minutes.' Private Harry Esler was surprised to find he was 'calm, no fear,

because I could see a target'.[31] The surviving Viet Cong to the left of
10 Platoon veered away; their cadre could be heard above the sound of
battle and the Viet Cong broke contact. As recalled by Kendall, 'We
probably knocked over 15 or so of them, on their right element. The
other guys just turned left as on an order. There were bugles blowing all over. I don't distinctly remember hearing a bugle but they just
turned sharp left and trotted away and we were still knocking them
over as they went away. They then got out of sight and out of range.'[32]

11 Platoon assaulted and 10 Platoon assists

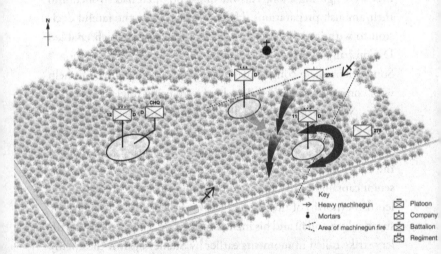

Around 4.45 p.m.: 12 Platoon has moved into CHQ position, while 10 Platoon tries to extricate
11 Platoon, which is pinned down. In doing so they disrupt a Viet Cong attack that is trying to
surround 11 Platoon.

That's when they got hit with concentrated enemy fire – from the
front and left. Kendall remembered: 'We were still on the ground,
and we copped it then with a hail of fire . . . and a couple of the
guys were wounded, some badly.'[33] Like 11 Platoon, they were now
fighting defiantly to hold back a strong and determined enemy force.
With the first burst of enemy enfilade, Kendall's radio operator, who

was standing beside him, was hit. 'My signaller, Brian Hornung, was hit with a round through the top of his shoulder. The bullet spun him round and I saw the red patch of blood near his left collarbone. My platoon sergeant, Neil Rankin, and the stretcher-bearer treated his wound while Brian, to his great credit, tried to help me get the radio set working. But it was no use – the radio was wrecked.'[34] Kendall now had no communications; he and his men were on their own. He looked over at Corporal Ross 'Black Mac' McDonald's section and saw that a number of McDonald's men had also been hit. They were still under heavy suppressive fire and it was difficult to get orders to his section commanders. The noise was absolutely deafening.[35]

The young lieutenant recalled that they had been forced to ground and were in a prone position, fighting off the attempts by the Viet Cong to surround them. The 2IC of his forward section on the extreme left, Private John Cash, the machine gunner for 1 Section, was badly wounded in the right leg. Cash recalled that it 'all went pear-shaped pretty quickly'.[36] Kendall reckoned that anyone about a metre above the ground was certain to get hit – the fire was truly horrendous. Kendall and Rankin crawled around as best they could to organise the wounded, telling them to crawl back out of the area and try to get to CHQ, which should be about 300 metres back. Kendall told Cash to 'tell the boss that the radio's gone and what does he want me to do'.[37] With the help of the wounded 2 Section commander, Corporal Thomas 'Buddy' Lea, Cash made his way back to CHQ.[38] Not far away, one of Kendall's men, Private Peter Doyle, was trying to find the 'biggest puddle of water, or the biggest puddle of mud? And I actually got into the biggest puddle I could find, simply because where the water was lying, that meant there was a depression in the ground. It would have been a depression maybe only 2 or 3 inches [5–8 cm] deep, but it made you a lower target.'[39]

Back at the Task Force base and still in the TOC, US Lieutenant Gordon Steinbrook vividly remembered hearing that D Company CHQ had lost contact with 11 and 12 platoons:

> As I remember, the company commander lost radio contact with his lead platoon, the one that first ran into the VC; and then lost contact with the platoon that had gone up to support the first. The radio blared with the pleading of operators attempting to raise the two platoons. Meanwhile, on the artillery radio net the D Company FOO [Captain Stanley] was calling in fire – first 161 Battery, then the Australian artillery, and then finally the big guns of my own battery. Even though the afternoon monsoon rains were coming down in sheets, we could hear the rumble and roar of Aussie and Kiwi 105s and of A Battery's six 155mm howitzers as their shells screamed over our heads from the other side of the base camp to fall around the cut-off and surrounded D Company. The orders, appeals, and pleading over the radio continued as D Company tried to re-establish radio communications among themselves as well as calling for assistance from the battalion. The situation got so bad that at one point I heard a terror-stricken radio operator say, 'They're gone!'[40]

The dispersed position of D Company made it difficult to wage a defensive battle. The two forward platoons were out of visual contact; neither could provide supporting fire to the other. The men of 11 Platoon had gone to ground in extended line, which left each flank exposed to enfilade and attack even though they had managed to form some type of defensive position. Artillery support also had to be switched from one platoon to the other, given the overwhelming enemy attack against the dispersed company formation. Both 10 and 11 platoons were fighting individual battles at this point, and even with the available artillery support, things were becoming increasingly desperate. Even so, the dispersed nature of D Company helped them in that the Vietnamese troops found it difficult to find their flanks, and the sudden unexpected appearance of another enemy force in the shape of 10 Platoon convinced the Vietnamese that they had collided with a large enemy force. First they had unexpectedly collided with 11 Platoon, 30 minutes later they were hit by 10 Platoon north of 11 Platoon, and soon they would collide with 12 Platoon, which would move up to try to extract 11 Platoon. Indecision was creeping into the minds of the senior Viet Cong commanders.

Major Smith radioed Lieutenant Colonel Townsend and explained the gravity of his situation, saying that with each minute the situation was deteriorating. He recalled personally asking his CO for urgent reinforcements to be flown into the area by chopper near where he had met B Company. However, Townsend believed a landing zone within the area would not be safe and even so there was no ready reaction force available. Smith understood from his CO that they would be sending out a company to support them in APCs as soon as possible. For the next two hours, Smith would desperately try to bring his dispersed force together in order to define a defensive perimeter – but the odds did not look good.[41]

At this point, it was only the training and guts of the men from 11 Platoon and the artillery fire being brought to bear against the enemy troops surrounding them that kept the men in the fight. Private Brian Halls recalled that at the time 'everybody knew what the bloke next to him was doing, and how he was reacting. It was like a very tight family. We all worked very well together. That control came from Sharp, down through the section commanders, and after he was killed the control was still there in Bob Buick, who took over the platoon.'[42] It was now that Private Peter Ainslie saw the Viet Cong advancing straight towards their scattered firing line 'in extended line: it seemed they would attempt to attack very strongly one part of the platoon; that would wither a bit; then they would attack another part very strongly'.[43]

Halls had a near miss when a sniper targeted his position; he called out to Magnussen, who quickly spotted the enemy sniper and killed him. The sniper was about 'five rubber-trees out from us, up in the branches. He had killed the person [Australian] on my other side with a bullet in the head. Presumably he got him initially and was coming across the section for the rest of us.'[44] The headquarters of 11 Platoon, consisting of Buick and privates Vic Grice and Barry Meller, were being specifically targeted. Maybe the Viet Cong had spotted the radio – regardless, this small party seemed to be taking the brunt of the renewed enemy fire.

Meller would be wounded twice during the battle but somehow survived. Buick realised that leading parties of Viet Cong were less than 30 metres away. He and Meller took turns at spotting and shooting the enemy as fast as they could while trying to remain in as much cover as possible, but just as Meller began to direct fire for Buick, the private was shot in the mouth. Buick later remarked that Meller was lucky it happened when it did, because if he'd had his mouth closed at the time the bullet would have shot away his lower jaw. Instead, it tore out of his right cheek. Buick also recalled that he did not remember Meller flinching – he just kept on talking.[45] Buick still had no idea where the rest of the company was, but he yelled to those within hearing distance that the rest of the company was on the way, and the remainder of the battalion was now in APCs racing to the rescue – just hang on a little longer.

17

'. . . you better put the stuff on top of us'

1650–1700 hours

Back at Nui Dat, at 4.50 p.m., Brigadier Jackson and Lieutenant Colonel Townsend were deciding their next course of action. Townsend wanted to send out A Company to reinforce D Company, but he could not do so until he had cleared it through the Task Force commander. Jackson, however, was concerned for the safety of 1 ATF base. He was still unsure of the whereabouts of the Viet Cong *274* and *275 regiments*, although he suspected from Major Smith's description that at least a battalion from *275 VC Regiment* along with *D445 VC Battalion* was attacking D Company. That left two battalions from that regiment and the whole of *274 VC Regiment* unaccounted for.[1]

If Townsend got his way, the whole of 6 RAR along with 1 ATF base's artillery would be committed to the battle raging in the rubber plantation. This would leave the base exposed to an enemy attack, even though by now 5 RAR had returned, minus one company. While the artillery could be switched back to support any attack against the base, this would leave 6 RAR with minimal or no artillery support. However, the base was considerably well placed to withstand any serious attack against it, even without 6 RAR – it could call in strategic reserves from II FFV (the US Field Force) if required, and air support was close by.[2]

Jackson eventually agreed that A Company could go out to support D Company, but he was not going to let them go until he thought it absolutely necessary. He also agreed that Townsend would accompany A Company to take command of his battalion in the field when it moved out, and it was arranged for US ground-attack aircraft at Bien Hoa air base to be placed on air alert to deliver a napalm strike against the enemy massing in the eastern half of the plantation.[3]

The official history of the Vietnamese *5th Infantry Division* confirms that Smith and his company were facing the three battalions of the Viet Cong *275 Regiment* along with *D445 Battalion*. However, the Vietnamese were suffering heavy casualties from the Anzac artillery:

> The enemy began to fire artillery and their rear elements split into two wings along the axis of Route 52 to concentrate on striking and rolling up the 2nd Battalion . . . The 3rd Battalion and an element of the 1st Battalion attacked the enemy in the decisive area of the battlefield. The Australian troops regrouped and resisted while calling intense artillery fire into our vanguard elements and the blocking elements of the 1st Battalion and D445 Battalion . . . the situation of our leading elements was difficult due to the enemy's artillery and firepower that blocked us, and we were unable to achieve encirclement of the enemy battalion. The 1st Battalion and the 3rd Battalion suffered high casualties. At 5 p.m., the battlefield headquarters ordered our units to withdraw to the regrouping position.[4]

Back at Smith's position, about 500 metres west of 11 Platoon, Smith reported to Townsend at 4.53 that enemy troops were moving to his right (south) at position 485668.[5] A few minutes later he reported that CHQ was located at 479674; 10 Platoon was still about 200 metres east of his position, while 11 Platoon was at 484670. Smith estimated that the enemy they had previously seen moving around his right was about three companies strong.[6] By now, Lieutenant David Sabben and 12 Platoon were at CHQ. He noticed how the tracer rounds buried themselves in the mud to his front, indicating that someone was in the trees firing down at them. Sabben recalled that the radio traffic was constant, with 11 Platoon reporting on the tactical situation and helping Captain Stanley adjust the falling artillery shells. Listening to the transmission from 11 Platoon, the sound of the small-arms fire was loud and sharp, but from his position about 500 metres to the rear the sound had 'lost its *crack*'.[7]

Smith now ordered Sabben's 12 Platoon to move forward towards 11 Platoon, and Sabben left Corporal Merv McCulloch's 9 Section to help defend CHQ's position. Moving out with 12 Platoon was Private Alan Parr, the machine gunner for 7 Section, along with his mate and No.2 on the gun Private Noel Grimes, who was carrying the spare machine-gun barrel and extra ammunition. On hearing the order that they were moving forward, Parr recalled: 'I looked at Noel and said "Now we're going to find out what it's like to be in action," and with that we jumped up with the rest of the platoon and headed in the direction of the first shots we heard.'[8]

Meanwhile, Private Terry Burstall of Sabben's 9 Section recalled going into all-round defence with his section placed on a slight slope looking back towards the Task Force area, facing away from the sound of the firing. They were to dig in, so he and the others of the section threw off their packs, got out their entrenching tools and started to dig shell scrapes. They had no idea what was happening just a few hundred metres behind them.[9] Sabben and the rest of his platoon (now just two sections strong), Corporal

Laurie Drinkwater's 7 Section (Drinkwater had served in Malaya) and Corporal Kevin Miller's 8 Section pushed forward in a south-east direction into an enemy maelstrom of small-arms, RPG and mortar fire with the aim of trying to extract and rescue 11 Platoon. Unknown to Burstall and the others of 9 Section, as Sabben and his men moved out, Smith and CHQ moved forward with them.

By now, the wounded Private Brian Hornung, radio operator for 10 Platoon, had arrived at the former CHQ position, the rear of which was still being held by 9 Section. Burstall recalled seeing him come in: 'He was bleeding down the front of his shirt and hold-ing a field dressing on a wound low in his shoulder, almost in his chest. He looked at me, blank-eyed, and said, "There's hundreds of them out there." I looked at [privates] Brian Reilly and [Richard] Shorty Brown and I think we all wondered, "What the hell have we hit?" Hornung moved through us and over the slight rise and disappeared.'[10] Burstall could not help thinking that something was wrong, and he moved over the rise to see that CHQ had gone. He grabbed his rifle and ran through the rubber to the east towards the sound of the firing.[11]

Meanwhile, CHQ had only gone about 150 metres when it was forced to bunker down. The casualties from 10 Platoon began to arrive at Smith's position, including the wounded machine gunner from 10 Platoon, Private John Cash, with Corporal Buddy Lea.[12] Miller, commanding 8 Section, 12 Platoon, recalled that as other wounded started coming in from 10 Platoon, some were saying 'there were heaps of Charlie out there . . . Buddy Lea was wounded and his eyes had become as big as saucers and he was saying "Don't go up there". . . . He said there's "thousands of them".'[13] A rough company aid post was quickly established in a slight hollow in the ground.

With this, Sabben and his two sections continued their advance to try to extract 11 Platoon. They headed towards the tapper's hut to get their bearing; from there they would turn east and head for 11 Platoon's position. Smith halted CHQ because with the wounded from 10 Platoon they were now committed to remain static. Stanley recalled that it was also impossible to control the situation on the move: he had two lots of radios sorting out information, and the artillery needed to know exactly where each platoon was located, so they were forced to stop.[14] The situation had deteriorated considerably and Smith knew that neither he nor Stanley could perform his critical role while moving around the plantation. If they failed their command and communication tasks, the platoons would be in even more dire straits. They stopped to establish a secure area for the wounded, and as they did so the torrential rain continued, seemingly getting heavier by the minute.[15]

At this point Smith was focusing on trying to establish some sort of defence position and Stanley found that he and his radio operator, Lance Corporal William Walker, had plonked themselves into the same hole. Walker was carrying Stanley's radio, while Bombardier Murray Broomhall was temporarily manning a machine gun. While Murray was only 10–20 metres away, in the current conditions Stanley recalled that this was a very long distance.[16] Indeed, Smith's signaller, Corporal Graham Smith, who would remain at his CO's side throughout the battle, having the critical role of maintaining communications, recalled that 'once company headquarters had gone to ground we could actually see some enemy and it was pissing down rain'.[17]

By now Burstall had found CHQ. He recalled that on seeing Sergeant Major Jack Kirby he yelled at him 'did he want us up there, and he almost turned purple. "Of course I want you up here, you stupid bastard!" he called back. I ran back again to the section and we collected our packs and came up to Company Headquarters.'[18] As they arrived, Kirby put them in a line facing south, covering the right flank, and they saw enemy movement through the rubber trees. Even though it was still daylight, the distance was too far for effective fire and they had been told to conserve ammunition, so they held their fire. It is likely these enemy troops were advance elements from *D445 VC Battalion*, although they may have been elements of *275 VC Regiment* who were trying to locate the southern flank of the Australian position. Burstall and his mates lay prone in the mud watching and listening to the sound of the firing to their left, and watching the artillery explode further to the left near 11 Platoon. They were still in the dark about what was happening.

At this point it looked like the enemy did not know of the presence of CHQ and 12 Platoon, although probes by small groups were beginning to be attracted to Smith's position. The perimeter of CHQ to the right (south) was relatively flat, but to the left (north) and front (east) it sloped downwards. Here they were in among the young rubber trees, which Burstall later remembered as not being very high – not high enough to form a canopy – and the ground was fairly clear and clean with little undergrowth.[19]

Company No. 2 signaller Private Bill Akell, attached to CHQ, recalled that 'the noise was frightening, just like sitting in the middle of a company rifle-range, with the crack of shots falling all around you. I was wet, cold and frightened.'[20] Word reached CHQ that the radio of 10 Platoon was out of action. Smith ordered Lance Corporal Dennis Spencer to advance to 10 Platoon with the spare company radio; however, Spencer didn't get far before he was wounded. He moved off in the general direction of 10 Platoon but got no further than 20 or 30 metres when he saw a line of mortar bombings exploding along his path. He later said that he didn't remember much after that. He reckoned he was unconscious for about ten or 15 minutes, because when he regained his senses it was still daylight and the battle was still raging all around. It soon became clear to him that he had shrapnel in his back and in both legs. He managed to crawl back to CHQ.[21]

Private Bill Akell now turned to Kirby, telling him he would go down to 10 Platoon with his radio to re-establish contact. Regimental signaller Graham Smith recalled: 'We had a spare radio set at company headquarters and . . . my number two radio operator, who was Private Bill Akell . . . picked up the radio set and took off with it.'²² Akell recalled:

> Brian Hornung was the radio operator for 10 Platoon and he was on the company internal radio net [CHQ – platoon communications net] and when he came in [wounded] I heard him talking with Jack Kirby CSM and Jack Kirby was trying to organise the wounded into a small depression just to the rear of company headquarters and they were trying to get them into that small depression to keep them out of the small-arms fire and Hornung came in and said something like 'I've been shot and the radio is stuffed' because a round went through the radio. It was then that I realised that 10 Platoon had no internal communications, they had no way of talking to Harry Smith and because the radio set that I had was serviceable, but on the wrong frequency, it was on the air admin [administration back at base for supplies, etc.] I decided to turn the channels and get onto the company internal frequency. I just said to Jack Kirby, who was looking after Hornung, that I've got a spare radio set and I'll go forward and Kirby was a big, big bear of a man and I say that in the nicest way . . . he was a typical CSM, kind when he needed to be, rough when he needed to be as well, and firm as well. Anyway Kirby in his usual bear-like manner just yelled out 'Go, go, go!' He was more worried about the wounded then anything else, he just said go, go, go and I just took off. Unfortunately when I took off I [only] had a rough idea where 10 Platoon was, but I certainly had no idea where [Lieutenant] Geoff Kendall would have been and I was really running blindly when I took the set forward.²³

Akell bolted into the bullet-swept no-man's land, trying to find 10 Platoon among the exploding mortar and RPG fire, falling trees and torrential downpour. He recalled that as he was searching for 10 Platoon 'there was a mortar round that landed relatively close to me as I was heading forward'.[24] As he raced down the slope he came across two Viet Cong coming towards him on his left. Armed only with his World War II vintage 9mm Owen submachine gun, he swung around and squeezed the trigger, firing the whole magazine into them. They both went down, and he kept running towards where he hoped 10 Platoon was located. He recalled that as he ran forward, 'I was very concerned. I won't say I panicked, I didn't panic, it was a matter of I needed to get this radio to Geoff Kendall . . . as I said I had no idea where Kendall was.'[25] He saw a couple of 10 Platoon soldiers, each behind a rubber tree, and 'I just yelled out where's Mr Kendall, and they just pointed to their right and I just moved around yelling "Mr Kendall, Mr Kendall" until I made contact with Geoff Kendall'.[26] Indeed, many men from 10 Platoon remember hearing through the noise of battle, someone shouting 'Mr Kendall, Mr Kendall'.[27] Kendall recalled seeing Akell running up through the rubber having completely disregarded his own safety – he came running through the hail of fire directed at Kendall's platoon, and Kendall couldn't believe that Akell not only survived but managed to find him among the confusion of battle.[28]

Akell himself can't explain how he survived his dash through the torrent of enemy fire being poured into and around D Company's position: 'I have no idea how I didn't get hit. Even to this day I realise just how bloody lucky I was to make it through there – rounds were binging off everywhere. People talk about hearing the round passing you, and that's a true thing – you virtually can hear it – and how I didn't get hit I don't know. Somebody was looking after me that day and that's for sure.'[29] Akell gave the radio set to Kendall so he could speak directly to Smith. Thanks to the Victoria Cross–like actions of Akell, communications were restored – but 10 Platoon, like 11 Platoon, was still fighting for its very existence.

Private Akell now took up a position close to Sergeant Neil

Rankin, armed with his World War II submachine gun, to help repel the Viet Cong assaults against 10 Platoon. 'Neil and I just kept firing to our front because they just kept coming and coming and you would see the yellow-type blast of the artillery rounds, and how they didn't turn around and flee – I wouldn't have had the guts that the Viet Cong had to run through that artillery barrage [in fact he had just done something similar]. It was almost suicide. Up front it was small rounds coming our way, it was the enemy coming our way, and of course the artillery just kept pounding away.'[30]

What was left of 11 Platoon was just hanging on. Private Brian Halls heard, even above the sound of battle, a lot of yelling coming from the enemy. He reckoned they were trying to get adrenaline pumping through their veins – they were charging through an Anzac bombardment of shells and needed something to steady their nerve. Australian survivors of the battle would later talk about hearing a loud babbling sound in the rubber, followed by a yell, and the Viet Cong would then come on. The babbling was the enemy psyching themselves up before the attack, and that's when a bugle would sound – a short, sharp, hair-raising blast.[31] The Vietnamese troops would bravely stand up and advance towards the thin Australian firing line among a hurricane of exploding Anzac shells. They didn't run – they just advanced. In all, however, there 'was only one sort of a wave at a time,' recalled Halls. 'I couldn't say how many in all . . . one would finish and another would come in.'[32]

Similar attacks were happening all along the scattered firing line of 11 Platoon. Something had to give – it was just a matter of time. In the centre, close to 4 Section and platoon headquarters, the Viet Cong had heavier weapons, including what some believed to be .50-calibre heavy machine guns, one of which was seen to be moving to the right. Halls of 5 Section recalled how their machine gunner, Private Ian Munro, protected their position by pouring enfilade into the Viet Cong machine-gun crew that had just taken up a position in front of Halls' section. He also recalled that after the battle they found the .50-calibre machine gun right out in front of their position, with the crew's bodies slumped over (it turned out to be a pre-World War II Soviet vintage 7.62mm heavy machine gun).[33]

Private John Heslewood and his mates were under no illusions about their chances of getting out in one piece, but they laughed and joked their way through it all in a desperate optimism:

> The five of us were pinned down and we were joking. It was pouring, really pouring. It was real thick mud and a bullet would hit the mud and fly up and you'd say that if it was coming straight then it couldn't kick the mud up so there must be someone in the tree shooting down at us. So snipers in the trees. And one of the blokes looked up and said, 'There's one up in the trees, six rows back, three wide.' And you'd say, 'It's your turn, have a go at him.' This went on. And you might miss him and someone might say, 'You idiot, I'll get him.' So that's what kept everyone going. There was no real panic. Everyone just fed off each other.[34]

Meanwhile, a few hundred metres behind and north of 11 Platoon, Lieutenant Kendall had ordered his men of 10 Platoon to get up and renew their advance through enemy fire towards the stranded platoon using fire and movement. They advanced in two leaps, one section offering suppressing fire and the other section advancing. However, because of the rain and exploding ordnance it was difficult to spot individual targets. They managed to push on another 50 metres. Kendall recalled: 'I tried to go forward by fire and movement, but we took more casualties. Our guys couldn't see while they were firing, because they [Viet Cong] were on the ground, it was bucketing down rain . . . and they were firing an absolute sheet of small-arms fire at about 8 inches [20 cm] from the ground.'[35]

At the same time, Corporal Ross McDonald and his men of 3 Section, along with Corporal Buddy Lea's 2 Section, attempted to move forward using fire and movement tactics, but they did not get far as the fire was too heavy. They were forced to ground, firing at opportunity targets, and their position was hit by a number of mortar bombs. Kendall had no choice and gave the order to hold where they were, at least until he could organise the wounded. He knew it was hopeless: there was no point in going further, as he would lose more of his men for no purpose to an enemy they could no longer even see.[36] Private Tony Stepney of 3 Section distinctly remembered 'it was pouring down rain, it was absolutely black, the only thing you could see was our tracers going out and that's how they worked out where we were . . . we had gone to ground and we couldn't see a thing.'[37]

Even with the rain pouring and the battle raging around him, Rankin believed he could hear the firing of 11 Platoon up ahead; all around it he noted a barrage of shells exploding. Some were likely from the Anzac batteries that had been ordered to fire against the enemy force to the left of 11 Platoon. Rankin was calling to no one in particular to lift the artillery fire when he saw a blue flash at his feet and felt the air suck him up into the rubber trees, with his marker-panel bag being torn from his shoulder. He landed with a thud but miraculously was unhurt. He wasn't sure whether it had been an artillery shell or a mortar bomb, but he was happy to have survived. Kendall was just then turning around to call to his sergeant when he saw the explosion and Rankin seemingly disappear. 'Gee, there goes poor old Neil Rankin, gone west!' thought the lieutenant, but to his immense relief he soon saw his sergeant back in action.[38]

Now back in radio contact with CHQ, Kendall radioed Smith to tell him that he was in contact with the enemy and had tried to go forward but was not able to get far using fire and movement. He asked his CO what he wanted him to do, and Smith said, 'Withdraw to me.'[39] Frustratingly, 11 Platoon was only about 200 metres from 10 Platoon's position – not that Kendall knew it at the time. Even so, there was no way of breaking through the enemy force that had almost surrounded 11 Platoon and was now pouring heavy fire into 10 Platoon's position.[40]

Like the rest of 10 Platoon, McDonald and his men of 3 Section were still pinned down and found it difficult to fall back. Even though they had orders to withdraw, they couldn't do so straight-away as one of their riflemen was wounded somewhere close by and had to be found before they could move out.[41] Kendall begun pulling his men back as best he could, using fire and movement, with the section to the left giving covering fire while the section on the right fell back; when they went to ground they provided covering fire to the left, leapfrogging back towards CHQ as best they could.

They soon managed to break out of the immediate area being blanketed with enemy fire and were apparently now out of sight, as they were able to get back to Smith's position without further casualties.[42] The young lieutenant recalled walking 'straight into company headquarters – there wasn't a platoon in front, for example. Lieutenant Sabben had already left [and there was] some sort of preliminary defence for the company headquarters. I walked straight up to Harry and asked, "What do you want me to do?"'[43] Smith told him to put his men around CHQ in all-round defence and that he had kept a section of 12 Platoon (9 Section) back with him.

Lieutenant Kendall organised his men, placing McDonald's section left forward (north-east), with Lea's section right forward (south-east) and Corporal Doug Moggs' section behind platoon HQ. It was still possible to see the enemy moving to the east, although in most cases they were too far away to waste a shot on. Kendall was unsure whether or not the Viet Cong knew his platoon had withdrawn; if they did, the Australians could expect to be attacked at any minute from a number of different directions by an overwhelming enemy force.[44]

Of the 28 men in 11 Platoon, only about ten were now able to fire
their weapons – the rest were either dead or seriously wounded. Halls
remembered Corporal Bill Moore, commander of 5 Section, ordering those with automatic weapons to 'fire only single rounds, not
to fire them on "automatic", to conserve rounds'.[45] Buick reckoned
they had at most about 15 minutes, more realistically ten, and after
that all bets would be off. Without being ordered to, men began to
gather up all the hand grenades and ammunition they could from
the dead and wounded; machetes and entrenching tools were also
laid out in arm's reach ready for a last-stand defence.

Private John Heslewood recalled that at this point things did
'not look real good . . . when we started to run out of ammo.
Some blokes had used more than another. I had a spare 30-round
magazine for the SLR [self-loading rifle] which is for an automatic
SLR which we didn't have, but an SLR back then was 20 rounds
and somehow I came across this 30-rounds one so I kept that, but
it wouldn't work on the rifle because the spring was too strong
for the mechanism . . . for an automatic one, so the spring could
pump them out quicker. I just had it in my pack so I had an extra
30 rounds that we shared around.'[46]

Buick knew that the rest of the company would be trying to
help extricate them, but he had no idea how this could be done. He
radioed Stanley, asking him to bring the artillery fire right down on
top of them – he had no choice, as the enemy was closing in. He
yelled into the radio that Stanley had 'better put the stuff on top of
us because there is only about a dozen of us left out of 28 that [are]
still capable of firing . . . Morrie being a good artillery man and a
Kiwi wasn't prepared to shoot his guns onto Australians.'[47] Stanley
informed Buick of the danger and told him that unless his troops
were dug in, he was not prepared to adjust the fire onto Buick's
position.[48] Even so, Buick was able to adjust the fire until it landed
exactly where he wanted it, recalling that the artillery was coming
over the top of their heads and landing about 50 metres in front.

The 'whole ground was shaking. You could feel the blast on the side of the face. It was lots of flash, lots of smoke, lots of noise.'[49]

Buick directed the fire as the first rounds came in: '*Drop 100, 25 right, drop 50 – now give it all to them!*' He recalled that there was nothing more 'spectacular or truly frightening as being near artillery gunfire when it lands close to you – the closest artillery round hit 25 to 30 metres in front of me'.[50] Each shell contained around 15 kg of high explosive and when it exploded the shell shattered into shrapnel shards of metal, with the shrapnel flying towards the front of the exploding shell. Because D Company was behind the shells when they exploded, the destructive force of the explosion and resulting shrapnel impacted against the enemy to their front, much to the relief of the Australians.[51] The Viet Cong front line was blasted to pieces, the forward attacking force completely obliterated.

Private Brian Halls watched as another human wave came in, and remembered that it just 'disappeared in a howl of artillery fire! At the right time, *very* close, too close! The ideal thing, just what we wanted.'[52] However, it was inevitable that the next wave a few hundred metres behind would quickly take their place and attempt to wipe the Australians out.[53] Private Ian Munro was out of ammunition and reduced to cheering on the Anzac gunners as their barrage exploded among the Vietnamese to his front. The Viet Cong were being blown away 'almost in front of your face. It was very, very close and we were very, very grateful.'[54]

Indeed, when the request from Stanley reached the artillery command post to lower the range just in front of 11 Platoon's firing line, Sergeant Jim King was in the post and remembered someone yelling '"Drop 50" [metres] and someone else saying that the rounds would be on their heads if this occurred. There were some choice words being said over the radio. I suddenly realised just how close we were firing in front of our own troops. With that in mind I remember telling the detachment to make sure their laying and corrections were "spot-on", as this was really close. For the rest of the battle, accuracy was paramount in our minds.'[55]

Meanwhile, Townsend had warned A Company at 4.58 p.m. to prepare to move out at once to the scene of the fighting.[56] The company had only just returned from their patrol; even so, they were the best situated to go – although they were tired, they had all their gear ready and it was only a matter of reissuing them with rations and ammunition and they were set to go again.[57] Captain Charles Mollison of A Company was with Townsend discussing the best way of deploying his company when all transmissions on the battalion-command net frequency went blank and were replaced with Vietnamese music blaring out of the speakers: the Viet Cong were jamming communications. This required some sophistication, and emphasised that the force to the east of Nui Dat was not merely the local *D445 VC Battalion*. Standard operating procedures specified that a previously declared frequency should be used if any trouble was experienced, and communications were quickly re-established.

The men of A Company had come back from their three-day patrol and most had had a shower and put on a clean uniform. They were entering the mess, which had tables full of food, including steak, chicken, turkey, hamburgers, fish, spaghetti and rice, and, most importantly, ice-cold beer. There was much discussion about the sudden large-scale artillery mission and the situation that D Company had apparently got itself into, but none had any idea how serious the situation was. Recent replacement in A Company Private Mick Greenwood was talking with his new commander, Lieutenant Trevor Gardiner, who had made his way to the mess after having been 'chucked out' of battalion headquarters, when a runner came down from company HQ telling them not to put their gear away as they would likely be going out again. Greenwood suggested to the lieutenant that he should wait until they came back to be allotted to a section. Not so, Gardiner informed him: 'Just put your gear down there. You'll be coming with us if we go out again.'[58]

Corporal Rod Armstrong was close by talking to two other replacements assigned to Lieutenant Peter Dinham's platoon. All were keen to get stuck into the feast laid out before them. Private Peter Bennett, a machine gunner, had just managed a mouthful of hamburger when the company sergeant, Major Jack Roughley, came in, ordering everyone to be ready to move out in five minutes, taking only basic webbing. Bennett recalled that it was 'the best meal I had seen since the last one with my parents before leaving Australia. I had no sooner started to bite into a beautiful hamburger when the company sergeant major rushed over and announced that Delta Company was in big trouble and we were to get our gear back on and go out to their rescue. I managed to squeeze two hamburgers into my basic pouches before we had to dash off and get ammunition out of our ammunition bunker to load into the APCs.'[59] Their previous relaxed demeanour vanished as the men ran back to their tents to get their gear; many changed back into the wet, smelly greens they had been wearing for the last three days. As they headed to their rendezvous point, the sergeants were handing out as much ammunition as any man wanted. Greenwood recalled: 'I was fairly shitting myself'.[60] At the time he was not to know that one of his mates, 21-year-old postman and national serviceman Private Col Whiston, had already been killed in action.

Townsend told Major Bob Hagerty of 1 APC Squadron that along with A Company they were to advance east of Nui Dat to the Long Tan rubber plantation. Townsend planned to use a helicopter to get close to the battle zone to meet up with the APCs.[61] Hagerty had already briefed Lieutenant Adrian Roberts of 3 APC Troop that one of the companies in 6 RAR was in trouble and that he should take his troop across to 6 RAR battalion headquarters for orders.[62] The troop would normally consist of 13 APCs, allowing three APCs per platoon (one per section) and one for CHQ, but

Roberts informed his CO that only seven APCs were currently operational. Much of 3 Troop had spent the day on track repairs; only seven of his 13 carriers had been brought to a serviceable state due to lack of track parts.[63] Hagerty provided Roberts with three additional APCs from 2 Troop; these were all missing their .50-calibre gun shields, but all ten had radios and functioning intercom systems. However, they were still three APCs short.

All the carriers had previously been armed and fuelled, and Roberts and his troop set off for 6 RAR headquarters to confer with Townsend before picking up the men of A Company.[64] Even so, this did not enable the infantry commander to allocate a platoon of infantry to a section of APCs, which would fragment his company command. Why another three APCs were not allocated to bring the squadron up to strength remains unknown – they certainly should have had enough carriers on hand. Indeed, at some point Hagerty went to the FSCC to request permission from Jackson that another troop be sent out to Long Tan in case the first troop of just ten APCs was ambushed. Jackson by then had left the FSCC and Hagerty found him sitting in his tent. When he requested that an additional troop be sent out, Jackson refused.[65]

In the 6 RAR area of Nui Dat, Major Brian McFarlane and his men of C Company had long ago left the last concert on hearing that their mates from D Company were in trouble. Most were in their tents getting their gear together, expecting to be called to assist their brother company. As they packed, they listened in silence as the voices of the men from D Company came over their radio – the radio net had been jerry-rigged to speakers so the men did not have to sit with their ears glued to the handsets.[66] The radio traffic indicated that these men were fighting for their lives just five kilometres away. Private Norm Wotherspoon was there and recalled: 'I felt, "Shit, this is really bad," because you couldn't do anything and it was pissing with rain and it seemed to be all chaos. There was all this happening on the radio, but absolute silence in the tent. It was just the enormity of it all. I think we were all stunned that this huge attack should be happening so close, only a couple of miles away.'[67] He was especially concerned as he had originally been assigned to D Company and had made some good mates there, but had later been transferred to C Company.

The batteries continued their murderous fire and everyone could feel the shock waves from the shells as they passed directly overhead to slam into the rubber plantation of Long Tan and nearby hills of Nui Dat 2.[68] As recalled by Major McFarlane:

> During the late afternoon I could only sit with my staff, dry and secure, and listen to the unfolding drama on the radio nets and the accompanying sounds of battle from across the valley of the flooded Suoi Da Bang. We listened with difficulty though. We were in a direct line between the guns and D Company. All the barrels of the four batteries were pointed in our direction and the rounds all going overhead. With the field artillery this was not so bad, but the 155mm US howitzers made a terrible blast when they fired and the giant rounds broke the sound barrier sending shock waves right through our bodies. Better than being out there at the other end.[69]

Things were developing at an alarming rate. It had been only 50 minutes since the fighting at Long Tan had broken out.

'. . . the din of the engines and the noise of war'

1700–1715 hours

Flying above the exploding trees and the battle was 6 RAR intelligence officer Bryan Wickens, in the Sioux helicopter being piloted by Lieutenant Rob Rich. He was trying to contact D Company without success, a task made more difficult by the Viet Cong jamming communications – this confirmed that the enemy below included at least elements of a main force and not just the local *D445 VC Battalion*, as the local insurgents had demonstrated no expertise to date with such techniques.[1]

Below in the plantation Major Smith radioed in at 5.01 p.m. 'En [enemy] GR [Grid Reference] 487669 NORTH to 487672 penetrating both flanks and to NORTH and SOUTH'. This was followed by another message, at 5.02 p.m., that they were 'running short of ammo require drop through trees 475674'. Smith stated that they would use red smoke to designate their position. He received word that 1 ATF had requested US air strikes with 'napalm GR 487669 to 487672 [with] 1000lb' bombs to take out the Viet Cong mortar positions – this was the area north, close to Nui Dat 2.

At 5.06 p.m., Smith radioed in that he would 'accept napalm within 100 metres' of his own position. He would use red smoke to designate their position and the required target would be 200 metres north-east of red smoke.[2]

The need for ammunition was now paramount. While the 60 rounds that each rifleman normally carried was sufficient for the contacts experienced so far, the current battle meant the men by necessity were expending their supply at a fast rate. The situation for 11 Platoon was especially desperate. Smith requested that the ammunition be dropped by helicopter about 400 metres behind CHQ. This position was behind a small knoll and would offer a better position for all-round defence, but he soon realised that many of the wounded could not be moved. They would have to stay put and make do with their current position, which did offer some protection because of a reverse slope away from the enemy.[3]

Back at Nui Dat, Lieutenant Colonel Townsend had passed on Smith's request for an ammunition drop to Brigadier Jackson. The brigadier turned to RAAF Group Captain Peter Raw and asked for helicopters to deliver the ammunition as requested, but Raw demurred. His orders were that his helicopters were not to operate in the immediate area when enemy resistance was present or expected. Undoubtedly the battle raging just 5 kilometres away would put his choppers in very real danger as they hovered above the battlefield at treetop level – to make matters worse, during a torrential downpour. They would be sitting ducks. Relations with the Air Force had always been strained, with previous complaints voiced by 1 ATF concerning a lack of support from 9 Squadron. Now Raw was voicing his concerns about losing his helicopters, stating that he would need to get approval from Canberra. Jackson, however, interrupted, telling the group captain in no uncertain terms: 'Well, I'm about to lose a company. What the hell's a few more choppers and a few more pilots?'[4] In frustration, Jackson turned to the US Army aviation liaison officer, who told the Australian commander, 'Well, Brigadier, I dare say my guys can help out' and said the choppers would be at Nui Dat in 20 minutes.[5]

Meanwhile, the two Australian helicopters that had brought the Australian entertainers to Nui Dat earlier that day were sitting a few hundred metres away. At some point during the debate, flight lieutenants Frank Riley and Bob Grandin had made an appearance at 1 ATF HQ on learning that an infantry company was in serious trouble. All they could hear was radio messages coming in from D Company requesting ammunition urgently.

Raw explained to Riley that D Company was in trouble and needed ammunition but they could not go in because it was unsafe: the flying conditions were terrible, there were too many Viet Cong out there, the squadron's helicopters were not support helicopters, and they were not designed for this type of operation. Riley wasn't concerned about the reasons why they couldn't do it and said, 'Well, I don't care. I'll go!'[6] He was commander of the aircraft in the field and had the right to make tactical decisions regarding his aircraft and crew.

Jackson was relieved to 'see some guts' from an air-force officer and turned to Raw for his response. Raw, likely humiliated and embarrassed that US pilots were willing to support the Australian infantry while he was talking about contacting Canberra, ceded to Riley. The flight lieutenant would take responsibility for the helicopters and the mission. The two helicopters, commanded by flight lieutenants Riley and Cliff Dohle, would conduct an ammunition airdrop to assist the embattled infantry. Most, including Grandin, considered it a suicide mission, but all of the flight crews agreed to go.[7]

Meanwhile three US F-4 Phantom fighters had taken off on their napalm bombing mission; they were soon over the target area.

This meant that the artillery fire missions had to be called off while aircraft were in the immediate area – an anxious time for Smith and his men, as they were denied the critical support of the artillery and would have to deal with any human-wave attack using small-arms fire alone. Smith had earlier requested that the deadly incendiary fluid be dropped north-east of his position by an airborne fire controller in a light aircraft, who would identify their position by a red-smoke grenade. However, the fire controller was unable to see the red smoke defining 11 Platoon's position because of the treetop cover and rain. Smith tried to radio the airborne spotter aircraft several times but was unable to make contact. He then radioed the Task Force base, knowing that he could not hold the Viet Cong off without the artillery support. He told BHQ to send the aircraft away as he needed the artillery fire back urgently.

Sergeant Buick and Captain Stanley went back to calling the artillery fire in front of 11 Platoon.[8] The fighters were ordered to drop their napalm on the forward slopes of Nui Dat 2 – it was here that the enemy command element was assessed to be positioned. On doing this, they were to immediately vacate the area.[9] Stanley recalled the enormous confusion and resulting strain he felt – many others would have cracked under the pressure:

> . . . the tremendous din gave the effect of a continuous violent thunderstorm. As a result of all the noise, my observation of hundreds of 105mm shells falling reasonably close to us plus the periodic suspension of fire from Nui Dat for air clearance purposes, I became somewhat unsettled. I reported on the artillery radio: 'The situation is too confused to use the guns.' I might as well have said to my battery commander 'Help'. My call for help was answered by [Major] Harry Honnor, who suggested a safe grid reference at which I could recommence firing and adjust as necessary. I will be forever thankful for the way he restored my confidence.[10]

At another point, Stanley asked for 'ten rounds gunfire' using a superseded British mode of ordering artillery fire. An Australian gun position officer requested that Stanley correct his order with the accepted 'ten rounds fire for effect'; this officer rightly got an immediate tongue-lashing from Lieutenant Colonel Richmond Cubis, who told him in no uncertain terms: 'When he asks for gunfire, you give him bloody gunfire!'[11]

Back at the Task Force base, both Townsend and Jackson were concerned that they were sending the APCs and A Company into an enemy ambush: setting an ambush for a relief force was a favourite tactic used by the Viet Cong. This was indeed almost certainly part of their plan for the next day's ambush. Smith became increasingly concerned about the ongoing debate on whether the APCs and infantry relief force should come to his rescue. At some point he retorted to his CO in frustration: 'If they don't hurry up and get here then they might as well not come at all!' or words to that effect.[12] Townsend and Jackson finally agreed that the APCs and the relief force should be sent out.

The APCs of 3 Troop, commanded by Lieutenant Adrian Roberts, while they had both gun shields (which turned out not to be bulletproof) and radios, both supplied by the Americans, were still far from battleworthy. They had been operating with 1 RAR, their tracks and suspension were worn and, while they had radios, they were largely primitive; however, they did enable the commander to speak to his driver as well as the commanders of other APCs, but background noise made communications difficult at best. The commander was able to speak to base, but it meant cutting communications with the rest of the troop – this also applied when listening to D Company's transmissions. The commander had no communications with the infantry he was carrying, other than shouting above the din of the engines and the noise of war.[13]

The additional three carriers from 2 Troop supplied to Roberts' squadron were commanded by Sergeant John 'Bluey' O'Reilly and were in better condition than the other seven APCs, having only recently arrived from Australia. However, while they had decent radios, they were missing their .50-calibre machine-gun shields.[14]

Most of the men posted to 3 Troop were national servicemen and had trained at Puckapunyal in Victoria, which was remote from the infantry battalions and meant they had little combined-arms training. Their experience since arriving in Vietnam had been mostly road convoys and Roberts himself had trained as a tank commander before being assigned to 3 Troop. His command was normally held by a captain. The 2IC was Lieutenant Ian Savage, a National Service officer recently graduated from Scheyville.[15] However, Roberts and his men of 3 APC Troop had gained some experience during Operation Hardihood when, in May 1966, 1 APC Squadron helped US forces clear Long Phuoc village before 1 ATF was established at Nui Dat. The role of 1 APC Sqaudron had been a blocking position east of the village and they had conducted patrols along the line of the Suoi Da Bang between Long Phuoc and Long Tan villages. During this operation Roberts and his men became familiar with the terrain around the plantation and discovered a stream crossing used by the Vietnamese bullock teams, beside an agricultural dam. This intelligence was crucial for crossing the stream, especially now that it was swollen by a tropical downpour.[16]

When Roberts arrived at 6 RAR headquarters, he found Townsend and majors Harry Honnor and Brian Passey (the operations officer) in a heightened state. On looking at one of Roberts' maps, Passey drew a circle in grid 4767, scaled at about 1000 metres in diameter – this was the general location of D Company according to the most recent information.[17] Roberts was ordered to convey A Company, 6 RAR to join D Company, 6 RAR and break up the attack.[18] No other orders were given, and nor was a route to the battle area provided. Roberts quickly boarded his carrier and with the other nine APCs headed to A Company lines, where the infantry was waiting. It was now around 5.15 p.m. Meanwhile, Captain Charles Mollison, commanding A Company, had been provided with his orders: he was to move by APCs to the AO (area of operations). His men were to relieve the pressure of the Viet Cong attack against D Company by attacking from the south, reinforce D Company, repel any attacks, and secure the AO to enable D Company to evacuate the wounded.[19]

'Keep this for me, skipper'

1715–1730 hours

The artillery was crucial in the Battle of Long Tan, and apart from the professionalism of the gunners and their officers, other factors contributed to the effectiveness of the fire support: the 'convenient range of 5000 to 6000 metres; the infantry being on a line between the guns and the target area on the near side of the target to the guns; the rubber trees causing airburst and creating maximum destruction by scattering splinters down on the exposed enemy; [with] unlimited ammunition'.[1] Even so, the guns and associated communications equipment were not designed to operate in tropical conditions, which became evident not long after the Australians arrived in Vietnam.

Sergeant Jim King of 105 Battery recalled how, during the battle, a bolt of lightning took out the tannoy system, disrupting communications between the gunners and the command post. Orders had to be shouted down the line until the system was repaired. When it was finally repaired it was again put out of action by shorting due to the rain. Condensation also continually fogged up the gun sights. King remembered:

> To keep firing my gun, we finished up using a bicycle torch
> attached to a star picket as a GAP [gun aiming point]. I know
> the other guns used the same or similar GAPs . . . It was soon
> realised that with the number of 'ten rounds, fire for effect'
> and the periods of 'continuous fire', which meant for 10 to 12
> minutes at a time, we would soon run out of ammunition.
> This was reported to the command post and a massive
> ammunition resupply from the ammunition dump to the
> guns was put into effect. Cooks, clerks, medics, Q Store staff,
> technicians from the RAEME [Royal Australian Electrical
> and Mechanical Engineers] workshops, and members of
> 131 Divisional Locating Battery assisted in resupplying the
> gun line.[2]

Some cooks, however, remained at their post, supplying the men
with something hot to eat and drink during the torrential downpour; an unknown New Zealand gunner recalled how cooks came
'looming out of the rain from time to time with a huge pot of stew
and a ladle to keep us all going'.[3]

Another problem was that the ammunition itself, which was
principally supplied by the US Army, and which the Australian
government paid for, was unreliable. The Australians were the only
allies of the US who paid their own way, paying for everything from
ammunition to razor blades; all other allies had their 'costs' covered
by the US government.[4] The accuracy of the US-supplied shells
depended on the batch number – quality control during production obviously being a major problem – some from one lot might
be accurate, while shells with a different batch number could be up
to 400 metres out. To help counter this, the Anzac gunners adopted
a policy of having two different types of ammunition: 'close target',
where one batch of a lot number known to be accurate was used

by all guns when firing in direct support of Australian troops, and inaccurate, which were different-weight projectiles used to harass the Viet Cong by firing at irregular intervals to keep them wondering where the next round was going to fall.[5] The latter were only fired when no Australian patrols were in the area and a 400 'drop short' would not endanger the lives of Australian infantry.

New Zealand signaller Patrick Duggan was in the thick of it, and later recounted how 'the position looked like hell on earth, with clouds of cordite smoke gusting across as the rain hammered down . . . the noise was unbelievable. There was no let-up, and while we were concentrating on the task at hand – for me, empty-ing charge bags into casings and screwing on their deadly, high-explosive noses – we had no real sense of how the fortunes of the battle were running, whether it was won or lost.'[6]

The rain and continuous firing were creating a potentially seri-ous situation for those manning the guns and the battery positions. When each shell was fired it resulted in toxic fumes, which are normally dispersed – but the storm, lack of wind, and continued firing were preventing the toxic cloud from dispersing and it was lying all around the battery positions.[7] Some were forced out of the battery area to vomit and after a short break would head back into the toxic mix. Gunner Jason Neville of 105 Field Battery recalled: 'While we were belting out the rounds some of the dig[gers] from our Battery were fainting as the smoke (cordite) was inhaled by all and caused [them] to stop . . . breathing. Some only vomited but nobody was really bad as our medic pull[ed] them through.'[8] Indeed, at no time during the battle did a gun stop firing because of a shortage of ammunition or a reduction in its crew.[9]

Back in the plantation, Lieutenant Sabben and his two sections from 12 Platoon had continued their advance towards 11 Platoon. They took a line slightly east of south and were soon approaching the old tapper's hut. Sabben was acutely conscious of the gap into their rear, and that they could themselves be easily cut off from CHQ if they moved too far forward. He was desperately hoping that 11 Platoon would be able to withdraw to his position.[10] They made it about 200 metres when they were hit with overwhelming fire from a number of different directions.

Private Alan Parr, a machine gunner for 7 Section, recalled: 'Across to my right front I could see a hut and in the top window I noticed tracers screaming from a machine gun in our direction. I fired off a burst – about 60 rounds from the M60 – at the window but word came to hold fire as they didn't know exactly where 11 Platoon were. Even though I'd stopped firing, it was obvious it wasn't 11 Platoon in the hut. The VC were taking advantage of the height, sweeping fire down into the rubber trees.'[11] Nearby, Private Max Cameron also knew that those firing at them were Viet Cong. Fire was coming from the hut to their right, and bugles could be heard blowing out orders. At one point a bugler was hit by Private Bryan 'Bushy' Forsyth, but within seconds another Viet Cong took up the bugle in his place.[12]

Private Stan Hodder, who was part of platoon headquarters, recalled being immediately 'pinned down by heavy fire from a machine gun – you just couldn't move'. This was soon added to by small-arms fire, including submachine guns from a number of different directions, most of it from the direction of the tapper's hut to their right. They were now met by a large enemy force, about a company strong, coming up on their right (south) flank.[13] Sabben and his men fired and with their first volley dropped about a dozen of the enemy, but were forced to ground as concentrated return fire tore into their position and the enemy continued to advance upon them.[14]

Sergeant Bob Buick was not far away, and recalled that the light over the battlefield was now very gloomy as a result of a 'combination of the failing natural light as darkness approached and the severe tropical thunderstorm that was lashing the Long Tan plantation. The smoke from the intense small-arms and artillery gunfire was creating a dense fog, which was hanging low over the battlefield.'[15] He and his men could see the enemy moving around in the mist, trying to find their exposed flanks. They were taking fire from three directions, but while the poor visibility was to their advantage, any movement would bring a hail of concentrated enemy fire. It was impossible to withdraw with the large number of casualties.[16]

In the rain and mist, Sabben and his men, a few hundred metres behind 11 Platoon, saw haunting and fleeting images of indistinct shapes: groups of enemy troops, moving to the north-east and south-east. Sabben distinctly recalled movement to his front, converging from left and right, and when they met he knew that they were getting in between his platoon and 11 Platoon. He and his men fired on the concentrating Viet Cong and they immediately scattered left and right. The Australians attempted again to advance but only managed another few metres, when they were hit with tremendous fire, appearing to be overshoots from 10 and 11 platoons' areas as well as other Viet Cong who were firing directly at Sabben's advance. It was now only their presence that stopped the enemy from completely surrounding 11 Platoon, and it was their fire that kept a corridor open.[17]

Before long, additional parties of Viet Cong were identified to their front, trying again to sandwich themselves between the two Australian platoons. This allowed them to attack 11 Platoon from the rear, cutting off all avenues of escape for the platoon's survivors.[18] Parr recalled how the enemy were trying to circle around 11 Platoon, because 'they didn't know how many of us were there . . . [soon it] looked as though they were coming out from behind the hut. I reckon there was a couple of hundred Viet Cong marching away from Eleven Platoon, heading around behind company head-quarters, dark figures moving through the trees in a line. Because I was facing Eleven Platoon, I ran across into the rubber trees and plonked down facing that group of men I could see, and fired another burst.'[19]

With every passing minute the torrential downpour and developing mist made it more difficult to see the enemy, with rain from the Australians' raggedy hats drenching their faces and nothing dry to wipe away the water from their eyes. Sabben recalled:

Above us the thunderheads were lightning, and we had the effect of lightning subdued but under the clouds. It would be like flashbulbs going off, but not startling, just dimly. When the artillery flashed it was the same thing, except you could hear the noise and see the vapour of the blast. You could see the lightning and because we were right under it, you could hear the thunder straight away. But it was low rumbling. That feeling you have when you're sitting in the theatre and they put on the earthquake sounds, and your guts churn. Everything instantly is wet around you, and the rain is coming down so hard it's going straight through the leaf canopy, it pushes the canopy out of the way, and it's like little bullets hitting the ground. And once the ground was wet, once it was saturated – because it was level and there was nowhere for the water to go – it just lay there, so the pools formed within a few minutes. And once the pools formed, the rain was pelting into the pools, and the pools were dissolving the surface mud, and the pools then were splashing. And the rain was heavy enough to raise that little splash mist about a foot [30 cm] above the ground. So we were lying on the ground in that mist and, from 25 yards [23 metres] away, if you looked, you'd just see the uniform reddish-brown mist. But occasionally you'd see a hat sticking through it.[20]

At 5.17, Major Smith radioed to battalion headquarters that 11 Platoon was surrounded at position 485670, while 12 Platoon, which had gone forward to try to extricate it, was itself pinned down taking heavy fire and was being directly assaulted; its position was 481672. He also confirmed that the enemy force was 'generally EAST and also SOUTH of 670 Northing'.[21] Private Noel Grimes, No. 2 on Parr's M60, recalled: 'Originally 11 Platoon got pinned . . . meanwhile we all stayed put where we were and we could hear the gunfire up ahead. We're thinking, "What's going on, what's going on?" with a bit of confusion obviously and then 10 Platoon went to their aid and they got pinned, and then in our turn we went up and we got pinned – we were all pinned and quite frankly no one knew where anybody was. The sig sets were jamming because it was so full on and they were all trying to talk to each other.'[22]

Even so, Sabben and his men managed to fight off the enemy to their front, allowing a tentative corridor to exist between the two platoons. Sabben, like Lieutenant Geoff Kendall before him, was now unable to advance to 11 Platoon. He was not completely sure how far in front 11 Platoon was positioned, as visibility was down to 70 metres. The young lieutenant and his men had been in the thick of it for over 30 minutes but still held their ground, determined to keep the passage open between them and 11 Platoon somewhere up ahead.[23]

At 5.20, Smith requested Lieutenant Colonel Townsend to send in a 'heliborne assault', but given the weather, appalling visibility, approaching darkness and lack of a secure landing zone, Townsend replied that this was 'totally impossible'. Townsend told Smith that a company in APCs would soon be leaving Nui Dat to come to their position.[24] Smith informed Townsend that the 'enemy [were] dressed in green camouflage' and positioned in 'general area Pt 66'.[25]

Meanwhile, Sabben knew that if his platoon tried to advance any further they would be surrounded, and given the overwhelming number of the enemy force around them, they couldn't hope to survive an assault from more than one direction at a time.[26] He was correct to be concerned, as Corporal Laurie Drinkwater recalled. When they got pinned down there was some movement to their rear, but Drinkwater and the others couldn't distinguish who was there, friend or foe. They were aware that B Company was on its way to their position – was it them? He remembered that troops were wandering around and looking at them, and looked back at them. Private Grimes recalled that with the appalling 'monsoonal conditions, torrential rain and slush and poor visibility [along with] the Viet Cong looking just like us in jungle greens . . . at one stage we were told to cease firing because we thought it might be B Company coming through the rubber trees'.[27] Private Neil Bextram of 7 Section was adamant that they were not the men from B Company and, yelling to those around him 'B Company be fucked!', started firing on them. Sabben's platoon now took fire from at least three directions; there was just no way forward.[28] Private Kevin Graham was shot in the chest and, as recalled by Parr, was asked if he could make his own way back to CHQ: 'He replied, "Fucking oath I can" and took off like a scalded cat.'[29]

Sabben and his men lay in the downpour firing into the approaching enemy troops, hoping to see the survivors of 11 Platoon making their way towards them. The enemy continued to probe their position, unsure of their strength. If they had known, they would have steamrolled right over the top of them. Sabben remembered that they were being probed on both flanks and that the enemy were likely reporting back on his position in order to put in a concentrated assault against his two sections. Worryingly, he still had had no contact with 11 Platoon.[30] Indeed, it was now that he received a message from CHQ that enemy troops had bypassed them and were probing CHQ's position from the north – these were likely enemy troops following up on 10 Platoon's withdrawal back to CHQ.[31] Sabben recalled that on two separate occasions enemy troops to his north 'undertook a flanking move on Company [HQ] that brought them towards us and to within firing range, so we opened up on them. This caused great confusion both times and resulted in one instance of them changing direction towards us in a feeble attempt at an assault. The group was small – some ten or twelve – and they were easily beaten off, leaving behind half their number dead.'[32]

Private Alan Parr, still behind his M60, also recalled the enemy movement towards CHQ, but this time from the opposite flank. From near the hut 'a large group of Viet Cong bunched quite close together were moving through the rubber trees around towards the rear of company headquarters. It looked like hundreds of them, and I think then all realised we were in big trouble. I moved position so I called fire at the line of VC; I let off a burst of rounds . . . It was in this spot, lying there with my M60 tucked in against my shoulder, when a bullet struck my gun. Punching a hole straight through the barrel just behind where the spare barrel fits on, and only a foot from my head – the gun was ratshit.'[33]

The main threat to 12 Platoon remained the enemy troops massing south of their position. Sabben recalled, chillingly, that 'when the enemy went to ground, we couldn't find them . . . they may well have crawled towards us, and we wouldn't have seen them until they could see us, but when they stood, and when they advanced on us – because they had to advance; we were in defence, almost all the time – we could see them standing above the mist, so we could hit them and they didn't know where the bullets were coming from. They could see the muzzle flashes but, so long as our aim was good, by the time they saw the flashes, it was too late for them.'[34] By now Parr was anxious for a few shots at the enemy; Bextram had been blasting away when Parr asked him for a loan of his rifle. 'Straightaway he handed it to me and I blasted a few rounds off at the VC then handed it back. It always amazed me how Neil just handed his rifle over to me. We never did talk about it.'[35]

Sabben and his men focused on keeping the tenuous corridor between his platoon and the men from 11 Platoon open. He just hoped that the survivors of 11 Platoon would realise that there was little fire coming to them from the rear, indicating that their avenue of escape lay there. He gave orders to the section on his right not to fire on any targets until they had been positively identified as enemy troops. Casualties continued to rise, and Private Terry Ryan, who was next to Sabben, was hit in the elbow. Luckily for him the bullet was an overshoot and had lost most of its velocity, allowing him to pluck it out and hand it to his officer: 'Keep this for me, skipper. I wanna get the bugger that sent it.' He continued to fire.[36]

Parr, who was close by, recalled that amid all of the fighting and exploding ordnance, 'even though it was so frightening, if Lt Sabben or one of the corporals had said, "Jump up! We're going through the gates of hell!" we would have followed them through. It has always amazed me how a person can function under such extreme conditions . . . Maybe it's the mateship, training and the not-wanting-to-let-anyone-down that makes you get up and move when you know you have to.'[37]

20

'Bugger you, George, I'm coming too'

At 5.30 p.m., B Company, halfway between Nui Dat and the plantation, was finally ordered by 6 RAR commander Lieutenant Colonel
Colin Townsend to return to the plantation to support Major Harry
Smith and his men. Private David A. Thomas recalled how earlier
'it [had] started to rain, and we were drinking water off the banana
leaves. It was a fair while before we were told to go back. I think
they'd basically forgotten us.'[1] Major Noel Ford radioed back that
his depleted company (now at platoon strength) was 'moving to
D Coy HQ at 477675'. Ford was heard to ask over the radio,
'What do you want us to do when we get there?' The reply by
Major Brian Passey, 2IC of the battalion, was 'Kill the enemy'.[2]
Soon, however, they themselves were being targeted by Viet Cong
60mm mortar fire. So far they had suffered no casualties, but the
enemy clearly knew they were moving back towards Long Tan
Plantation.[3]

Sergeant Major Jack Kirby and Major Harry Smith, who commanded D Company, test firing a Viet Cong heavy machinegun captured on the Long Tan battlefield. Many veterans of the battle believe that Jack Kirby should have been awarded the Victoria Cross for his actions.

Young National Service Officer Lieutenant Gordon Sharp commanded 11 Platoon, D Company. During the opening hour of battle he was killed in action, while risking his life to call in artillery to protect his men.

Lieutenant Adrian Roberts, commanding 3 APC Troop; Lieutenant David Sabben, commanding 12 Platoon, D Company; and Lieutenant Geoff Kendall, commanding 10 Platoon, D Company: all were in the thick of the fighting at Long Tan, and showed true leadership during the chaos and horror of battle.

LEFT: New Zealand Forward Observation Officer Captain Maury Stanley provided critical direction to the Australian and New Zealand batteries during the battle of Long Tan.

RIGHT: Sergeant James 'Paddy' Todd (12 Platoon, D Company) went off on his own when wounded, to not remove any men from the firing line, and somehow made it back to D Company HQ.

Lance Corporal Geordie Richardson (D Company HQ) and Sergeant Bob Buick (11 Platoon, D Company), who commanded 11 Platoon after Lieutenant Sharp was killed, attend to Private Jim Richmond (11 Platoon, D Company) the day after the battle. Wounded, Richmond had remained on the battlefield overnight, the Viet Cong all around him.

The fatherly figure of 10 Platoon, D Company, Sergeant Neil Rankin with one of his men, Private Don Montgomery, during quieter times.

LEFT: Lieutenant Colonel Townsend, who commanded 6 RAR at the time of the battle.
RIGHT: Brigadier David Jackson, commanding 1 Australian Task Force at Nui Dat.

Helicopter Flight Lieutenants Frank Riley (left) and Cliff Dohle (right), both of the Royal Australian Air Force (RAAF) No. 9 Squadron, dropped ammunition supplies to the stranded D Company at tree-top level while the battle raged 10 metres below – a near suicide mission.

Artillery offering fire support from Task Force base during an unknown operation. During the battle the toxic fumes around the guns made many gunners sick – but they all stayed beside their guns throughout the action.

The destruction of Long Phuoc Village in early June 1966 was meant to clear out the Viet Cong from the immediate area of the Australian Task Force base at Nui Dat.

Private Barry Meller (11 Platoon, D Company), who also remained overnight on the battle-field, being treated in an armoured personnel carrier (APC), 19 August 1966.

Private Jim Richmond being evacuated from the battlefield by medevac, 19 August 1966.

Intelligence officer Captain Brian Wickens of 6 RAR interrogates a captured Viet Cong the day after the battle, 19 August 1966.

LEFT: Corporal Buddy Lea (D Company, 10 Platoon), who ventured behind enemy lines in the heat of battle to bring in the wounded Sergeant James Todd.

RIGHT: Corporal Graham Smith (D Company HQ), who kept communications going throughout the battle.

LEFT: Corporal Kevin Miller (12 Platoon, D Company), who went forward with two sections of his platoon in an attempt to extract 11 Platoon.

RIGHT: Corporal Phil 'Doc' Dobson (D Company HQ), who saved lives tending to the wounded during the battle.

LEFT: Lance Corporal Denis Spencer (D Company HQ), who was wounded while trying to get a spare radio to the stranded 10 Platoon.

RIGHT: Sergeant Major Jack Kirby during better times.

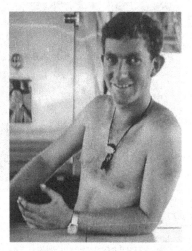 

LEFT: Private Harry Esler (10 Platoon, D Company) recalled that he felt calm during the battle when he could see a target.

RIGHT: Private Les Vine (10 Platoon, D Company) recalled Sergeant Major 'Big' Jack Kirby running around distributing ammunition to his diggers under intense fire from the Viet Cong.

LEFT: Private John Heslewood (11 Platoon, D Company), who was in the thick of the fighting from the opening round, and among the last to leave their position.

RIGHT: Private Paul Large (12 Platoon, D Company), recently engaged to be married, was among the last Australians to be killed during the battle of Long Tan.

LEFT: Private Ray Stewart (D Company HQ), recently promoted Lance Corporal Ron Eglington (11 Platoon, D company), and Private Allen May (11 Platoon, D Company). Ron Eglington was a machine gunner and was awarded the Military Medal for his actions at Long Tan.

RIGHT: Private Dave Beahan (12 Platoon, D Company) was to be the best man at Private Large's wedding, and was close by when Large was killed.

LEFT: Private Robin 'Pom' Rencher (D Company HQ) had transferred to the Australian Army from the British Army and was 'officially' recognised by his mates as 'Australian' after the battle.

RIGHT: Private Russ Parendis (D Company HQ), when firing his M60, kept his ammunition belt in a puddle of water to stop the mud getting into it and jamming the mechanism.

LEFT: M60 machine gunner, Private Alan Parr (12 Platoon, D Company), advances with his mates to try to extract 11 Platoon.

RIGHT: Lieutenant Peter Dinham (A Company), who turned around from Nui Dat to reinforce D Company upon returning from a three-day patrol.

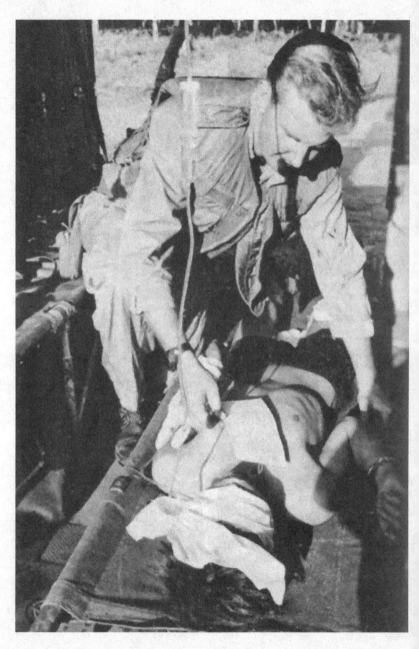

Leading Aircraftsmen B. Hill treating wounded Viet Cong in an APC, 19 August 1966.

Lieutenant Trevor Gardiner and Captain Charles Mollison (commanding A Company), on their return to Nui Dat after their company's three-day patrol, 18 August 1966. At the time this photograph was taken battle had just broken out 5 kilometres to the east. *(Mollison 2005)*

Only confirmed image of a member of D445 Viet Cong Battalion, with a rocket-propelled grenade (RPG). *(Courtesy Ernie Chamberlain)*

Major Smith (left) briefing officers and NCOs, D Company, before returning to the battlefield the next day.

Lieutenant David Sabben, commander of 12 Platoon, on the battlefield the following day.

LEFT: Part of the Viet Cong weapons collection after the battle.

RIGHT: Privates Stan Hodder (D Company HQ), Terry Burstall (12 Platoon, D Company) and Peter Dettman (12 Platoon, D Company) with weapons collected on the battlefield, 19 August 1966.

Australians of D Company after receiving dolls and gifts. Front: Pte Noel Grimes, Pte Allan May, Pte 'Yank' Akell, Pte Neil Bextram, LCpl Bill Roche. Rear: 2Lt Geoff Kendall, Sgt Bob Buick, Pte Geoff Peters, Cpl 'Bluey' Moore, LCpl Barry Magnussen, Pte Ian Campbell. (Ranks as at time of presentation.)

Australian soldiers of Long Tan holding awards presented in lieu of medals by the South Vietnamese government.

Erecting the Long Tan Cross at the scene of the fighting in the plantation on the battle's third anniversary, 18 August 1969.

Flight lieutenants Frank Riley, Bob Grandin, Bruce Lane and Cliff
Dohle, along with their flight crews, knew that their mission to
resupply D Company was going to be extremely hazardous. The
weather presented truly atrocious flying conditions: not only was the
rain pouring down, but it had now turned into a tropical thunderstorm, with low-lying clouds. The amount of enemy ordnance flying
around the battle zone, including mortar bombs, could easily bring
down a helicopter that was hovering 10 metres from the ground.
Added to this was the fire from the ground from small arms and
RPGs. They were also aware that Major Smith and his men would
be open to mass infantry attacks without artillery support while
they were flying in the area. It was crucial that they get in fast and
get out even faster so the artillery could recommence laying down
the vital artillery barrage against the enemy forces massing around
the stranded infantry below. Indeed, finding D Company in these
flying conditions was going to be a major task in the nondescript
rubber plantation. If they failed to see the smoke grenade, the mission would be over, and D Company would likely be overrun within
minutes with no ammunition and no artillery support while the
helicopters were flying around trying to find the smoke.[4]

Earlier, Lieutenant Adrian Roberts, in command of 3 Troop, had
arrived at A Company lines. The men and their officers were anxious to be on the move, and the young lieutenant expected a quick
discussion regarding the route to be taken and other particulars.
But there seemed to be no time – the infantry and their officers just
wanted to push on and get to the scene of fighting as soon as possible. Not being able to allocate each of his platoons to an APC section, given Roberts' troop was down by one APC section, Captain
Charles Mollison ordered his platoon commanders to load up
from the front of the column of APCs.[5] This meant that not only
would the vehicles be overloaded but there would also be a mix of

men from differing sections in each APC. Sergeant Jim Myles of
1 Platoon recalled that as they began to mount up, one of the corporals from the carriers was handing out shell dressings (bandages). Myles didn't ask why; he just stuffed them into his shirt.
He and the others were informed of the seriousness of the situation – D Company had taken a lot of casualties.[6] They were soon
aboard but still pretty much in the dark about what was happening and what their specific objectives were, other than to relieve
D Company.

Fortunately Roberts knew of the ford across the stream and that
is what he headed for. It was the best way of crossing the swollen
stream, whose banks in almost all other areas were steep and difficult to negotiate at the best of times. He had already discussed this
with his commander, Major Bob Hagerty, who had approved his
proposed route to the plantation. However, once across the stream
all bets would be off, as there was no way of knowing what awaited
them at the crossing and beyond; the situation was extremely fluid
and largely unknown.

Three Troop and A Company did not leave their company
lines until 5.35 p.m. Sergeant O'Reilly's APC was in the lead as he
was most familiar with the crossing point and had crossed many
times while working with D Company.[7] There were only a few gaps
in the base's wire defence wide enough to enable the carriers to
pass through. Normally, when exiting south-east, they would pass
through a gap in the engineers' area, but the road here was blocked
because of roadworks. Roberts was forced to take a circuitous route
through the base, heading north for a known gap in the wire. Time
was ticking away.

Meanwhile, Warrant Officer George Chinn, the regimental sergeant
major of 6 RAR, could not stand by as the men of D Company
were in danger of being overrun. He organised volunteers to carry

the heavy boxes of ammunition to the helicopter pad. Thought was given to whether they should open the boxes and fill magazines or just drop the boxes as is. It was decided to wrap the boxes in blankets and push them out. Even so, some were opened and ammunition belts were placed in a number of sandbags to make it easier for D Company to distribute the ammunition quickly. Soon, Major Owen O'Brien, commanding 6 RAR's Administrative Company, joined Chinn in organising the men.

As this was going on, the pilots were discussing how they intended to carry out their critical mission. As recalled by Grandin, they would use a technique they had perfected when inserting SAS behind enemy lines. The lead helicopter, with Riley and Grandin on board, would take a lighter load of ammunition and go out at a height of about 600 metres to help locate the target zone. The other helicopter would fly at a lower level and be directed by Riley to the drop zone. After it had dropped its ammunition to those below, Riley would dive down and drop the other supply. This would improve their safety, as at height the probability of being hit by small-arms fire was unlikely and at treetop level the window of opportunity to fire an accurate shot was very much reduced. O'Brien informed the pilots that it was imperative they get in and out as soon as possible as the artillery fire would have to be suspended while they were flying in the battle zone, and D Company was just as reliant on the artillery fire to stop the enemy overrunning its position as it was on ammunition.[8]

Because the onboard door machine gunners had to man their weapons, several soldiers volunteered to board the aircraft to assist in dropping the ammunition. However, RSM Chinn was adamant that he would accompany the drop. O'Brien pointed out to Chinn that he was responsible for organising the ammunition and not for delivering it. However, Chinn almost insubordinately informed the major that he was going, come what may.[9] O'Brien had served with Chinn in the SAS and had known him since he had joined the army 12 years before. He merely replied, 'Bugger you, George, I'm coming too.'[10]

With the ammunition boxes stowed away and O'Brien and Chinn aboard, they were soon airborne and following the track that the APCs were using, which would take them into the plantation and hopefully to D Company. Grandin recalled that with O'Brien and Chinn aboard, 'Beauty – two more to go up when our load of ammunition exploded with a hit from the ground.' But another surprise awaited them: 'To the east was a large thunderstorm with intense rain falling over Long Tan.'[11] Of major concern now was the reduced efficiency of the rotors in the torrential downpour, which could result in the engine 'flaming out'. Dohle recalled that it was an extremely 'uncomfortable' situation[12] – an understatement if there ever was one.

Meanwhile, Sabben and his men were still fighting to keep a corridor open between them and the men of 11 Platoon. Enemy fire was still pouring into their position, even though the mist made it difficult to target individuals – most of the enemy fire was too high and hit the rubber trees. Sabben recalled that as the bullets pierced the tree trunks, the bark ruptured and the latex sitting beneath it leaked out. It didn't dissolve, despite the rain, and a couple of minutes after a bullet pierced a tree, pure-white latex would dribble down the bark. There was no 'dust or mud at that level, and the water isn't going to dissolve it. It's just there, like blood. It looked like the rubber trees were standing there bleeding.'[13]

At this point, an enemy heavy machine gun was sweeping their position with tracer, and with every burst of fire leaves and twigs showered on Sabben and his men. He was increasingly concerned that 11 Platoon might not be aware that 10 Platoon had retired to CHQ, and that they might think 10 Platoon was still on their left – if so, they might attempt to move in that direction to link up with them, which would be disastrous.[14]

12 Platoon tries to extract 11 Platoon

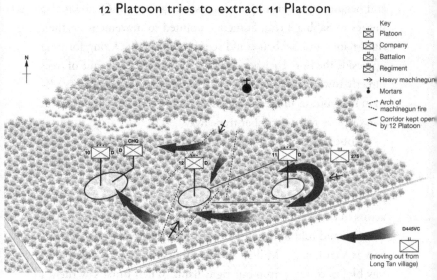

Around 5.30 p.m.: 12 Platoon is pinned down, having moved out to try to extract 11 Platoon and, by providing covering fire to the rear of 11 Platoon, creates a potential corridor of escape for 11 Platoon to its front. Meanwhile other Viet Cong units move towards CHQ and 10 Platoon's position, while D445 VC Battalion attempts to swing around from the south in a blocking position.

Sabben knew that time was running out, not just for 11 Platoon but for his own men. He was continuing to take casualties and the enemy were becoming increasingly aggressive, perhaps now finally realising, with their continued probes against Sabben's position, that they were facing at most one Australian platoon. They would soon have to retire to CHQ. However, he decided to hang on a little longer, hoping against hope that the survivors of 11 Platoon about 200 metres in front would make a break for it and head for his position through the corridor they were managing to keep open – just. Within minutes, however, his worst fears looked as though they were about to be realised.

Another large enemy force was seen forming up near the enemy heavy machine gun and was soon moving to the right of Sabben's position, near the tapper's hut – but it seemed to be ignoring them and beginning to form up for an assault against CHQ, about 200 metres to Sabben's rear. Someone pointed to movement on their right flank, and Sabben could see a group of Viet Cong forming up beside the hut. They very quickly moved up the avenue of trees directly towards CHQ position. This force was bypassing his platoon by about 50 metres and crossed the front of 12 Platoon, about two or three rows of rubber trees away.

Sabben was still unsure of the position of Major Noel Ford and B Company, who were likely making their way back to the plantation – were these them? He got Corporal Kevin Miller to move his M60 machine gun into the centre of their position, pointing across to the avenue of trees that the advancing troops would have to cross, and told him to fire it only if they were positively identified as Viet Cong.[15] Miller, commanding 8 Section, recalled: 'We saw blokes coming from our right flank. When I first saw them I thought they were our blokes. They just looked like our fellas – they were almost dressed the same as us.'[16]

As these troops got closer, he and others recognised the curved and round magazines that identified the weapons as AK-47s. Sabben ordered his men to fire and recalled the enemy's complete surprise: it looked like they had knocked over the first line of that advance with their concentrated fire. The others broke and ran south, back towards the area of the tapper's hut. At this point Sabben heard on the radio that the ammunition resupply was on the way and the choppers would soon be overhead, and that CHQ would throw a smoke grenade to confirm their position.[17]

This gave Sabben the idea of using coloured smoke to try to gain the attention of 11 Platoon – it would provide a rallying point for the survivors of the stranded forward platoon. He would use yellow smoke as it would be the easiest to see through the trees. Even so, it would also attract the attention of the enemy force all around his position. He called up Corporal Laurie Drinkwater, who threw a smoke grenade well to their front and clear of their position. This was immediately followed by a hail of enemy fire, including from the heavy machine gun, with tracers crisscrossing the area, which was now covered in smoke. Sabben recalled being glad he ordered the grenade to be thrown well clear of their position.[18]

Behind Sabben and 12 Platoon, Smith was telling his men that the choppers would soon arrive with an airdrop of ammunition – great news. But this also meant the artillery support would be called off while they were in the area – not so great. He advised his platoon leaders that they would lose the guns while the choppers were near and they should be prepared for any Viet Cong attack. He didn't need to tell them that during this period they would be extremely vulnerable and on their own.[19]

21

'I just screamed at him to piss off'

1745–1800 hours

Lieutenant Adrian Roberts and his troop were arriving at the northern passage through the wire when he received a message from Lieutenant Colonel Townsend via the radio that Townsend had changed his mind: he would not be approaching the battle area by helicopter but would accompany his men in the APCs. Roberts was forced to detach two of his precious carriers under the command of Lieutenant Ian Savage in APC 30B, together with Corporal Paul 'Jock' Fottrill's 33A, to go back and pick up Townsend's group. He was already short by three APCs, and now he was short by five. The remaining eight carriers continued their approach to the hole in the wire. However, when they got there, to Roberts' frustration – and that of Captain Mollison and his men of A Company on board – it had been closed off with a mass of newly installed barbed wire. Further delay was encountered as they tried to find someone to show them the new passage through the perimeter. Everything seemed to be working against them.[1]

A few hundred metres in front of 12 Platoon, Sergeant Bob Buick was still searching for a way to extricate what was left of his platoon. He figured he had about ten men left alive, two of them wounded. He had few alternatives and for a moment contemplated a charge straight through the enemy: 'Do I go forward straight through these bastards and keep running?'² This idea was quickly dismissed. Behind him was the only place where no Viet Cong had been seen, so the company must still be behind them. He decided to go back in that direction; if he couldn't make contact with the rest of the company, the survivors of 11 Platoon would take cover during the night somewhere along the Suoi Da Bang. Buick passed the word that when he said, 'Go!', they were to 'get up and go like hell and help anyone they could'.³

The ongoing shellfire had devastated the front and flanking attacks of the Viet Cong and a momentary lull had developed, with the enemy seemingly deciding on its next course of action. It was now or never. He yelled for the men to 'Go!'⁴ A number heard him yell 'Every man for himself!' The enemy saw the platoon head-quarters get up and head for the rear and they immediately opened up with a heavy burst of fire. Radio operator Private Vic Grice, a 21-year-old storeman from Ballarat, was killed, while Private Barry Meller was wounded a second time. He recalled: 'There was Bob Buick, Vic Grice and myself. Vic Grice was in front of me and he got shot, and I said to someone, "What happened to Vic?" and I don't know who it was said, "He's dead." About 10 or 20 metres after that I got shot in the leg and went down. I took off my pack and threw my rifle away because it was out of ammunition.'⁵ Private John Beere recalled that Buick ran over to help him with the wounded Private McCormack⁶, who soon died. Both then made their way back towards CHQ's position.⁷

Minutes earlier, Private Ron Eglinton, who had been manning the machine gun and protecting the extreme right of the platoon, was heading back into the platoon area. Private Allen May saw him 'coming back from the right flank and I could see him coming towards me and there was one hell of an explosion and a shell hit, and I said to Bluey Moore, "Ron's gone" and as far as I was concerned poor old Ron was dead . . . The next thing I knew was Bob Buick in his guttural voice yelling out "Every man for himself". I didn't get any warning about moving but it could have been delayed getting to me.'[8] Eglinton was very much alive, and recalled hearing the yell from Buick to clear out.

Private John Heslewood of 5 Section, on Buick's right, recalled: 'I didn't hear the order passed along by Bob Buick about getting ready to withdraw, and none of the others near me heard it either. The first we knew was when Bob Buick yelled out, "Every man for himself" and the others got up and went and we were left there, just the five of us.'[9] Among them was Lance Corporal Barry Magnussen, who recalled hearing the 'loud voice of the platoon sergeant, Bob Buick, yelling out "Every man for himself!" I looked behind me to see him taking off to the left. The rest of us could not leave as we were still pinned down by heavy fire. Some little time later, we had a better chance to return fire.'[10] Even so, some enemy troops got up in front of the small group; it was then that Private Ian 'Darby' Munro 'dispatched them. We could hear a whistle blow from time to time, seemed they were coming again . . . they were. Darby knocked them over again . . . John Heslewood and Allen May [were] still alive and . . . on the job. Allen had an Armalite but John had an SLR and he gave me half of his 8 rounds.'[11]

The wounded Corporal John Robbins on the left, one of only two survivors from 6 Section, remembered hearing Buick yell 'We're gonna get out of here!' and saw him 'pissing off . . . and I thought, *Fuck, I'm going to have to do it this side* . . . I thought *This is it, we're gonna have to make a run for it*, so he took off and I yelled out to anyone else around, I thought I was the only one alive . . . I had my backpack on . . . I ran the way he [Buick] went, and I went to ground.'[12] The already-wounded corporal was hit in the hand by shrapnel and losing a lot of blood. It was more painful than the wound to his arm; he thought he had lost his hand and was too scared to look at it. He soon came across a 20-year-old regular soldier from Thurgoona, NSW, Private Ernie Grant, who had also managed to escape. Grant asked the corporal, 'Are you hit?' and he replied, 'Yeah.' Grant then said, 'I'll get rid of your backpack,' and was taking the backpack off when he was killed instantly by a shot through the head. Before he could react, Robbins saw a number of Viet Cong so he took off, zigzagging, and made his way into a shallow gully.[13] He took a breather but soon saw the yellow smoke thrown by Sabben's platoon and quickly went in that direction. He was relieved to find himself surrounded by the Australians of 12 Platoon and was soon being seen to by the medic, Private Graeme Davis. Robbins asked for some morphine; there wasn't any. Davis was starting to bandage Robbins' wounds when the medic was shot in the shoulder. Sabben recalled that 'Doc' Davis was hit in the upper arm with a tracer lodged in his chest while he was attending Robbins.[14]

Meanwhile, Heslewood and his mates made a break for it to the rear. Another two men were wounded in the withdrawal, one for the second time. They hit the ground for cover and to check on their wounded mates. Heslewood recalled that they probably made about 30 or 40 metres at a time, and when they heard the fire starting to build up, would go to ground again. They sought cover from the shattered trees and branches and then, after getting their breath back, would all get up and run another 30 or 40 metres. That went on for 300 or 400 metres.[15] With Heslewood was Private Brian Halls, who remembered: 'Once [we] got that initial break we got up and ran. Then we'd hear a burst of fire – didn't matter where it was coming from – and we'd hit the ground and *slide!* about 10 yards. It was raining, with very red mud . . . we were gaining ground every time we went down.'[16] Heslewood and his small party did not see the yellow smoke and missed seeing Sabben's platoon altogether – they got up and continued their withdrawal with their wounded mates. In the confusion, Heslewood lost contact with his party. At some point he dived behind a tree with Private Frank Carne and a few others. They reckoned they must be less than 100 metres from CHQ and soon heard Australians calling out to them, so they took off in that general direction.[17]

Magnussen had also become separated from 4 and 5 sections after they had made their break and came across the wounded Private Meller. Meller recalled how the lance corporal dragged him for a fair way on his back, but Meller knew this was getting them nowhere and told Magnussen to let him go, arguing with him to go on ahead and saying that he (Meller) would make his own way back or hide in the debris of battle. It was the only sensible thing to do, as his pain was unbearable with every step. The enemy was also closing in and both would surely be killed. Magnussen reluctantly put him down and headed for where he hoped CHQ was. Within minutes Meller spotted six or eight Viet Cong moving back through the area he had just come through. Then to his horror he looked up and saw a Viet Cong standing over him with a grenade in his hand – but no rifle. He didn't know what to do so screamed at him 'to piss off'. That did the trick – the enemy soldier did just that and headed back the way he had come. Meller crawled for a small way, coming across a dead enemy soldier. He pulled the soldier's gear apart and found a groundsheet, took it and looked around for a place to settle in for the night.[18]

Earlier, Sergeant Buick was heading towards where he hoped CHQ was located when he collided with Private Ron Crane of his platoon and together they went down into the mud and slid for a short distance. Both noticed the yellow smoke and made contact with Lieutenant Sabben's 12 Platoon. Buick later recalled that he could hardly believe his eyes – he had found D Company.[19] Private Alan

Parr of 12 Platoon recalled that the first person he saw come in from 11 Platoon was Buick, who had a 'stunned look on his face – I'll never forget it. Little did I realise at the time we all would have looked the same. I saw a few more of the boys come into our position but by this time we had started to take a few casualties.'[20] Close by was Corporal Laurie Drinkwater, who had thrown the smoke grenade. He recalled that they were still pinned down but soon saw some men from 11 Platoon making their way to their position. He and others were calling out to them and he thought the first in was Buick, but very few came in after him.[21] Private Stan Hodder of 12 Platoon also recalled few from 11 Platoon making their way to their position: he could remember seeing only 'Bob Buick and a couple of others . . . when they came to us Bob Buick was the only one I can remember as he came into platoon headquarters.'[22] Corporal Kevin Miller recalled how 'Bob Buick lobbed himself right next to me' and a few others arrived. One asked if he had 'any ammunition, so I threw one of the blokes a magazine, as they were out of ammo, some of them'.[23]

Another who made his way to Sabben's platoon was Eglinton, who recalled making it back to 12 Platoon's area with some relief and seeing Robbins, who had been wounded twice.[24] Buick recalled that by this time around six men from 11 Platoon had made their way to Sabben's position.[25] Sabben recollected some shouts and waves as they made their way to him in ones and twos.[26]

Buick remembered that the first person he saw from 12 Platoon was the recently engaged Private Paul Large, who was taking cover behind a tree trying to unjam his Armalite rifle. Then Buick came across Sergeant James 'Paddy' Todd, who gave him a cigarette. Buick recounted that Todd appeared to be wounded as he could not move his feet; even so, he was relatively calm as they lay there sharing a smoke. Buick made the comment as they smoked in the downpour with bullets cracking over their heads: 'Paddy, you're getting too bloody old for this shit!'[27] Todd, a veteran, had been wounded in

Korea and was now in a rubber plantation in Vietnam wounded in both ankles. Sabben recalled that his sergeant had been in a prone position when a 60mm or RPG round came screaming through the trees and landed between his ankles, burying itself in the mud before exploding. Todd recalled that when it exploded he felt like both his legs had been hit with a baseball bat. He couldn't find any wounds, but shrapnel fragments had buried themselves in his ankles. He couldn't see the puncture marks in his boots and the pain soon went away – he counted himself lucky.[28] Buick checked him over but could find no wounds or signs of blood.

Buick soon moved off to speak to Sabben, and Todd tried to get up but 'fell arse over tit . . . I got up to go again and fell over again.' He fell into the deep mist among the branches that covered the ground. 'I tried again to stand and couldn't, so I started to crawl back [towards CHQ] and the rain really came down.[29] When asked later why he didn't call for help, Todd told Buick that he 'didn't want to be a burden on the others so he decided to make his own way back'.[30]

Meanwhile, Private John Heslewood and his small party, who had not seen the yellow smoke, had come across CHQ instead. The first person they saw, to their great relief, was Sergeant Major Jack Kirby. 'All I could see was him and he said, "Are you all right, soldier? You're not wounded?" I said, "No, sir, I'm all right." He said, "Right" and pointed us somewhere to the back, saying to go down there and he'd bring us some ammunition. And sure enough he turned up with some ammunition and said, "That's your area out there – just watch out there from now on."'[31] Indeed, Heslewood would recall how 'Big' Jack Kirby's frame kept coming back into his mind – he seemed to be everywhere.[32] They weren't the only ones who had not seen Sabben's smoke and had made their way directly to CHQ. Magnussen, after a lot of 'falling over in the mud and slush . . . saw the large figure of Jack Kirby standing in front of Company HQ. Looking for his charges, I suppose – a great sight! Maybe I had made it to safety. Harry Smith came over to me for a report. I told him I knew who had been killed.'³³

Privates Allen May and Doug Fabian had also failed to see the smoke and would eventually come straight into CHQ's position. As May withdrew he was hit in the back, but luckily the bullet hit his entrenching tool; even though he was thrown to the ground by the impact, he was unhurt. He got up and took off his backpack and webbing, keeping his rifle as he had about four rounds left, and moved off again. It was then that he heard his mate Fabian yelling out that he was hit. His reaction was 'Shit, should I leave him?' He and Fabian were good mates, and there was no way he was going to leave him behind, so he was turning to head back for him when he saw Fabian running towards him. As far as they were concerned they were the only survivors of 11 Platoon – no one else could be seen or heard. As Fabian came along, they spotted a rubber tree that had been blown apart and decided to hide in the branches until daylight.³⁴

The two sections of 12 Platoon, with Buick, Crane, Robbins, Eglinton and a few others from 11 Platoon, quickly re-formed. Sabben had earlier been ordered to withdraw to CHQ, but the fire was still pretty intense, as recalled by Drinkwater: 'I think the radio was out at the time, and we didn't have communication with company headquarters. I remember looking at the platoon commander and yelling out, "Do you think there's any chance of getting out of this?" and he said, "I don't think so", which really made my old stomach turn over.'³⁵ At this point, Sabben ordered Miller to try to make his way back to CHQ, leading the survivors of 11 Platoon towards Smith's position. Sabben asked Buick to organise the retirement of the wounded: Todd as he begun to crawl back towards CHQ saw Buick grab the wounded medic Davis and help him get back to CHQ with the others.³⁶

Just as the last of 12 Platoon were getting ready to head back to

CHQ after the wounded and survivors of 11 Platoon had moved out, Sabben and those around him were surprised to see another large enemy force just south of their position, coming up behind the rubber tapper's hut. No sooner had 'we got up than someone said, "Hey, look at that", and we all sat down again. On the far side of the hut was line on line of enemy in the rubber trees. They were forming up, one to each tree, and a few minutes later they came up, about three ranks, about 50 in each. They couldn't have known we were there – they were just standing there waiting for the whistle to blow.'[37] Sabben ordered the team from his remaining M60 to sight their weapon down the avenue of rubber trees. If they had been aware of his presence, Sabben believed the Australians would have been mistaken for Viet Cong given their dark, wet uniforms, floppy hats and basic webbing – similar to what most of the enemy were wearing.

A few minutes later, the Viet Cong moved out in three ranks of about 20 each. In less than a minute, their slow, steady pace had them passing Sabben's platoon at less than 50 metres. He waited for the first rank to pass through the gun sights and then ordered his men to open fire on the second and third ranks. The enfilade of M60 and small-arms fire devastated these lines of troops; both ranks simply collapsed in a heap. The startled first rank then turned and ran back the way they had come, which meant they raced straight into the two fire-lanes that had torn through their comrades. Few made it. For a few minutes, surviving elements of the enemy force fired into Sabben's position; this resulted in additional casualties to his two sections, which had originally numbered 20. He was down to 14 rifles.[38]

There was a momentary lull in the firing; it appeared the enemy were forming up to attack Sabben's position. That being said, Hodder recalled that while it had died down, it was all relative – it dropped from '10 000 bullets per second to about 5000. I've never ever seen or heard anything like it in my life, it went on for three and a half hours – it was full on. I don't know where they got all the bloody rounds from.'[39] It was time to get out while they still could.

Sabben ordered those remaining to head back to CHQ; Miller's 8 Section would remain as the rearguard while the others cleared out. The young lieutenant and Private Tom Newall thought they were the last to leave. Sabben checked to make sure none of the wounded had been left behind and waited another minute or so to make sure no others from 11 Platoon were still heading their way, then headed back towards CHQ. They had five weapons to carry back between them; one was a seized-up M60. Sabben decided not to carry this back and put a round into the trigger housing and another into the gas regulator to make sure it was useless. He looked around again to make sure there was no one left behind and made his way back towards CHQ without having another shot.[40]

However, still there, unknown to Sabben, was Hodder, part of the platoon headquarters section. Hodder recalled: 'I looked around and they were all gone. [I] saw Sabben and followed him and quickly overtook him.'[41]

Meanwhile, back at 11 Platoon's original position, the wounded Private Jim Richmond of 6 Section had been drifting in and out of consciousness as he lay helpless among his dead mates. He felt the air being sucked in and out of the wound in his back every time he breathed. He tried to keep awake, but the pain was terrible. There was no way he could get a dressing onto it, so he rolled over into the mud on his left side, hoping that the mud would dry out the wound and help stop the bleeding.[42] All around him enemy troops were moving forward. He'd placed the live hand grenade nearby, the only thing stopping it from detonating being the flimsy elastic band wrapped around the mechanism.

———

Back at Nui Dat, Townsend and his staff were preparing to board the two APCs sent back by Roberts, commanded by Lieutenant Savage. Nearby, army chaplain Les Thompson and medical officer Captain Vic Bampton decided that they should go with the CO to offer assistance to the men of D Company. The chaplain approached Townsend, who denied the request. Because of the heavy rain and darkness, the wounded would likely be brought back to the battalion lines, and Thompson and Bampton would be needed there when they came in. Thompson went back and told Bampton, and they stood there chewing their fingernails.[43]

22

'Well, let's go – because it's no good staying here'

1800–1820 hours

The two RAAF helicopters from 9 Squadron captained by flight lieutenants Frank Riley and Cliff Dohle were now approaching the battle zone. Bob Grandin recounted that 'the rain was heavy, visibility was very, very poor, we could not quite pick out our position. When we slowed down and did this we realised we'd gone past the position, to just past Long Tan [village], so we turned around and came back at about 20 to 30 knots, above the trees, as we had to get up for visibility. We were in rain, we identified the rubber plantation, and moved slightly to the south, as we were over the position given as the enemy's.'[1] Grandin also remembered drawing himself back into the armour-plated seat trying to be a smaller target.[2] Coming in low at treetop level with the bulk of the ammunition were Dohle and Flight Lieutenant Bruce Lane. Lane glimpsed something through the pouring rain: leaping out of the brush below was a 'dark moving mass, a big bird, animal or human – unknown, but enough to frighten him as they swept over it'.[3]

By now the Anzac artillery had stopped firing, and some of the enemy troops took advantage of the momentary lull to press their advantage in numbers and push forward. Others could be seen collecting their dead and wounded from the battlefield. Sergeant Neil Rankin, who at the time was at CHQ's position, recalled: 'It was while we were waiting for the helicopter with the ammo that Jack [Kirby] and I noticed a constant flow of enemy moving to the road, carrying their dead and wounded. In a matter of about 15 minutes, about 100 metres away, I estimated at least 400 passed us.'[4] Rankin also heard firing from another enemy assault against one of the platoons to his front and, given his men's return fire, he knew they were making every shot count. It was here that privates Harry Esler and Doug Mitchell from 10 Platoon were positioned. Esler recalled making a bet with Mitchell: '"OK, you're supposed to be a crash-hot shot . . . I'll bet you a can of beer you can't hit that bloke in the stomach." He'd have a shot, then say to me, "A can of beer if you can hit him in the head . . ."'[5]

It wasn't long before Esler took note of an individual 100 metres to his front.

> There was this big fellow running around in a white dustcoat.
> He seemed taller than the rest, giving orders, shouting
> orders . . . Anyway, I had a few shots at him. I don't know
> if he had on a bulletproof vest or if I'm a lousy shot, but I
> couldn't get him. Corporal [George] Green in 11 Platoon [*sic*
> CHQ] said later that he got the bastard, but he was never
> found among the dead. I remember him as a big, tall bloke,
> and whether he was a medical officer or one of the big nobs,
> I don't know.[6]

Meanwhile, Sergeant Major Kirby was collecting as much ammunition as he could. He approached Captain Morrie Stanley, asking, 'Excuse me, sir, could I have your spare ammunition?' Stanley recalled: 'The way he did that was so typical of the man. Anyway, I told him to help himself from the small pack I had on my back, and he may have taken four M16 magazines, leaving me with the one on my rifle.'[7] It was not only Stanley who gave away his ammunition, as recalled by Corporal Graham Smith, who was desperately focusing on keeping the critical communications open with the Task Force at Nui Dat and by this point had already given away 'most of my ammunition and had it sent forward'.[8]

Flight lieutenants Riley and Grandin made radio contact with Major Harry Smith and called for the smoke grenade to be released. Within seconds, Grandin could see 'orange smoke – it was supposed to be yellow'. Hearing this, Graham Smith yelled into the handset, 'No! No! Wrong! Wrong!' The helicopter broke contact, as it was feared that the enemy were listening to their communications and had thrown a decoy grenade to disrupt the ammunition resupply. Another grenade was thrown, this time red, and this time Grandin saw red smoke. D Company assured them that red was the correct colour. The red smoke was located very close to the 'orange' smoke. Later it was assessed that the orange smoke observed by Grandin was likely yellow, but the rain, and enemy mortar bomb bursts, dispersed it, making it appear orange.[9] The logbook for 105 Battery records a radio communication stating 'Just seen red smoke' at 6.07 p.m.[10]

Grandin now called in flight lieutenants Dohle and Lane, guiding them to D Company's position. He quickly saw their helicopter with the red light on the top and directed them to the position, giving them left and right steering directions at treetop level, and as they approached 'we told them to break and they rolled onto their side over the position, all of the ammunition being able to fall down into the company while they were turning already on their way back'.[11] Major Owen O'Brien recalled that he and Warrant Officer George Chinn could clearly see members of D Company below as their helicopter came in at treetop height to make the drop. Although they could see no Viet Cong, they did see 'tracer rounds arcing into the air from unfriendly weapons some distance away'.[12]

O'Brien and Chinn, located behind the pilots, assisted by kicking the boxes out of the helicopter, 'right into the CSM's lap', as recalled by Major Smith. As soon as the ammunition had been dropped, both pilots noticed the helicopter lightening as the boxes crashed through the canopy to the ground below. The helicopter quickly disappeared as it flew west. Now Riley and Grandin 'dived from the height that we were sitting on up above and did a steep turn, which allowed us to push all the ammunition out . . . and headed off back to the Task Force'.[13] Graham Smith was talking to the pilots and recalled how the helicopters were hovering above them when the 'ammo came crashing through the trees . . . and I said, "You bloody beauty! Right on target!". . . and that chopper moved off and then another came in and the stuff just screamed through and they didn't even stop – they just banked and tipped it [out] . . . Lucky there was no one under it.'[14] Major Smith later commented that his radio operator was way in front of him in getting his radio tuned into the 'Albatross' helicopter VHF radio net and directing the choppers in: 'He did a great job that day.'[15]

Within minutes the Anzac artillery began to fire again. Remarkably, while most expected this to be a near-suicide mission, the enemy apparently were completely oblivious to the helicopters: they received no enemy fire. The battle raging on the ground and the pouring rain seemingly made them invisible to the enemy below. Grandin recalled that on landing, 'Frank [Riley] was quite high, he really felt it was the right thing to do and nothing was going to happen in these sorts of things. We then sat around trying to keep tabs on how things were going.'[16] This skilful and daring feat by the RAAF pilots marked the beginning of improved relations between the army and air force and a new era of inter-service cooperation and understanding.[17]

Later the commanding officer asked why a company commander and the regimental sergeant major had gone on a dodgy resupply mission instead of staying at Nui Dat doing what they were paid for. They could only say it seemed like a good idea at the time, and the commanding officer said, 'Bloody silly thing to do, but well done.'[18]

Kirby, Rankin and others immediately set to work opening the boxes and supplying ammunition to the men holding the fragile perimeter. Rankin recalled that the helicopters 'arrived through thick rain and threw out the ammunition boxes wrapped in blankets for our wounded. The blankets were given to [Corporal] Phil Dobson, the company medic, who [with Lance Corporal Geordie Richardson] was trying to attend to a hell of a lot of wounded at this stage. We attempted to break open the boxes, as they were still banded. We hacked away with entrenching tools and anything we had, cursing the incompetent pricks in Task Force who didn't have the sense to see we were desperate and may not have had the time for this. Luckily at this point we did have the time, although only just.'[19]

Lieutenant Geoff Kendall remembered the boxes apparently being kicked out of the helicopter and Kirby running around with bandoliers over his shoulder throwing them out to the men as he made his way around the defence perimeter.[20] He also recalled that distributing the ammunition was particularly dangerous, as at this point, even though there was a distinct lull in the battle, 'there was still enemy moving in the general area, but too far away to engage. You couldn't see them all the time . . . It was dangerous business distributing the ammunition but the CSM [Kirby] took care of it.'[21] The belts for the machine guns had already been loaded with ammunition, but the rifle ammunition came in bandoliers and had to be loaded into 20-round magazines. The men had to try to keep them dry and clean while they were lying in the rain and mud.[22]

It was then that wounded CHQ radio operator Lance Corporal

Dennis Spencer at the company aid post saw the first of the survivors from 11 Platoon coming in with some from 12 Platoon. Among them was Corporal John Robbins. Spencer asked where the rest of the platoon was, and Robbins just looked at him and said they were dead; the ones here were all that were left. That really shook Spencer up, as 'they were all blokes I knew well. I was stunned. I started to ask names and said, "Where's Kenny Gant? Where's Kenny [Glenn] Drabble?" and he said, "They're gone, mate, that's it."'[23] Robbins recalled on reaching CHQ 'such a sense of relief for me. And Jack Kirby got all of the wounded into one area. I was walking around. I thought, *Shit, I'm pleased to be here*, and the next thing – bang! – he crash-tackled me, knocked me arse over head, and said, "You get down, you stupid bastard! Get down!"'[24] Private David Beahan of 12 Platoon also recalled that 'Kirby, a big man and an easy target, was dashing around picking up people and carrying them back . . . To see that man run here and run there was just unbelievable.'[25] Private Len Vine of 10 Platoon also recalled seeing 'Big' Jack Kirby providing the men ammunition: he 'exposed himself all the time, he should have got a VC . . . He was like our father, he was the head of the family.'[26]

Meanwhile, Corporal Graham Smith recalled seeing Buick leading the survivors of 11 Platoon who had made it to Lieutenant David Sabben's platoon back into CHQ's position.[27] Kendall recalled Buick coming in. He asked him, '"Where's Sharpie?" Buick said, "He's been dead for a long time." This was a bit of a shock because Gordon and I were pretty good friends.'[28] He recalled with grief how 'Sharpie' 'was my mate, the guy who had stopped a milk truck on Lutwyche Road at two in the morning and convinced the driver to back up to a lamppost so he could souvenir a construction sign that said "Delta". The same guy that walked into the private bar at the Majestic and said, "I'm here for the photo" and souvenired the Penthouse Pet photo that graced our mess right through the Vietnam tour. I guess I knew that 11 Platoon had been in big trouble, but the extent of the trouble didn't sink in until then.'[29] Kendall also remembered the wounded being brought in being in a shocked and dazed condition – they moved through his position.

Those not wounded from 11 Platoon were positioned by Kirby to defend the rear of the position, facing west. Not long afterwards 12 Platoon came back, but Sergeant James Todd was missing and nobody knew where he was. The men of 12 Platoon moved through and were organised to help define a company all-round defensive position.[30] Among those returning was Private Alan Parr, still carrying his 'ratshit' M60. He recalled that as he arrived at CHQ he came across Kirby, who was 'directing traffic. I ran straight up to him and, showing him the M60, said, "Have a look at this, it's fucked!" I threw the gun into the trees – I'll never forget the look on his face. He realised how uptight I was, raced over and got me a rifle, and I was on my way to our new position.'[31]

Sabben came in just behind the last of his men and was instructed to position his platoon within the north-east part of the perimeter. It was around 6.10 p.m. Parr recalled taking up a position with his mates of 7 Section, privates Noel Grimes and Neil Bextram, either side of him, with about the distance of a tree between them. Close by were Sabben and Corporal Laurie Drinkwater, and here they stayed for the remainder of the battle. At this point there was still a lull in the fighting, which Sabben recalled persisting for five to ten minutes. The Anzac artillery was still falling outside their perimeter and there was the odd Viet Cong mortar bomb exploding on the southern side.[32] Kendall recalled that there 'was certainly a lull in the battle for quite a while. We could see movement and the rain also eased a bit, which made it easier to see people moving. They were in range of maybe 200 metres, but you're probably wasting a round if you fired at them . . . Certainly almost direct east of where I was there was a big body of blokes there. We had dropped our packs which we used during the first assault and we saw the enemy get into our packs. We fired a few rounds at them but whether we knocked them over it's difficult to tell at that distance in the rain.'[33]

Meanwhile, M60 machine gunner Private Russ Perandis of CHQ had moved out to support Kendall's platoon. He recounted 'rain bouncing off the machine gun, hitting me in the face and eyes, making it hard to see. I had to keep my ammunition belt in a puddle of water to stop the mud getting into it.'[34] With the arrival of 12 Platoon and the survivors of 11 Platoon, Major Smith was able to further consolidate his company's defensive position. For the time being the enemy had broken contact as they did not follow up.[35] Smith organised his three battered platoons for all-round defence. Undoubtedly they would soon be surrounded by a large enemy force – there was no way the Australians could withdraw with the wounded – they would fight it out here.

Unbeknown to Major Smith, the enemy force confronting him consisted of the Viet Cong *275 VC Regiment* and *D445 VC Battalion*. Excluding casualties, they still numbered around 1700 troops (not including non-combat support elements). By now Smith probably had fewer than 70 effective men. The odds against them had increased to 25:1. Smith recalled:

It was [now] obvious that we were up against uniformed and well-equipped regular Main Force VC, rather than the black-pyjama-clad local force. I had no doubt we were in for a tough fight. I knew we could not withdraw and leave our casualties. That was not an option. So we were here to the end. I hoped that reinforcements would eventually get here, as the bottom line was that we were obviously outnumbered. But on the plus side, we had our company team spirit, we had the guts and will to survive, we had plenty of ammo, [and] we had the artillery . . . In the lull I was able to walk around often and coordinate the defence with platoon commanders and talk with some of my soldiers. I recall one of my soldiers, Shorty Brown I think, asking me, 'Do you think we'll get out of this, boss?' I just knowingly winked back at him, confidently indicating I thought we would.[36]

Moments earlier, just a few hundred metres away, privates Allen May and Doug Fabian of 11 Platoon, who had taken shelter among the shattered remains of a rubber tree, saw the smoke grenade that had been thrown by CHQ for the ammunition resupply. May looked at Fabian and asked, 'What do you reckon?' Fabian replied, 'Well, let's go – because it's no good staying here.' The firing had died down at this stage so they were able to run straight in to CHQ. May recalled that he could not remember much after that – he was suffering from shock.[37]

It was only now that Lieutenant Adrian Roberts' APC force was finally moving through the wire, out of Nui Dat and heading for Long Tan. They were soon skirting north-east of the destroyed village of Long Phuoc, with the rain pelting down. Roberts was sitting on a plank across the open hatch so he could see above the machine-gun shield and recalled that the rain was 'absolutely blinding'.[38] The force was moving in column formation and began their ascent to the Suoi Da Bang. Given the heavy rain, the stream was swollen more than usual, with the current running at between 6 and 7 knots. The carriers could manage only half that speed in water. Things were even worse for the carriers of 3 Troop, as their pivot-steer systems were worn out, making it difficult to steer the carriers when afloat. This was weighing on Roberts' mind, as just a few weeks earlier, as part of Operation Hobart, 1 APC Squadron had been sent out to support 6 RAR but could not negotiate the same stream and had to return to base having failed to accomplish its objective.[39] Come what may he knew he *had* to get his carriers and infantry across the swollen river. Roberts was sure that they would come under mortar fire before making it to the stream – the

VC likely had observers positioned along the high ground east of the stream – but no such fire eventuated. It was possible that the rain hid them from view. To help further hide their presence, the APCs advanced towards the stream with their lights off.[40]

Back at the Task Force base, Brigadier David Jackson ordered 6 RAR's C Company to be prepared to move out at first light via helicopter. He also ordered 5 RAR, which had returned from Operation Holsworthy, to take over the security of the base and place a company on one hour's standby to be ready to reinforce 6 RAR if required; D Company, 5 RAR was nominated.[41]

Major Smith's position in the rubber plantation was defined by the gentle reverse slope away from the enemy's front. A smooth crest was present about 50 metres to their front. About 1000 metres north-east was the steep, jungle-covered, elongated hill of Nui Dat 2. Partly helping to screen their left flank here was an impenetrable wall of bamboo and scrub. The remainder of their perimeter, however, was open ground defined by rubber trees. Any northern approach to Smith's position would channel the enemy into a narrow front-age because of Nui Dat 2 and the bamboo. Smith assessed that the most likely direction for a major assault would be directly east and south-east. He and Kirby had already placed the survivors of 11 Platoon to defend the north-western side of the perimeter, while 10 and 12 platoons were positioned to the southern and eastern approaches respectively. He placed CHQ with the wounded in the south-western part of the perimeter.

Sergeant Bob Buick recalled that 11 Platoon's position was defined by a gentle slope away from the direction of the enemy assaults to the perimeter's front. All the 'small arms and green tracer fire arced harm-lessly over our heads. After hitting trees some bullets deflected away, providing a deadly fireworks display. In our area you could walk around upright but everyone instinctively crouched and crawled. Some of the diggers jokingly said that they moved like that for days after the battle.'[42] Private John Heslewood recalled that at this point it 'was getting on dark . . . but it still wasn't pitch black – you could see the shapes, and you could see faces, but it was getting darker.'[43]

Most of the machine guns had by now malfunctioned due to overheating and the thick mud getting into the mechanism. It was not only the machine guns that were jamming: Rankin had trouble with his weapon as he had to place each round 'up the spout by using my finger, as the mud had started to seize the working parts and would not allow the breechblock slide to go forward enough'.[44] However, machine gunner Perandis of CHQ was still able to operate his M60 and had been duelling with an enemy heavy machine gunner 'using a .30 gun on wheels, which we later captured. When it opened fire, I was behind a small rubber tree. I could see the red-and-green tracer coming. I didn't know a person could move around so quickly on his stomach.'[45]

While Private Alan Parr's M60 was useless, he had kept its ammunition belts. Now firing the Armalite that had been given to him by Kirby, he quickly emptied the 20-round magazine and reloaded it by taking time to prise the bullets out of his M60 belts. He also noted the enemy heavy machine gun: 'Up the line of trees about 200 yards [180 metres] away I could see a machine gun with a rounded shield steel plate on its front, firing. The streams of tracers were going right over the top of D Company's position. I fired quite a few rounds at that gun, but couldn't tell whether I hit it.'[46]

As this was going on, Stanley was plotting new defensive-fire missions for the artillery, taking care to mark the former position of 11 Platoon to be avoided as it was possible Australian wounded were still out there. The lull continued and it enabled Major Smith to dart around among the men, checking their situation and the condition of the wounded, boosting their morale with words of encouragement.[47]

Meanwhile, the wounded Sergeant Todd was still crawling, trying to make his way to CHQ. Some feared he had been killed, or worse. There was no let-up in the rain – it was the heaviest he could remember. Even though he had done a couple of tours in Borneo and Malaya, he had never seen rain like it. 'Down it came,' recalled Todd, 'and I was crawling through the mud. I kept on crawling, and I think I crawled about 100 yards [90 metres] when to my right I think a couple of Viet Cong troops were coming towards me. I don't think they'd seen me, because by this stage with all the mud I would have just looked like a log or something. I killed these two. I'm sure I killed one and may have only wounded the other, but they both went down.'[48]

He continued to crawl towards where he estimated CHQ was located, and after another 15 or 20 minutes he could see the Australian perimeter. He started yelling all the Australian adjectives he could think of, and the wounded Corporal Buddy Lea, at great personal risk, scrambled out of the perimeter to help him in. However, the Australians were not the only ones who had heard him, and Todd looked over to his left and saw a couple of Vietnamese coming straight towards them, about 50 metres away. 'I said to Buddy, "Look out!" and Buddy said, "It must be our blokes from B Company coming back to us." I said, "You'd better have another look." Buddy stepped behind a tree, and I got down behind this big log, and when they were about 10 yards away Buddy stepped out, but the other fellow was too quick, and Buddy got hit in the shoulder. Somebody off behind us had seen what happened and killed both of them.'[49]

With the help of Sergeant Neil Rankin and Private Billy Roche, both wounded men were brought in, but it was now that Lance Corporal Jack Jewry was killed while trying to put a dressing on Lea, his section commander.[50] Both Lea and Todd were very quickly with the medics in the slight hollow where the wounded were located. Both were given a shot of morphine to ease their pain, but all they could do was lie there and wait, recalled Todd.[51] He was the last to come into CHQ position.

The lull in fighting continued – the Vietnamese commanders were obviously assessing the situation and manoeuvring their forces for a final assault, as word had reached them that the entire enemy force was bottled up in a shallow defensive position. The Viet Cong were no longer facing three desperate forces but one Australian force judged to represent just a single company that had already taken significant casualties. All that was needed was one coordinated all-out assault to destroy the Australian force in detail. Even so, the rain and the ongoing Anzac artillery were disrupting communications and the Vietnamese were sustaining significant casualties with little to show for it. The senior commanders surely also knew that an Australian relief force would be on the way and they were in no position to take on another enemy force, given the current confusion and dispersal of Viet Cong units within the plantation. Time was slipping away.

To the west, Roberts' APC force was following a bullock track down to the edge of the Suoi Da Bang. Lieutenant Peter Dinham of A Company, along with his radio operator and platoon sergeant Frank Alcorta, was sitting on the edge of the open hatch. Dinham looked into the APC where the men of one of his sections were positioned. They all seemed to be looking up at him, so he 'had to be fairly cool and calm. At that time I realised I had their responsibility on my hands.'[52] Alcorta recounted that they had absolutely no information on D Company's position or casualties sustained, but he reckoned something serious was up due to the hurriedness of everything. He had no real idea just how serious the situation was, and wouldn't until he reached the battlefield.[53] Sergeant Jim Myles looked on as they reached the stream crossing, which was now, with the torrential downpour, flowing fast. It had swollen to about 30 metres wide with the increased quantity of water flowing into it, and the carriers fanned out into formation, stopping at the river bank.[54]

Roberts began 'swimming' the carriers across the swollen stream, which here had a small dam. As each moved into the water, the current took hold and it swung around unyieldingly, colliding with the dam. However, each made its way across, gaining traction on the eastern bank, and pulled up waiting for the next carrier. All the time the plight of D Company could be heard on the radio. They sounded desperate, doubting whether they could hold on for much longer.[55] Roberts, now on the eastern side of the stream, knew the urgency of the situation and had no time for a reconnaissance of the immediate area. He pushed forward through the paddy fields heading for Long Tan Plantation, leaving one APC behind under the command of Corporal John 'Tiny' O'Shea, with its infantry section, to protect the stream crossing and act as a guide to Lieutenant Colonel Townsend; 3 Troop was down to just seven carriers, and was effectively an infantry platoon short, but they pressed on towards the sound of the fighting.[56]

Roberts then received a message from Townsend that he was to halt and wait for Townsend's party, in the other two APCs, to catch up. Roberts must have been flabbergasted, to say the least. Not only had he been forced to send back two of his precious carriers (and their infantry) to pick up the battalion commander; now, with the men of D Company fighting for their lives just a few kilometres away and seemingly about to be overrun, Townsend wanted him to wait at the Suoi Da Bang so he could catch up and take command. Roberts recalled shouting the message down to Captain Charles Mollison but having the intention of pressing on regardless of his reply. Mollison did not argue the point with Roberts and used a hand gesture to tell him to keep moving forward.[57] The seven APCs proceeded towards the sound of battle.

Unknown to the survivors of D Company, the two wounded men from 11 Platoon were still alive, trapped forward of their position. Private Barry Meller had taken up a position with his Vietnamese groundsheet and 'settled' into the scrub for the night, while Private Jim Richmond, with the live hand grenade next to him, was slipping in and out of consciousness among the dead mates of his section.

23

'Got that bastard, sir'

1820–1830 hours

At 6.20 p.m., Major Smith radioed in that the enemy appeared to be massing just east of their position, likely reorganising for an attack. He reported that '2 platoons are about 75% effective [10 and 12 platoons]. 1 platoon has been almost completely destroyed. [11 Platoon] . . . reorganising for all-round defence.'[1]

It was then that his position was targeted by concentrated enemy heavy machine-gun fire, sweeping the company with streams of bullets and tracers. Most of the fire originated from the east and south-east – the enemy were re-engaging for an all-out assault, just as Smith had feared. The Australians could see them moving through the trees at a range of 150–200 metres to their front. The men opened fire but soon stopped, as they were wasting ammunition – the range and conditions made it pointless. Even so, the enemy veered to the north for a short distance.[2] Then another large enemy force was observed massing to their front; the Viet Cong quickly fanned out and prepared for an advance along a broad front that would sweep around the Australian position. Bugles were blowing and the enemy concentration advanced. Smith and his men watched as the human waves to their left and front prepared to break over them. It was about this time that Private Stan Hodder heard Major Smith yell into the radio handset something like: 'I've got quarter of an hour and if the APCs are not here, we won't be here!'[3] Private Tony Stepney also recalled hearing something similar: 'If you don't send someone out in ten minutes, forget us – we'll be gone!'[4]

Lieutenant Sabben recalled seeing the Viet Cong forming up and moving around down the avenue of trees. Their officers and NCOs were using the same tactics used by the Australians: the spacing, the rate of movement. It was all so similar to their own training back in Australia, but then they would hear the bugles and whistle and the enemy troops would move off.[5] Many of the survivors of D Company believed they had little hope of repelling this enemy attack – their time was apparently up.

Not far from Sabben was Private Alan Parr, who recalled seeing a line of Viet Cong with 'tree branches for camouflage advancing towards our position. They would move 20 or 30 yards and hit the deck, then repeat it again. When it looked like they were getting fairly close, I called out to Sabben for some artillery to our front (I think it was "Get some fucking artillery!")' Whether Sabben heard or not is unknown, but within seconds artillery came 'screaming in overhead, right in amongst the VC'.[6]

Smith reported back to Nui Dat that a continuous assault of human waves at battalion strength was falling against his perimeter. He requested that the guns 'drop 50 metres' – drop the shells 50 metres in front of his eastern perimeter. However, there was a great reluctance to do so as this could result in casualties to Smith's company from 'friendly fire'. Smith was not having a bar of it. He was the commander of the ground, he needed it close and he needed it now. He recalled grabbing the radio handset from his signaller, Corporal Graham Smith, and telling 6 RAR to instruct the gunners to fire the 'bloody guns where I want them or they will lose the lot of us!'[7]

At 6.17 p.m. B Company radioed that they were approaching the plantation.[8] At about 6.25 p.m., 1 ATF radioed B Company urging them to 'press on 476676 – Loc D Coy' while telling the APCs with A Company to 'press on 500 metres NE'.[9] Lance Corporal Phil Buttigieg of B Company recalled hearing a radio message from Major Smith calling for the immediate relief of D Company, as they were about to be overrun: 'We stopped moving via our covered creek-line approach and turned directly towards the main firing.'[10] Corporal Robin Jones of B Company was on the right flank and recalled that 'it was now raining heavily. We moved back across the paddy, and waded across the Suoi Da Bang. It was rising fast, being fed by the downpour.'[11]

As they scrambled onto the other side, they followed tracks back to the western edge of the plantation, near where they had earlier found the enemy rocket-launcher position. They had the grid reference of D Company's position, although, as recalled by Jones, they didn't really need it with the sound of the firing. When they got into the rubber they moved with two sections forward and one behind. The tropical downpour had increased and it was getting dark very quickly.[12]

The men of this composite platoon were soaked and their uniforms looked black in the shadow of the rubber – even so the enemy knew of their approach, as indicated by the earlier mortar fire against them as they headed back east towards the plantation. Visibility would have been down to about 50 metres at best, and they came under heavy small-arms fire with a lot of tracer from a Viet Cong force that was forming up between them and the rear of D Company.[13] This was likely scouting elements of *D445 VC Battalion*. It was now that 1 ATF received a radio message from

Major Noel Ford that they were approaching the western edge of the plantation and would soon be in a position to offer direct fire support to D Company. Ford drew his empty pistol, organised his composite platoon into assault formation and pressed on towards D Company, which was somewhere east of their position.[14]

It was also at this point that another radio message from A Company in the APCs reached Brigadier David Jackson that they were 1000 metres south-west from D Company and could see 'firefight to right moving now'.[15] The seven APCs under the command of Lieutenant Adrian Roberts had reached the junction of the east–west Route 52 to Long Tan and the main north–south bullock-cart track that led into the plantation, directly to the battle area. Private Peter Bennett of A Company, in one of the APCs, began to hear the sound of battle even above the noisy engines of the carriers. He and his mates started to psych themselves up, with Bennett thinking of his mates in D Company whom he was desperately wanting to help.

Not far behind was Lieutenant Ian Savage carrying Lieutenant Colonel Townsend and his staff. He had tuned his radio to Roberts and back to squadron HQ while Townsend was on the air to D Company and issuing instructions through Savage to Roberts.[16] In one of these APCs was Lieutenant Trevor Gardiner, who recalled crashing through banana plantations as they pushed on towards Long Tan when one of the aerials on the carrier dislodged a nest of angry green ants, which fell into the APC. Private Bill Reynolds remembered 'heaps of ants dropping into the APC . . . and they were biting the shit out of everyone'.[17]

Townsend radioed back to 6 RAR headquarters at Nui Dat to inform Lieutenant Gordon Steinbrook of some unwelcome news: 'Inform American OP [observation post] officer that his sergeant is with us.' The young US officer was more than a little startled: 'I couldn't believe it! In all the excitement my FO [forward observation] team reconnaissance sergeant had gotten his equipment together and gone with the APCs and A Company reinforcements. I swore, assuring Major [Harry] Honnor that my sergeant was acting on his own and that when I got my hands on him, if he survived the battle, I'd court-martial him.'[18]

Meanwhile, up ahead, Roberts had halted the column and, using the bullock track as the centre of his line, deployed the three carriers of 32 Section, commanded by Sergeant Ron Richards, to his right (east) two carriers up, and the three carriers of 23 Section in the same formation under the command of Sergeant John O'Reilly to his left (west). Each section commander's carrier was between the two other carriers in the section for control purposes, while the troop leader, Roberts, was in the centre of the two sections.[19] Within minutes, the carriers were advancing north in a broad frontage of about 300 metres into the heart of the plantation. To the left of them thundered the artillery at Nui Dat about 5 km away – it was common for the enemy to set up an ambush along the likely routes any relief force would take. All were tense as they waited for the likely opening shots of RPGs and machine-gun enfilade to tear into their small force of seven APCs.

Sergeant Frank Alcorta, still sitting exposed on the back of one of the APCs, was drenched and looking down at his men in the semi-darkness of the M113 carrier. He noticed they were silent. 'Usually there was a lot of bantering and jokes between the diggers who rode on the APCs, but not this time. They were silent, as if they suspected a test of some kind, perhaps even on their lives, might be imminent.'[20]

Roberts recounted: 'I had a board across the hatch, and sat on that. A silly thing to do, but that's how I was, head and shoulders up. I had to be like that, I had to be able to see what was going on. My troop sergeant was behind me, with the infantry company commander. It wasn't written down then, but in those days we were in command while we had the infantry aboard.'[21] That certainly was not how Captain Mollison, commanding A Company, understood it: as far as he was concerned he was in charge of the troop. He was continually ordering the APCs to go faster, but it just wasn't possible – they were already going as fast as they could, given the appalling conditions and the danger of a Viet Cong ambush.

As the APCs moved out into formation before heading into the plantation, Roberts got another message from Townsend: he was to halt and wait for the battalion commander before going any further. Roberts again ignored the message and ordered his driver, Trooper Bill O'Rourke, to push on. It was now 6.25 p.m., almost 90 minutes since 3 Troop had arrived at 6 RAR headquarters. Mollison confirmed their position with Roberts (GR 473659) and radioed back to 6 RAR headquarters. In response he was advised that D Company was located at 476676.[22] There was about 30 minutes of daylight left, but the heavy rain and black clouds gave the impression it was already night, favouring the enemy, who were now in large numbers surrounding D Company. Indeed, Roberts and his men would soon collide with the enemy troops of *D445 VC Battalion*, who were trying to swing around D Company from the south to attack them in strength from the rear, sealing the fate of the Australians.[23]

The lead elements of *D445 VC Battalion* were heading east, just south of D Company's position, with the intent of cutting off any line of retreat. This would completely encircle the beleaguered enemy position and result in its total destruction. Even so, things were not going well for the troops of *D445 VC Battalion*. The ongoing Anzac artillery missions were devastating, as recalled in the battalion's official history:

> The battle became close combat, fought in groups and by areas – it was difficult for our infantry and artillery [mortars] to support one another . . . our forward position [held by 275 Regiment,

3rd Battalion] was able to force the enemy into the killing zone. Our rear element began to storm into the killing zone [and] our flank-attacking group advanced. The enemy regrouped . . . we were unable to move even a half-metre to finish off the enemy because of their rain of artillery.[24]

In the thick of this devastating artillery barrage, Viet Cong company commander Chin Phuong and her 80 or so medical staff of the *Civil Labour Company*, mostly female, along with a transportation unit, continually ran through the 'rain of artillery' explosions to bring in the wounded and dead from the battlefield.[25]

By now Major Smith had gotten his way with his request for the artillery to drop 50. He and his men were holding their fire waiting for the human avalanche that was about to fall upon them. Lieutenant Geoff Kendall recalled that the enemy came straight down the same line that 12 Platoon and the survivors of 11 Platoon had taken to get back to CHQ, which was right towards the centre of his two forward sections. He could see the Viet Cong forming up in a large assault line, which soon advanced at a slow walk. As they advanced about 100 metres, another assault line formed up behind them.[26] He recalled:

We didn't fire until they were probably about 30–35 metres at the most out, for a couple of reasons. First of all we didn't want to disclose our positions – we were low down on the ground with buckets of rain, and being prone on the ground is a good place to be. You don't want to give that away unless you're going to do something . . . We actually waited until the enemy was close and then we fired and . . . we managed to stop the front line. The second line was always about 100 metres behind them and . . . in both cases [they were] very

badly knocked about by the artillery. A lot were killed but
others stayed behind and sniped.[27]

The Anzac artillery came in and completely wiped out the enemy
attack. Kendall recalled that they were just like a 'pack of cards
falling down. This was a big factor in assisting us in stopping the
assault.'[28] Private Grimes of 12 Platoon recalled 'Harry Smith calling in the artillery that was hot on our heels – it was the most
frightening thing of the day really in my view, the artillery, but
they did save the day . . . but it was frightening, the whole thing
was obviously frightening . . . but they just go off with such a big
bang and big flash that they seemed to [explode] right in front of
us . . . I've got to give Harry Smith full credit for he was calling
in the artillery.'[29]

Major Smith's radio operator, Graham Smith, recalled: 'The
main factor that saved our arse that day, or preserved it . . . was the
artillery, absolutely magnificent [even though] it was very, very close
at times and I know the artillery signallers had some communication problems . . . There was so much smoke and enemy moving
on the battlefield silhouetted against the smoky background and
I'm wanting to shoot a couple and Harry is saying "No" – he was
firing plenty of shots.'[30] Major Smith needed his chief radio operator to focus on keeping communications open between him and
the Task Force base.

Sergeant Bob Buick recalled that at this time the 'rising mist
and gunsmoke from the battlefield was . . . aiding the . . . company.
The enemy, who most surprisingly were walking around the position, could easily be seen because they were silhouetted' against the
exploding shells.[31] The Anzac artillery no longer had to offer support to differing platoons but were now focusing all of their fire at
the same target: the encroaching enemy north, east and south of
Smith's position. It was later estimated that about 1500 kg of high-
explosive shells landed on the enemy troops every few minutes – 18

guns firing at least five rounds a minute at the enemy troops that were still massing around their position.[32]

Lieutenant David Sabben looked on as the wall of high explosive and shrapnel tore into the ranks of the advancing enemy line. He recalled how the results were nothing like they were portrayed in the movies: 'The typical idea of artillery firing is a flash and bodies hurtling and so on . . . but in reality . . . there's a sudden impact where you see the whole environment just shudder, just vibrate, and then everything is just steam and smoke and you don't see anything, and anything that might have been shattered has gone and as the smoke and steam dissipate you see the leaves just falling down or whatever else was there just falling down . . . and then they weren't there.'[33]

Close by, Private Bill Doolan of 10 Platoon looked on as the main assault came on. There seemed to be hundreds of Viet Cong advancing in formation straight towards him. He and those around him kept firing, but then Doolan's Armalite begun to misfire. He remembered he couldn't get it firing properly and was cursing and swearing to himself as the rain poured down and the enemy troops advanced to his position.[34] He wasn't the only one having problems with his weapon – next to him, a machine gunner had been wounded. Doolan got on to the M60 and could not get it to work. He was cocking it and 'belting it against a tree and carrying on with it, and the bastard of a thing wouldn't work . . . I remember someone asking whether we had bayonets; I didn't have one so I got my machete out and lay that near me because I didn't know whether we'd have to stand and fight them.'[35]

A number of the enemy troops in the first-line assault managed to gain a position just 20 metres from the Australian firing line. Major Smith's men opened fire, causing the enemy survivors to take cover in the mist and shattered foliage. These Viet Cong troops began to snipe at the Australians while another human wave was forming up behind them just 100 metres back. However, Kendall saw to his relief that the Anzac artillery, being directed by Captain

Morrie Stanley, was knocking out the reserve line that was forming up.[36] Stanley himself, in a brief respite, heard an Australian
next to him calmly saying to himself, 'Steady . . . aim . . . fire!'
and was reassured by the calibre of the men defending the position.[37] Even so, Major Smith recalled that the Viet Cong would
pick themselves up and re-form and once again advance, over
the top of their dead comrades. They just kept pushing forward.
Something had to give.[38]

Now individual duels between Australians and Viet Cong took
place, each trying to pick off any movement. Small groups of Viet
Cong began to move around the perimeter in an attempt to block
any avenue of escape. Bullets slammed into the Australian position.
Sabben recalled: 'When a soldier is killed, it's an unbelievable thing.
You don't believe that's happening. You can see a soldier lying there
and there's a flinch and they go slack . . . it's not a hysterical fling-
ing of arms in the air and a double somersault backwards . . . If
he's standing up it's like his legs are just cut out from underneath
him. He just collapses . . . and lies still. If he's lying on the ground
there's just a flinch.'[39]

As the firefight continued, some of the enemy troops were able
to creep ever closer to the Australian perimeter. One Vietnamese
soldier managed to get behind the forward troops and was just
5 metres from Lieutenant Geoff Kendall when the ever-dependable
Private Bill 'Yank' Akell again came to his rescue. 'I don't know
whether it was just before the second assault or not, but I remember Yank Akell, the reserve signaller, who was on the other side of
the rubber tree . . . still had an Owen gun because we hadn't been
issued with very many Armalites then. Anyway he looked around
the tree at me at one stage and had a silly grin on his face and said,
"Got that bastard, sir." I looked to the front and there was a Viet
Cong lying I suppose 3 metres from us. He'd obviously crawled
up between the assaults, and old Yank had let him have it straight
through the top of the head.'[40]

Akell recalled how he and Sergeant Neil Rankin were positioned behind one rubber tree:

> The next tree was where Geoff Kendall was, so we were only a couple of metres apart and the problem that we had was that we were wearing jungle-green uniforms . . . [which] because of the torrential rain [quickly] took on a very dark colour . . . the Viet Cong were in dark-coloured uniforms. They were crawling towards us and the problem we had was that we knew there was probably some of our wounded who were trying to make their way back to company headquarters; so anybody crawling towards you, and a lot had mud splattered on their faces as well from the rain, [meant] it was very, very difficult. If you saw someone 20 metres out you couldn't afford to take the shot because you weren't too sure if it was one of [our] wounded coming up or it was a Viet Cong; you really had to wait until they got close enough for positive identification and . . . that's the main reason I suppose you would say the enemy were allowed to crawl as close to us as they did. It was out of fear of shooting one of our wounded who might be crawling back towards us.[41]

24

'We're not going to get out of this – no way'

Now the second assault line against CHQ's position had formed up. Bugles were blaring and the line advanced against the small pocket of Australian defenders. Yet again, the artillery was called in, smashing the organised attack, but survivors from this wave managed individually to push forward to link up with those from the first wave. An unknown Australian later stated 'a solid line of them – it looked like hundreds – would suddenly rush us. The artillery would burst right in the middle of them and there would be bodies all over the place. The survivors would dive for cover beside those bodies, wait for the next attacking line, get up and leap over the dead to resume the rush. They were inching forward all the time over their piles of dead.'[1]

Lieutenant David Sabben recalled that even with the intense artillery bombardment, a number of enemy troops made it through. When the survivors of one wave went to ground, a bugle would sound and another wave would charge forward, and the survivors from this line would drop down beside those who had made it through the first time. Then the bugle would blow again and another line charged forward. This was repeated time and time again, with each major assault coming in about five minutes after the previous one. First from the south-east, then from the north-east, then another from the south – they were uncoordinated and the next direction of assault was unknown. In between, some would attack in small groups, or there might be a lull of up to several minutes between assaults.

These brief lulls in human-wave assaults gave the Australians the chance to spread their ammunition around, reload their magazines and check on those who were either side of them. However, each time they saw the enemy re-forming for another major attack and heard the bugles and whistles, they wondered whether this would be the one that would break through their weak perimeter and overrun the heart of their position.[2]

One of Sabben's men, Private Noel Grimes, recalled how the enemy bullets crisscrossed through their small defensive position, and while the branches from the rubber trees were falling everywhere, the enemy just pushed on. There were many of them, and they darted from tree to tree and dived in among the dead and wounded – they didn't just stand there. They were continually on the move and all seemed to be heading straight for him.[3]

Lieutenant Geoff Kendall recalled seeing a 20-year-old regular from Perth, Private Rick Aldersea, with one of the few working machine guns firing into the line of oncoming enemy troops. He moved to another spot to get a better position and was killed. His No. 2, a 22-year-old army regular from Goondiwindi, Queensland, Private Max Wales, took over the gun, but within seconds he was also killed.[4] Private Len Vine recalled: 'You couldn't lift your head up . . . all of our machine gunners got hit because with an M60, [if] you had a stoppage, you had to lift your chest up to open the butt up to clear the round. They all got shot in the chest, all our machine gunners got hit [that way], except Rick Aldersea, who stood up and

he was more or less firing from the hip. He got hit straightaway.'[5]
Nearby was Private Tony Stepney who recalled: 'Johnny Cash, a
mate of mine, was shot in the knee . . . [then there was] Jack Jewry
up a little bit further from me and then there was Rick Aldersea
who was just about three or four guys down from the other side
of me, and when you hear they've been killed you think "Oh my
God". . . . All you could hear when they were attacking was these
blessed bugles . . . and they just came in waves and if someone fell
others would pick him up and take him back and the rest would
continue on.'[6]

Company No. 2 signaller Private Bill Akell recalled: 'If you ask
anyone who was at Long Tan what's one of the things they remember, they'll always tell you the bugles . . . That's the way they com-
municated, it was by bugle, to charge, retreat, left or right, whatever,
it was their bugle calls. It was such a piercing [sound] . . . the shriek
of the Viet Cong bugles . . . you'll always remember the bugles.'[7]
Indeed, these diggers' forefathers at Gallipoli would have had similar memories of the Turkish bugles, using the same communication system to help them launch human-wave attacks against the
Anzacs 50 years before.

If this assault continued for much longer, the overwhelming
number of enemy troops had to break the Australian defence. While
the Viet Cong were suffering large numbers of casualties with each
human wave, some managed to push through the barrage and con-
gregate close to the Australian perimeter. Private Vine recalled:
'They were 100 metres from us, less than that . . . they were chant-
ing . . . psyching themselves up . . . you'd see them in lines . . . then
the bugle would go and they'd charge us and they'd walk through
our artillery fire, which was just wiping them out . . . If we didn't
have that [artillery] we'd have been dead.'[8] As each main assault
line advanced, 'the fallen of the previous assault . . . who had been
lying there joined the attackers in a rolling effect, which gave an
impression of invincibility.'[9] Lieutenant Geoff Kendall remembered

thinking that they weren't going to get out of this. He thought of his wife, who was about to give birth to their first child, and how 'lousy' it would be for his son or daughter to be born after his or her father had been killed.[10]

While fire had been brought to bear against Nui Dat 2, Viet Cong heavy and light machine guns positioned along its forward slopes had been active throughout the battle and continued to pour fire into what they believed to be the Australian position. However, the area was so broad and visibility so limited that the Viet Cong could not directly observe their targets. It was not long before Sergeant Major Jack Kirby and others realised that another heavy machine gun was being established just 50 metres to their front (east). The warrant officer, alone, moved out of the perimeter, killed the machine-gun crew and somehow made his way back unhurt – undoubtedly this action saved the lives of many Australians and helped to further secure their tenuous defensive position.

Regimental signaller Corporal Graham Smith recalled: 'I never fired a shot in the battle, even though I wanted to. I could see plenty of enemy, but Harry Smith said "No, you stay on the radio."' Major Smith told him later that this 'enabled him to concentrate on other things, I was experienced enough to be able to tell B [Battalion] HQ exactly what was going on. Occasionally the commanding officer, Townsend, needed to speak to Harry directly and I handed the radio set over.' He too remembered Kirby in action: 'I saw Jack Kirby do some absolutely wonderful things . . . I would certainly have gone along with Jack Kirby [getting a Victoria Cross]. He did take out an enemy machine gun and he told me as soon as he'd done it; and he was just guiding people around and giving them moral support.'[11]

Private Akell, who himself acted courageously in running through the gauntlet of enemy fire to get his radio to 10 Platoon, agrees with his mate Graham Smith: 'How Jack Kirby was never awarded the Victoria Cross I will never know, because of what he did. He was the one who broke open the ammunition when the boxes were dropped from the helicopters after our resupply; he was the one who pulled out his bayonet, cut the wires and forced them [the ammunition boxes] open, and this is with rounds pinging off everywhere; he was the one who ran forward and distributed that ammunition – nobody went back for the ammunition, he took it forward; he took out the [enemy] heavy machine gun there. To this day I will swear to anybody that Jack Kirby was well deserving of a Victoria Cross. I have got no doubts about that whatsoever.'[12]

Indeed, many others recalled that despite the fire coming into their position, Kirby moved around the men inspiring them, joking, encouraging them to hold on, distributing much-needed ammunition and helping the wounded. A long-standing joke in D Company was that the sergeant major always referred to Private Harry Esler as 'Private Ralph', who had last been seen while on a patrol in Malaya. Every time he approached Esler in the thick of the action, Kirby would say to the private, 'You remind me of that bludger', and on his journeys around the perimeter he would remark, 'How are you, Private Ralph?' and 'You're not going to get back if you don't watch out.' Undeterred, Esler would reply, '*I* will. You make sure *you* do.'[13]

Private Bill Doolan recalled seeing Kirby running around everywhere screaming encouragement to the men, like: 'Keep it up, fellows', 'You're doing great, fellows', and things of that sort.[14] At some point during the thick of the fighting he made an appearance at the aid post having dodged a round of fire, as recalled by the wounded Corporal John Robbins. He yelled words of encouragement to the wounded, but also yelled for the men to keep down. According to Robbins, he was lying 'on top of me. He said, "I'll get you out of here, mate, don't worry," and I can remember saying, "I hope you can, but I won't need the VC to kill me because you'll bloody well kill me yourself if you don't get off me." I thought he was terrific the way he got about and organised things and kept blokes' spirits up. How he never got hit himself I'll never know. The size he was, it's a miracle.[15] Private Tony Stepney recalled: 'I really do believe that

CSM Kirby should have got a VC for what he did. We're almost short of ammunition and he'd come along . . . with bandoliers of ammunition and he'd put it next to our arms and say, "You have to load your own magazine, mate."[16]

Another who was recognised for his outstanding bravery and service was the company medic, Corporal Phil Dobson. Major Smith recalled how he gave a 'magnificent amount of first aid to the wounded'.[17] Esler said that Dobson should have been awarded the Victoria Cross for what he did: 'You'd see him run up front, out of sight, bring back a wounded fellow, patch him up, and away he'd go again. He was a champion, that bloke.'[18] Private Peter Doyle also recalled that 'Doc' Dobson was doing everything in his power to attend to the wounded and stressed: 'He's a Band-Aid putter-on and "Here's an Aspro" – every one of those people that he treated lived. Not bad when you've got blokes with severe gun-shot wounds.'[19] Eventually 23 wounded men were under the care of Doc Dobson, some of whom would surely have died without his skill and dedication.[20]

There was no let-up. The main frontage of the attacks was from the east and south, where 10 and 12 platoons took the brunt of the fighting, but other smaller uncoordinated attacks were developing around the remainder of the perimeter. Major Smith and Captain Morrie Stanley were tasked with keeping the company together as a fighting unit, keeping track of ammunition supply and, most important of all, directing the fire missions that were keeping them in the fight. Without them, they had no chance of surviving the enemy assaults. Smith's task was to work with Stanley, and he recalled that Stanley did an excellent job with the artillery. He later stated that it was the accurate artillery fire, along with the fact that they were positioned on a small slope and not on flat ground, that saved them from being overrun. He also recalled that he and CHQ virtually sat there calling in the artillery and watching events unfold as almost impartial observers. The Viet Cong would assault and withdraw, assault again and withdraw. They attacked from a number of different directions, but fortunately for him and his men, had not yet assaulted them from behind – their weak spot.[21] Even so there were concerns, as a number of enemy troops could be seen in that very direction.

Corporal Laurie Drinkwater was positioned along the left flank of 12 Platoon and, through the driving rain, saw enemy troops trying to flank them to the north. He and those around him were firing at the oncoming troops when he looked back towards his mate Private Paul Large, who was only a few metres behind him. 'I just looked around and I saw him with his head down. I didn't know whether he was packing it in or not, so I was yelling out at him and throwing rocks; [Private] Neil Bextram crawled over to him and looked over to me and said, "Paul's dead." I said, "Can you get him back to the aid post?" and Neil and [Private] Noel Grimes dragged him back.'[22] Indeed, just before, Sabben had witnessed the 22-year-old manager from Wellington in NSW, Private Large, being shot in the forehead and knew he must be dead.[23]

Privates Bextram and Grimes, under fire, managed to get Large back to the CAP (company aid post) and then returned to their firing positions. Private Alan Parr also got up to help, but there was no point in three doing it, so he immediately went back to his position to offer covering fire – this incident would haunt Private Parr for many years.[24] Close by was Large's best mate in the army, Private David Beahan. He recalled that hearing his mate had been killed 'really knocked the shit out of me . . . I just cried and cried and cried. I think we all prayed and cried. I don't believe there's one that wouldn't have cried during the battle.'[25] Beahan would never get to be the best man at his mate's wedding.

Since the depleted company had gathered together, Major Smith's command had suffered another ten or 12 casualties, with four of these having been killed. Something had to give. As they were removed to the aid post, Smith had no choice but to shrink his perimeter to help with its defence.[26] The wounded Private John Cash, located within the first-aid post, recalled that at this point 'a few times you thought that's the end of things . . . Lying there you can't do anything – you can't fire back because you've got no rifle.'[27]

The enemy, seemingly not short of troops or ammunition, continued to press forward, certain of victory. The low crest to their front meant that a large amount of the Viet Cong small-arms fire passed overhead. The grey mist rising from the ground was still present, providing an 'eerie appearance to the protruding heads of the Australians as they raised themselves to fire'.[28] Drinkwater was sure that his time had come when Kirby came along and plonked himself down next to him, saying, 'Do you know that bloke out there?' and pointed to some Viet Cong to their front; the private replied, 'No' and Kirby said, 'Well, shoot him . . . Shoot anyone you don't know.'[29]

Kirby continued around to the northern perimeter, carrying bandoliers of ammunition, and came across privates Terry Burstall and Richard Brown of 12 Platoon. While they had seen the main attacks focusing to their right along the eastern part of the perimeter, they had also seen a number of Vietnamese probing their position. Kirby told them to be prepared: 'because he reckoned that any moment they'd twig [to] where we were, and send a large group around through the thick scrub on the edge of the plantation and assault straight up the rise into our position'.[30] Sure enough, within minutes tracer fire came into their position from this direction, one of which found a mark in Private Harley Webb, who was hit in the neck and began rolling rounding in agony. Burstall was just setting out to bring him in when, seemingly out of nowhere, Big Jack Kirby 'came thundering down the slope behind me. He raced past me and got down to the bloke – it was young Webb, the reinforcement who'd only just joined us. Kirby scooped him up and threw him on his shoulder like a bag of spuds and started back.'[31] Undoubtedly this act saved the young national serviceman's life.

Brown turned to Burstall, who had made his way back to his position, and said 'we weren't going to get out of this, and all I could say was "I know that". We both thought we'd had it.'[32]

As had occurred with the previous defence of 11 Platoon's position, most of the rubber trees within and around D Company's defensive position had now been raked with bullets, while some had been torn apart by RPG fire. A never-ending supply of tracer rounds slammed into the trees or flew just centimetres above the men's heads. Major Smith remembered looking in front and seeing Sergeant Don 'Jack' Thompson, his mortar-fire controller, lying behind a rubber tree. Smith noted that it wasn't 'great cover because the rubber trees are [not] that [broad] and his head was that wide, so it really wasn't of much use, but it was psychological protection and . . . I remember looking at Jack and looking over him towards the enemy and seeing the tree just above his head being peppered by tracer rounds just going straight through it.'[33] Smith also recalled that these rounds had the appearance of fireflies as they came towards them.

While the slight rise offered some protection to his men, the defensive position that D Company was required to take meant that all the initiative was with the enemy – they could dictate events. It was the key link between Stanley and Major Harry Honnor back at Nui Dat that kept D Company in the fight. Stanley remembered as the rain poured down that his 'judgment of distance was assisted by the observation (or lack of it) of flash against this screen [of rain] and the enemy were silhouetted as were our own troops'.[34]

Major Smith was concerned that should the enemy change tactics and launch multiple attacks against his perimeter at the same time, the artillery defensive fire would be divided and the enemy would push further towards the perimeter, beyond the ability of the artillery to fire out of fear of hitting then men of D Company itself. The enemy were now using their proven tactic when fighting against those with artillery support: 'holding the belt with one hand

and punching with the other'. Already a large force of fresh enemy troops had been seen moving to the south and west of their position, in an attempt to encircle them; these were members of the local *D445 VC Battalion*. Smith and his men were wondering whether their relief troops would arrive in time – it was now approaching 6.40 p.m.[35] Indeed, Corporal Kevin Miller of 12 Platoon, even with the ammunition resupply, was down to just two rounds. He recalled thinking, '*This is it – we're not going to get out of this.* Nobody thought we would.'[36]

Close by was Sergeant Neil Rankin of 10 Platoon, who was facing the third major assault against his position. The Viet Cong just seemed to keep on coming. He watched as the assault came in 'picking up cable from the ground. I later found they laid cable on the move. They hit us with heavy machine-gun and small-arms fire from a wide front, and we opened fire on them at a distance of 60 to 80 metres, cutting into them. After about ten minutes, they broke contact.'[37]

Luckily for Smith and his men, the Viet Cong commanders were at certain points relying on telephone cables for communications, and when the artillery fire cut the cables, communications turned into a shambles, with runners and bugles having to be increasingly used to try to direct the battle. Confusion set in and a true fog of war developed. Among the men trying to fix the cables and act as runners were those from the transportation unit that was assisting Ms Phuong Chin's *Civil Labour Company*. This confusion undoubtedly assisted in the relief force not being ambushed by the Viet Cong – a common tactic.

Soon Rankin's position was hit with mortar fire, bombs exploding in and around them: 'We were trying to dig in with our bare hands, as our entrenching tools were with our packs, out somewhere the enemy held. I could see them moving forward collecting their dead and wounded, along with weapons.' Seeing the enemy picking up weapons from the fallen, he yelled at his men: 'Shoot them before they pick up the bloody things!'[38] He would later feel remorse about this order, but he simply had no choice in the matter. By now Kendall and others had become aware that it was the enemy wounded from the assault waves and those taking cover among them who were causing the most casualties to the Australians. 'They just lay there, waiting for the next assault wave to come in, and between-times they'd crawl forward and snipe at [any of] our fellows they could see.'[39]

Private Stepney recalled how each man knew he could depend on those around him, especially their platoon commanders: 'Geoff [Kendall] was great, [Neil] Rankin was great.'[40] Rankin recalled that conditions remained atrocious as the rain bucketed down. By the time of the third enemy withdrawal, things were looking pretty grim. They got more ammunition sent up during this slight lull, but even so it was not long before they needed more, and most of the machine guns had packed it in and were useless.[41] With each assault the enemy seemed to be getting closer, and he began to think that either the enemy would overrun them or the enemy force would have to withdraw as they had lost so many men; he desperately hoped for the latter. He remembered praying and thinking of his parents back home – he had little prospect of seeing them again.[42]

Lieutenant Kendall, whose position had been taking the brunt of all attacks to date, was thinking the same thing, that time was pretty much up. He had already replaced his Armalite, which had malfunctioned, and it was getting dark, which would assist the enemy in getting in among them. Most of the men didn't carry bayonets 'and a lot of the boys had entrenching tools and machetes out beside them'.[43] Akell vividly remembered the call of the bugles and their deadly intent: they were 'shocking, that was horrendous. You saw them lining up, you heard the awful sound. They were spread out in an extended line in the pouring rain. You could see these black figures coming your way. Your mind is going a hundred miles an hour. I thought, *This is my last moment on earth*.'[44] He had again taken up a position with Rankin and recalled at this point 'looking at Neil when the Viet Cong massed themselves for what was to be the final push, the final assault upon us. I looked at Neil and we just sort of shook our heads and thought, *Nah, this is going to be it. We're not going to get out of this – no way . . .* They started with their bugles blowing and they started to advance on us.'[45]

Moments earlier, Lieutenant Adrian Roberts, leading in the centre of the line with his seven APCs in open formation, had entered the plantation. He was still unsure of the exact position of D Company, but the sound of battle was getting louder as they advanced, providing him with a general direction to take. At first, when they had entered the young rubber of the plantation, where the small trees were only 2–3 metres high, the branches created havoc for the commanders in their open hatches. Between the young rubber trees, waist-high scrub grew in profusion. Corporal Rod Armstrong of A Company was riding on top of an APC and saw more mature rubber trees exploding a few hundred metres to his front. He noticed the 'orange glow as a shell would hit a tree; there'd be a ball of fire . . . It was about that time [that I decided] I didn't care how crowded it was inside the carrier, I was getting inside! I couldn't see anything anyway; I had spots in front of my eyes.'[46]

As the carriers forced their way through, those positioned in the open hatches could see, even through the pouring rain, troops moving across their path about 100 metres in front. These troops, representing a company at least, wore webbing, were dressed in army greens with cloth hats, and were in an open arrowhead formation, seemingly oblivious to the APCs. The rain and sound of battle were 'hiding' the APCs' advance. Were these members of D Company? Roberts, sitting up on his wooden plank completely exposed above the command hatch, recalled that the ground seemed to 'stand up . . . across our entire front as [we saw] this great group of infantry moving from east to west in pretty determined fashion and in formation'.[47] Sergeant Jim Myles of 1 Platoon saw this large force of Viet Cong as they moved across his front at a very rapid rate. He was sure that they didn't know the APCs were there due to the torrential downpour and the artillery and small-arms fire that was occurring to their front and side.[48]

Lieutenant Peter Dinham, commanding 2 Platoon (A Company), was in the right-hand carrier and looking through an open hatch. He recalled that these troops were not aware of their presence until 'we were right in amongst them, and these people suddenly stood up, in the thick scrub and rubber immediately in front. We had come out of the rain surprising them as much as us. There we were on top of them.'[49] Dinham saw that some had camouflage nets on their hats, while others were wearing pith helmets. Recognising them for who they were, he shouted to the carrier commander of 32B, Corporal Richard Gross, to open fire. That was enough for the young corporal, who commenced firing within seconds. The rest of the troop joined fire.[50] Roberts remembered hearing via the radio from the APC on his left, commanded by Gross, 'It's the enemy!' and with that everyone opening with machine-gun fire against the Viet Cong.[51] Seconds before, Armstrong, in another carrier, had ordered his machine gunner, Private Leo Kucks, to open fire, but Kucks had replied that they might be Australians. Armstrong turned to the APC commander who was busy watching the troops in front through his field glasses, but before Armstrong could say anything the commander dropped his glasses, grabbed the .50-calibre machine gun and opened fire.[52]

25

'They're forming up to hit us from behind!'

1840–1900 hours

The commander's log for 105 Battery, smudged with the red mud of Nui Dat, states at 1840 'Q/FIRE 10 SEC', underlined multiple times in red ink.[1]

Corporal Tommy Douglas was sitting on top of the APC carrying the battalion from 6 RAR headquarters, heading for the stream crossing. They had 'no trouble following the tracks in the mud and were pleased to see another APC (33B) had waited for us. But the swollen stream was a bit daunting . . . At least now we had three APCs to fight our way through any enemy ambush we might encounter on the way.'[2]

Lieutenant Ian Savage's driver, Trooper Geoff Newman, hit the stream at full speed and didn't even bother to lower the board at the front, which helped prevent water going into the open hatch. Savage recalled: 'My driver did a marvellous job, crossed it no problem, made it flat strap.'[3] The momentum of the fast-moving carrier pushed it through the water and they made it onto the other side seemingly in one movement. The other APC crossed in similar fashion and joined up with Savage and the reserve carrier left behind by Lieutenant Roberts. All three took off in pursuit of the relief force.

Up ahead, the fire from Roberts' 3 Troop tore into the ranks of the unsuspecting elements of the heavy-weapons company of *D445 VC Battalion*, who instinctively turned to meet the immediate threat and put down a heavy barrage of fire into the approaching carriers. Sergeant John O'Reilly and the APCs from 2 Troop were covering the left flank of their advance and for the first few seconds O'Reilly wasn't sure whether the men from A Company had dismounted from some of the carriers, as there was a whole group of them wearing greens and webbing like the Australians.[4] However, Sergeant Jim Myles of 1 Platoon, who was in one of O'Reilly's carriers, saw to his horror among them a Viet Cong 57mm recoilless-rifle crew dragging their weapon. One hit from this gun would completely obliterate an APC. One of the Viet Cong turned back and saw the carriers. Myles saw them stop, but he wasn't sure whether they stopped to try to fire the weapon or were attempting to escape the onrushing vehicles. Within seconds, another APC put on a great burst of speed and ran straight over the top of the gun and its crew.[5]

To the right, Lieutenant Peter Dinham and Sergeant Frank Alcorta were riding exposed on top of Corporal Richard Gross's carrier when the enemy swarmed around the APCs, targeting them with concentrated small-arms fire. The sergeant immediately jumped off the carrier while his officer dropped into its open top hatch. Dinham immediately ordered Gross to stop the carrier and open the rear hatch – they were not going to leave Alcorta out there. Within seconds, men were pouring out to support their stranded sergeant. Alcorta was seen emptying his magazine into the enemy all around. When he fired the tracer round, indicating he had only one round left, it exploded into the face of a Vietnamese soldier and the 'whole thing disappeared in a mess of blood and flesh'. Alcorta was thankful that his machine gunner, Private Ron Brett, had jumped off the carrier firing his weapon; he recalled that the private 'saved my life, because he gave me a chance to bring a fresh magazine from the pouch'.[6] (In a later action as part of Operation Bribie in February 1967, Alcorta repaid his debt to Brett, whose legs had been shattered by Viet Cong machine-gun fire. Alcorta ran forward under a stream of machine-gun fire, picked up the wounded private and carried him to safety. He was recommended for the Military Medal, but Lieutenant Colonel Townsend rejected his nomination, allegedly stating, 'He already has the MiD' (Mentioned in Dispatches).[7]

Other APCs carrying 2 Platoon also stopped, and these men were soon joined by their officer, who quickly ordered them into extended line formation, firing as they advanced towards the enemy troops. Private Laurie Bodey, one of the replacements who had just that day joined A Company, was among these men and recalled:

> There was much yelling as we all tried to get out. At first the APC driver would not lower the back ramp, but some well-chosen words from Corporal Louie Stephens soon persuaded him to change his mind. Down came the ramp and out we went, [with me] keen to do my new job as number two on the machine gun. The rain immediately pelted in my face. It was gloomy and smoky. Red and green tracer trails crisscrossed the scene . . . All my senses were in overdrive.[8]

Lieutenant Dinham recalled: 'I had the platoon out, forming an extended line, and while we were doing it . . . dozens of the enemy – some dressed in pith helmets, some in floppy hats, a lot with a form of netting hanging over the back as a type of camouflage – started standing up in front of us.'[9] The young officer stood slightly behind and to the left of one of his section commanders,

Corporal Stephens, so he could observe and direct his platoon. He was standing beside a rubber tree, and opened fire on some enemy troops who appeared from nowhere. He watched with relief as they dropped, then noticed that 'something flicked at my face, sufficient to distract me. I looked up to see two fresh bullet holes [in the tree trunk] at about eye level. I immediately adopted a lower profile. In this brief exchange I fired 16 shots, the only shots I fired in anger throughout my time in Vietnam.'[10] Stephens also recalled how his men immediately joined in combat with the enemy, including Brett, Bodey, Max Vickers, Tom Burke, David Harwood and Bruce McLay. They could hear some firing from behind, and Stephens looked back to see his platoon commander, Dinham, firing from a standing position against a tree.[11]

Alcorta was surprised by the response of the enemy to their sudden appearance, which seemed to rattle them. He reckoned that given their numbers, if they had pressed an attack the Australians would have been overwhelmed. At this point, the APC force consisted of a depleted infantry company with just one Australian platoon engaged, and there were only seven carriers – and the Viet Cong had RPGs, which they 'abandoned, and with which they could have taken the APCs almost at will. There were hundreds, literally hundreds of them around us. Yet they broke and ran. We were grateful anyway, and exhilarated, as we were out of immediate danger.'[12]

Roberts also recalled that 'the right-hand infantry got out of the tracks and went forward. I yelled at the infantry commander [Mollison], and we got'em back in again.'[13] He was concerned that these men might become casualties from the APC fire, even though the infantry had veered to the right of the carrier troop. They were needed at D Company's position, not conducting a firefight south of it. Indeed, his orders from Major Brian Passey were that he was to take A Company to relieve the hard-pressed D Company.[14] Mollison had not ordered the platoon to directly engage the enemy and radioed that they were to immediately get back into the carrier.

Private Tom Burke recalled: 'When we got the order to remount, I adopted the tactic of fire and movement to withdraw back to the APC. But when I looked around, I was the only one left. I think I collapsed out of sheer fright but Corporal Stephens picked me up.' Stephens vividly recalled the incident: 'Burke was the last one in, and about 2 metres from the APC he went down. My heart sank, but looking up, he gave a silly grin. He had just slipped on the wet ground – gave me a bit of a fright, though.'[15] Within minutes the infantry were back in the APCs and Roberts' small force advanced north through the shattered enemy formation with their machine guns tearing into the survivors and in some cases running them over and grinding them to pulp beneath the tracks of the APCs. These Viet Cong retreated towards Long Tan village.[16]

Roberts and others noticed how some enemy troops had cane-loops tied to their calves; they would use these to help drag their wounded away while a fellow soldier offered covering fire. The Viet Cong suffered a number of casualties but the Australians suffered only one wounded who received a bullet graze to an eyebrow. By all accounts Alcorta's assessment that the Viet Cong had been totally surprised by their sudden appearance and were rattled is the only reason that can explain the lack of Australian casualties.[17]

Still in assault formation, 3 Troop pressed on, following the track into the heart of the plantation towards D Company's last reported position. The scrub and small trees had now turned into mature rubber trees, some 10 metres high, which allowed increased visibility and enabled the carriers to increase their speed. On advancing another 200 metres they came into contact with another, even larger enemy force streaming across their front, completely oblivious to their presence. These were likely the lead elements of *D445 VC Battalion*, who were south of D Company and moving west to cut off any line of retreat by that company. With no hesitation, the carriers opened up with a 'broadside' of .50-calibre machine-gun fire. A number of enemy troops fell to the ground, and the survivors turned to open fire on the advancing enemy vehicles. It was then that an explosion occurred in front of Corporal John Carter's carrier, 39M, just across the road from Roberts' APC. Carter's vehicle had been fitted out as an ambulance but did not have the huge Red Cross markings signifying it as such.[18] A 57mm RCL just missed the carrier, but its round slammed into a tall rubber tree, which fell onto the vehicle. This weapon was later recovered by the Australians after the battle, and luckily for Carter, the aiming apparatus for the weapon was found to be internally fogged over, making it impossible to use. The operator had to sight the target using the barrel alone – a far from accurate method.[19]

With his .50-calibre jammed, Carter took a 9mm Owen submachine gun from his driver, Trooper Paul McNamara, and, standing fully exposed on top of his APC, saw the two-man RCL team just 15 metres away preparing for another shot. He immediately fired into them, just as they launched another round. There was another explosion but they only managed to hit the same tree that had fallen on top of the APC. Remarkably, Carter was unhurt and his driver passed up more magazines to him. Once the smoke cleared, the corporal saw that the RCL crew had been killed by his original burst of fire. He emptied another three magazines into the enemy troops around him before he scrambled into the APC. The only damage to his carrier was that his aerial had been shot away – he was now without radio contact.[20]

Roberts, still sitting on his wooden plank exposed above the .50-calibre/command hatch, saw the initial explosion and believed that 'they'd had it. I couldn't get them on the radio but could see them, just across the road. There was an RCL team with it on their shoulders, and the fellow firing it was down, and the one loading it was kneeling at the back just like in a military textbook. They fired a second round, and it hit the branches of the tree they'd just shot down.'[21] Roberts also saw Carter on his carrier with the Owen, killing 'the crew and a few people around. He was standing on top of the vehicle, and the driver was throwing up magazines.'[22]

Roberts knew that the Vietnamese RCL teams tended to operate in groups of two. He had to identify and destroy the second weapon before pushing on – the APCs were easy targets for these weapons and he did not want to advance into an ambush until he had destroyed the second team or was sure they had retreated with the rest of the enemy lead element. Any shot hitting an APC would kill all inside. However, Mollison was adamant that they push on and shouted so to Roberts. The lieutenant ignored him – as far as he was concerned he was in charge while the infantry were in his carriers. Mollison began to argue the point, but it was Roberts' decision. It was 6.53 p.m., and Roberts radioed through to 6 RAR headquarters: 'One APC hit – will keep moving'.[23]

At this point, back in D Company's shrinking perimeter, the enemy could be seen re-forming north-east and east of their position for another attack. Major Smith radioed 6 RAR headquarters: 'Enemy to East and NE – reforming to attack again' and warned that the APCs, when they arrived, should come in from the north-west.[24] Smith's men were doggedly holding their position, with the Anzac artillery barrage exploding close by. Sergeant Major Kirby was, at great risk to himself, continually running the gauntlet to resupply his men with the last of their ammunition. Coming across Private Harry Esler, whom he still insisted on calling Ralph, he asked, 'You all right, Private Ralph? Doing the job?' and dropped 12 rounds by Esler's side. Esler was to make each one count.[25]

Meanwhile, just after renewing their advance, the three APCs of 3 Troop, covering the left flank, were hit with heavy machine-gun fire. These were the three carriers that had no gun shields on their

.50-calibre machine guns. With this fire, Corporal Peter Clements, a 21-year-old regular-army soldier from Cunderdin in Western Australia, who was exposed above the hatch with the .50-calibre and no gun shield, fell back into his carrier mortally wounded with a shot to the stomach; he would die from his wounds on 28 August. The carrier immediately turned and drove right over the top of the machine gun. Another two infantrymen in the carrier were also wounded.[26]

The vehicle soon stopped, as did the other two carriers of the section. The commander of this section, Sergeant John O'Reilly from 2 Troop, had received a bullet-graze to the forehead, which knocked him unconscious momentarily. Roberts, aware of the attack against his left flank, had come to a stop and ordered his troop sergeant, Noel Lowes, to get out and race across the bullet-swept space to Clements' carrier to take command. Mollison was 'urging me to get on, but he was down inside, and here am I sitting up on the board, taking in the whole scene'.[27]

Sergeant Lowes grabbed his gear and without hesitation left the APC via the rear hatch and charged through the area. He came up to a carrier among the exploding shells – but it was the wrong APC. He yelled at the commander: 'I was told you were wounded.' 'No, not me. That one over there,' said the commander, pointing to Clements' carrier. 'Aaargh, shit!' yelled the sergeant as he jumped off the vehicle and headed towards Clements' carrier, APC 23B.[28] Roberts recalled how Lowes demonstrated extreme bravery with his run between the carriers across the battlefield while under fire, and said he deserved to be remembered.[29]

Lowes radioed back to Roberts that Clements was badly wounded and they had sustained other casualties; Roberts said, 'Right, take the carrier back.'[30] Mollison argued against sending the carrier back, and to make matters worse, Clements' carrier, unbeknown to Roberts, was carrying Mollison's 1 Platoon headquarters element, including its radio. Roberts later admitted that the carrier should have remained.[31]

Final stages of the battle

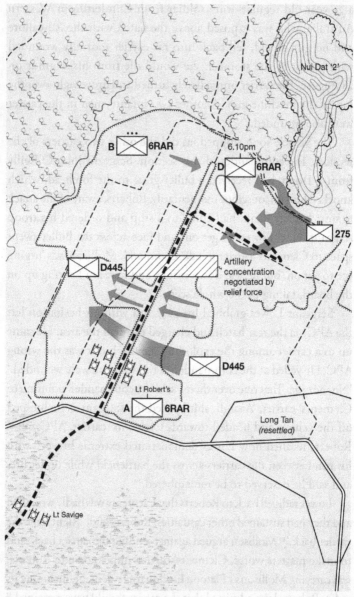

Around 6.30 p.m.: The APC force south of a united D Company hits *D445 Viet Cong Battalion* (including its heavy weapons unit) and possibly elements of *275 Viet Cong Regiment* that are attempting to surround D Company. D Company is still just managing to hold back multiple human-wave attacks against its position.

However, as stated by Major Brian McFarlane, 'Everyone makes mistakes, particularly under circumstances such as these, and during a year in very serious action in Vietnam, if this was the worst mistake made by the gallant young Lieutenant Roberts, then he was doing better than many I can think of.'[32]

Now believing he was relatively close to D Company, Roberts was concerned that their own machine-gun fire might result in friendly fire against the stranded Australians. He would have been doubly concerned if he had known that B Company was also approaching D Company's position.

Just moments before, one of the .50-calibre machine guns from O'Reilly's section covering the left flank had become jammed with a round in the barrel. The unnamed driver of the APC, a national serviceman, brought it to a halt, stood up out of the driver's hatch and, completely exposed to enemy fire, 'calmly' replaced the barrel; the unnamed commander of the APC, another national serviceman, assisted.[33] Within seconds of this, the APC was again advancing, with its .50-calibre firing into the enemy troops. When later asked about the incident and how he had been so cool under pressure, the driver said, 'It was all right. If I didn't look at them, they wouldn't bother me.'[34]

Meanwhile, the APC section on the right, commanded by Sergeant Ron Richards, was unaware that Roberts and the left section had come to a halt, and they continued their advance. The troop commander ordered the headlights of all carriers be turned on to help blind the enemy.[35] Carrying 2 Platoon, Richards swept on through Anzac artillery fire that had been ordered by Major Smith against an unknown enemy force south of D Company's position. This was the same enemy formation – *D445 VC Battalion* – that 3 Troop was doing battle with. Corporal Ross Smith, a section commander of 3 Platoon, A Company, recalled as they passed through the Anzac barrage that the 'ground [was] being pulled to the sky by some evil force, with no reason, and I realised we were in the midst of the artillery. Everyone got inside, the driver went blind over trees and outside we could hear the RPGs and small arms firing.'[36]

Lieutenant Dinham also remembered that the noise was 'tremendous: the Task Force guns, enemy mortar fire, constant small-arms fire, and the roar of the tracks. The only way I could communicate with the vehicle commander – we didn't have intercom – was by standing up, putting my mouth to his ear and yelling. You could almost feel the concussion pressing in around you.'[37] Next to Dinham, Alcorta remembered the overpowering smell of explosive from the exploding artillery as he reloaded his empty magazines, while Korean War veteran Corporal Max Vickers was busy emptying his magazines into the enemy from an open hatch in the M113.[38]

Not far away, Major Smith was waiting for the Viet Cong human-wave avalanche to fall upon them when he turned around and distinctly saw, through the fading light, another mass of enemy troops forming up. He yelled out to Esler: 'Righto, Private Esler and you others had better turn around and look behind you.' 'What, sir?' asked Esler. 'Can't you see them?' yelled Smith, but Esler and those around him could not. Smith yelled impatiently, 'They're forming up to hit us from behind!' This was their weak spot and the enemy had finally found it.

The Australians saw the movement of the Viet Cong formation – individuals moving between the trees, then taking up positions in a patch of thick scrub – and, chillingly, heard above the sound of the exploding ordnance a bugle being blown. Then they saw the enemy troops, camouflaged with tree branches, moving towards them. 'Christ!' yelled Esler. Major Smith opened fire, but for no apparent reason the troops suddenly turned and headed away from them. Smith heard a dull rev of engines 'like a couple of bulldozers . . . and then all of a sudden it struck me. It was the nicest sound I'd heard in my life!'[39] Corporal Kevin Miller recalled: 'We could see these lights coming through the rubber trees and they were firing, and it was the armoured personnel carriers coming in with another company – A Company.'[40] It was then that the cheering started.

Sergeant Richards' section, with headlights beaming, was thundering just south of D Company's position into the enemy formations to the west. Men from D Company 'stood and cheered. The appearance of the "tracks" truly signified both their relief and their deliverance.'[41] New Zealand bombardier Murray Broomhall recalled: 'You could hear the roar of the engines and they would fade away again and you would hear another engine roar up . . . Suddenly they came roaring up towards us and spinning on the wet laterite mud under the rubber – they really slewed, weaving from side to side.'[42]

The carriers charged through the mass of enemy troops that had been forming up, and many Viet Cong were crushed to a pulp by the M113s as they fell under the tracks. One attempted to throw a grenade at an M113: the commander tried to fire his .50-calibre but it would not depress sufficiently. Esler and Private Doug Mitchell from 10 Platoon saw it just in time and both fired, and the enemy solder was hit and collapsed with the grenade exploding next to him as he dropped it.[43] Private Len Vine vividly recalled that at this point 'three VC had a recoilless rifle set up and they were going to hit one of the ACs and I thought, *I've gotta get this fella*. I shot the bloke that was going to fire, another bloke went over to take his place and I shot him, and another went and I got him . . . I'm still shaking now when I think about it.'[44]

Sergeant Bob Buick, on seeing the APCs pushing through, jumped up, yelling and waving to 'identify our position, just like in the movies. I felt like one of those Yankees saved from the Indians.'[45] Private John Heslewood used a similar analogy: 'Ah yeah, it was great – [just] like the cavalry coming in, as they say.'[46] Lieutenant

David Sabben recalled that the APCs finally arrived with their head-lights on and guns blazing; it was great to see the tracers from the carriers bouncing off the trees, and he appreciated being behind them.[47] Lieutenant Geoff Kendall also recalled the APCs coming in. They approached to his right with a 'roaring sound and three APCs charged through the rubber firing their machine guns'.[48]

Close by were Sergeant Neil Rankin and Private Bill Akell, who just moments before had resigned themselves to the fact that they were about to be overrun by the Viet Cong human wave. Now they saw the APCs charging through the enemy lines. Akell recalled that 'they were a wonderful sight, pushing through us with their machine guns firing and so forth, straight towards the enemy, and at that particular stage, our internal feelings just completely changed. It went from one that we were going to die in the next few minutes, to one of complete relief, excitement – it [now] looked that we just might get out of this.'[49]

Just east of them, Major Noel Ford and his men from B Company, representing a composite platoon of just 31 men, had been moving towards D Company's position. They pushed on, expecting at any moment to encounter a major enemy force or to be trapped in an ambush. It was around 6.50 p.m. when they began to come up to D Company's position within the rubber. Corporal Robin Jones and the rest of the platoon were proceeding at a fast steady pace until they came under fire with a lot of tracer. These enemy troops soon disappeared and minutes later they came up against another, larger enemy formation about 200 metres west of D Company. These enemy troops at first didn't fire on B Company, probably thinking in the dark and rain that they were part of their *D445 VC Battalion*. Jones remembered that at this point he and his machine gunner were just about among them when suddenly the enemy opened fire on the Australians; somehow both managed to escape.[50]

However, Private Tom Burke was wounded in the arm and as they moved over the crest of a hill they ran into a fence; just then the APCs roared past them and looked like going straight into the Viet Cong group they had just passed.[51] Private Bernie Wesiak of A Company, on board one of the APCs, was standing 'up at the top hatch of the APC and saw what I thought were VC. I aimed my SLR and was just squeezing the trigger when someone called out, "Cease fire!" The person I nearly shot turned out to be Lieutenant John O'Halloran . . . I didn't know Bravo Company was there.'[52]

Not all were as fortunate, as recalled by Lance Corporal Phil Buttigieg. Alpha Company came in from the north mounted in APCs and mistook his group for assaulting Viet Cong and began firing into them. The section beside his took casualties – luckily most were slight and all remained on duty. However, Private Carey Johnson, who was a machine gunner, was struck three times with bullets.[53] O'Halloran recalled that Johnson was extremely reluctant to leave his weapon when he was placed in the carrier that was also carrying A Company's medic, Corporal Peter Short. As the battle continued to rage, Johnson was heard to say in frustration, 'I've carried this bloody gun for months. I'm not going to give it up now, just when I need it.'[54] The very lucky O'Halloran, the boy-hood friend of the now-dead Lieutenant Gordon Sharp, moved up towards D Company's position in extended line.

Private David A. Thomas remembered that he was still on the left flank and was not sure how far D Company was extended when two men appeared out of a pile of shattered trees and branches. Thankfully he did not blaze away at them: they were men from D Company. The look of stunned relief on their faces was something he would never forget.[55] He also remembered that it was then that the enemy 'were running . . . they were doing the bolt. They'd had enough. They weren't worried about us. But in the rain we couldn't tell friend from foe. We got back in there before A Company on the APCs.'[56]

Realising for the first time that his troop section was on its own, Richards and his carriers now did a 360 to rejoin his troop, moving again through the Anzac barrage to do so. One hit on an APC would blow it apart. Rankin and others were concerned to see the carriers disappear. He could hear them to his right rear, and he also heard their .50-calibre machine guns chattering away. It wasn't long before he saw their headlights, and his heart was 'really thumping at that stage and I was almost crying with relief. A couple of minutes later I saw them turning away just as another assault started towards us, and I lost sight of them, which gave me a hell of a fright.'[57] The medic, Corporal Short, recalled racing ahead through the artillery barrage but losing sight of the carrier to their left. They went through the flank of D Company before turning round to go back and pick up a 'lad from Bravo Company [Johnson] who had been wounded in the arm'.[58]

Dinham, who was in one of Richards' carriers as it moved back through the Anzac barrage, could see rubber trees on either side of him disintegrating from the exploding shells – most were being blown apart from the resulting air bursts. Just south of D Company, Roberts and the remaining carriers of his troop were advancing towards that company's position. Richards and Roberts joined up just south of the artillery zone, about 300 metres south-west of D Company's position, and it was then that the troop section, commanded by Lieutenant Savage and carrying the battalion CO, Lieutenant Colonel Townsend, also arrived. The troop was finally together – minus the one carrier that had been ordered back to Nui Dat – all now moved forward through the ongoing Anzac artillery barrage. It was approaching 6.55 p.m. and darkness had just about truly set in.

Lieutenant Robert Toyer, A Company, 3 Platoon was travelling with the battalion commander and recalled pushing through the enemy with the Anzac artillery exploding all around them. He could hear shrapnel and small-arms fire pinging off the side of the APC.[59] Sergeant Myles, who was now commanding 1 Platoon after the evacuation of the carrier carrying the mortally wounded Clements (and 1

Platoon headquarters), recalled moving through the artillery barrage
with the hatches open and the carrier commanders completely exposed
as they directed their drivers through the fire. The machine guns were
firing as the drivers advanced through the artillery barrage with shells
exploding among them – shrapnel from the artillery was hitting the
sides of the APCs.[60] In the same carrier, Private David Hede recalled
that 'we were jammed in the APC like sardines in a can and I could
hear all this stuff hitting the sides. Our section gunner was firing his
M60 machine gun from the top hatch and the gun kept jamming
on every fifth round that was a tracer. We were scrambling around
extracting the tracer and passing these belts of ammunition back up
to the guys at the hatch . . . Sergeant Myles told us we would soon be
disembarking from the APC, that we were to fix bayonets . . . I don't
mind telling you that sent a chill up my spine.'[61]

Back at Nui Dat, Captain George Bindley of 103 Battery recalled
that there was still no let-up in the fire missions needed to support
6 RAR in the battle taking place in Long Tan Plantation. He noted
how each of his guns 'seemed to slip into another dimension like
some great engine of the Industrial Revolution, roaring and flaring
in great billowing clouds of smoke and steam. The fierce downpour
gave an eerie shine to the guns, reflecting the muzzle-flashes against
the gathering smog, which cloaked the movement of men toiling
with ammunition, their shadows showing only in the glare, while
the roar of the guns, with "fire for effect" in force, created a bedlam.
It was our El Alamein, but a little damper.'[62]

Just moments earlier, the North Vietnamese commander, Lieutenant
Colonel Tran Minh Tam, had called off the attack – as told to Long
Tan veteran Terry Burstall in the mid-1980s by operation officer
Nguyen Thanh Hong – Tran's 2IC:

When we could not destroy you in the required time frame we decided to withdraw. The artillery was hitting us hard and we knew reinforcements would be arriving and we did not have the strength to stop them. We were disappointed we could not overrun your troops but the weather was a factor which created problems with our communications. We were hoping you would follow us out to Ap Suoi Cat, out of gun range, but this did not happen. Much of the cleaning up, weapons and badly wounded were removed during the battle, and were carried to the Nui May Tao mountains.[63]

However, most of the attacking Viet Cong commanders had yet to receive this order, and those to the north-east had not seen Richards' APC Troop and continued to advance towards Major Smith's position, with renewed concentrated fire. Smith's men were not out of the woods yet.

Private Len Vine at this point was, like all the others, in the thick of it. He recalled 'lying on the ground and [feeling] this massive whack down the bottom of my left foot, down near the ankle, and I thought, *Shit I've lost me frigging leg . . . .* it was like being hit with a massive piece of clay or something. I really wasn't game to look down . . . but when it was all over a piece of shrapnel had taken the side out of my boot, made a massive hole in me sock and I didn't even have a scratch. How bloody lucky is that?'[64] Esler was close by and on hearing his mate had been hit he crawled over to him, looked down and told Vine his leg was still there. He examined it and recalled seeing a bit of shrapnel had 'cut through his boot, the ridge around the sole-edge, the laces and the top and even put a hole in his sock – that's how lucky he was. He must have thought his leg was gone.'[65]

On reaching the tapper's hut, Roberts and his APCs changed direction to reach Major Smith's position. However, Townsend ordered

Roberts to attack the enemy formations to the east, having already disrupted the enemy force that was attempting to block the line of retreat from the south and west. Roberts' 3 Troop was now directly taking on the human waves of 275 *VC Regiment* that had for hours been trying to overrun D Company's position from the north, south and east. With four carriers up front and three behind they advanced towards the enemy's position, passing D Company's perimeter immediately south of the enemy's line of attack.

The attack was almost over before it started, but even so, it was intense. 'All I can remember,' recalled Roberts, 'was that the tracer seemed to weave . . . at you in a way that you felt you could sway backwards and forwards and [dodge] it.'[66] Lieutenant Savage, Roberts' 2IC, was in the rear troop section and recalled seeing a mass of enemy firing and moving. He tried to fire his .50-calibre machine gun but in most cases couldn't depress it far enough to have any impact; he recalled that it was 'most frustrating seeing these fellows firing at you and trying to dodge the tracer. It seemed to be coming towards us in slow curves, but it was like ducking tennis balls.'[67]

Enemy fire tore into the advancing carriers from the front and flanks, while the Anzac artillery fire continued to fall to their right. Alcorta saw wounded Vietnamese unable to move out of the way being crushed as the APCs run over them. Not far behind, Savage was finally able to use his .50-calibre as he fired between Roberts' APC and another next to it – but 'Adrian got pretty dirty towards me as I was firing pretty close to his vehicle, so I eased off on my firing and concentrated on backing him'.[68] Roberts recalled that the fire that hit them was 'absolutely enormous: small-arms and machine-gun fire, from the front. I think that we survived because we kept coming on and they were firing high. I put my tin hat on, as an instinctive reaction.'[69]

They continued to push back the enemy force for about 500 metres until Townsend called off the attack and ordered them to return to Major Smith's beleaguered survivors.

26

'I'm a Yank! I'm a Yank!'

By now, word had got out in Saigon that the Australians were in trouble. Australian Red Cross volunteer and former journalist from Adelaide Jean Debelle had arrived in Vietnam just months before. Only male journalists were allowed to cover the war, so Debelle had volunteered with the Red Cross, hoping to cover aspects of the conflict in her spare time. That was not to be – what spare time?

That night she arrived with some US nurses at the Pacific Hotel for the usual 'bland offerings'.[1] However, this night was different: everyone seemed to be talking about a major battle the Australians were having with a significant enemy force about 70 kilometres away in a place called Long Tan, in Phuoc Tuy Province.

> 'Why is everyone talking about the Aussies?' I innocently asked an American. 'Ma'am, they're in serious trouble. They're fighting for their lives'. . . . I remember shivering despite the hot, humid air. I *had* to find out more, but making a phone call was not easy. The Vietnamese system, for all practical

purposes, was non-existent. Military phones were not
plentiful. While sending jumbled prayers skyward . . . I raced
back to the Villa to use the field phone there. I was switched
through to the American signals system and then heard an
answer at ALSG [Australian Logistic Support Group] in the
familiar Aussie accent: 'Emu.' I knew enough about the army
by then to ask for the duty officer. That night he was Major
[Athol] Nat Salter. 'Are the Aussies in trouble?' In the gentlest
voice imaginable, Nat said: 'Yes Jean, they are.' 'Are they being
brought into the 36th Evac?' 'Yes,' he replied.'[2]

Back in the plantation, the wounded Lance Corporal John Robbins
was still lying in a small depression among the other wounded in
the centre of the perimeter and remembered hearing the sound of
the carriers as they came in. He couldn't see them, but he could
certainly hear them, and the wounded who were conscious in the
muddy little ditch that went for an aid post got pretty excited,
even in their shocked and confused state.[3] He recalled that it was
'the most beautiful sound you'd ever hear, the roar of these APCs
and these big .50-cal machine guns up on the top, blasting away.'[4]

Moments earlier, Private David Beahan of 12 Platoon with his
mates was manning the perimeter and anxiously awaiting the arrival
of the carriers that were said to be coming to their rescue. He was
asking himself, as were likely many others, 'Where the f— are they?'[5]
Nearby, Private Peter Doyle of 10 Platoon was 'lying in the mud,
using my elbows, my knees and my bloody chin, trying to dig a
hole in the mud, and I heard the rise and fall of a diesel engine as it
revved and dropped and revved and dropped, and I thought, *F—k,
it's a carrier*. All the artillery was still dropping down. The next thing
I saw was this big grey shape coming through the rubber.'[6]

Even as 3 Troop arrived back at Major Smith's position, a Viet
Cong force from the north-east was continuing its attack, but within
minutes the enemy troops broke contact and headed back the way

they had come. In the near distance, even with darkness setting in, some Australians saw enemy troops rising from the ground, firing off a few rounds and withdrawing, receding into the rubber. Sergeant Bob Buick recalled that the Viet Cong had had enough and stopped their attacks – the battlefield suddenly went totally quiet. He saw the carriers coming through the line of rubber trees, or what was left of them, towards their position[7] and recalled how the Viet Cong started to get up in dribs and drabs right across their front. He couldn't believe how many of them had obviously been lying out there among their dead and seriously wounded, waiting for the next human-wave assault to come in. They just individually or in small numbers got up and trotted away to the north-east.[8]

A very relieved Major Smith, looking across to his right just before 7 p.m. recalled how 'all of a sudden amongst the noise of the machine guns and artillery there appeared the noise of diesel engines and here were these armoured personnel carriers coming though the gloom, guns firing, and some of my forward soldiers got up, because . . . as soon as these tanks arrived the enemy just turned and left.'[9]

Moments earlier, Lance Corporal Phil Buttigieg's section of B Company had become separated from Major Noel Ford's other two sections. Approaching the rear of D Company, the noise and poor visibility made knowing which way to go impossible. Enemy bodies were strewn throughout the rubber as some fading light got through large holes in the rubber canopy, caused by the artillery air bursts. Buttigieg and his men advanced towards where they hoped their OC might have gone. At one point he thought they might have to get through the night as a lone section, but then he heard his name being called to his left. They were soon picked up by some carriers just north of D Company's position, and were reunited with Ford and the rest of his 'platoon'.[10]

Ford and the men were now moving into the heart of D Company's position and radioed Task Force headquarters at Nui Dat: '493671 – Regimental target from CO. Now with C/S 1 [A Company] in C/S 4 [D Company] loc. D Coy is now non effective – estimates 25 KIA and 40 WIA. Planning to get A Coy to cover front [EAST] and south of D Coy whilst reorganising. Not ready for dust-off at this stage.'[11] Corporal Robin Jones came directly into D Company's position and was shocked by the scene of utter destruction that greeted him. He and the others realised that this had been a real-life Custer's Last Stand in a very small, circular, deadly space.[12] One of the first he came across was Sergeant Major Kirby, who was walking around giving orders and encouragement; Kirby's actions during the whole battle had placed his life at great risk, and he was still potentially exposed to fire. Jones recalled thinking to himself: 'Get down, you big bastard.'[13]

Jones noticed how the wounded had been collected in a small depression just off to the side of the command position, and reckoned there were around 20 of the 'poor bastards, with all sorts of pretty horrible wounds. Some were unconscious and others were doped up with morphine. The whole company, wounded or not, was definitely all shell-shocked, as everyone just looked at us blank-eyed and tried to say things without much success. It was a pretty devastating sight to see those guys in that condition, filthy, wet, shocked and exhausted, and to realise it could be any one of us the next time.'[14] It was sometime just after 7 p.m.[15]

Smith and his men were now able to stand for the first time in relative safety, even though intermittent fire continued from just beyond the Australian perimeter. Smith apprised Ford of the situation and their position as they walked the perimeter, and asked him to place his men to defend to the south-west to western area as they had earlier seen Viet Cong trying to get around their position from there.[16] These were the troops from *D445 VC Battalion* whose advance had been shattered moments earlier by the APCs.

The sound of battle had ceased and had been replaced by the noises of 'moaning wounded out to the front', recalled Smith, 'and then the jubilant talking among the company at having survived.'[17]

The APCs had circled around the position and the rear hatches came down. The men of A Company, going to ground between, were facing the enemy. On leaving the carriers they had no idea that the firing had mostly stopped, having been trapped in their noisy confines, but as the last of the men slid into position a silence fell on the plantation – the Anzac guns finally fell silent. It was only broken by the now-gentle rain and the clicks of the APC engines as they began to cool down.[18] 'I think a lot of my soldiers,' recalled Major Smith, 'thought that they were never going to arrive and that we would never get out of it, and a lot of them stood up and went over and gave the carriers a gentle pat on the side and certainly shook the hand of the armoured corps guys and probably some of the A Company guys that came out of the carriers. We were certainly very pleased to see them, to say the least.'[19]

Private Peter Bennett of A Company, likely still with his cold hamburgers in his pouch, was probably among the first to be thanked as he walked into D Company's position. He held his fire as he approached the general location – the last thing he wanted to do was hit one of the survivors from D Company.

Captain Charles Mollison, with his 9mm pistol in hand, came across Captain Morrie Stanley, who had for hours been calling in artillery strikes against the Vietnamese human waves. His men had suffered from mortar and heavy machine-gun fire, had seen napalm drops against Nui Dat 2 and had experienced ongoing fire from RPGs and RCLs, and looking at Mollison, with his seemingly toy-like pistol, Stanley almost broke into laughter – until he realised that Mollison was part of the infantry relief force. They had finally arrived.[20] Stanley was not the only one who was amused by

Mollison's pistol in the circumstances. Lieutenant Geoff Kendall recalled smirking to himself and being a bit bemused that Mollison was carrying this pistol.[21]

Lieutenant Peter Dinham recalled seeing the New Zealand officer 'calmly calling down the fire from a crouched position behind a tree'. Within seconds the Anzac artillery fire ceased and 'all was very quiet'.[22] In all, the Anzac and US batteries had fired a total of 3440 rounds in just four hours, some as close as 30 metres from D Company's perimeter.[23] Bombardier Murray Broomhall recalled that 'the sudden silence was nearly as deafening as the thunder of the guns . . . No tree was unmarked. Most of them looked as if someone had hit them with a giant flail – there were no leaves, no twigs, shattered stumps, fallen branches and whole trees toppled over.'[24]

Corporal Rod Armstrong, a member of Dinham's platoon, saw Major Smith 'standing there waving his arms around, giving directions to his survivors of D Company, while close by Sergeant Jim Myles witnessed Jack Kirby, who had somehow not only cheated death but had escaped being wounded, supporting two Australian casualties, one over each shoulder.' He thought that they must be dead because that was not the normal way to carry a wounded soldier.[25] Close by, Private Russ Perandis discovered that his M60 had been crushed by a carrier so he picked up an SLR, checked it over and got ready to continue the fight, if necessary. Private Ken Branch of 10 Platoon came across his mate Private Rick 'Doug' Aldersea: 'I passed Doug, my fellow scout and mate, lying there with a hole in his head, and I thought sadly, *Well, well* and just burst into tears.'[26] Private Terry Burstall was walking around as if in a trance, amazed at his survival – but it didn't take long for some reality to hit:

I can recall walking in a sort of a daze towards the area where the wounded were and saw some Australian troops coming towards me. John Loader, a bloke I was with in Kapooka, said something to me but I don't know whether I answered him or not. They had two carriers in the centre with the back hatches down and were doing something with the wounded. I came across Peter Dettman and Dave Beahan [both 12 Platoon], and poor Dave was just hanging on to a rubber tree with his head down. I thought he may have been hit but Peter grabbed me and told me that Paul Large had been killed. Dave and Paul had been good mates and Dave was taking it pretty hard.[27]

Private John Heslewood also recalled feeling stunned after the adrenaline of being in battle subsided: 'After Alpha Company arrived and the firing died down, we started to move around and regroup into our sections. It was only then that the full picture became apparent. It was a very sobering sight to look at the aid post with the wounded being treated and realising a lot of blokes had not made it back at all.'[28]

Robbins commented that the badly wounded were placed inside two of the carriers, where medics worked on them. He remembered sitting with Heslewood, who was smoking, and thinking that he had never seen him smoke before; he certainly went through a few that night. Kendall had also made his way to the aid post to check on the wounded. He estimated that Corporal Phil Dobson had been caring for about 18 wounded. Most of the unconscious had their tongues pinned to their bottom lips with a safety pin so they wouldn't swallow them and choke.[29]

Meanwhile, Lieutenant Adrian Roberts had swung his carrier force into a north–south line to the east of D Company's position. On his own initiative, Dinham advanced his platoon to take up a position between the carriers to help provide a line of defence against any enemy attack. Mollison soon called Dinham on the radio and told him to secure the newly established eastern part of the perimeter. Dinham called back to say he'd already done so.

What Roberts remembered most vividly after setting up his

defensive position was 'this silvery blue of the cordite from the artillery that had been dropped. It was floating like a mist and you could hear the groans of the wounded and what have you out to the front and you were sort of straining, looking into the mist, and then the darkness came on and you couldn't see anything after that.'[30]

It was then that Corporal Ross Smith's forward scout yelled out, 'Contact front!' The corporal recalled: 'Heeding Captain Mollison's warning, I stopped him opening fire. As we ran forward, this figure jumped up with his "hand" in the air yelling, "I'm a Yank! I'm a Yank!" I had captured a goddamn Yank! He was one scared soldier.'[31] Lieutenant Gordon Steinbrook's missing NCO was missing no more. Corporal Smith also recalled trying as best they could to improve their position: 'I have never seen a defensive position dug so quickly, even though the trenches filled with water as soon as they were dug. I heard someone calling out, "Help me! Someone please help me!" I looked up and could just see a soldier dragging another soldier by the yoke of his webbing. I'm no hero, so I told Bruce McLay to go and help. "Thanks a bunch," was his muttered reply. When he came back, I asked how the other bloke was. Bruce told me he thought he was dead. What impressed me at the time was, that soldier was not going to leave his mate behind no matter what.'[32] Also digging in with Corporal Smith was his new-found best friend, US sergeant Frank Beltier. 'As soon as I stopped digging, I threw my entrenching tool to the Yank so he could dig his personal swimming hole also.'[33]

Townsend now took command of his battalion. All expected a renewed attack at any time. Alcorta, who was with Dinham along the eastern perimeter, recalled that suddenly the Viet Cong had vanished: only the moans of the enemy wounded and the jungle silence remained.[34] They were not to know that the Viet Cong commanders had no intention of renewing the fight and that what was left of the *275 VC Regiment* and *D445 VC Battalion* had melted away, heading east. A company commander from *D445 VC Battalion*, Nguyen Duc Thu, later recalled: 'We saw the tanks [APCs] coming and we knew that we did not have the weapons to fight them.'[35]

While the rain had slackened off, it would not be long before it again came down in a torrential downpour.

27

'Frank said we would
take the bodies'

1930–2400 hours

Australian Red Cross volunteer Jean Debelle was anxious to make
her way to the US 36th Evacuation Hospital to help any Australian
wounded who were brought in. She asked her supervisor, Hilda
Zinner, 'Are you coming with me to the 36th Evac?'[1] However, the
older and more experienced Red Cross officer knew that at this point it
was up to the medical staff to receive and treat the wounded, and that
she and Jean would only get in the way. She replied that she was not
going, and nor should Jean. 'I was dumbfounded,' recalled Debelle.
'Wasn't this what we had been sent to Vietnam for? "I'd like to go
tonight," I persisted, but Hilda was adamant that there was nothing
that couldn't wait until morning and that I would be in the way.'[2]

The Red Cross was stationed with US military doctors and
nurses at the 'Villa' and these personnel were all being called back
to the hospital even though most had just completed an exhaust-
ing shift, as Australian wounded would soon be arriving. Debelle
believed she could be of some use, if only by holding the hand of a
wounded or dying soldier and letting him hear an Australian voice

among the cacophony of Americans – hear a voice from home. She later wrote: 'I pleaded, but to no avail. Inwardly pouting, but fearful of disobeying a direct order, I went to bed early, planning to be at the hospital at dawn. The decision not to go to the hospital that night still bothers me today.'[3]

Back at 1 ATF, the expenditure in artillery shells had been extremely heavy and the batteries needed urgent resupply. US Army Chinooks were made available to fly in the heavy payloads of shells. While the choppers brought in the resupply, 5 RAR was sent to patrol the outer area around Nui Dat. Others from the headquarters company of 1 ATF were sent out as working parties to help the exhausted gunners bring in the rounds. All of this had to be done in the dark and rain.[4]

Brigadier David Jackson and others were still concerned that the base might be the ultimate target – he had only five companies available to protect his long perimeter – but he was also aware that further attacks might be conducted against the depleted 6 RAR, still in the plantation 5 kilometres away. By now, Wing Commander Ray Scott had assembled six RAAF helicopters at Kangaroo Pad at 1 ATF. He recalled that they were not about to leave their helicopters because 'I'd been told that we had a very critical situation on our hands . . . It was quite some time before we had anyone come down from the Army Ops Room to tell us what it was all about.'[5] Among the helicopters were those that had flown in the original ammunition-resupply mission. Flight Lieutenant Bob Grandin recalled being 'nervous all the time, the sort of nervous energy that keeps you on edge . . . but we remained ready to do whatever we had to do'.[6]

Back in the plantation it was 7.38 p.m. when Lieutenant Colonel Townsend radioed Jackson at Nui Dat to tell him: 'D Coy is to reorganize his force. I propose for D Coy to withdraw to a likely LZ [landing zone] to regroup and evacuate casualties or they may die. The proposed LZ is 750 metres NW of this loc. Dustoff expected in 60 minutes approx.'[7]

Lieutenant Roberts now set about reorganising his troops for all-round defence. The men were anxious and expected to get the call to re-form and move up to 11 Platoon's former position to recover the Australian dead and hopefully find some wounded among them. As they waited, Roberts heard a lot of sniper fire but there was no assault.[8]

Private Terry Burstall and the other survivors of D Company had collected into one area fairly close to the carriers. 'Blokes were sitting and standing in little groups, just staring and smoking. Everyone gave anything to whoever asked for it. Blokes gave away their last cigarettes without even hesitating. I have never experienced before or since such communal unselfishness, and it disturbs me to think that it takes a tragedy to produce this spirit. All any bloke cared about was helping everyone around him.'[9]

At 8.35 p.m. Townsend and Jackson discussed the possibilities of try-ing to move forward to 11 Platoon's original position to recover the dead and any wounded who might still be out there. They agreed that they would have to wait until daylight, and that the current position could not be made secure and the force should retire to the west to help cover the evacuation of the wounded at the pro-posed landing zone. Townsend also reported that the casualties so far known were five dead, 16 wounded and another 16 missing; he mentioned the enemy had clearly suffered heavy casualties from D Company and the Anzac and US artillery.[10] Jackson concluded that Townsend was preparing to 'evacuate area to secure an LZ with the troops available'.[11] Jackson was clearly distressed by the Australian losses. Once he had finished talking to Townsend he sat down on a chair and stayed there for some time, seemingly alone, with his head buried in his hands. One platoon destroyed, one company non-effective, 16 men missing – it looked like a disaster.[12]

Meanwhile, the wounded and dead were being loaded into the APCs for the movement to the landing zone about 750 metres west of the present position, just beyond the rubber plantation. The handling of the dead and wounded took some time and the severely wounded had now been without professional medical care for several hours. Three of Major Smith's wounded volunteered to remain on duty. The centre of the landing zone was just 200 metres from the earlier rendezvous position between majors Smith and Ford six hours before.

The wounded Corporal Robbins remembered that time meant nothing to him at this point, and he even managed to have a light sleep. When he woke up, someone told him that they were clearing an area for the helicopter medevacs.[13] At 8.45 the Task Force was advised that the 'LZ GR 470670 [was] to be ringed by APCs with their red tail lights at extreme of LZ. Should be ready approx 1 hours time.'[14] However, the APCs with the dead and wounded would not leave the battlefield for the landing zone for another two hours.

Major Smith had no time to reflect on what had happened – he was still in command of D Company, and he and his men still had plenty of work to do. Lieutenant Sabben recalled that Sergeant Major Kirby had several parties organised: one group of NCOs supervised the distribution of ammunition and water bottles, while another cared for the wounded and helped load them and the dead into the carriers. Yet another was collecting all of the unclaimed gear, including damaged and undamaged weapons, while NCOs were doing roll calls and consolidating a list of missing and casualties. At a quieter time, Smith reflected on their survival against overwhelming numbers:[15]

We only lost four killed in the final company defensive area – albeit not dug in – thanks to the gunners and their accurate artillery fire, and to the courage, tenacity and resilience of my own company in giving the VC back as much as we were receiving. My soldiers just kept up a steady and accurate volume of small arms fire into the assaulting VC, who were surging forward over the bodies of their fallen comrades. Thank heavens we had ample ammunition. Although not a religious person, I recall thanking God for the RAAF choppers and the gunners. Morrie Stanley and his crew were outstanding. Although Morrie was later to place much of the praise on his battery commander, let me make it very clear Morrie was the man on the spot and he called the tune of the song we wanted to hear to the guns back at base.[16]

At 10.30 p.m. Jackson, back at Nui Dat, was informed that D Company was still in its original 'location as the casualty loading is pretty slow and should leave in approx 15 minutes. Remainder here will follow later. A Coy patrol is investigating groaning to their front.'[17]

Indeed, some of the men from A Company had been concerned for a while that some of the injured moaning out beyond the perimeter might be Australians. Company Sergeant Major Jack Roughley, a Korean War veteran and former member of the AATTV, crept out beyond the perimeter on his own initiative to investigate the moans originating to the north. While he was out there the moans begun to cease, and he made his way back to the perimeter having come across no one.[18]

Another who conducted a self-appointed recce was Corporal Ross Smith, who searched the area south-east. He had warned Lieutenant Robert Toyer that they would be going out – the last thing he wanted was to be shot by 'friendly' fire. On hearing that Corporal Smith was going out, Private Peter Bennett volunteered to go with him as 'one of my very good friends was still lying out there [Lance Corporal Jack Jewry – who had been killed earlier at 11 Platoon's original position]. I wasn't sure whether he was dead or wounded. I wanted to locate him or any other Australian before the Vietcong did so.'[19] Toyer passed on the request to Captain Charles Mollison, who refused the mission; Smith and Bennett went out regardless.[20]

As they crawled out into no-man's land, Smith with an Owen submachine gun and Bennett with an SLR, they began to think it wasn't such a good idea. Bennett understandably got the shakes, but to his credit he pressed on. 'It was unbelievable. It was dark, there were people groaning and moaning everywhere . . . I didn't really know who we were trying to make contact with. We just continued to crawl along the ground to that noise, to the groan . . . obviously hoping that we'd locate one of our own. The thing that I noticed was that as we got closer, the groans would move away . . . we seemed to be losing whatever contact we made. It was very dark – you couldn't see a few feet in front of you – and raining.'[21] It was only later that they realised the groaning was likely from Vietnamese wounded being dragged away.

It wasn't long before Smith and Bennett saw enemy troops that seemed to be moving about. Smith was the first to see them. 'When the lightning flashed in the distance, we saw these people, the enemy, in front of us. Peter Bennett grabbed my leg – my leg was shaking enough to fall off, and his hand was shaking – and said "Did you see that?" and I said, "Shit, I saw that too. They're in front of us – they're coming in from both sides too."' Smith looked at his night compass and held out his arm, providing a direction back to the Australian position. He whispered to Bennett: 'When I start shooting, keep going – don't stop.'[22] Both men crouched, ready to fire, but the lightning had ceased and they managed to get away without having to fire a shot, making their way back to the Australian perimeter.

Soon after, they went out again, this time with permission

from Mollison. They took with them their radio operator, Private Ernie Dare. As they crawled, and at great risk to themselves they would call out was there anyone from Sydney, or who had won the rugby league grand final?[23] They never got a reply, and returned to A Company's position having found none of the missing Australians. Smith recalled returning to their platoon location empty-handed and pretty much dejected, having nothing to show for their effort.[24]

Townsend approached Major Smith and suggested that he and the other survivors of D Company be evacuated back to Nui Dat and from there on to Vung Tau. The major was strongly opposed to this. He insisted that the missing were from his company and there was no way he and his men were not going in to retrieve their dead and hopefully bring in any wounded who might have survived the night. It was also imperative to him that he and his men 'assert a psychological dominance over the area'.[25] They had been thrown off a metaphorical horse and needed to get back on.

Smith further argued that apart from the wounded, they should maintain their present position and not withdraw from the plantation. They now had a consolidated force, with A Company and a platoon from B Company, along with the APCs. There was also a regiment of artillery zeroed in, and they could have US air support in terms of helicopter gunships and strike aircraft overhead on immediate call. He argued further that their presence would keep the enemy well away from the missing:[26] Smith and others had heard terrible stories from the Americans up in the northern provinces about atrocities committed on American soldiers captured on the battlefield. Smith tried to argue with his immediate superior that they should stay on the battlefield all night but he didn't win the argument and was forced to withdraw to a safer area to get his casualties out.[27]

Townsend was adamant about evacuating the present position. He did not have an intact battalion: A Company was down to two effective platoons (with the withdrawal of 1 Platoon and CHQ), B Company consisted of a composite platoon, and D Company was a spent force.[28] While Smith didn't win the argument about maintaining their existing position, he and his men would remain in the vicinity of the landing zone in order to go out at first light to look for the missing Australians. They would not be heading back to the Task Force base.

With the wounded now loaded, the lead APC, with its headlights on, moved out for the landing zone with the other carriers close behind. The lead carrier was commanded by Lieutenant Ian Savage, whose vehicle contained the Australian dead. Companies A and B would walk out 45 minutes later.[29] Mollison, commanding A Company, recalled that during the next hour he and the others 'crouched down in the watery shell scrapes we had dug and tried to present as small a target as possible. We shivered in the cold night air, staring into the pitch black, trying desperately to see the enemy before he saw us. We had only a handful more men than Delta Company had started with, and the enemy now knew exactly where we were. Time passed: 10 minutes; 20 minutes; our nerves were stretched to breaking point. After 40 minutes passed without incident, we started to relax.'[30]

When the time came, they moved out towards the landing zone to the west and before long the artillery got the word to start firing into their old positions – but not around 11 Platoon's original position. The artillery also targeted suspected enemy escape routes; added to this, aircraft began to bomb in depth to try to disrupt the enemy's retreat.[31] Corporal Robin Jones of B Company recalled moving out after the APCs had gone. He soon received an order from Major Ford to set his 'compass on a bearing and the bearing was checked by the OC. I was to lead Alpha and Bravo companies back to the area of the evacuations. This was a case of blind navigation, as you couldn't see your hand in front of your face. We stopped numerous times after falling over or running into a tree. Obstacles were numerous. We made the rubber's edge about an hour or so later. I never liked night navigation ever again.'[32]

Lieutenant Peter Dinham recalled moving out in single file, the complete darkness requiring each man to grab hold of the webbing of the man in front. His platoon was the last to leave the battlefield, with Mollison's tactical party just in front of his one remaining section, followed by platoon HQ representing the rearguard. It seemed to take forever to move a relatively short distance – approximately 1000 metres.[33]

At the very end of the line was Private Trevor Atkinson, who was acting as 'tail-end Charlie' – always a stressful and unwanted position. He recalled that whenever the line stopped, he faced back the way they had come, but every time this happened the 'line seemed to take off twice as quick. Many times I lost contact with the man in front of me. It was a matter of stumble on in the pitch-black, hoping to catch up. I remember thinking once that, if I didn't find the end of the line in the next minute, I was going to dig the deepest hole possible and wait there till daylight.'[34]

The APCs had arrived at the makeshift landing zone at around 11.20 p.m. Corporal Kevin Miller recalled arriving at an 'old banana plantation which was reasonably clear – we could clear it and get the helicopters in'.[35] Roberts organised his troop to form a square around the makeshift helicopter pad with all their hatches opened; they turned on their interior lights to guide the choppers to their exact position.[36] The first to arrive was a US Army helicopter, just before midnight. With its lights beaming, it took on board the three most serious cases on litters. This was followed by other US helicopters. The RAAF helicopters followed, commanded by Wing Commander Scott. They were ordered not to use their landing lights and it took them longer to arrive. Sergeant Bob Buick recalled that the first helicopters to come were the US Army choppers, which flared dramatically just before landing. As the pilots made their steep descent onto the pad, they turned their landing lights on about 7 metres from the ground. The Australian pilots were a bit slower in their landing as they did not use lights and were far more deliberate in their approach. 'It would have been a worrying time for the Australian chopper pilots,' recalled Buick, 'as they were new to this type of operation, especially at night. Although slower, the 9 Squadron RAAF pilots and crews did a great job of getting the dead and wounded out.'[37]

Wounded lance corporal Dennis Spencer of CHQ was among the last to be lifted, and one of his greatest memories was the medevac helicopters lifting off and taking him and the others to Vung Tau. They could see the lights coming up fairly quickly, and he recalled how unreal the world was up there, totally unrelated to the hell they had just been through. There was a sense of safety.[38] Robbins recalled some of his mates walking him over to the helicopter: 'I can remember that clearly and the bloody red lights flashing . . . the Yank machine gunners . . . I remember the ride . . . as clear as anything and just how good it was, the best taxi ride I ever had.'[39] Private John Cash found himself on a chopper with another from 10 Platoon, Corporal Buddy Lea, who had helped him get back to CHQ, along with Sergeant James Todd and Private Grant Davis, both from 12 Platoon. All were conscious and no doubt pleased to have got out alive.[40]

There was no let-up for flight lieutenants Frank Riley and Cliff Dohle and their crew, as they too were involved in the evacuation of the casualties. Grandin recalled how they moved to the holding position and 'circled waiting for the aircraft before us to pull out. There was a hold-up as one pilot was having some problems with his approach. Then it was our turn . . . We slid smoothly into the position. Someone ran forward and said that there were no more wounded. We could go, or maybe take some bodies out! Frank said we would take the bodies.'[41] Four Australian dead were placed in the chopper and it lifted off, then turned and headed for Vung Tau. The wounded and dead were evacuated to 36 Evac Hospital at Vung Tau, with the last of the helicopters carrying Australian casualties leaving the battlefield area at around 1 a.m.

While all of this was going on, Private Bill Akell recalled hearing 'the artillery pounding away. They were firing at what they suspected to be the enemy withdrawal routes. It was a terrible night really.'[42]

Back at Nui Dat, Lieutenant Gordon Steinbrook was preparing to go out into the plantation at first light. He spent the evening of 18 August preparing himself – he had never been out in the bush before except for 'one little A Battery patrol, nor had I ever operated with the infantry. I had been with the infantry three whole days, and now it appeared my initiation would be an experience to equal the worst nightmares. I packed my gear, oiled my Owen submachine gun, removed each 9-mm round from the magazines, checked for cleanness, and then reloaded . . . I went to bed that night praying, finding some peace.'[43]

Not far away, in the 6 RAR operations tent, the battalion second-in-command, Major John Hooper, operations officer Major Brian Passey, and the adjutant, Captain Max Turrell, had been discussing events when word came through from US Defense officials in Saigon asking about the big battle that had been fought in the Long Tan rubber plantation. What was the name of the operation being conducted? Operation Vendetta concluded at 11 p.m. 18 August 1966 and was replaced by Operation Smithfield.[44] Turrell recalled that 'our policy at the time was that operations were named after Australian towns and cities. Somebody had remarked that [Major Harry] Smith was having a field day. So the decision was taken to name the operation "Smithfield" after the town of that name and the officer commanding Delta Company. This decision was passed to HQ 1 ATF and to the commanding officer, Lieutenant Colonel Townsend, out in the field.'[45] The later unofficial 'amalgamation' of Operation Vendetta into Operation Smithfield by Townsend and other senior commanders would result not only in much confusion but also controversy.[46]

Part Three
AFTERMATH

Dear Mum, Dad & All

Well, I suppose you got my letter saying we were going out on another Operation . . . I suppose you heard about the company on radio and TV that was surrounded by three battalions of Viet Cong and the bitter fighting. Well that was us. Seventeen of our mates were killed and twenty-four wounded . . . I know you worry about me, but I don't want you to worry too much. I was close to death the other day and I thought I'd never see you all again but I came through. I don't understand what we're really fighting for but we're all mates here and I think we fight to save ourselves and each other. It's a funny thing, it doesn't matter how bad it is, you won't run out on your mates, and we all really thought we were going to die. It looked so hopeless and there were so many of them, but everyone who died, died like a man. You feel sorry for the ones killed but when you see them lying there you thank God it's not you, I'll be glad when it's all over.

Letter from Private Alan Parr, 7 Section, 12 Platoon,
D Company 6 RAR to his parents, 21 August 1966

28

'. . . I must say that I was troubled all night'

During the early hours of 19 August, Major Harry Smith and his men were still in their soaking-wet greens, huddled in and around the APCs. After the evacuation of the dead and wounded, the officers of D Company organised their survivors. A roll call was held, with a number of names going unanswered. The officers tried to establish who was missing and, of these, who was known to have been killed. This was a trying and difficult task for all concerned. Some were in a state of depression, some were clearly in a state of shock, and some were on a short-lived high having escaped what had appeared to be certain death.

Sergeant Bob Buick had understandably mixed emotions and, while numb, was on a 'high, but not tired. There was too much to do, and I was still thinking about the guys in the battle area. How many were still alive?'[1] He spent most of the early morning in Lieutenant Adrian Roberts' APC with Lieutenant Colonel Colin Townsend while his battalion commander set about drawing up plans and orders for the return to the main battlefield area. The operation was given the codename of *Smithfield* at about 2300hrs on 18 August.[2] Private Kev Branch of 10 Platoon was 'remorseful, shaken up, wet as a shag, and couldn't relax. *Maybe* I caught twenty minutes or an hour's sleep, then it was daylight.' Private Bill Akell of CHQ didn't remember much of that night as his mind was 'blown [away] at what had happened . . . in too short a time to be able to think straight. It wasn't till days later that we knew what had happened. I appreciated a hot cup of coffee and a cigarette, followed by a cold can of meat and a packet of dog-biscuits.' Private Russ Perandis, also from D Company CHQ, remembered someone giving him a 'raincoat to sleep in, and in the morning I found I'd been sleeping in a thorn patch and didn't know. I was numb.'[3]

Private Brian Halls of 11 Platoon was sitting in an APC also feeling pretty numb and 'probably going into a bit of delayed shock . . . Buggered. Drained, but not ready to sleep.'[4] Close by were privates Terry Burstall and Richard Brown, both from 12 Platoon, hardly speaking to each other. Burstall recalled that it was 'pitch dark where we were and I just sat there, staring into the bush. Gun pickets were changed in silence and a numbness seemed to hang over the whole area. I couldn't even cry, although I know I wanted to. I kept thinking of Paul Large wrapped in a groundsheet somewhere, seeing nothing with his blank eyes and cold skin.'[5]

Lieutenant David Sabben, after putting the events of the previous 12 hours into some kind of sequence and perspective, recalled having something to eat and a hot brew while trying to answer the questions of the A Company and APC troopers.[6] He then sought out another platoon commander and both sat against a carrier 'looking into the darkness. There was nothing to discuss. What could I say? I was just deflated, I suppose. A drained feeling. I remember drinking a lot of water.'[7] He eventually found some uncomfortable and fitful sleep.[8] His fellow platoon commander Lieutenant Geoff Kendall was feeling extremely anxious about the fate of their missing men. 'We were really afraid that night, waiting to go back in or do what we were going to do the next day – that they'd get our guys . . . We don't know if they're all dead or if any are alive.' He

was terrified that the wounded who were still alive in the plantation might be mutilated. 'We were also pretty worried that we were
going to go in the next morning and find it's all been swept clean,
there's nothing there, and no matter what we say for the rest of our
lives nobody'll ever believe us. They'll say, "Well, they had a bit of
a scrap, lost 18 guys and went home with their tails between their
legs.'[9] Kendall sat back and waited for dawn with these and many
other thoughts going through his mind.

Captain Morrie Stanley desperately wanted to collapse into
sleep, but he had too much to do. His OC, Major Harry Honnor,
wanted to make sure he had a fire plan to harass the withdrawing
enemy force and target any who might still be lurking in the plantation. He found that 'an APC made a comfortable enough place
for me to prepare the small fire plan and after sending it by radio
to Nui Dat, I probably sat there and fell asleep. The guns fired
during the night at a more leisurely pace and that was virtually the
end of my fire support duties at Long Tan . . . I hoped ATF would
organise a US Army block to the east of the Long Tan area to cut
off the withdrawing enemy, but as [we] later discovered, this did
not happen. Like the return to the battlefield on the 19th, nothing
was to happening quickly.'[10]

Out in the battlefield area, two wounded Australians from 11 Platoon
were hoping to survive the night. Private Jim Richmond of 6 Section
was fading in and out of consciousness but knew he had to try to
stop the bleeding:

> I thought . . . well, I'll have to try and survive the night and the
> only thing to do with me wound was to lay in the mud and try
> and pack the wound with mud to try and stop the bleeding.
> I knew that I had a bad wound because before we went
> overseas they take you through with the doctors . . . [who]

give you a lecture on all types of wounds you could have, and I remembered this one was a sucking chest wound because I could feel the air being sucked in through me back. So I knew what sort of a wound I had because that's what he told us it would be like. So I just packed it full of mud and rolled on my side and just tried to survive the night, which was fairly long. I yelled out a couple of times in the night for a medic but just got fired upon so I kept quiet and tried to survive the night and the artillery kept pounding me all night. I did hear movement around me but none of it was friendly so I just tried to keep as quiet as I could.[11]

A few hundred metres behind Richmond, Private Barry Meller of platoon HQ was wrapped in an enemy groundsheet and trying to lie undetected in low brush. He tried to get as much sleep as he could, but shells were exploding all night through the trees. Luckily for him, they were not exploding in his immediate area as the gunners were careful not to fire where Australian wounded might be located. All around, the Viet Cong were in search of their own wounded and collecting weapons and ammunition. After a few hours Meller reckoned they had cleared out as he had not seen or heard them for some time. By now he was so fed up that he decided 'Stuff the Viet Cong' and tried to light a cigarette, but he couldn't get his lighter to work.[12]

The Australian wounded who were conscious and had made it to the large US 36th Evacuation Hospital finally felt safe. Lance Corporal Dennis Spencer of CHQ recalled as his helicopter landed how several medics were waiting. An American asked him where he was hit:

[He] picked me up and just bolted straight into an open operating theatre which was like a huge hangar that was lined full of beds, doctors and surgeons. He placed me on a table and brought out the biggest pair of scissors I'd ever seen in my life, and I lost my boots, shirt, trousers, and the whole lot in about three snips. I was lying there naked on the table with the surgeons and nurses working and talking to us very quickly, finding problem spots and sorting things out. That didn't seem to take very long and then we were in a ward having a hot meal. I suppose at that time it would have been about 3 a.m. All of us who had been attended to were lying there just looking – we were all pretty much stunned by the events, I think.[13]

Corporal John Robbins of 11 Platoon, doped up on morphine and undoubtedly dazed and in shock, remembered landing at the hospital; most of the nurses who met and helped him and the other Australians were male, mostly African Americans 'and good fellas, too'.[14] His recollections are similar to those of Spencer:

A team met each chopper – there were other choppers coming in when we came in, and there was a team there that met them. I can't remember who else was on the chopper with me, but there was a team more or less that was met for every person . . . [that's] how organised they were. I don't think I walked in – I think they put us on a stretcher and took us in and they get these bloody big scissors and just cut all your gear off because you're covered in mud and blood . . . cut all your gear off including your boots, throw everything in a big bin and wash you down, and talked to you trying to make you as comfortable as they could. The next thing I remember was going into the operating theatre; it was something I'd never seen before . . . There was a lot of pain in there, yelling and things happening, doctors and tubs and bottles and all the rest of it . . .[15]

Private Ron Eglinton, also of 11 Platoon, recalled when the 'chopper was coming down there were about a dozen or so people lined up and as soon as the chopper put down they just grabbed you and raced you inside.' His most vivid thought was the feeling of being safe.[16]

Major Smith's exhausted radio operator, Corporal Graham Smith, recalled being in the back of an APC with the headquarters group, including Major Smith. For hours the corporal was in radio contact with the Task Force base and at one stage he was 'asleep and they [the headquarters team] could hear from my handset so they didn't bother waking me up but as soon as I did get a call, I'd wake up and answer it anyway'.[17] Corporal Ross McDonald of 10 Platoon was near Corporal Smith at the time when a radio message came in from Task Force headquarters stating that they could withdraw back to the base so as to reorganise, and from there they could spend a couple of days' leave at Vung Tau – but Major Smith was adamant and replied 'No', saying that at first light he and his company would be moving back into the battle area to collect any wounded and dead.[18]

The enemy had almost certainly departed and there was now an ample force available to search for the missing Australians from 11 Platoon, who were still in the heart of the plantation. Major Smith was aware that the men of his company were in a dazed and confused state and needed to take psychological control of the battlefield to shake them out of their malaise. In the distance the Anzac batteries continued to fire into the plantation, targeting likely escape routes.[19] Corporal Smith was immediately privy to Major Smith's decision to return to the battlefield at first light and recalled being 'very apprehensive of what we would find because we had heard stories of enemy mutilating bodies and so on and we had so many missing at that point'.[20]

Townsend was given a relatively free hand by Brigadier David

Jackson to conduct operations over the next three days as part of Operation Smithfield. D Company of 5 RAR, under the command of Major Paul Greenhalgh, was also placed under his command. Townsend wanted his force to move back into the battlefield area in the APCs at first light[21] but, as recalled by Major Smith, Townsend was distinctly unhappy that the Task Force commander was apparently trying to get in on the act, taking kudos away from 6 RAR.[22] Buick also remembered Townsend resenting the intrusion of a 5 RAR company, which would make it a Task Force operation. That said, Smith himself was unimpressed with Townsend, as he was doing exactly the same thing in relation to downplaying D Company's role in the battle by emphasising that it was a battalion operation that had started on 17 August, with the battle for Long Tan being part of a broader 6 RAR operation. Indeed, some reports and histories have 'deleted' Operation Vendetta from the pages of history and replaced it with Operation Smithfield, indicating that the latter operation commenced on 17 August, as opposed to the final hour of 18 August.[23] There were two distinct operations; Operation Vendetta led by Major Smith which resulted in the battle of Long Tan; and the second Operation Smithfield commanded by Lieutenant Colonel Townsend which was involved in following up the enemy after the battle.

At 3 a.m. Townsend called his orders group together in one of the carriers and issued verbal orders for operations to be conducted on 19 August:

> 6 RAR will be reinforced by more APCs and Delta Company 5 RAR. Provided the reinforcements arrive in time, our advance to contact will start at dawn. Delta Company 6 RAR and Delta Company 5 RAR, both mounted in APCs, will lead the advance. Alpha and Charlie Companies are to set off on foot back towards the battlefield and then mount the APCs used initially to carry the two Delta Companies. Alpha

Company's task is to then sweep the area to the east and south of the battlefield, to engage any enemy found and to protect Delta Company's clearance of the battlefield.[24]

At 4 a.m. Townsend requested that all available APCs bring in his battalion headquarters, the men from C Company under the command of Major Brian McFarlane, and a section of mortars. He also obtained a US helicopter lift for D Company, 5 RAR. The first of these reinforcements left Nui Dat at 6.55 a.m.[25] Townsend was making plans for the movement back into the plantation and clearance of the battlefield, including follow-up operations against the Viet Cong; however, he was not to conduct operations beyond the range of the artillery, which severely limited his ability to pursue the fleeing enemy.[26]

'He's still trying to dig in'

Private Alan Parr, the machine gunner in Lieutenant David Sabben's 12 Platoon, was awake and lying beside a carrier as the sun begun to rise: 'I honestly thought I'd never see another sunrise and to be lying there near an APC and see that sun come up was the most glorious thing in my life at that time.'[1]

Corporal Peter Short, the A Company medic, recalled seeing in the early-morning light some of the men from D Company: they looked like old men. He nearly walked 'right past my friend Phil Dobson (Delta Company Medic). There was something very different about them.'[2] Another from A Company, Corporal Ross Smith, awoke to the sound of the US helicopters bringing the men of D Company, 5 RAR in to the makeshift helipad just beyond the plantation. He recalled a friend of his from this company, Bob Simpski, on seeing him saying, 'God, mate, you look as if you've been through bloody hell. How are you?'[3] An exhausted Corporal Rod Armstrong of A Company awoke and recalled looking around their harbour position and noting that 'it was nothing like a textbook, blokes were just where they'd dropped. I saw Bob Buick standing on a carrier – they must have slept around them or in them.'[4]

Indeed, Sergeant Buick distinctly recalled that as dawn broke the birds were singing and as he stood on the carrier he saw a circle of APCs with his men crammed into the perimeter of the small clearing created for the medevac helicopters. He recalled thinking that the day was going to be a great test for them all.[5]

Sabben saw the men of D Company, 5 RAR being flown in by helicopters and recalled how some put down their packs and set up for a quick brew and breakfast. He made his way over to them – he and his men had been forced to leave their own packs in the battlefield area and they asked questions about the battle but seemed more interested in their role and what they would be doing next. He couldn't help them, but knew that Major Smith had an orders group planned for 0800hrs; he told them the orders for the day would be given then – they would know soon enough.[6] With the wounding of Sergeant James Todd of Sabben's platoon, Corporal Merv McCulloch was acting sergeant. He and Sabben went through the platoon roll and decided that, even with their casualties, 12 Platoon would maintain a three-section structure rather than merging into two sections. This meant that two of the sections would be at half-strength.[7]

Meanwhile, Major Brian McFarlane had been among the first to arrive in the morning to get orders for C Company. His company, under the command of Captain Peter Harris, would arrive later via APCs. He remembered meeting Major Smith for the first time after the battle. Their association in combat operations went back 'ten years to Charlie Company 2 RAR in Malaya and now I was so proud of him and his company that for the first time in my life I was speechless. I could only stand there like a dodo and shake his hand. I hoped that no hint of a tear would well up and invade my eyes to display my emotions. Speech would not come. I let go of the poor fellow's hand and went off without a word to seek out the colonel and receive my orders.'[8]

Earlier, Private Peter Doyle of 10 Platoon had woken up in the mud and all he had was the clothes he stood up in, the webbing and the ammo belt: 'Our packs, we dropped in the initial contact. We were stuffed and far from home, rotten dirty, as usual. By then, the brass were flying in, in helicopters, there were APCs – there was more people there than you could point a stick at.'[9] Indeed, Private Terry Burstall remembered the helicopters bringing in a lot of 'bigwigs from somewhere all telling us what bloody great fellows we were, which didn't seem to make a lot of sense to anyone very much. All we knew was we'd been caught in something pretty rugged and were lucky to have got out at all.'[10]

Private John Heslewood recalled something similar, with daylight seeing the arrival of all the 'experts and the heroes from the Task Force and Vung Tau . . . all the people who wanted to be involved once it was all over. All I wanted to do was get out of the bloody joint. I didn't want to be there at all.'[11] Signaller Graham Smith recalled how it was a bit of a bad 'joke because time had pushed on and nothing was happening, and we still hadn't begun to go back into the battlefield and the Task Force commander had come out [along with] the press and just arseholes all coming out to have a look, and they really gave all of us the shits. We just wanted to get back in and retrieve our mates, and it just wasn't happening.'[12]

Buick later described with some understandable bitterness how the 'wonder workers' arrived by helicopter from numerous headquarters. These were the 'blokes who slept in beds with sheets, had three cooked meals served to them and always had a cold beer on call. They flew in from Nui Dat, Saigon and other places. They were all officers – there were no gunners invited to witness what they had done for us.'[13] Those 'baggy-arse diggers,' recalled Buick, 'who had worked through appalling conditions to get rounds on the ground because we needed them . . . could not be spared from their duties, so just the shiny-bums from various headquarters came out to the bush. Perhaps it was their very first and only "trip to the bush" during their tour of duty.'[14]

The gunners were indeed busy, but most of all they were completely exhausted. Sergeant Jim King recalled that most had not slept
much since the night of 16–17 August and by 7 a.m. of 19 August
were suffering from extreme fatigue. The ammunition expended
during the battle phase of the operation was 3198 rounds of 105mm
and 242 rounds of 155mm. The men of the batteries were now tasked
with bringing the guns back to full ammunition entitlement, tidy-
ing up the gun positions, and removing spent cartridges and cordite
bags. These jobs left King and his men 'quite bluntly, buggered'.[15]

Earlier, at first light, Lieutenant General Jonathan Seaman, commanding 1st US Infantry Division, sent Australian major Alex Piper,
the assistant planning officer with headquarters II FFV, and a number of US staff officers to Task Force headquarters at Nui Dat to get
a briefing on the battle. Brigadier Jackson, ashen-faced and almost
speechless, told Piper that the companies had yet to move back
into the plantation battle area and that one platoon had been lost
and they had nothing to show for it. Indeed, Piper recalled that 'far
from feeling that we'd had a major victory, we believed that we'd
had a significant defeat'.[16]

Four kilometres away, just outside the plantation, this certainly
was not Lieutenant Colonel Townsend's understanding. He assessed
that D Company had taken on and beaten a major enemy force,
probably regimental in size, with at least one enemy company dug in
before the battle; he estimated that around 150 Viet Cong had been
killed. However, 15 Australians remained unaccounted for. Piper
was soon on a helicopter to discuss the situation with Townsend
and Major Smith and brief Seaman at Long Binh. Sometime after
that he would be in Saigon to brief General William Westmoreland,
the commander of all forces in Vietnam, after Westmoreland had
returned from his own first-hand inspection of the battlefield.[17]

At around 7.30 a.m., Brigadier Jackson made his way to

Townsend's forward position just as he was giving his final orders for the day to 6 RAR. Jackson would remain there for another two hours; in the distance the Anzac shells were still exploding in the heart of the plantation and airstrikes could be heard further east against suspected enemy retreat routes, including a number of air strafes using 20mm Gatling guns. US Lieutenant Gordon Steinbrook had arrived by now in one of the APCs and remembered seeing US jet aircraft roaring overhead and hearing machine guns being fired, which sounded like 'cloth tearing, not at all like rapid machine-gun firing. The Gatlings fired so fast that the sounds ran together. The aircraft were strafing possible enemy escape routes.'[18] At around 8.45 a.m., the Australians began their move back into the battle area, including the survivors of Major Smith's D Company. Smith was distinctly unhappy about the delay in moving back into the plantation: as far as he was concerned, they should have moved out hours ago.[19]

Meanwhile, Corporal Ross Smith of A Company and his American friend Sergeant Frank Beltier had parted company as the Australians were to head back into the bush. Smith recalled that as he was waiting for the order to move back to the battlefield, his platoon commander told him he was needed nearby and pointed him in the general direction. On arrival he was greeted by his Yank 'prisoner' and Steinbrook.[20] Steinbrook thanked Smith for looking after his sergeant on the battlefield. Beltier had decided to get a close-up look at the Viet Cong and had taken the opportunity of jumping onboard an APC as the Australians passed through the gun area on their way to Long Tan. Steinbrook recalled wanting to 'chew [Beltier] out, but the sight of him, so pleased with himself, and the relief that thank God he was all right mellowed my anger. I don't remember saying a cross word to him then, nor did I ever mention the court-martial I had threatened the afternoon before.'[21]

Earlier the men from D Company, 6 RAR, had learnt that they were to lead the advance back into the battle area that morning. No. 2 signaller Private Bill Akell recalled that 'the word came down that the battalion was assaulting back into the battlefield. We didn't know . . . if the VC had come back into the rubber plantation and re-established themselves and we were surprised to learn it was Delta Company [6 RAR] that would lead the battalion back in to the assault. Bear in mind we had lost a third of our company either killed or wounded and we were pretty well . . . exhausted after the battle and also after a sleepless night, but still it was us to go back, that was the commanding officer's call . . . and we did.'[22]

Most of Major Smith's officers and men, when informed they were tasked with going back into the plantation, were distinctly unhappy. At the time, Lieutenant Geoff Kendall remembered thinking, 'Jesus Christ, haven't they [the enemy] given us enough of a hiding? Why don't they pick one of the fresh companies to go back in first?'[23] Private Noel Grimes of 12 Platoon felt something similar, recalling that the general reaction was 'Why us?': 'That wasn't just me, that was everybody. "Why us?"'[24] Buick, now 11 Platoon's acting commander, was also unhappy about going back into the plantation as he believed the Viet Cong were likely still out there and he was not keen for a repeat performance; he believed that 11 Platoon had been hurt enough and could not understand why A or B company could not conduct the operation. Let them take on the Viet Cong; 11 Platoon, and D Company more broadly, had already done enough and suffered a high price for it.[25]

Private Peter Doyle of 10 Platoon, on hearing Major Smith announce 'Saddle up, D Company – we're going back in', reckoned his company commander had had an 'aneurysm – he'd blown a piston in his head. In hindsight, it was a brilliant command decision. If we'd have gone back to base with our tails between our legs, it would've taken a bit to get back on the horse.'[26] Private Stan Hodder of 12 Platoon remembered thinking that they were being 'pushed too hard and the men really didn't want to go back in'.[27] Private Brian Reilly, also of 12 Platoon, was likewise not happy, but he, like the rest of them, would later appreciate the deliberate decision to send them back into the battlefield area, as it was crucial that they 'finish the job'.[28] It was probably at this point that the Long Tan 'survivors' became the Long Tan veterans.

Just before moving out, the men of 6 RAR, D Company were checking their gear, as recalled by Parr: 'I was standing near Cpl [William] Bluey Moore – he was 5 Section commander in 11 Platoon – when he said to me, "Have a look at this." Going through his backpack, he pulled out his Dixie and there was a bullet hole straight through it. 11 Platoon would have still had their packs on when they came under that intense fire and hit the deck, not like us where we ditched our packs. How many more incidents like that happened on the 18th?'[29]

The start of the advance back into the plantation closely followed the axis followed by D Company the previous day, close to where the abandoned enemy mortar base plates had been found and where B and D companies had met up during the afternoon of 18 August – a lifetime ago for many. Earlier, three carriers from 2 Troop, with call signs 8, 98 and 9 Echo Troop, had left Nui Dat to team up with their mates from 3 Troop to assist in the clean-up and follow-up operations. The battalion was organised into assault formation. D Company, 6 RAR would lead the force back into the plantation, with D Company, 5 RAR covering their left flank. Behind these two companies were the men of A, B and C companies, 6 RAR on foot. The lead companies were to sweep through the battle area in the carriers and then the men from D Company, 6 RAR would dismount on approaching the main battlefield area and commence the search for their dead, and hopefully find some survivors. The other companies on foot were to clear the surrounding areas and start the follow-up operation against the fleeing enemy. However A Company was first to go back to where, with 3 Troop, they had fought and broken through the southern force of the Vietnamese *D445 VC Battalion* that had been trying to cut off any line of retreat by Major Smith's beleaguered garrison during the final 20 minutes of the battle.[30]

As the battalion moved into the plantation, not a shot was fired. The APCs moved slowly and purposefully through the rubber trees and low brush, heading for the tapper's hut. Burstall, who was inside an APC, would have preferred to be moving up behind the carriers on foot, even given the possibility of a Viet Cong ambush: 'For me, locked inside the carrier, it was a bad trip back. Travelling in a carrier is like being inside a washing machine. The roar of the motors is deafening and if the hatch is open all that can be seen above the four closed walls are the sky and trees. The movement is very rough and the passengers are constantly thrown around as the vehicles change direction.'[31]

Doyle had a similar feeling about going in a carrier: 'I got back into an APC with other blokes . . . In an APC you sit against the wall, facing inwards with the rifle between your knees. Normally you're talking shit, a bit of bravado.'[32] That certainly was not the case this time. The men sat in the semi-darkness in quiet; even with the noisy engine, quietness seemed to prevail as each became lost in his thoughts. Doyle went on to say that there was 'not one bit of black humour, bullshit – there was nothing. I was more terrified than I was during the actual contact, I think because we didn't expect it. It erupted, it was on, then it finished.' However, now he and the others knew what they were in for. He recalled how the 'pins and needles started in my feet, went up through my legs, up through my body, up through my head, up through my ears, and I was numb. I believed 100 per cent, *Okay, we got out yesterday by the skin of our teeth. We're going back in. There's heaps and heaps of them. We ain't gonna see the sun go down.* When the back of the carrier dropped down and we shot out, I thought, *The shit is just gonna hit the fan.*[33]

Private Alan Parr was on the same carrier as Private Doug Langland of 12 Platoon; both were sitting on top of the APC. As it pushed on, Langland somehow got his rifle caught in the vegetation and tree branches; by the time he was able to pull free, recalled Parr, 'the barrel was bent at right angles. Doug looked surprised.'[34]

The majority of the veterans from D Company sitting on and in the carriers were hoping that the bulk of the enemy force had fled, but it was possible a company of Viet Cong had been left behind to ambush the Australians to help deter them from pursuing the main force. It was around 9.20 a.m. when the men of D Company, 6 RAR reached the area of the battlefield. Private Harry Esler of 10 Platoon recalled that as soon as 'they let that back door down we bolted out. We looked around and didn't know what to expect. As I got down I accidentally stood on a bit of an arm – half an arm of a VC. I picked it up and said, "How would this go hanging up in the canteen?" And whoever it was nearby said, "Put that bloody thing down!"'[35] Undoubtedly Doyle and many others were happy that no shots were fired as the rear doors of the carrier opened and they dismounted. Doyle recalled that the plantation was 'absolutely shredded. It was stark, just like a giant tumultuous thing had decimated the place.'[36]

Sergeant Buick was still twitchy and tense as he began to move back through the plantation on foot after leaving his carrier. His apprehension increased as he moved though the battle area, but the feeling changed as he was confronted with the devastation of the battlefield.[37] He and his men had been trained to kill the enemy – that was their job – but they were not trained to go back into a battlefield the next day to witness the carnage and clean up the stinking mangled bodies. They were not prepared for 'what you witness when you go in . . . I had no idea just what happened at Long Tan. I knew what happened in my little bloody paddock but I had no idea what happened 30 or 40 metres away behind me, 100 metres behind me and so on.'[38] Lieutenant David Sabben recalled seeing as he moved towards the final company headquarters position during the battle:

> a crescent of absolutely destroyed trees, and what I can only describe as a slaughterhouse of bodies. And not many of them were full, complete, identifiable bodies either. They were just body parts and pieces of flesh. Up until then, we really had no idea of what damage we had inflicted. Because of the heavy rain, because of the necessity to survive, we hadn't really sat back and taken stock of what was actually happening. And all the assaults that came in on Twelve Platoon's front and Ten Platoon's front. They were just beaten back and we got onto the next thing. We didn't worry about what was out there. And the next morning when we got back, we found what was out there was actually row upon row of bodies . . . [that] had been churned up by the fact that we had artillery rounding twenty-five yards [23 metres] from us for the last ten minutes of the battle, so anything that had already been shot was being churned up by the artillery.[39]

Somewhere nearby, Captain Bryan Wickens, the intelligence officer of 6 RAR, recalled how eerie it was going back 'onto the battlefield, with bodies everywhere. There were an awful lot. It wasn't raining. I was up close – in fact, right up front. You see a rifle, a man in a black uniform behind a tree, pointing at you . . . you'd fire. It's the natural thing. I didn't fire a shot at anyone. The riflemen alongside me would give a burst. The VC were dead already, but propped against a tree they looked alive.'[40] Indeed, orders had been given, as recalled by Lieutenant Geoff Kendall, that if anybody was in a fire position and you did not know if he was alive or dead, you were to shoot him.[41] Kendall recalled seeing dozens of enemy in such positions, and a number of shots rang out from Australian rifles but almost 'invariably they were shooting dead people . . . The Viet

Cong are notorious for having live guys among the dead guys and shooting people, so if you are in any doubt, put a round into them and make sure. If he puts his hands up and wants to give up, good, we'll take him prisoner. If you can see he's alive and he's helpless, okay, fine, we'll help, but don't take any chances.'[42]

At 10.20 a.m., D Company, 6 RAR asked that a bulldozer be sent to their former CHQ position to help bury at least 100 Viet Cong. In the end it never arrived as the Suoi Da Bang was still in flood. Just after 11 a.m., a total of 113 enemy bodies and two wounded enemy troops had been located and the information radioed through to Task Force HQ at Nui Dat. In some cases the enemy dead lay in heaps where an assault wave had attacked over the bodies of fallen comrades. As the hours passed the number of enemy dead increased, as did the realisation that D Company, 6 RAR had had a significant victory over a much larger enemy force.[43] One of Major Smith's radio operators, Private Robin 'Pom' Rencher, recalled being very 'surprised at the number of bodies and amazed at the devastation. The first body I saw was a VC whose clothes had been stripped away by [a] blast and whose skull was half missing, and with an arm blown off. It was the first badly mutilated body I had ever seen, but it didn't touch me. I felt nothing for it.'[44]

Close by, Private Tony Stepney recalled seeing the destruction: 'Ah, it was out of this world. We were only 21 years of age and we'd never seen anything like it in our lives . . . and I think that's when the regulars didn't think the nashos were so bad and were good soldiers. It brought us a lot closer together after that.'[45] Hodder recalled years later that his most vivid memory was the smell of the 'human dead. You never forget it – the sweat clawing, that's what you remember for the rest of your life.'[46] APC troop commander Short recalled the devastation as they swept through the area. Some enemy bodies were 'lying as if ready to fight, some torn apart, some just crumpled over. The battlefield itself looked to me like a badly filled rubbish tip. Bits of webbing, rags, black plastic, hats, weapons. I couldn't believe anyone could have lived through it. The sun was streaming through the shattered rubber trees. The latex resin running down the trees as if they were crying. As we set off to follow up the enemy, all I could think of was "At least we didn't get burial detail".'[47]

Coming up behind on foot was Private William Reynolds of A Company, who saw an enemy soldier who had been run over by a carrier the night before. All he could see were 'two ankles and feet sticking out of the mud. Even in that gruesome setting, wry Australian humour forced its way to the fore. Someone remarked, "Look at this keen bugger. He's still trying to dig in."'[48]

30

'The squelch sound was still coming through his handpiece'

The men from D Company, 6 RAR approached the front-line position of 11 Platoon at around 11 a.m. Lieutenant Geoff Kendall recalled that 'we met no opposition. Just walking through on this bright crystal morning, and seeing the absolute carnage that we'd caused the day before – it was a sight you couldn't imagine. An area as big as two or three football fields and several hundred bodies spread all over the place. Also, as we topped the first rise, we saw old "Custard" Meller leaning against a rubber tree, weakly waving his hand. That was pretty marvellous.'[1] Nearby was D Company HQ radio operator Corporal Graham Smith, who recalled: 'We were expecting the worst, but all was relatively quiet. Then, to my utter disbelief, leaning against a rubber tree was Private Barry Meller . . . he waved and I almost burst into tears I was so happy . . . I didn't know Meller at the time but his name was one of those on the list of "missing in action" I had radioed through a few hours earlier.'[2]

Meller had left his hiding place and walked for a short distance. His mates rushed to his side on seeing him, he said, 'You took your fuckin' time, didn't you!' Lieutenant Adrian Roberts of 3 Troop was present and remembered seeing an Australian soldier 'standing up. He was wounded, in a state of shock, had somehow contrived to walk himself to the spot.'[3] As Meller was getting his wounds seen to, Private Robin 'Pom' Rencher walked past and said, 'G'day, Custard.' Meller looked up and replied, 'G'day, you pommy bastard.' As described by Vietnam War veteran and historian Lex McAulay, Rencher walked on with lightened spirits. He had been in Australia for only 15 months and in 6 RAR for five months. Rencher acknowledged Meller's reply as 'the finest acceptance speech I had ever had'.[4]

The advanced battlefield area was covered with trees that had been blown apart by Anzac artillery fire and Viet Cong mortar and RPG fire. White latex covered the shattered trunks. It harked back to the Flanders fields 50 years before, but without the trenches and devastated villages: it was shattered 'woodland'. The dead Viet Cong lay all around and some of the Australians found their equipment, weapons and ammunition in small, hastily dug weapons pits. Lieutenant Colonel Townsend later estimated that at least 50 per cent of the Viet Cong dead had been killed by Anzac artillery fire, although this was difficult to accurately assess as those killed by small-arms fire were often also later hit by the artillery shells. Sergeant Buick recalled that 'there were areas about a hundred metres square with all the trees smashed and broken. Latex sap poured down the trunks. There were branches and crowns blasted from trees with the impact of high-explosive shells and rocket-propelled grenades. The stench of death from the bodies wafted through the air. Weary, but alert, the diggers carefully looked around and under the smashed vegetation expecting to be fired on at any second.'[5]

Lieutenant David Sabben had moved forward from the CHQ position and soon came to the spot where he and his men had tried to provide an open corridor for 11 Platoon. They found their backpacks, which 'appeared to be intact, but we retrieved them carefully, in case of booby traps. Of note was the extraordinary quiet of the area. It was as if we were walking in an empty cathedral and everyone was constrained to talk only when they had to, then only in whispers . . . at one stage I crouched down beside a rubber tree, facing a wheeled . . . machine-gun, its crew lying dead beside it. The PR photographer snapped a few photos, the noise of the shutter unnaturally loud in the stillness of the place.'[6] One of these photographs has since become perhaps the most iconic image of the Battle of Long Tan, showing the young lieutenant kneeling next to a rubber tree with the deadly heavy machine gun in the background, the scene covered in the debris of battle.

Private Terry Burstall of Sabben's 12 Platoon recalled coming across the same enemy machine gun as they swept through the southern parts of the plantation towards 11 Platoon's position during the main contact. He and others in his section began to see increasing numbers of enemy dead and very quickly came across 'almost straight ahead of me, a heavy machinegun on wheels. We went to ground; it was terrifying, with everything very quiet, very still. We stopped for a minute or two and it was about then, while everyone was really looking hard, that I started to focus on bodies. There was a body wherever I looked. Within my vision, which wasn't all that wide, there must have been twenty bodies. I think everyone was stunned.'[7] Private Alan Parr recalled that after dismounting from the carriers they started 'moving through the trees when I heard a shot and was later told someone had shot a badly wounded VC. All through the area where the action took place was a real mess – tree branches, weapons, VC bodies.'[8]

Close by, Buick came across a wounded Vietnamese soldier whose guts were spread over the ground. He took a closer look, only to see that most of the man's head had been blown off, exposing parts of his brain. Buick couldn't believe he was still alive – his arms and legs were twitching, while his face was in the 'dirt with his entrails pierced by sticks. His bloodied body was covered in dirt and leaves, and digested rice was oozing out of the large shrapnel wound in his slashed stomach. Maybe his nerves were causing the

twitching, the poor fucking brave bastard, his heart was still working; a quarter of his brain spilling out of his skull and most of his
guts was lying over the ground. I couldn't handle this . . . I aimed
my rifle and shot him twice through the heart . . . I have never
considered what I did morally right or wrong – it was something I
just had to do.'⁹ A spontaneous act of mercy.

Sabben had a similar experience after moving away from the
enemy heavy machine gun, although this soldier was conscious and
while seriously wounded had a chance of surviving his wounds:

> We heard a shallow whimper, as if a small cat was meowing.
> We approached carefully and found a wounded VC
> under . . . foliage. We covered him with our rifles and removed
> the branches, but he was not dangerous any more. He had a
> hideous wound that had opened up his entire abdomen. His
> gut was plainly visible, looking like plastic in the dappled
> sunlight. Even as we looked, we could see maggots moving
> around his intestines. He put two fingers to his mouth in the
> international appeal for a cigarette and someone obliged. We
> called the Doc forward, and he administered a painkiller, but
> the guy had already passed the pain threshold. I didn't know if
> he could survive, but I called for a stretcher and we moved on.¹⁰

All through the battle the night before, Australians recalled how
brave Vietnamese soldiers would dart out and collect their wounded,
dragging them away even as the Anzac shells exploded all around
them. By the time the Australians re-entered the battlefield the next
day, the Viet Cong had done a pretty good job of collecting their
wounded comrades.

Up front, Captain Bryan Wickens came to a halt and saw all
around a mass of enemy dead. He noticed a few Australians in
prone position, ready to open covering fire should the Viet Cong
conduct an attack, and asked one of them if he had seen 'any sign

of movement on the left flank?' No answer, so he asked again. Silence. He walked up to the line of dispersed men and found that the 'platoon I thought were protecting me were all dead. I thought, "Crikey, where am I?" and looked around. Everybody else was way back!' Many years later he recalled that 'every soldier was still in a firing position. They'd stuck to their guns, they really had. It was the bravest thing I'd ever seen, and I've been in seven theatres of war.'[11] Indeed, this ex-British Army soldier later claimed that the experience of seeing these brave men compelled him to change his nationality to Australian.[12]

It was not long before Buick came up; he had managed to keep things together until then, but was staggered and upset to see his men face down still holding their rifles, killed while firing their weapons. 'Private Vic Grice,' he recalled, 'was sitting with a grin on his face and looked so peaceful. The radio on his back was still working. This showed that the VC had not been in the platoon area. The rain had washed the battlefield clean but the bodies were beginning to swell and that sweet sickly pungent smell of rotting human flesh permeated . . . the still morning air.'[13]

The APCs moved forward and cut off their engines. Lieutenant Ian Savage of 3 Troop moved up on foot towards Lieutenant Gordon Sharp's last position. He recalled it was an 'eerie situation, because all the dead were lying there in firing positions, and they looked as if they were alive except for the pools of blood underneath them. I remember Gordon Sharp, shot running from cover to cover. His radio operator [Grice] had been shot in the chest, was sitting upright, and the squelch sound was still coming through his handpiece. This upset everybody.'[14]

Rencher so far had seen it all – enemy bodies blown apart, trampled into pulp by the carriers – but had remained unmoved: 'I came to the 11 Platoon position. My mates lying in an arc, facing outwards, with rifles still in the shoulder as if they were frozen in a drill and it only needed a touch to bring them back to life again.

They hadn't been touched by arty [artillery], thank goodness, and the rain washed off any blood. They looked very peaceful and dignified, dying in place, doing their duty. And that's when the tears started. I don't suppose anyone was dry-eyed. I know I wasn't.' He came across his dead officer, 'the young, fun-loving National Service commander, not the most brilliant soldier in the world, but one of the nicest and most well-liked people in the company'.[15] Parr recalled that 'the most haunting part of all to see was the line of 11 Platoon soldiers, each beside a rubber tree, all facing in the same direction. It looked as though they were just resting there . . . it's something that no one can be prepared for; you're going on with your life and theirs had just finished at 21 years of age.'[16]

However, one soldier from 6 Section was found to be alive: Private Jim Richmond, who had been shot twice through the chest. Buick recalled that among the 'carnage there was one joyous moment for me. I heard a voice calling my name. It was Jim Richmond, a member of 6 Section, the section that had been on our left flank. Jim and John Robbins were the only two survivors from that section.'[17] Buick dashed over towards his wounded soldier, calling for a medic and assistance. The wounded private recalled earlier hearing the APCs coming towards him and some voices he didn't recognise. They came 'closer so I yelled out. I heard Sergeant Buick's voice so I just put [my] hand up and yelled out to him and that's when they found me.' He told them of the live grenade to his front. On seeing Buick he vividly recalled thinking he's not a 'good-looking bloke, Bob, but I nearly could have kissed him that day! . . . They patched me up on the field there and then and called in the armoured personnel carrier. They put me in the back . . . and then they got me out to a landing zone so that the American helicopter would take me back to 36 Evac Hospital in Vung Tau.'[18]

Radio operator Graham Smith was elated on hearing that Richmond had been found alive, but then to 'see the blokes from 11 Platoon, most of whom were still in their firing positions – one bloke even had his rifle still supported on his hand and shoulder and in fact when they took the rifle from him it discharged. Most of those blokes were shot through the head or chest and they died facing the enemy.'[19] Private Allen May of 11 Platoon recalled that there were yells all over the place that they had found Richmond alive although he had a serious shrapnel wound to his chest.

The group May was with had the job of picking up the Australian dead. He remembered helping wrap up Private Doug Salveron, who was a good friend of his, and it making him pretty bitter.[20] He was not the only one feeling bitter. Private Terry Burstall recalled coming across a wounded Viet Cong propped up against a tree; he was in his late teens. The wounded soldier was holding in 'his stomach with both hands and he indicated to me he wanted a drink. When I pulled his hands from his groin his bowels started to roll out, so I let his hands go and he pushed his bowels back in and held them with the tail of his shirt. I gave him a bottle of water, but it wasn't because I felt sorry for him. I knew water was bad for gut wounds so I let him drink as much as he liked.'[21]

Earlier, Sergeant Jim Myles of A Company and his men had been searching the area where the dirt road ran through the middle of the rubber plantation, just north of the 11 Platoon site. He recalled seeing a mass of dead enemy troops lying everywhere. Most had been killed by artillery, as indicated by the utter carnage and body parts strewn all over the place. Myles and his men moved up through the main battle site in formation and came to where the casualties from D Company were located. He recalled a whole line lying there, all facing towards the enemy, most having taken cover next to a rubber tree.[22] Private Peter Bennett, also of A Company, recalled seeing the Australian dead lying on their stomachs in prone position with their weapons at the ready, their heads along their rifles. He also remembered someone trying to remove Sharp's weapon, but that his finger was on the trigger and it went off.'[23] Private Brian Reilly remembered the incident and the burst of fire being heard all around, with many men dropping down ready to return fire before they realised it was a false alarm.

Private Trevor Atkinson of A Company later approached the scene of 11 Platoon's battle and stood there transfixed: 'I can still see those 11 Platoon soldiers lying in a straight row, their weapons at the ready . . . After a while, a Delta Company officer came up and asked me what the hell I was doing. I could see he was in shock so I just quietly moved away.'[24] Another from A Company, Private David Hede, remembered 'recognising my old friend Warren Mitchell. I had spoken to him only a few days before . . . I could do nothing for him. I guess I just stood there looking at him. Sergeant Myles came over and gave me a blast. Told me to move on. I remember thinking what a prick he was but, on reflection, I guess he was just trying to hold things together.'[25]

Meanwhile, Captain Alan Hutchinson, FOO for D Company, 5 RAR, who thought he had conducted his last operation and was to fly home to Australia the next day, was in the plantation and recalled: 'I must confess that I was less than impressed . . . you become a little superstitious at doing another operation when you thought you had completed your last . . . When we arrived at the battlefield we found utter devastation. Every rubber tree, or so it seemed, had been hit by artillery and there were bodies everywhere. We even found Private "Custard" Meller . . . The VC thought Meller was dead and one had tried to remove his boots in the middle of the night but ran off when Custard cursed him.'[26]

By now, Private John Heslewood was approaching the right flank where he and his mates had fought back the Viet Cong human waves. It was there that he found his friend Private Kenny Gant: 'he was a fair way, probably about 50 metres, [to the right] from where

I was positioned'.[27] However, the fact that two of their mates who had been given up for dead had been found alive helped to lift the spirits of the men. Meller and Richmond were quickly evacuated to hospital, where they recovered from their wounds. A total of 13 dead Australians were retrieved on the battlefield, which meant that all the missing Australians had been accounted for.[28]

Burstall recalled at about this time coming across Heslewood and asking him if he was all right. He replied, 'OK, but bloody hungry.' Burstall hurried to his pack and soon had a 'tin of meat, some dog biscuits and a brew [on] for him. He was all right, but definitely shocked. I went over to Peter Dettman and Stan Hodder [of his platoon] to have a smoke and a bloody photographer came around snapping pictures. I don't know where he came from but there were all sorts of types in the area by that stage. We just carried on like zombies for the rest of the day, checking gear and bodies.'[29]

Indeed, General William Westmoreland, with a large number of staff, journalists and photographers, had arrived on the scene. Private Bill Doolan of 10 Platoon was with some of his mates digging graves for the dead Viet Cong when the general walked up and said, 'You've done a good job, fellows, but this is the dirty part.' Doolan's reply made newspaper headlines: 'She'll be right, mate. We can handle it.'[30] Others were more edgy and increasingly upset that the battlefield and their casualties had become a scene of voyeurism for 'every man and his dog'. Heslewood recalled (and he certainly was far from alone in his assessment):

All the generals and the photographers and a lot of them were getting around the area. They were getting around in their nice starched greens and pointing a rifle at a dead body and their mates were taking photos for them. They would come up and talk to you and a few of the boys told them to get out. They didn't want to talk to them. Didn't want to talk about

what happened. That upset the blokes more than anything
else. All these people from Saigon and Vung Tau coming out.
They came out to the battle scene so they could report to
their superiors and that sort of stuff . . . to be part of it. The
brigadier [Jackson] came to have a look around to say he had
been there. But they brought a lot of hangers-on with them.
There were hundreds of weapons and other equipment and at
that stage we had it all bundled up in this big area and they
were all coming up and picking up weapons, cocking them
and playing with them and this sort of stuff. We were sitting
around having a smoke at this stage and saying 'Have a look
at those posers.'[31]

Indeed, Buick became increasingly upset with some of the recently
arrived high-ranking staff, who were intruding on his men's raw
emotions less than 24 hours after the battle. He was understandably reaching boiling point as these individuals walked around
the dead of 11 Platoon taking photographs and making thought-
less remarks, and ended up punching a major who made what he
considered undignified and unwarranted remarks about the dead:
'I cannot remember his words today but at the time his words caused
me to explode in anger. Had it not been for RSM, WO 1 George
Chinn, I would have been in deep trouble.' Buick was also close
to shooting a 'pommy' journalist who would not leave him alone.
The last thing 'we needed', he recalled, 'were the wankers from the
base areas, be they officers or news journalists, coming for a sticky-
beak, to write a story, commenting on what they saw without any
apparent empathy or compassion'.[32] At this point, Sergeant Major
Jack Kirby ordered Buick to move out of the immediate area and
search for Viet Cong dead, giving him a chance to cool off. Buick
collected Private Dettman, the machine gunner from 12 Platoon,
and they headed south-east from 11 Platoon's position, Dettman carrying his heavy machine gun 'should an enemy lying doggo decide

to have a go'.[33] Shortly afterwards, the journalist was still being an insensitive bastard to all and Kirby had had enough; he hung him up in a rubber tree by the collar of his shirt and left him there, to the relief of all around.[34]

Meanwhile, the recently arrived 6 RAR, D Company chaplain, Les Thompson, was distraught at seeing the dead from both sides: 'Dead bodies everywhere. As you jumped off the chopper, they were there. There was a lot of activity. The guys from D Company were worn out, they were pretty edgy, they were sweaty-dirty, they had looks on their faces which showed quite clearly that they'd been through a horrendous ordeal and were still toey.' As he walked among the dead enemy troops he imagined their families and could see them receiving the letter: 'at the same time I could see our families receiving the letter about our men. And they seemed to be together, there didn't seem to be distinction then of an enemy, and of us and them, it just seemed to be "us" in this tragedy. It was a difficult situation. I remember one burial . . . I went and stood there, and I wanted to do something, I wanted to pray for the fellow and his family, and I most certainly did.'[35]

New Zealand captain Morrie Stanley and two of his men were within the battlefield area. He had no feelings when viewing the destruction that the artillery had brought to bear against the enemy – he just felt tired. He noticed how the infantrymen were collecting and burying the human wreckage all around. They silently cleared the area of enemy weapons and equipment. Kirby came up to him and asked if he had any objection to his two men helping recover the Australian dead.[36]

Corporal Robin Jones of B Company was allocated to a burial detail and recalled burying about 80 bodies that afternoon and during the early hours of the next day. They didn't get much of a grave, as the hole was shallow. Usually a shell hole was used and the body rolled in and a bit of dirt thrown on top. Most of the men he worked with managed to keep up a fairly 'humorous attitude throughout the time, which was just as well under the circumstances. I remember thinking that at least the poor bastards were getting buried, and I tried to maintain some dignity. I noticed a few blokes I was with crossing themselves as they worked at shovelling dirt on to the bodies.'[37]

Private Robin 'Pom' Rencher made his way back to CHQ's last-stand position and had a 'heart-stopping' moment when he came across the rubber tree he had called home for a few hours, 'to find, not far away, a tripod-mounted 57mm RCL, loaded and cocked, pointed right at the CHQ position, the VC dead all around it'.[38] Somewhere nearby, privates Peter Doyle, Harry Esler and others from D Company, 10 Platoon were burying some enemy dead when they turned one over and beneath him they found two pearl-handled Colt .45 pistols. 'Look at this,' said one of the Australians. 'This would be a good souvenir to take home.' From behind came the voice of Major Smith. 'Aren't they beautiful?' said the officer. The soldier reminded the major that he had seen them first, but Smith pointed to his badges and said, 'They're mine' – privileges of rank.[39] Smith kept one of the pistols, which turned out not to be a Colt .45 but rather a Russian-made Tokarev.[40]

Meanwhile, Savage took two of his carriers, commanded by Corporal John Carter and Corporal Paul Fottrill, back to where they had broken through the Vietnamese heavy-weapons company to the south of D Company's CHQ – also where, the night before, Carter had conducted his own personal war against the enemy while standing on top of his APC.[41] They searched the area and recovered a Viet Cong prisoner who had been wounded in the leg. He'd been hiding in long grass and only stood up when he was about to be run over by one of the carriers. Later, Sergeant Frank Alcorta took charge of the prisoner, who was a 'terrified young fellow of about 17, who'd had the fight knocked out of him altogether. In fact, about the only thing he wanted to do was crouch and kiss my feet.'[42] The troop headed south to sweep the area, but one of the carriers overturned when it accidentally drove into an old trench; Savage and his troop spent the rest of the day trying to upright it.[43]

The decision by Major Harry Smith to send his veterans back into the plantation had originally upset many men from his company, but, as later stated by Private John Heslewood of 11 Platoon, being sent into the battlefield turned out to be the 'best thing we could've done, because they let Eleven Platoon find our own dead. And it was sort of a closing. You picked up your own mates, rather than hearing that somebody else had found so-and-so. Plus, we knew where they were, so we just sort of wrapped them up and put them in APCs to take them back to the heli-base.'[44] Graham Smith remembered vividly how their dead were eventually collected and wrapped in their groundsheets: 'straight out in a row they were loaded into a couple of armoured personnel carriers . . . and taken back to Nui Dat and that was a pretty terrible sight'.[45] Private Noel Grimes sadly remembered 'putting our guys into body bags and loading them into the APCs', where they were driven to the western edge of the plantation and later flown out by helicopter.[46]

31

'The Claw'

Not long after midday, D Company, 5 RAR reported discovering a large bunker complex just south of the main battlefield area. Soon Lieutenant Colonel Townsend made an appearance.

The bunker was around 500 metres south-east of 11 Platoon's forward position and was set out in concentric circles, the outer row holding about 100 pits. In all there were about 200 pits, each one about 2 metres long and 1.5 metres deep (not unlike Australian weapons pits) and covered using wood, bamboo, dirt and stone. At each end the pit was left uncovered to allow firing positions. In all, it was estimated that this position could hold around 400 troops – about the size of *D445 VC Battalion*, who were later assessed to have occupied Long Tan village and the southern outer parts of Long Tan Plantation before and during the battle. The design of the system was not for an ambush, but likely for a rest and defensive position. Three Viet Cong bodies were found, along with webbing equipment, food, two machine guns, ammunition and hand grenades – all suggesting a hurried evacuation of the position. Not long after this, another similar but smaller complex consisting of around 100 pits was found to the east of the main battlefield;

it was assessed to be a fallback defensive position.[1]

As the first bunker system was discovered, one of the main escape routes used by the Viet Cong was found, running due east from the battle area. Narrow, at just 1 metre across, the amount of traffic had been sufficient to gouge out about 30 centimetres, making it a shallow trench. Bloodstains and muddy handprints were seen on tree trunks where wounded soldiers had staggered along, while numerous shallow fresh graves, discarded equipment, used bandages and parts of weapons indicated the hurried nature of the withdrawal. The quantity of lost enemy equipment was significant as a result of the number of Viet Cong withdrawing during the night, in the rain, with a command system in tatters. Caches of cooking oil, kerosene, rice and fish heads were also found.[2] Corporal Peter Short recalled seeing fresh blood trails against tree trunks and bushes – he reckoned that 'you could smell them'.[3]

On being informed of the discovery of the track, Townsend immediately radioed Brigadier Jackson for permission to follow up on the retreating enemy force. With his battalion, carriers and a supporting company from 5 RAR, Townsend assessed that he had sufficient strength to conduct such an operation – and all on the ground within the plantation seemed to want to push on and finish the job. However, Jackson refused, only allowing him to push on down the track another 1000 metres: beyond that, he would be out of artillery range. Nor would Jackson sanction moving his batteries forward to increase Townsend's operational area.

Jackson was still concerned about the safety of the Task Force base at Nui Dat and had yet to assess that Major Smith and D Company had inflicted serious casualties against a superior enemy force, resulting in a significant victory. Major Alex Piper recalled at the time that no one at the Task Force base 'was in the frame of mind to go charging off into the jungle chasing the enemy when we thought we'd been done'.[4] While some at the time criticised Jackson for his 'cautious' approach, Townsend later conceded, when writing his after-action report and discussing the situation many years later, that Jackson had been correct. Considering the risks of following up a strong enemy force (whose strength at this point was still unknown) and considering the state and strength of his own force, it would have been folly to conduct such an operation. Townsend concluded that it would have been 'unwise to have thrown caution to the wind . . . despite the temptation'.[5]

While Townsend's force on paper looked pretty strong, the troops were exhausted. D Company was still suffering from its ordeal and was represented by two battered platoons; A Company had been thrown into the battle after having just completed a three-day patrol; B Company had a strength of just 32 men, as those on R&R were not scheduled to return until 4 p.m. the next day, and essentially B Company represented a composite platoon; and the APCs were vulnerable to ambush from RPG and recoilless-rifle teams. The only 'fresh' companies at Townsend's disposal were C Company of 6 RAR and D Company of 5 RAR.

Corporal Robin Jones of B Company was part of the element that moved down the newly discovered escape route for about 1000 metres. The track had obviously been used by the enemy to withdraw from the battle. As they advanced, they came across about eight fresh graves and signs of a rapid withdrawal. They continued following the track, which took them in a northerly direction to the western arm of Suoi Mon River. Jones had been ordered to go no further and turned back and headed back to the battle site. Sergeant Jim Myles of A Company was also sent forward, to investigate one of the withdrawal tracks to the east. It was apparent that a very large enemy force had moved off and had subsequently broken into smaller groups, making it extremely difficult for Myles to follow up. He and his men followed the track to Suoi Mon River, where it swung north. Like Jones, he was to go no further and returned to the main battlefield area.[6]

By now it was mid-afternoon and Corporal Rod Armstrong,

also from A Company, was keen for a shave, but his gear had been left back at Nui Dat and they had only brought out their basic webbing. So he searched a number of Viet Cong packs in search of a razor blade. He found 'a couple of razor blades (French – you could tell by the wrapping), and it was just my luck: they were blunt. I wanted a drink, as our resupply had not come, so I opened up one of their bottles, and it had grass in it. I opened another one, and it had grass in it too. I never found out why they had grass in them.'[7]

Likely close by was Private Bernie Wesiak of Armstrong's company, who was burying an enemy soldier. 'A Kiwi soldier [one of Captain Morrie Stanley's men] and myself were ordered to dig a grave and bury a VC body we had found. After we dug the grave we found it was too short. I was reaching for the shovel to lengthen the grave when the Kiwi soldier said, "Don't bother." He then jumped on the legs until they fitted. I shuddered but carried on with the burial because I didn't want to display any weakness in front of the Kiwi.'[8] Private Alan Parr recalled seeing something similar that made him sick to his stomach. An Australian had just finished burying a body in a shallow grave but one of the legs was 'sticking up from the knee, so he was hacking at it with a machete to get it in the grave'.[9]

Back on the main battlefield site, Private Bill Akell and others of D Company, 6 RAR were in the midst of the slaughter burying the dead. The signaller recalled that 'you lift them, and you've got the brains pouring out the back of the head . . . I mean, it was grim stuff, it really was.'[10] He also recalled that the graves were extremely shallow as all the Australians had to work with were their entrenching tools, 'so there wasn't six-foot graves, they were only very shallow, but at least we buried the dead that were there . . . Artillery does a terrible thing to the human body and quite honestly there were bits and pieces of bodies all over the place. And even today, I still think about picking up the odd arm and throwing it into the hole . . . There was this, and I'll never forget it, what I would call a young kid – he probably looked about 15 or 16. He was a Viet Cong, and there was only half of him – the bottom half was missing from just below the ribs down – and he was just lying there, and I'll never forget that image until the day I die.'[11]

Parr recalled how, because of the torrential downpour of the night before, 'everything in the area was so clean. One VC body that has always stuck in my mind was just lying there, face down, clean black hair . . . with a triangle piece missing from the back of his skull.'[12] Private Tony Stepney of 10 Platoon recalled that 'there were bodies everywhere, bits and pieces everywhere. It was gory. We were trying to dig holes to bury them, but it just wasn't possible . . . it was horrendous, horrendous.'[13] Private Noel Grimes of 12 Platoon recalled that 'with all of the artillery it was literally a bloody mess, with bodies and body parts and in that heat – because it always hot over there, it's either dry or wet – it was so wet and humid overnight . . . the bodies were not good . . . The burial of the Vietnamese was gruesome. Fortunately we had shell holes from the artillery and that's how we buried them . . . we'd drag four or five into one hole and try and cover them up . . . I could have done without it.'[14] Things were no better for Corporal Laurie Drinkwater of Grimes' section. It was his birthday, and as he dug one of his mates yelled out for all to hear: 'Happy birthday, Drinkie!'[15]

The exhausted men, especially of D Company, 6 RAR, had to continue to work among the mass of dead and now-stinking enemy bodies. Not only this, but they were also very much aware that they could be attacked at any minute. More than once a shot rang out as an enemy soldier was seen behind a tree with his weapon aimed at the advancing Australians. When the enemy soldier was approached, it became clear he had been dead for many hours – but understandably no one was taking any chances. Had the advance 'been from a different direction and not straight back into the teeth of the previous day's attacking enemy, the unnerving phenomenon would not have been so marked.'[16]

As the mopping-up continued, Major Smith at one point saw two very much alive and armed Viet Cong less than 30 metres away from his front-line troops – but before they could fire, they were killed. Another Viet Cong was later found and shot, but whether this was an act of mercy or the result of a perceived threat remains unknown. Major Paul Greenhalgh, commanding D Company, 5 RAR, queried the incident on the radio and Townsend's operator confirmed it was the killing of a hopelessly wounded man; he recorded it as such in the signal log.[17] In all, three wounded Viet Cong were captured and given emergency medical treatment before being evacuated. One of them was found by Sergeant Bob Buick and Private Peter Dettman, who were searching for bodies. They came across a terrified teenager who had been shot in the groin. Dettman placed the muzzle of his M60 on the soldier's forehead and called for a medic; one soon made an appearance. A bottle of iodine was poured over the boy's wound and maggots were picked from it before it was dressed – Buick never saw the boy again and wonders to this day if he is still alive.[18]

Soon after this Buick and Dettman had had enough of working among the mangled bodies and headed back towards the position of 11 Platoon's stand. Buick walked up close to where he had been positioned during the height of the battle fought less than 24 hours before and saw an Australian near the Viet Cong wheeled heavy machine gun. He stopped and watched as the soldier pushed a 'piece of bone, a little bigger than a fifty-cent piece, back into the skull of the dead Viet Cong. The machine gunner had been killed – shot through the front of the head. The exiting round had caused a wound at the back of the skull. Every time he pushed the piece of bone back into the skull it fell out again and hung there with a flap of skin acting like a hinge. After a few minutes I left, but the digger was still there ten minutes later.'[19]

Enemy bodies were found up to 500 metres south-east in front of 11 Platoon's final position. By mid-afternoon the body count had increased to 168 and by 4.15 p.m. it was 180, with evidence that other dead and wounded had been dragged away. On most occasions the Viet Cong had been able to retrieve weapons and equipment, but clearly they had not bothered to do so during or immediately after the battle in some areas of the plantation, as vast numbers of precious weapons were recovered. They included the heavy wheeled machine gun along with a 60mm mortar, two recoilless rifles, four rocket launchers, 33 AK-47 assault rifles, assorted US carbines and other types of rifles, thousands of rounds of ammunition, 300 grenades, 100 mortar bombs and several rockets.[20]

Private Peter Doyle remembered that 'we'd sit down on a log, or sit out in the dirt, and we'd be having a bit of crap Australian 24-hour ration-pack food, and there'd be a body here, a body there and a bit of body there. We'd just stop for a feed, or boil up some water and make a tea or a coffee or something . . . Because of the humidity and the heat, things go off real quick . . . The first day wasn't too bad, but by the time we got towards the end of it, the whole thing was getting pretty ripe. We were handling bodies with our bare hands. We didn't have gloves. The only water we had was in our water bottles.'[21] These and other soldiers' memories are similar to reminiscences from an Australian battle 50 years before: Lone Pine, Gallipoli, August 1915.

Doyle also recalled that after returning from the day's burial detail, the men 'took all of our clothes off because we were rotten, and we had all of our clothes – which was only a shirt and a pair of pants, and a pair of boots and socks – put in a big heap, covered in dieseline and burned. We had a Vietnamese well, and canvas buckets we used to lower into the well – which was full of frogs and shit anyway – and haul it up into a tree, and that was our glorious shower centre. We had a bit of a scrub-up and a feed.'[22]

By 6.10 p.m. the body count had reached 188 with evidence that more would be found, with a number of drag marks and blood trails being identified. Shallow graves were still being dug and the enemy dead were buried pretty much where they had fallen.[23]

The men settled down for the night, sleeping on the battlefield with around 250 dead bodies strewn around or buried – they slept not worrying too much about it. During the night the corpses stiffened due to rigor mortis and escaping gases flexed muscles and changed the posture of the dead. The next morning the Australians awoke to find that parts of the enemy dead had emerged, arms and legs protruding from the shallow graves. Before too long some joker hung a sign from a protruding arm, calling it 'The Claw'.[24]

32

'They had to face that all over again'

20 August 1966

The Australians arose and set about continuing the grim task of burying the enemy dead. The men of D Company were on 'automatic' and most did not register much of what happened during that third day in the plantation. For most of the day they were assigned to the burial details, while other companies were sent out to sweep the area.

Lieutenant David Sabben recalled that they had to 'go through every identifiable piece of body we could find and see if there was any intelligence on it – paperwork in the pockets, diaries, wallets, everything like that. Anything that was ex-human we had to bury. Anything that was metallic we had to put in one spot – all the ammunition, all the weapons, the magazines.'[1] What particularly upset him and others was coming across wallets, which invariably held photographs of families: 'Mum and Dad and the kids and there were photographs . . . wrapped in plastic against the humidity. There were little letters, books, dried flowers pressed in the pages of a book.'[2]

Private Alan Parr had a similar experience: 'We searched a lot of the VC bodies looking for documents and collecting weapons. I found a wallet on one VC and, when I opened it there were photos of his wife and children . . . a very sobering experience.'[3] Sabben recalled that while photographers were taking pictures of enemy dead and the stockpile of enemy weapons, 'no one turned around and took a picture of a pile of notebooks, diaries, wallets, plastic envelopes of family photographs. No one took that photograph and no one will ever know how pathetic it was to see them sitting there just under a rubber tree, collected lives sitting there waiting to be disposed of. It was terrible.'[4]

While there was some sense of victory over the enemy, the prevailing sense was of 'letdown, this awful dread that we were witnessing,' recalled Sabben. 'Not that we had caused it, because most of it we weren't witnessing people that we had actually shot, we knew that artillery had fallen or someone else in the company had shot them or something. It wasn't a personal guilt but it was just overwhelming dread of just loss. I mean, yes, they were enemy soldiers but by that stage we knew that they were like us.'[5]

Private Peter Doyle of 10 Platoon recalled 'hunting around [and] when we'd find a body, we'd use a toggle rope, six or eight foot [1.8 or 2.4 metres] long. We'd tie it around a leg or an arm and pull them over, just in case they were booby-trapped. We buried about a hundred a day, and we just had little pack shovels. They were going to send a bulldozer in, but the Suoi Da Bang river was flooded, it wasn't even possible. We couldn't do a sterling job; no one was given a six-foot-deep grave. Basically, we dug a shell scrape and buried them the best we could. I found a body, and it was severed through the nipple line. I found the lower part. He looked like he had been cut with a sheet of corrugated iron, like a ripple effect.'[6]

The other companies scoured the battlefield and surrounding region for up to 1500 metres east of the main field of combat, including Long Tan village itself and to the north beyond Nui Dat 2; they too were involved in burying the enemy dead they came across. Major Brian McFarlane recalled how one of his men, Corporal Ray Barnes of C Company, 7 Platoon, was using a toggle rope tied to the ankle of a dead enemy soldier to pull him to a shallow grave and as he did so, Barnes 'saw that the man's brains had spilled out and left a trail over the ground. Corporal Barnes was an experienced soldier and an excellent section commander, but I remember Corporal [Geoff] Jones, my medic, telling me of the horror that Ray felt on this occasion.'[7]

Beyond the immediate battlefield area, the men from these companies found a number of tracks with telephone lines running along their side, drag marks indicating the removal of dead and wounded, and indications that the tracks had recently suffered major and heavy traffic by both oxcart and people on foot.[8] Private Peter Bennett of A Company recalled seeing 'numerous tracks, made when taking most of their dead, but there were quite a number of graves found'.[9]

The men of D Company, 5 RAR swept the northern area of the plantation, moving out of the plantation and coming across a small enemy supply dump containing 27 gallons (123 litres) of kerosene, 21 gallons (95 litres) of cooking oil, 20 pick heads and clothing. They then swung west and found two large, freshly dug weapon pits that had been evacuated in a hurry as a lot of personal gear was there, including wallets, photographs and a pile of documents.[10]

The men of C Company, 6 RAR moved forward through the plantation heading east and came across discarded equipment, ammunition, webbing and clothing. As they continued their advance they came across more tracks and signs of heavy enemy movement. They soon came to a track junction and it became obvious that the bulk of the enemy had used these two tracks to withdraw; one led in a northerly direction, the other in a south-westerly direction. At this junction they found a telephone cable that led back west towards the main battle site. The site was likely a key command post and as they continued to sweep the area a number of body parts were located.[11]

In the afternoon there was a rapid burst of automatic fire, which probably brought many men of D Company out of the malaise that had set in. Private Terry Burstall recalled that 'it was a strange feeling. Everyone in the area of my vision froze and I know I grabbed for my rifle and just stood listening, hardly daring to breathe. The troops all around me stayed quite still except for their hands feeling their weapons.'[12] Burstall was not far from the company commanding officer, Major Harry Smith, who had his signaller with him. Smith grabbed the radio and a few seconds later said very loudly for all to hear, 'OK, no worries, a prisoner tried to escape, and he's now dead.' Burstall said, 'Everyone grinned or laughed with relief and carried on with what they were doing, but the sound of firing had shaken us all.'[13]

Overnight the unburied dead had become hardier to bury as the bodies had become very stiff with rigor mortis and could not readily be pushed into a shell hole and covered; some extra digging had to be done to cover up the remains. As recalled by Burstall, it was mind-numbing work that was carried out automatically and in an off-hand manner. Private Allen May of 11 Platoon recalled seeing one soldier trying to bury a body, but every time he threw dirt on it an arm would keep popping up. After two or three attempts to get it covered, he gave up and pulled out his machete, chopped off the arm and threw it down beside the body, and was finally able to cover it all up.[14]

Sergeant Bob Buick had become seemingly immune to the smell of the dead, having lived side by side with them for almost three days. One of his mates from A Company, 6 RAR, Sergeant Jim 'Snow' Curtis, came across Buick and they sat down on a fallen rubber-tree trunk and shared a cigarette and a mug of coffee. As they sat there, Curtis said, 'There is something dead around here!' Buick thought he was making a bad joke and let out a loud laugh.

Curtis had been away to the east of the main part of the battlefield and had become unaccustomed to the ongoing stench of death and decaying mangled corpses from the 'perfumed garden of rotting bodies', recalled Buick. Earlier Buick and others had cleared the area of any bodies and body parts they could find; even so, there were still many bodies surrounding them that needed to be buried. Buick recalled that he had 'missed the four bodies under the foliage of the tree [where] we sat. The horror on [Curtis's] face must have prompted some smart remark from me because Snow did not stay too long afterwards. He went back to his company muttering, "Buick, you're bloody mad".'[15]

The enemy dead were finally tallied at 245. However, this was a gross underestimate as weeks later patrols would come across decomposing bodies, other areas that had not been searched were found to contain remains from the Anzac barrage of 18–19 August, and other parts of the battlefield had been cleared by the Viet Cong before the Australians reoccupied the plantation during the morning of 19 August. The degree to which the Viet Cong were able to clear the battlefield is attested to by the fact that they left only three wounded behind (one from *D445 VC Battalion* and two from *275 VC Regiment*) to be captured by the Australians.[16] A diary of a senior Vietnamese commander of the battle was later discovered by US troops and it stated that the *5th VC Infantry Division* during the battle for Long Tan had suffered over 500 killed and 1000 wounded, while other captured documents, including some from enemy hospital units, placed the casualties for the battle at over 800 killed and 1800 wounded.[17]

That night, C Company set up a harbour position to the east of the battle site, but had to request a helicopter to evacuate one of their men. It was later learnt that close by there had been a Viet Cong field hospital, likely Company Commander Chin Phuong's medical unit, that until then had not been aware of the closeness of the Australians; the helicopter alerted them and the Viet

Cong were able to clear out undetected. Even from C Company's advanced position, the dead bodies could be smelt and somewhere to the east a number of bugles were heard. Sergeant Neil Rankin of D Company, 6 RAR, located at the main battle site, recalled how the sound of the bugles on the still night air, even given the great distance they were at, was enough to make the hair stand up on the back of his neck.[18] The men of D Company, 5 RAR had set up a harbour position north of the battlefield area and they too smelt the decaying bodies and heard the bugles.

As the men tried to sleep in the graveyard of the main battle site, movement was heard: it was wild dogs and pigs scrimmaging around the shallow graves, attracted by the smell.

Early on 21 August the veterans of D Company, 6 RAR were relieved and sent back to Nui Dat; from there they would head out for two days' R&R at Vung Tau. Not long after they left the plantation, it was the turn of those from D Company, 5 RAR to leave for Nui Dat to rejoin their brother companies of the battalion. Meanwhile, the remainder of 6 RAR, including a now up-to-strength B Company, continued on with Operation Smithfield. These men came across another track that led east between Suoi Mon River and the eastern arm of the Suoi Da Bang. The company moved north from this position and came across a large camp that had only recently been evacuated; it was assessed to have contained around 300 individuals. At about 11.30 a.m. they found what was obviously the main crossing point of the withdrawing enemy force across the eastern branch of the Suoi Da Bang. Several hundred metres further on they discovered a fortified enemy position that had been held by a delaying force to keep back any attempt by the Australians to pursue their retreat. It was assessed that the enemy had only left the night before, leaving behind clothing and equipment.[19]

The main Viet Cong evacuation track leading east through the plantation and the areas in the immediate vicinity were the focus of the operation. The men of A Company, in their sweep further south, found a number of recently evacuated defensive positions, likely constructed to help hinder any Australian advance against the fleeing main force. An additional bunker system of about 40 weapons pits, constructed long before the battle, was also found, but there was evidence it had only recently been evacuated.[20] They found evidence as well of a large force moving towards the eastern tributary of Suoi Mon River – an additional track leading to the river was also gouged deep into the mud and like previous tracks all of the tree trunks were marked with mud and bloody handprints, while used bandages and torn clothing littered the area.[21]

Not far from this bunker system the men from C Company, on their renewed sweep to the east, came across a small enemy camp – likely the field hospital that had been evacuated the night before – with a few huts and 14 fresh graves. Defending this field hospital were a number of weapons pits, topped with corrugated iron that had been covered in earth. McFarlane could see that his men 'were dead tired and I worried once again, as I did constantly, that a moment's inattention might bring disaster to one or more of them. My silent prayers were answered when the rear-link radio operator told me that we were to move to a rendezvous for return to Nui Dat by air . . . C Company's brush with the Battle of Long Tan had ended.'[22]

Meanwhile, an observation helicopter had spotted scattered groups of what appeared to be civilians, some with oxcarts and many carrying bundles, bags and baskets suspected to contain medical supplies, travelling along the road between Long Phuoc and Long Tan. The largest group consisted of around 40 Vietnamese, mostly women. An APC troop with infantry was sent out to investigate, and 24 males of military age were apprehended and held for questioning.[23]

By midday, Lieutenant Colonel Townsend's force of infantry and APCs had completed their searches, and just after 3 p.m. they had concentrated on the edge of the Long Tan rubber plantation, 500 metres north-east of Long Tan village. From there the force withdrew to the Task Force base at Nui Dat, with the infantry in the carriers and others getting a ride via helicopter. Operation Smithfield resulted in the discovery of more graves, food and ammunition caches, trails and small camps, but there was no further contact with the enemy. This operation was followed by US corps-level Operation Toledo (supported by Australian troops), which swept the area but found nothing of significance.[24]

With all of Brigadier Jackson's force now back in base, Operation Smithfield was declared ended at 5 p.m. on 21 August 1966. The total tally of enemy dead left on the battlefield was listed as 245, with three captured. The Australians suffered 17 killed in action, one dying from wounds, and 24 wounded; of these, D Company suffered 17 killed and 19 wounded – around one-third of its total strength. Of the 17 killed in action, 11 were national servicemen.[25]

A few days after the battle, Major Smith made a special visit to RAAF No. 9 Squadron to personally thank the crews of the two helicopters – A2-1020, commanded by Flight Lieutenant Frank Riley, and A2-1022, captained by Flight Lieutenant Cliff Dohle. These men and their crews had supplied the ammunition drops to his men that were so crucial in helping D Company push back the enemy human waves against their final positions in the plantation on 18 August. In a later ceremony at Nui Dat, 6 RAR presented to the squadron one of the AK-47 assault rifles captured during the battle.[26]

Lieutenant Adrian Roberts recalled with pride how, not long afterwards, Major Smith made him and his men honorary members of Delta Company's mess.[27] B Company also had an honorary member in their mess back at Nui Dat. During the burial detail they had come across a decapitated enemy head and took it back to the Task Force base with them. After the ants had picked it clean, they hung it above the door to their 'boozer', which soon became known as 'The Skull Cave'.[28]

As the veterans from D Company, 6 RAR arrived back at Nui Dat in the late morning they were in for 'another whammy', as recalled by Lieutenant David Sabben. The quartermaster staff had gone through the belongings of the dead and wounded who would not be returning to the company, and all of their kit had been 'collected and put into the Q store. So these soldiers, who were still getting over the loss of their mates, came back to their tents and next to them was an empty bunk where their mate used to live. They had to face that all over again.'[29]

Indeed, Sabben had shared a tent with Lieutenant Gordon Sharp and remembered that 'half the tent was now just an empty bed'. He sat and stared at it for some time, coming to grips with the fact that his friend was dead. He could not help but wonder whether some-day soon someone would be sitting there looking at Sabben's own empty bed in the same way.[30] Parr recalled that when he returned to Nui Dat and entered his tent 'all of Paul Large's gear had gone'.[31]

Corporal Kevin Miller also distinctly remembers returning to Nui Dat and realising that 'all of our friends we had shared our tents [with were gone] . . . half the company area was empty. The tents were bare because of the killed and wounded. They weren't there – we'd lost half the company.'[32] Sergeant Neil Rankin, who had originally commanded 11 Platoon, D Company before being transferred to 10 Platoon, stood among the empty tents of his old platoon at Nui Dat and burst into tears.[33]

33

'OK, fellows, see you later'

In Australia the news of the battle hit radios, newspapers and television screens on 19 August, with the casualty figures being released before any of the families had been informed whether their loved ones were safe or had been wounded or killed. They spent an anxious night trying to ascertain what had happened – the army switchboards were immediately jammed by calls from anxious relatives and friends. Private Terry Burstall's mother told him later that 'she was in a terrible state for a while, especially since she had gone through the ordeal once before when her father had been wounded and later died' in World War II.[1]

Suzanne Jewry was the wife of Lance Corporal Jack Jewry, the 21-year-old apprentice electrician from St Marys in NSW. The couple had married three weeks before he left for Vietnam, and while serving there, Jack had been informed that he was going to be a dad. Jack was with 6 Section, 11 Platoon and now lay dead. On being informed of his death, Suzanne miscarried the next day. Jack's family received letters from him just hours after they were told he had been killed in action.[2] His mate, 21-year-old Private Glenn 'Ken' Drabble, a window-blind installer from Zillmere in Brisbane, died with Jack close by. He had written just before the battle to his girl-friend, Beverley Pilkington, asking her to make arrangements for their wedding on his return from his tour. She recalled: 'I should have been so happy, but now this is the saddest day of my life.'[3]

Beryl Gant, the mother of Kenny Gant, the machine gunner of 11 Platoon who had been killed in action, was sitting by a window listening to the radio and reading a book when she noticed a green army car coming down the road. She had not yet been informed that her son was dead.

> I didn't put much to it, you know. I thought, 'Oh no, he's only been away a little while.' But the next thing a knock come to the door and my husband went out and it was one of the army men and the army chaplain . . . I went out, and straightaway I knew that something was wrong and they told me Kenny had been killed. I couldn't get it into my head though. I couldn't believe it. I just said, 'No.' I said, 'It can't be him!' and we didn't get the news until the Saturday morning. He was killed on the Thursday.[4]

It would be another three weeks before the families would get to bury their sons, brothers and fathers.

Corporal John Robbins' first memory after leaving the operating theatre was a Vietnamese individual 'giving me a doll – he gave all the wounded a doll . . . I may have even been in recovery [room]. I was really out of it when this bloke was giving it to me. I really didn't want to talk but he gave us one.' Robbins recalled that after he 'recovered' from his surgery he saw seeing the wounded of the battle lying in bunks around him early the next morning – 19 August.[5] Soon they were all trying to find out from each other what had happened to them: 'How did so-and-so get on? You don't know about his section or whatever – who did you lose? And he doesn't necessarily know so there is a lot of anxiety about who made it and who didn't. What's happened since? Did they come back the next morning? You just don't know. Well, I knew that I was going home. And that was a relief.'[6]

Early that morning, Jean Debelle, the Australian Red Cross worker, was finally able to make her way to US 36 Evac and the wounded Australians. 'As I looked at the rows of casualties in the unnatural quiet,' she recalled, 'the stunned and wounded eyes, as much as the damaged bodies, identified those who had survived the battle in the rubber plantation. There were no friendly smiles, yet I heard no moans or crying. I was mentally prepared for tears from the men. I saw none. Some men avoided meeting my eyes, perhaps scared to reveal their emotions. A soldier might give way to grief in front of his mates, but not in front of an outsider.'[7] She moved from bed to bed, unsure of what to say, and gave each man a gentle touch on the arm, asking if there was anything she could do: 'Would you like me to send a message home? What can I do to help you?'[8]

Robbins and the others weren't informed of those who had been killed until the next day – 20 August. It was also then that he learnt that Private Jim Richmond had been found alive on the battlefield. This was a great relief to him, as he now knew he was not the sole survivor of his section; up until then that had been his belief. Even so, the shock of hearing of the casualties was horrendous and quite a few in the hospital broke up.[9] Private Dennis Spencer recalled that the day after the battle they didn't know who had been killed or wounded. However, the day after that they received a copy of the Brisbane *Courier-Mail*, which had photographs of all the men who had been killed, including 'Dougie Salveron, Kenny Gant, Ken Drabble, Jimmy Houston and all the other guys; I think that really hit home then. There was a lot of quiet sobbing going on in the ward and I remember looking across at John Robbins. John was really taking it hard. He was sitting on the side of his bed with tears streaming down his face, and it was just hitting home to everybody what had happened.'[10]

Meanwhile, Col Joye and Patricia Amphlett (Little Pattie) visited the wounded at the hospital. Both were a little apprehensive about their ability to keep it together in front of the men. Amphlett recalled: 'We were feeling pretty teary and sad and propping each other up. Eventually the door opened and we went inside and, of course, we didn't cry. But much later I did. Just seeing the many wounded and young faces, you know. They all looked like my brother. They all looked so young . . . And they were just baby-faced, brave, terrific Australians. [It was] really something that day, for me. I suppose if there's a turning point – we all have turning points in our lives, you realise later on where you grew up, and I grew up that day. I really did. Big time.'[11] Debelle was there and recalled Joye spending considerable time talking to each wounded man and that the visit 'could not have come at a better time. The happy diversion did much for everyone's morale.'[12]

A few days later, the rest of the men of D Company were on their way to Vung Tau, heading for the hospital to see their wounded mates. Robbins recalled that 'they came and saw all of us in hospital and you could see the look on their faces, because we'd been through a hell of a bloody turn-out really, and you could see that they knew we were going home and they weren't. I guess we were happier than they were.'[13] He felt some guilt as his mates would be stuck in South Vietnam for another nine months – that's if they weren't killed or wounded first.[14] Private Noel Grimes recalled: 'We'd only been there three months when it happened and it was a 12-month stint, and that was our biggest worry. We'd only been here three months and we have to survive another nine.'[15]

The veterans of Long Tan spent a few days trying to unwind at Vung Tau, which was used as a rest centre for Allied units – and allegedly by the Viet Cong. The men from D Company found that they had little in common with those around them and clung together in small groups, alone in the crowded 'resort' area. Some relived the battle, the many near-misses and the loss of friends; others remained silent, likely clutching another can of cold beer. Private Alan Parr recalled he 'got as pissed as a parrot and punched a mate, Max Cameron, in a bar. To this day I don't know why.'[16] Parr and another of his mates Private Neil Bextram thought that two days wasn't enough, so they 'took an extra day and copped an AWOL charge' on their return to Nui Dat, resulting in three weeks' loss of pay and three weeks' corporal punishment, consisting of no free time when they returned from patrol or ambushes; the Task Force always needed plenty of holes to be dug and backfilled.[17]

One incident involving the wounded veterans of D Company 6 RAR was soon doing the rounds, not only at Vung Tau but also back at the Task Force base – as recalled by Sergeant Bob Buick:

The story goes that they had left the hospital in pyjamas and slippers to get on the grog, all bandaged, some on crutches, one in a wheelchair and others pushing a trolley with drip bottles attached. A truck driver, an American, crashed his truck as he looked in amazement at this band of crazy Aussies going on the piss. Some were refused entry to the club because they had no shirts or tops. It did not take long before their mates returned with jackets and they all had a good time. When the doctors and nurses got wind of it there was all hell to pay but no retribution. This was the first time the Yank hospital, the 36th Medical Evacuation Hospital, had had so many Aussie patients at one time. Our Delta Company blokes set the tone for future patients at the 36th Medevac Hospital.[18]

Jean Debelle didn't hear about the booze-up until the next day; she recalled that 'the hubbub had subsided, but the hospital staff was still laughing'.[19] One American nurse, Polly Parrott, later admitted: 'We tolerated shenanigans from the Aussies that none of our men ever would be allowed to get away with. That "escape" by rule breaking, living by their own code, was one of the things that made the Aussies so attractive to us.'[20]

The South Vietnamese government recognised that the battle was a major victory over the Viet Cong and planned to honour the Australians of D Company, 6 RAR. The commander of the South Vietnam Armed Forces and chief of state, General Nguyen Van Thieu, arrived at Nui Dat to award them the South Vietnam Cross of Gallantry, but with the ceremony about to begin, an urgent message arrived from some pen-pusher's desk in Canberra that foreign awards were not to be recognised because they did not have Her Majesty Queen Elizabeth's approval – only gifts could be presented. The same applied to unit citations. Although they accepted the decree from Canberra, the South Vietnamese government persisted. The ceremony was put on hold for an hour while General Nguyen's staff went in search of something to present. In the end the president presented to the Australian officers lacquered wooden cigar boxes; the NCOs were presented with cigarette boxes and the privates received dolls in Vietnamese national dress.[21]

The US would also recognise the brave actions performed by the men of Major Smith's company. A United States Presidential Unit Citation – the second-highest military award for gallantry that can be awarded – was presented to the men of D Company, 6 RAR. Many years later Smith recalled that it was truly embarrassing to think that the Americans and South Vietnamese rewarded them but the Australian government 'put us down'.[22]

Indeed the Australian government and military authorities showed an appalling lack of respect for those who had fought at Long Tan. At the time a quota system was used in the allocation of military awards. New Zealand captain Maurice 'Morrie' Stanley was awarded the Order of the British Empire, but while Major Smith was recommended for the Distinguished Service Order (DSO), a superior 'downgraded' it to Military Cross. Company sergeant major Jack Kirby received the Distinguished Conduct Medal (DCM), as did Corporal John Carter of 3 Troop. Both Sergeant Bob Buick and Private Ron Eglinton received the Military Medal (MM). Smith had recommended Lieutenant David Sabben and Lieutenant Geoff Kendall for the Military Cross (MC), but unbelievably because the quota of MCs had been reached – awarded earlier to others for excellence in non-combat duties – these recommendations were denied and each received a Mentioned in Dispatches (MiD). Also to receive MiDs were Lieutenant Adrian Roberts of 3 Troop, Company Sergeant Major Jack Roughley, Corporal Phil Dobson, Corporal William Moore and Private William Akell – Smith had recommended that Akell and Moore receive the MM.

Smith recommended a number of others for awards, including the wounded Sergeant Paddy Todd, and privates Max Wales, Paul Large and Glenn Drabble, all killed. However, he was forced to withdraw his recommendations as on presenting his list to Lieutenant Colonel Townsend his CO stated: 'You have far too many for the battalion quota. What if we have another big battle next month?'[23] Again that bloody quota system! Other soldiers put forward by Smith for MiDs but struck off by others further up the line were Bill Roche, Geoff Peters, Ian Campbell, Barry Magnussen, Allen May, Noel Grimes, Neil Bextram and Gordon Sharp.[24] At the same time, cooks and postal-service officers working in Vung Tau were being nominated and 'awarded' MiDs.[25] Lieutenant Gordon Sharp – who had led his men from the front and died fighting with his platoon, refusing to withdraw as it would mean leaving his wounded behind – was recommended for an MiD but received nothing because at the time army regulations stated that those killed in action could be nominated only for a posthumous Victoria

Cross or MiD (this is no longer the case). The most distinguished awards were allocated to the Task Force commander, Brigadier David Jackson, and commander of 6 RAR, Lieutenant Colonel Colin Townsend, who both received the DSO – apparently for showing up. This is the same award that was denied to Major Harry Smith, who gallantly led his company throughout the Battle of Long Tan.

In 2008 an Australian parliamentary 'review' of the awards provided to the Long Tan veterans was conducted. Major Smith's award was deservedly upgraded to Australia's Star of Gallantry (previously the DSO) – second only to the Victoria Cross – while lieutenants Kendall and Sabben had their original recommendations for the MC upheld and were awarded the Medal of Gallantry, its present-day equivalent. In 2009 another inquiry was held that concluded that no other awards or upgrades should be considered, the sole exception being Flight Lieutenant Cliff Dohle, who was deservedly awarded the Distinguished Service Medal.[26] However, there has still been no justice for Lieutenant Gordon Sharp and many others of D Company. The awards 'system' applied by the Australian government and military to the veterans of Long Tan then and today remains nothing short of disgraceful. Harry Smith continues to fight for the deserved official recognition of his men of D Company, 6 RAR.

Vietnam's communist leadership maintained even after the war that they had won a great victory against the Australians during the Battle of Long Tan. Indeed the official history of Dong Nai Province, which includes Phuoc Tuy, states that the communist forces 'eliminated 500 Australians and destroyed 21 tanks' even though Australian tanks would not be present in Vietnam until 1967.[27] Also, there is no mention of Vietnamese casualties – they apparently suffered none. It has only been very recently that cracks have appeared in the official government mantra, with some hesitant suggestions that the battle resulted in a major defeat of Vietnamese forces. Even so, intelligence officer Captain Bryan Wickens learnt from captured Viet Cong documents that the VC held some grudging respect for Australians as they 'buried our dead – they are a true enemy'. That is, the Australians didn't abuse the Viet Cong dead like many Americans, who would cut off hands or ears or bury them with an ace-of-spades card sticking up.[28]

The war went on. Private Noel Grimes had shared a four-man tent but now it housed three with the death of Private Paul Large. He said: 'that empty bed space has always stuck in my mind, there were still three there but the fourth one has gone . . . some of the others, those from 11 Platoon, there was probably two or three from the one tent that wasn't there anymore – it would have been a lot harder for them . . . That sticks in my mind pretty much.'[29]

It wasn't long before the empty bunks of D Company were filled with new arrivals. Private Terry Burstall recalled that when they returned from Vung Tau, soldiers were transferred from one platoon to another and reinforcements quickly arrived.[30] Private Peter Doyle recalled that the new blokes were treated like outsiders, which with hindsight he regretted: 'I could not even tell you the name of one reinforcement. They came there not by choice; they came to replace dead or wounded blokes. I didn't care who they were. I wasn't interested in making friends with them. I didn't shun them, but I wasn't interested in knowing about them. And I think that was pretty universal. So it must've been hard for reinforcements. I couldn't tell you the name of the bloke who took Gordon Sharp's place.'[31]

Regimental signaller Corporal Graham Smith recalled that after their leave in Vung Tau 'that was that; there was no counselling or anything else. We had taken on quite a few reinforcements just before Long Tan and after Long Tan we took on quite a few more. But among the soldiers there was never any debriefing of any nature

that I can recall, and we just got on with the war and really Long
Tan didn't become a big thing until the 20th anniversary.'[32]

Indeed, the army at the time was keen to play down the action
and keep it low-key among the troops of 6 RAR. It was thought
that elevating one company to 'hero' status would lead to ill feeling among the other companies. Indeed, throughout the remainder
of the tour many units took a dig at the Long Tan veterans, with
comments such as 'D Company! That mob of bastards that think
they did something special' and similar jibes.[33]

Private Stan Hodder recalled that there was some talk about
the whole company being sent back to Australia a week or two
after the battle, but the idea was quickly dropped. He, like many
others, recalled that 'knowing what they know now, they probably
should have sent someone out because all we had was a church
service two or three days after we came back, and to make matters
worse, our 2IC arranged to have a [US] jet break the sound barrier over us the day we got back, and if you've ever heard someone
break the sound barrier, mate, it scared the shit out of everyone.
I think that's when my nerves really went . . . They broke it right
over our company area – it was supposed to be a welcome-home
victory thing . . . They didn't tell anyone and it scared the shit out
of me. It was like a hydrogen bomb going off.'[34]

Burstall recalled with appreciation how Sergeant Major 'Big Jack'
Kirby came into their tent one afternoon and sat down and asked
his men how they were. Each provided a similar answer along the
lines of 'No worries'. Burstall can still remember Kirby just sitting
there and 'looking at us all for about a minute and then he got up
quickly and said, "Yeah, OK, fellows, see you later", and headed
up the muddy path between the tents.'[35]

About six months later, on 6 February 1967, Kirby and the men
from D Company were on patrol when they made contact with the

enemy. The artillery was called in and 12 rounds were fired to help range in the artillery against the enemy position. Graham Smith, the regimental signaller, was present and remembers the incident vividly as one of the most traumatic periods of his time during the Vietnam War:

We had been patrolling in a company formation . . . with 10 [Platoon], 11 [Platoon] and an anti-tank [platoon] and we were in single-file formation on this patrol, with 10 Platoon out in front, followed up by company headquarters, anti-tank and I think 11 [Platoon]. The report came from the rear that we had enemy following us so we went to ground, pretty much each side of the track we were patrolling, and artillery was called for; they fired 12 rounds. They went over our heads and beyond and then a correction was made and I can remember the correction – it was add 200 – but when they started coming I thought, 'Fuck, these are going to land close' and the first one landed 15 metres away from me.

At that stage I was screaming 'Stop! Stop! Stop!' into my handset, which was heard in the forward patrol post but . . . they still continued to come. Anyway the company headquarters area was where the first shell impacted – surrounded in dust and smoke and so on, but as it cleared I could see Jack Kirby, he was sitting only about 5 to 6 feet from me . . . I was standing up by this time – he was clutching his chest and I could see blood coming from between his fingers and from his mouth and he just said, 'I'm hit', and all I can remember doing was shaking my head and my fellow signaller who was beside me, Robin 'Pom' Rencher, he was also hit in the neck, so I had his radio. The company commander wasn't Harry Smith, [it was] a fellow by the name of [Captain Murray] Weaver – he had his arm almost severed. I took

control for a little while – I ordered 10 Platoon to secure a
landing zone so we could get the choppers in and I reported
to BHQ what had happened . . . the next senior officer with
us was Lieutenant Paul O'Sullivan. I called him forward to
take over command of the company.

[Lieutenant] Colonel Townsend and medical officer
Captain John Taske arrived. Buick came up and Jack Kirby at
this stage was screaming, 'Bob! Bob!' Buick tried to give him
some comfort and then he took off . . . he headed back down
the line to perhaps investigate further . . . The doctor was
the last one who had contact with Jack Kirby [who] was in
[his] care, trying to give him mouth-to-mouth [resuscitation]
to keep him going and I remember him coming up and he
had blood all over his face, trying to breathe life into Jack
Kirby . . . This is one of my recurring nightmares, this whole
incident . . . We took stock of things – we had 13 wounded
and four killed. We got the choppers in to take the wounded
and the dead [and] they flew in Major [Owen] O'Brien to
take over the company and those of us who were uninjured
put our gear [back] on and continued the patrol . . . It was
a horrible, horrible day and in many ways it was worse than
Long Tan.[36]

Sergeant Major Jack Kirby, the backbone of the company, was dead.
When men heard, they couldn't comprehend that their loved and
respected warrant officer, who for many had become a father figure, was gone.

Just like in the aftermath of the Battle of Long Tan, nothing was
said. There was no debriefing or counselling – nothing from that
day to the next. They were to get on with the war. When Graham
Smith got back to Nui Dat, Harry Smith, who had been down in
hospital with pneumonia during the whole incident, saw him and
told his radio operator: 'I hear you did a pretty good job out there.'

Graham Smith said, 'I thought so' and Major Smith told him, 'I'm heading down to Vung Tau tomorrow – would you like to come?' 'And I said, "Yeah, I'd love to." And that was it.'[37]

Jim Richmond, like Graham Smith and so many others who survived not only the Battle of Long Tan but the Vietnam War, is still deeply affected. He has a recurring dream:

> The first day, the day I woke up in bed at the hospital, I had a dream the night after that and all the blokes in the dream were all me friends, all me mates that were killed and I just said to them, 'It's only a dream and when I wake up you'll wake up in the morning with me.' Well, that dream has kept with me from Long Tan till now . . . I don't know why, but the one that stays with me all the time is the young blokes – their faces are like they're still young . . . I see their faces, Doug, Shorty, Mitch, Glenn . . . and I still tell them that when I wake up that next morning, they'll all wake up with me. But they never do.[38]

Epilogue

On 17 August 1969, 6 RAR was in the middle of its second tour of Vietnam and A and D companies were preparing to launch an operation in the Long Tan plantation, two years to the day after the Battle of Long Tan. Some of the men were veterans of that battle.

Over the past 18 months the centre of Australian activity in Phuoc Tuy Province had shifted further north and few had visited the old battlefield, which lay just 5 kilometres to the east of the Task Force base. The men arrived via chopper and made their way to the site of 11 Platoon's stand against the human waves of Viet Cong. They swept the battlefield area, securing it, and with night approaching set up a defensive perimeter and waited for the arrival of the battalion's assault pioneers, who were due at first light the next day – 18 August.

Early the next morning the pioneers arrived and with the help of the infantry the immediate area was cleared of trees. A 3-metre-high concrete cross with a brass plaque attached, constructed by the pioneers, was flown in, suspended from an RAAF Iroquois chopper. The inscription on the plaque read:

In memory of those
members of D Coy and
3 Tp 1 APC Sqn who gave
their lives near this
spot during the battle
of Long Tan on 18th August 1966
Erected by 6RAR/NZ
(ANZAC) Bn 18 Aug 69

With the cross erected and a defence perimeter established, a number of APCs moved forward and formed a hollow square around
the immediate area of the cross. Ten veterans of the battle (nine
from D Company and one from 3 Troop) flanked the cross in an
honour guard while two pipers played a lament and a chaplain conducted a dedication. The ceremony was completed by midday, with
D Company the last to leave.

Very few Australians from the Task Force visited the area during
the remaining two years of Australia's involvement in the Vietnam
War, except as part of the odd patrol.[1] One person, however,
who made a number of patrols within and around the plantation was Warrant Officer Kevin 'Chicko' Miller, who had been in
12 Platoon during the battle. He was now part of the AATTV, commanding Cambodian troops, in his second tour of duty in 1971–72
and recalled going to Long Tan several times during this tour:

> I used to take my Cambodian [troops] out there to the cross
> that the battalion had erected on their second tour . . . and I
> took photos of it. The cross was there, but it didn't have the
> brass plate on it, and the chains that they'd put around it – it
> [originally] had four posts and a chain around it – the chains

had been stolen, they were gone, and they taken the brass plate. The cross was still there, but the grass and the bush was growing up right around it – it was overgrown, so I got the Cambodians to clean it up while I was out there. Just after we left there we had a contact about 300 metres from the cross and killed one VC that day. We operated all through that area on my second tour, while I was with the training team. But all of the other Australians had gone home – it was only us left there . . . all of the [Australian] battalion units had gone home. We were on our own, training Vietnamese or Cambodian troops.[2]

With the conclusion of the war, the cross was removed and used by local villagers as a 'headstone' for a local Catholic priest, Nguyen Van Minh, whose name was engraved on it. About ten years later the cross was removed by the Dong Nai Museum in Bien Hoa city, where it was put on display with a number of other artefacts relating to the Vietnam War. In 1989, Terry Burstall revisited Vietnam and saw the cross in the museum. It had been 'broken off from the concrete that had been poured around the base to hold it in place and there was a large fracture about 30 centimetres from the bottom. Two pieces of round reinforcing rod protruded from the end.'[3] In late 1989, the Dat District People's Committee erected a replica of the cross in the plantation with a new plaque, which read:

Socialist Republic of Vietnam
The Ministry of Culture
Recognises: Historic Place
Battlefield: D445 of Ba Ria – Long Khanh
Province
Contacted 6th Battalion of
The Royal Australian Army
Near Long Tan village on 18-8-1966

In April 2002, the Australian Vietnam Veterans Reconstruction Group with permission from the Vietnamese government completed the restoration of the replica cross and constructed a low-key memorial site. Many Australians today visit the memorial* and it remains one of only two foreign memorials relating to the Indochina Wars permitted on Vietnamese soil; the other is the French memorial at Dien Bien Phu.[4] The original Long Tan cross, with its plaque reattached, was loaned to the Australian War Memorial in mid-2012 and placed on display. It has since been returned to Vietnam.

After the war, the Vietnamese dead buried by the Australians immediately after the Battle of Long Tan were reinterred in a war cemetery in Hoa Long.

The No. 2 signaller from 6 RAR, D Company, Private Bill Akell, who bravely ran the gauntlet from CHQ to Lieutenant Geoff Kendall with the spare radio during the height of the battle, recently recalled his mixed emotions of that day, which likely apply to other veterans of the battle:

> Firstly, there was the normal 'We're just going on a patrol'. I won't say we were casual about it – once you moved outside the wire, nobody was casual. You looked ahead, you looked to your left and right, you looked up the trees, and you looked at the ground for booby traps. Your mind was active. Then there was in the first contact the excitement – we had made contact with the Viet Cong! And then there was the apprehension once the battle started about what had we got ourselves into. There was the feeling of 'I'm going to die' and

---

* The site is desolate, with the trees of the plantation having recently been removed. It is hoped that the plantation will be re-established.

that's a real feeling when they were lining up for their final assault. Then there was the exhilaration, excitement when the armoured personnel carriers arrived; then there was the complete exhaustion right throughout that night; and then the total sadness when we came across the bodies of our soldiers, mainly from 11 Platoon, that were lying there. So you can imagine in [less than] 24 hours you had that entire mixed emotion. The two things that stand out to me are the bugle calls and the artillery – I'll never forget it.[5]

Acknowledgements

In writing a work of recent history such as this, an author is dependent very much on first-hand accounts. I am most grateful to the veterans who kindly agreed to speak to me about their experiences, not just of the Battle of Long Tan but of the war in Vietnam more broadly. Without their generosity this book would never have seen the light of day. I am especially grateful to John Heslewood, President of the Long Tan Veterans Association, who was in the thick of the fighting and its immediate aftermath at the Long Tan Rubber Plantation. Not only did John agree to speak to me, but he kindly provided me with contact details of a number of veterans he thought might be willing to share with me their experiences. In alphabetical order I would like to thank these Vietnam War and Long Tan veterans who agreed to be interviewed for the book, and in doing so relived some of the most distressing events in their lives: Bill Akell; David Beahan; John Cash; Noel Grimes; Stan Hodder; Geoff Kendall; Kevin Miller; Alan Parr; John Robbins; Graham Smith; Tony Stepney; and Len Vine. Alan Parr his written a fascinating book on his time in Vietnam, *Memories of Vietnam* (2014), which is essential reading for anyone interested in Australia's involvement in the Vietnam War. To all these diggers I am extremely grateful, and I hope this book meets with their approval.

I also owe a special debt to two other Vietnam veterans turned writers: Ernie Chamberlain and Bruce Davies. Ernie has compiled and extensively reviewed the Vietnamese history of the Viet Cong 445 Battalion: *The Viet Cong D445 Battalion: Their Story* (2011) and *The Viet Cong D455 Battalion: Their Story and the Battle of Long Tan* (2016). Not only do these important volumes place the Vietnamese history in context of the Australian experience, but they provide significant analysis based on other primary and secondary Australian and Vietnamese sources. Ernie also kindly agreed to read an early draft of this book and provided invaluable critical comments, which did much to improve the final manuscript. My thanks also extends to Bruce Davies, who has written the definitive single volume on Australia's involvement in the Vietnam War: *Vietnam: The Complete Story of the Australian War* (2012). Like Ernie, Bruce provided valuable and extensive feedback on an earlier draft of this book. It goes without saying any remaining errors in the narrative and assessments made here are mine alone.

I would like to thank other Vietnam War veterans who allowed me to quote from their own books: Jean Debbelle Lamensdorf, *Write Home for Me: A Red Cross Woman in Vietnam* (2006); Charles Mollison, *Long Tan and Beyond: Alpha Company 6 RAR in Vietnam 1966–67* (2006); Lex McAulay, *The Battle of Long Tan: The Legend of Anzac Upheld* (1986); and *Blue Lanyard – Red Banner: The Capture of a Vietcong Headquarters by 1st Battalion, Royal Australian Regiment, Operation CRIMP 8–14 January 1966* (2005); and Brian McFarlane, *We Band of Brothers: A True Australian Adventure Story* (2000).

I would also like to thank the following publishers for granting me permission to quote from the following books: Hachette, *The Vietnam Year: From the Jungle to the Australian Suburbs* by Michael Caulfield (2007); Allan & Unwin, *All Guts and No Glory,* by Bob Buick & Gary McKay (2000) and, *The Battle of Long Tan: As Told*

By the Commanders by Robert Grandin (2004); and the University of Queensland Press, *A Soldier's Story: The Battle at Xa Long Tan Vietnam, 18 August 1966*, by Terry Burstall (1986).

I would also like to thank John Heslewood and other Long Tan veterans of the Long Tan Veterans Association for supplying the photographs used in this book.

At Penguin I would like to thank Ben Ball, my publisher, who has guided this book and my previous title, *The Battle for Lone Pine*, through to completion. The same applies to my editors Rachel Scully and Johannes Jakob – much thanks Ben, Rachel and Johannes. And a heartfelt thanks also to the rest of the team at Penguin. I would also like to thank my agent at Curtis Brown, Tara Wynn, for all of her ongoing help and support.

Finally, thanks to Emma, Anita and Lloyd for being there.

Notes

CHAPTER 1

1. See Caulfield, M. (2007) *The Vietnam Year: From the Jungle to the Australian Suburbs*, Hachette Australia, Sydney.
2. Kevin Miller interview, 8 June 2015.
3. See Burstall, T. (1986) *The Soldier's Story: The Battle at Xa Long Tan Vietnam, 18 August 1966*, University of Queensland Press, St Lucia.
4. See Caulfield (2007); John Heslewood to author, 29 September 2014.
5. McGibbon, I. (2010) *New Zealand's Vietnam War: A History of Combat, Commitment and Controversy*, Exisle Publishing, Auckland, p. 149.
6. See Mollison, C. (2006) *Long Tan and Beyond: Alpha Company 6 RAR in Vietnam 1966–67*, Cobbs Crossing Publications, Woombye, Qld.
7. Ibid., p. 114.
8. McAulay, L.F. (1986) *The Battle of Long Tan: The Legend of Anzac Upheld*, Hutchinson of Australia, Hawthorn, Vic., p. 30.
9. Ibid., p. 29.
10. Ibid., p. 30.
11. Mollison (2006), p. 114.
12. McFarlane, B. (2000), *We Band of Brothers: A True Australian Adventure Story*, B.W. McFarlane, New South Wales.
13. Mollison (2006), p. 114.
14. McAulay (1986), p. 31.
15. Blaxland, J. (1998) *Signals Swift and Sure: A History of the Royal Australian Corps of Signals 1947–1972*, Royal Australian Corps of Signals Committee, Canberra, pp. 201–2.
16. Steinbrook, G.L. (1995) *Allies and Mates: An American Soldier with the Australians and New Zealanders in Vietnam, 1966–67*, University of Nebraska Press, pp. 53–4.
17. Parr, A. (2006) *Memories of Vietnam*, Murray Tucker, Victoria, pp. 44–5.
18. See Grandin, B (2004) *The Battle of Long Tan: As Told by the Commanders*, Allen & Unwin, Sydney.
19. Australian Army commanders' diaries 6 RAR (AWM 95 7/6/5), 17 August 1966.
20. See Burstall (1986); McAulay (1986); McNeill, I. (1993) *To Long Tan: The Australian Army and the Vietnam War 1950–1966*, Allen & Unwin, Sydney; Smith, A.H. (2011) *Do Unto Others: Counter Bombardment in Australia's Military Campaigns*, Big Sky Publishing, Sydney.
21. McAulay (1986), p. 32.
22. Ibid., p. 33.
23. Mollison (2006), p. 113; see also Grandin (2004), p. 84.
24. Mollison (2006), ibid.
25. See Mollison (2006).
26. See McNeill (1993); McFarlane (2000).

CHAPTER 2

1. See Caulfield (2007); Davies, B. (2012) *Vietnam: The Complete Story of the Australian War*, Allen & Unwin, Sydney; Edwards, P. (2014) *Australia and the Vietnam War*, Australian War Memorial, Canberra & New South Books, Sydney; Fall, B.B. (1966) *Viet-Nam Witness 1953–66*, Frederick A. Praeger, New York; Nguyen, Lien-Hang (2012) *Hanoi's War: An International History of the War for Peace in Vietnam*, University of North Carolina Press; Pike, D. (1966) *Viet Cong: The Organization and Techniques of the National Liberation Front of South Vietnam*, MIT Press, Massachusetts; Schulzinger, R.D. (1997) *A Time for War: The United States and Vietnam 1941–1975*, Oxford University Press, New York.
2. Pike (1966), p. 22.
3. See Pike (1966).
4. See Caulfield (2007); Edwards (2014);

Palazzo, A. (2009) *Australian Military Operations in Vietnam*, Australian Army Campaign Series No. 3 (2nd edn), Australian Army History Unit, Canberra.

5. See Fall (1966); Frost, F. (1987) *Australia's War in Vietnam*, Allen & Unwin, Sydney; Pike (1966).

6. Pike (1966), p. 28.

7. See Davies (2012); Nguyen (2012); Pike (1966).

8. Palazzo (2009), p. 14.

9. Quote from Sexton, M. (2002) *War for the Asking: How Australia Invited Itself to Vietnam*, New Holland, Sydney, p. 29.

10. Quote from Giap, V.N. (1994) *Dien Bien Phu*, Gioi Publishers, Hanoi, p. 77.

11. See Davies (2012).

12. See Fall, B.B. (2002) *Hell in a Very Small Place: The Siege of Dien Bien Phu*, Da Capo Press, New York; Giap (1994); Windrow, M. (2004) *The Last Valley: Dien Bien Phu and the French Defeat in Vietnam*, Weidenfeld & Nicolson, London.

13. See Davies (2012).

14. See Edwards, P. (1992) 'Some reflections on the Australian government's commitment to the Vietnam War', in Grey, J. & Doyle, J. (eds) *Vietnam: War, Myth & Memory*, Allen & Unwin, Sydney, pp. 1–13; Edwards (2014); Palazzo (2009); Pike (1966).

15. 'Origins of the Insurgency in South Vietnam, 1954–1960' (1971), in *The Pentagon Papers* (Senator Gravel edition), Beacon Press, Boston, Vol. 1, pp. 242–69.

16. Palazzo (2009), p. 9.

CHAPTER 3

1. Fall (1966), p. 76.

2. See Davies (2012); Edwards (1992, 2014); McAulay (1986); Nguyen (2012); Palazzo (2009); Pike (1966).

3. Horner, D.M. (2000) *Defence Supremo: Frederick Shedden and the Making of Australian Defence Policy*, Allen & Unwin, Sydney, p. 320.

4. See Edwards (1992, 2014); Horner (2000); Palazzo (2009); Pike (1966).

5. Fall (1966), p. 138.

6. Truong, N.T. (1985) *A Vietcong Memoir*, Harcourt Brace Jovanovich, New York, p. 64.

7. See Davies (2012).

8. Watt, A. (1968) *Vietnam: An Australian Analysis*, F.W. Cheshire, Melbourne, pp. 81–2.

9. Dapin, M. (2014) *The Nashos' War: Australia's National Servicemen and Vietnam*, Viking, Melbourne, p. 11.

10. Fall (1966), pp. 185–6.

11. See Nguyen (2012).

12. Pike (1966), p. 81.

13. Pribbenow, M.L. (trans.) (2002) *Victory in Vietnam: The Official History of the People's Army of Vietnam, 1954–1975*, Military History Institute of Vietnam; University Press of Kansas.

14. See Pike (1966).

15. Truong (1985), p. 38.

16. See Frost (1987); Pike (1966); Race, J. (1972) *War Comes to Long An: Revolutionary Conflict in a Vietnamese Province*, University of California Press, Berkeley.

17. See McNeill (1993); Nguyen (2012); Pike (1966).

18. Ibid.

19. See Fall (1966); McNeill (1993).

20. See Davies (2012).

CHAPTER 4

1. See Davies (2012); Dennis, P. & Grey, J. (1996) *Emergency and Confrontation: Australian Military Operations in Malaya and Borneo 1950–1966*, Allen & Unwin, Sydney; Edwards (2014); Healy, J. (2008) 'A nine-battalion regiment: Australia, Malaysia and Singapore, 1965–73', in Horner, D.M. & Bou, J. (eds), *Duty First: A History of the Royal Australian Regiment*, Allen & Unwin, Sydney, pp. 149–69; Horner, D.M. (2008) 'Confrontation: Malaysia and Borneo, 1960–66', in Horner & Bou (eds), pp. 124–48; McNeill (1993).

2. See Blaxland, J. (2008) 'Consolidation and reorganisation: Australia 1950–65', in Horner & Bou (eds), pp. 105–23; Dapin (2014); Healy (2008).

3. See Dapin (2014).

4. Dapin (2014), pp. 27 and 69.

5. See Dapin (2014).

6. Davies, email to author, 8 February 2015.

7. Horner (2000), p. 306.

8. See Dennis & Grey (1996); Edwards (1992, 2014); Horner (2000); Palazzo (2009).

9. Horner (2000), p. 311.

10. Ibid., p. 320.

11. See Dennis & Grey (1996).

12. See Breen, B. (2008) 'The build-up: Vietnam, 1965–67', in Horner & Bou (eds), pp. 171–95; Edwards (2014); McNeill (1993).

13. See Krenpinevich, A.F. (1986) *The Army and Vietnam*, Johns Hopkins University Press, Baltimore.

14. See Davies (2012); Krenpinevich (1986); Palazzo (2009).

15. Ibid.; see also Nguyen (2012).

16. Davies, email to author, 2 January 2015.

17. See Dennis & Grey (1996); Bergerud, E. (1996) *Touched with Fire: The Land War in the South Pacific*, Viking, New York; Threlfall, A. (2014) *Jungle Warriors: From Tobruk to Kokoda and Beyond, How the Australian Army Became the World's Most Deadly Jungle Fighting Force*, Allen & Unwin, Sydney.

18. See Palazzo (2009).

19. See Davies (2012); Dennis & Grey (1996); Edwards (1992, 2014); Palazzo (2009).

20. See Davies (2012); Horner, D.M. (1995) *The Gunners: A History of Australian Artillery*, Allen & Unwin, Sydney.

21. Palazzo (2009), p. 19.

CHAPTER 5

1. See Avery, B. (2001) *Our Secret War: The 4th Battalion the Royal Australian Regiment: Defending Malaysia Against Indonesian Confrontation, 1965–1967*, Slouch Hat Publications, Victoria; Denis & Grey (1996); Smith, N.C. (1999) *Nothing Short of War: With the Australian Army in Borneo 1962–66*, Citadel Press, Victoria.

2. See Davies 2012; Horner, D.M. (2005) *Strategic Command: General Sir John Wilton and Australia's Asian Wars*, Oxford University Press, Melbourne; Palazzo (2009).

3. See Davies (2012).

4. See Palazzo (2009).

5. McAulay, L. (2005) *Blue Lanyard, Red Banner: The Capture of a Vietcong Headquarters by 1st Battalion, Royal Australian Regiment, Operation CRIMP 8–14 January 1966*, Banner Books, Queensland, p. 110.

6. Davies, pp. 146–7.

7. McAulay (2005), p. 144; see also Thomson, J. & MacGregor, S. (2011) *Tunnel Rats: The Larrikin Aussie Legends Who Discovered the Vietcong's Secret Weapon*, Allen & Unwin, Sydney, pp. 114–16.

8. McAulay (2005), p. 145; see also Thomson & MacGregor (2011).

9. Breen (2008), pp. 175–7; see also McAulay (2005); Davies (2012).

10. See McAulay (2005); Greville, P. J. (2002) *The Royal Australian Engineers 1945 to 1972: Paving the Way*, Vol. 4, Corps Committee of the Royal Australian Engineers, Sydney; Mangold, T. & Penycate, J. (1985) *The Tunnels of Cu Chi: A Remarkable Story of War*, Guild Publishing, London; Thomson & MacGregor (2011).

11. See Breen, B. (1988) *First to Fight: Australian Diggers, NZ Kiwis and US Paratroopers in Vietnam,1965–66*, Allen & Unwin, Sydney; Breen (2008); Blaxland (2008); Horner (2005); Palazzo (2009).

12. Breen (2008), p. 179.

13. See Palazzo (2009).

14. Breen (2008), p. 173.

15. See Breen (1998, 2008); McNeill (1993).

16. Breen (1988), p. 130.

17. Palazzo (2009), p. 26.

18. See Breen (2008); Ham, P. (2007) *Vietnam: The Australian War*, HarperCollins, Sydney; Davies (2012).

19. 'VC Dat Do district history' (2006) in Chamberlain, E. (2011) *The Viet Cong D445 Battalion: Their Story*, E. Chamberlain, Victoria.

20. Breen (2008), p. 178.

21. See Greville (2002); O'Keefe, B. (1994) *Medicine at War: Medical Aspects of Australia's Involvement in Southeast Asian Conflicts 1950–1972*, Allen & Unwin, Sydney.

22. Lieutenant Colonel Warr, 5th Battalion Royal Australian Regiment, Australian Army commanders' diaries, Operation Sydney 2, pp. 7–8 (AWM 95 7/5/6), 14 July 1966.

23. See McNeill (1993); O'Neill, R.J. (1968) *Vietnam Task: The 5th Battalion, Royal Australian Regiment*, Cassell, Melbourne.

24. O'Neill (1968), p. 65; see also Greville (2002); McNeill (1993).
25. See Horner (2005).
26. Horner (2005), p. 246.
27. See Horner (2005); Palazzo (2009).
28. Breen (1988), p. 70.
29. See Barclay, G. (1988) *A Very Small Insurance Policy: The Politics of Australian Involvement in Vietnam, 1954–1967*, University of Queensland Press, St Lucia.
30. McNeill (1993), p. 189.
31. Ibid., p. 240.
32. See Burke, A. (2005) *105th Battery: Royal Regiment of Australian Artillery: A Concise History*, A. Burke, Queensland; Horner (2005); O'Keefe (1994); Palazzo (2009); Picken, B. (2012) *Fire Support Bases Vietnam: Australian and Allied Fire Support Base Locations and Main Support Units*, Big Sky Publishing, Sydney.
33. Steinbrook (1995), p. 16.

CHAPTER 6

1. See Horner (2005).
2. See McNeill (1993).
3. Ibid.
4. See Horner (1995); Palazzo (2009).
5. See Davies (2012).
6. See Burstall (1986).
7. Buick, B. & McKay, G. (2000) *'All Guts and No Glory': The Story of a Long Tan Warrior*, Allen & Unwin, Sydney, p. 42.
8. See Buick & McKay (2000); Edwards (2014); McAulay (1986); McNeill (1993).
9. McAulay (1986), p. 8.
10. Ibid.
11. See Greville (2002).
12. Bishop letter to father (AWM PR91/18), 18 October 1966.
13. Signal Squadron Folio 1, Australian Army commanders' diaries (AWM 95 6/1/3 103), 1–30 June 1966.
14. See McNeill (1993).
15. See McAulay (1986).
16. McAulay (1986), p. 15.
17. Ekins, A. (2011) 'Unravelling the riddles of Long Tan', *Wartime: Official Magazine of the Australian War Memorial*, Issue 55, p. 44.
18. See Chamberlain (2011); Davies (2012).
19. See McNeill (1993).

20. Ibid.
21. Ibid.
22. See Chamberlain (2011, 2015); Dapin (2014); O'Neill (1968).
23. See Greville (2002).
24. McAulay (1986), p. 8.
25. Dapin (2014), p. 106.
26. See Davies (2012); Edwards (2014); McAulay (1986); McNeill (1993); Odgers, G. (1974) *Mission Vietnam: Royal Australian Air Force Operations 1964–1972*, Australian Government Publishing Service, Canberra.
27. McNeill (1993), p. 255.
28. See Greville (2002).
29. See Edwards (2014); Greville (2002); McAulay (1986); McNeill (1993); Odgers (1974).
30. See Dapin (2014).

CHAPTER 7

1. See Chamberlain (2011, 2015); Pribbenow (2002); Davies (2012).
2. See Chamberlain (2011, 2015).
3. See Pribbenow (2002).
4. Ibid.
5. See Chamberlain (2011); Davies (2012).
6. Ibid.
7. See Burstall, T. (1990) *A Soldier Returns: A Long Tan Veteran Discovers the Other Side of Vietnam*, University of Queensland Press, St Lucia; Chamberlain (2011); Davies (2012); Pribbenow (2002).
8. See Chamberlain (2011); McNeill (1993).
9. Davies (2012), p. 191; see also Dinh, P.Q. (2005) *History of the 5th Infantry Division*, People's Army Publication House, Hanoi.
10. See Chamberlain (2011).
11. Mollison (2006), p. 201.
12. See Chamberlain (2011, 2015).
13. Ibid.
14. See Chamberlain (2011, 2015); Davies (2012).
15. See Chamberlain (2011, 2015); Davies (2012); Dinh (2005); Pribbenow (2002).
16. Ibid.
17. See Chamberlain (2011, 2015); McNeill (1993).
18. Ibid.
19. Ibid.
20. Burstall (1986), p. 15.

21. See Burstall (1990); Davies (2012); Dinh (2005); McAulay (1986).

22. See Chamberlain (2011, 2015); Davies (2012); Dinh (2005); McNeill (1993).

23. See Buick & McKay (2000); Burstall (1990); Chamberlain (2011); Davies (2012); McNeill (1993).

24. See Chamberlain, E. (2014), *The Enemy, and Intelligence in Phuoc Tuy Province: Successes and Failures*, Phillip Island, National Vietnam Veterans' Museum (NVVM), unpublished transcript, 12 April 2014; Davies (2012).

25. See Chamberlain (2014).

26. See Smith, H. (2015) *Long Tan: The Start of a Lifelong Battle*, Big Sky Publishing, Sydney.

27. See detailed discussions in Chamberlain (2011); Davies (2012).

28. See Burstall (1990).

CHAPTER 8

1. See Burstall (1986).

2. Burgess, P. *Sydney Morning Herald*, 1 August 1966, p. 4.

3. See Buick & McKay (2000); Edwards (2014); Greville (2002); McGibbon (2010); McNeill (1993).

4. Major Ford, Operation Hobart 1 After Action Report, 6th Battalion Royal Australian Regiment Australian Army commanders' diaries (AWM 95 7/6/4), 1–31 July 1966.

5. See Chamberlain (2011).

6. Lieutenant Colonel Townsend, Operation Hobart 1 After Action Report, 6th Battalion Royal Australian Regiment Australian Army commanders' diaries (AWM 95 7/6/4), 1–31 July 1966.

7. Steinbrook (1995), p. 33.

8. Ibid., p. 35.

9. McNeill (1993), p. 298.

10. 1 ATF After Action Report, Operation Smithfield, p. 4 (AWM 181), December 1966.

11. See Blaxland, J. (2012) 'Listening to the enemy: signals intelligence played a key role in Malaya, Borneo and Vietnam', *Wartime: Official Magazine of the Australian War Memorial*, Issue 57, pp. 30–35; McNeill (1993).

12. Smith, H. (n.d.) *The Battle of Long Tan, South Vietnam: 18 August 1966, Biography Lieutenant Colonel*

Harry Smith, MC, SG <http://battleoflongtan.reddunefilms.com/wp-content/uploads/2011/03/Long-Tan-Harry-Smith-Biography.pdf>.

13. Ibid.

14. See Chamberlain (2011).

15. See Chamberlain (2011, 2015).

16. See Chamberlain (2011).

17. See Chamberlain (2014).

18. See Breen (2008); Ekins (2011); Ham (2007); McNeill (1993).

19. McNeill (1993), p. 309.

20. Ham (2007), p. 215.

21. See McNeill (1993).

22. Blaxland (1998), p. 244.

23. McNeill (1993), p. 309.

24. See Ham (2007).

25. DPI 200 interview with Brigadier Jackson (AWM 107), 1972.

26. Ibid.

27. See Mollison (2006).

28. Ibid., pp. 108–9.

29. Ibid., p. 111.

30. McNeill (1993), p. 311.

31. See Davies (2012); McNeill (1993).

CHAPTER 9

1. See Greville (2002).

2. See O'Keefe (1994).

3. See Ham (2007).

4. See Anderson, P. (2002) *When the Scorpion Stings: The History of the 3rd Cavalry Regiment, Vietnam, 1965–1972*, Allen & Unwin, Sydney; McAulay (1986); McNeill (1993); O'Neill (1968).

5. Major McQualter, B Company Operational Analysis, Operation Holsworthy, 5th Battalion Royal Australian Regiment, Australian Army commanders' diaries, Part 1 (AWM 95 7/5/7), 1–31 August 1966.

6. McNeill (1993), p. 296.

7. O'Neill (1968), p. 73.

8. Ibid., p. 70.

9. See McNeill (1993).

10. McKay, G. (1992) *Vietnam Fragments: An Oral History of Australians at War*, Allen & Unwin, Sydney, p. 99.

11. Ibid.

12. See Burstall (1986).

13. Ibid., p. 43.

14. Australian Army commanders' diaries 6 RAR (AWM 95 7/6/5), 17 August 1966.

15. See Grandin (2004).

16. See McFarlane (2000).

17. Dapin (2014), p. 107.
18. Australian Army commanders' diaries 6 RAR (AWM 95 7/6/5), 17 August 1966; see also Breen (2008); Burstall (1986); McKay (1992).
19. Ibid.; see also Mollison (2006).
20. See Burstall (1986); McNeill (1993).
21. See Horner, D.M. (1989) *SAS: Phantoms of the Jungle: A History of the Australian Special Air Service*, Allen & Unwin, Sydney; Horner, D.M. (2009) *In Action with the SAS*, Allen & Unwin, Sydney; Ham, P. (2007).
22. See Grandin (2004).
23. See Horner (1989, 2009); O'Neill (1993).
24. Ibid.
25. Horner (1989), pp. 191–2.
26. David Beahan interview, 30 May 2015.
27. See Mollison (2006).
28. See Grandin (2004).

CHAPTER 10

1. Smith, H. (n.d.) *The Battle of Long Tan, South Vietnam: 18 August 1966*
2. Smith, H. (2015) *Long Tan: The Start of a Lifelong Battle*, Big Sky Publishing, New South Wales.
3. Caulfield (2007), p. 259; see also McAulay (1996); Burstall (1986); McNeill (1993).
4. See Grandin (2004); Smith, H. (2015).
5. Ibid.
6. McAulay (1986), p. 34.
7. Ibid.
8. See Buick & McKay (2000).
9. See McAulay (1986).
10. Geoff Kendall interview, 6 October 2014.
11. Grandin (2004), p. 11.
12. Ibid., p. 12.
13. Tony Stepney interview, 17 April 2015.
14. Dapin (2014), p. 87.
15. See Dapin (2014).
16. Personal communication, Chris Roberts to author.
17. Dapin (2014), p. 99.
18. John Heslewood interview, 30 September 2014.
19. See Burstall (1986); McAulay (1986); also John Heslewood interview, 29 September 2014.
20. See Grandin (2004).
21. See McAulay (1996); Burstall (1986); McNeill (1993).
22. McAulay (1986), p. 22.

CHAPTER 11

1. 6 RAR commanders' diaries (AWM 95 7/6/5), 18 August 1966.
2. Ibid.
3. Ibid.
4. See Mollison (2006).
5. See McAulay (1986); Burstall (1986); McNeill (1993).
6. See Grandin (2004).
7. See McNeill (1993).
8. 6 RAR commanders' diaries (AWM 95 7/6/5), 18 August 1966.
9. Mollison (2006), p. 124.
10. 6 RAR commanders' diaries (AWM 95 7/6/5), 18 August 1966.
11. See McNeill (1993); McAulay (1986).
12. Ibid.
13. Mollison (2006), p. 124.
14. See Grandin (2004).
15. See Burstall (1986).
16. See Mollison (2006).
17. 6 RAR commanders' diaries (AWM 95 7/6/5), 18 August 1966.
18. See Burstall (1986).
19. See Mollison (2006).
20. See Burstall (1986); Mollison (2006).
21. See Coulthard-Clark, C. (1995) *The RAAF in Vietnam: Australian Air Involvement in the Vietnam War 1962–1975*. Allen & Unwin, Sydney; Grandin (2004); Odgers (1974).
22. See Caulfield (2007).
23. McFarlane (2000), p. 255.
24. Ibid.
25. See McFarlane (2000).
26. Ibid., p. 255.
27. Caulfield (2007), p. 257.
28. Bill Akell interview, 7 June 2015.
29. See Grandin (2004).
30. Parr (2006), p. 45.
31. Geoff Kendall interview, 6 October 2014.
32. See Buick & McKay (2000).
33. See Caulfield (2007).
34. McNeill (1993), p. 314.
35. Grandin (2004), p. 107.
36. Graham Smith interview, 26 May 2015.
37. See Parr (2006).
38. 6 RAR commanders' diaries (AWM 95 7/6/5), 18 August 1966.
39. See McNeill (1993); Mollison (2006).
40. See Mollison (2006).
41. 6 RAR commanders' diaries (AWM 95 7/6/5), 18 August 1966.
42. McNeill (1993), p. 314.

43. Burstall (1986), p. 46.
44. See McAulay (1986).
45. See Burstall (1986).
46. See Burstall (1986); Grandin (2004); McAulay (1986); McNeil (1993).
47. Ibid.
48. Ibid.
49. See Grandin (2004).
50. McAulay (1986), p. 43.
51. John Robbins interview, 20 May 2015.
52. See Dapin (2014).
53. Mollison (2006), p. 125.
54. Ibid., p. 126.
55. See Chamberlain (2011).
56. See Odgers (1974).

CHAPTER 12

1. Dapin (2014), p. 129.
2. See Grandin (2004).
3. See McNeill (1993).
4. See Grandin (2004); McNeill (1993).
5. Ibid; see also McGibbon (2010).
6. See McNeill (1993).
7. See Grandin (2004).
8. Geoff Kendall interview, 6 October 2014.
9. See Grandin (2004).
10. See McAulay (1986); Burstall (1986); McNeill (1992).
11. Graham Smith interview, 26 May 2015; see also Buick & McKay (2000).
12. See McAulay (1986).
13. See Grandin (2004).
14. Ibid., p. 112.
15. See Grandin (2004); McAulay (1986); McNeill (1993); Mollison (2006).
16. Ibid.
17. Burstall (1986), p. 51.
18. Caulfield (2007), p. 262.
19. Buick & McKay (2000), p. 88.
20. See Grandin (2004); McAulay (1986); McNeill (1993); Mollison (2006).
21. See Burstall (1990); Chamberlain (2011); Dinh (2005); McAulay (1986); Smith (2015).
22. Mollison (2006), pp. 122–3.
23. See Mollison (2006).
24. Steinbrook (1995), p. 49.

CHAPTER 13

1. Bill Akell interview, 7 June 2015.
2. Burstall (1986), p. 57.
3. Parr (2006), p. 46.
4. Smith (2015), p. 128.
5. See McAulay (1986).

6. See Caulfield (2007).
7. See McAulay (1986).
8. Ibid.
9. Smith (2015), p. 128.
10. See Smith (2015).
11. See Burstall (1986); Chamberlain (2011); Davis (2012); McAulay (1986); McNeill (1993).
12. See McNeill (1993); Mollison (2006).
13. See Anderson (2002); McAulay (1986).
14. Buick & MacKay (2000), p. 89.
15. See McNeill (1993).
16. John Heslewood interview, 30 September 2014.
17. McAulay (1986), p. 48.
18. Caulfield (2007), p. 271.
19. 6 RAR commanders' diaries (AWM 95 7/6/5), 18 August 1966.
20. See Burstall (1986); McAulay (1986); John Heslewood interview, 29 September 2014.
21. See Caulfield (2007).
22. Ibid., p. 263.
23. Dapin (2014), p. 129.
24. See Buick & McKay (2000).
25. Mollison (2006), p. 133.
26. John Robbins interview, 20 May 2015.
27. Parr (2006), p. 46.
28. See McAulay (1986).
29. McAulay (1986), p. 49.
30. John Heslewood interview, 30 September 2014.
31. McAulay (1986), p. 50.
32. Caulfield (2007), p. 267.
33. McAulay (1986), p. 48.
34. Geoff Kendall interview, 6 October 2014.
35. See Burstall (1986).
36. See Grandin (2004).

CHAPTER 14

1. 6 RAR commanders' diaries (AWM 95 7/6/5), 18 August 1966; Buick & McKay (2000).
2. McNeill (1993), p. 318.
3. Burstall (1986), p. 54.
4. Ibid., p. 56.
5. Ibid., p. 57.
6. See McAulay (1986).
7. Dapin (2014), p. 130.
8. See Burstall (1986).
9. See Buick & McKay (2000).
10. See Burstall (1986); John Robbins interview, 20 May 2015.
11. Burstall (1986), p. 54.

12. See McAulay (1986); Burstall (1986).
13. Dapin (2014), p. 131.
14. McAulay (1986), p. 51.
15. Ibid., p. 55; see also Grandin (2006).
16. McNeill (1993), p. 318.
17. 6 RAR commanders' diaries (AWM 95 7/6/5), 18 August 1966; Headquarters, 1 Australian Task Force Narrative Duty Officer's log, Part 1 (AWM 95 1/4/6), 1–31 August 1966; Headquarters 1 ATF Commanding Officer After Action Report Operation Smithfield (AWM 95 1/4/26), 1–31 January 1967.
18. See Smith (2015).
19. Ibid.
20. See Dapin (2014); O'Neill (1992); Smith (2006).
21. McKay (2014), pp. 100–1.
22. Dapin (2014), p. 141.
23. Mollison (2006), p. 133.
24. See Grandin (2004).
25. McFarlane (2000), p. 258.
26. See Grandin (2004); McAulay (1986).
27. Caulfield (2007), p. 278.
28. See McAulay (1986); McNeill (1993).
29. Ibid.
30. Ibid.

CHAPTER 15

1. See McAulay (1986); McGibbon (2010).
2. McAulay (1986), p. 71.
3. Graham Smith interview, 26 May 2015.
4. See Burstall (1986).
5. McAulay (1986), p. 50.
6. Kevin Miller interview, 8 June 2015.
7. 6 RAR commanders' diaries (AWM 95 7/6/5), 18 August 1966; see also Smith (2015).
8. McGibbon (2010), p. 152.
9. See McAulay (1986).
10. See Pound (2008).
11. Steinbrook (1995), p. 55.
12. McAulay (1986), p. 57.
13. See McAulay (1986).
14. Ibid., p. 65.
15. See McNeill (1993).
16. McAulay (1986), p. 54.
17. Ibid.
18. See Ham (2007); McAulay (1986); Pound, G. (2008) *What Soldiers Do: An Australian Artilleryman in Vietnam*, Australian Military History Press, Loftus, NSW.
19. See McAulay (1986).
20. McAulay (1986), p. 65.

21. Mollison (2006), p. 131.
22. 6 RAR commanders' diaries (AWM 95 7/6/5), 18 August 1966; Mollison (2006).
23. See Burstall (1986).
24. McAulay (1986), p. 50.
25. See Buick & McKay (2000).
26. See Burstall (1986); McNeill (1993).
27. John Heslewood interview, 30 September 2014.
28. See Buick & McKay (2000).
29. Burstall (1986), p. 77.
30. Graham Smith interview, 26 May 2015.
31. See Dapin (2014).
32. John Robbins interview, 20 May 2015.
33. See Burstall (1986).

CHAPTER 16

1. 6 RAR commanders' diaries (AWM 95 7/6/5), 18 August 1966.
2. John Heslewood interview, 30 September 2014.
3. Burstall (1986), p. 56.
4. Ibid.
5. Buick & McKay (2000), pp. 91–2.
6. See Buick & McKay (2000); McAulay (1986).
7. See Grandin (2004).
8. See Buick & McKay (2000).
9. John Robbins interview, 20 May 2015.
10. See Smith (2015).
11. McAulay (1986), p. 63.
12. See McGibbon (2010).
13. John Heslewood interview, 30 September 2014.
14. Chamberlain (2011), p. 35.
15. McNeill (1993), p. 320; see also Buick & McKay (2000).
16. Buick & McKay (2000), p. 92.
17. Headquarters 1 ATF Commanding Officer After Action Report Operation Smithfield, p. 6 (AWM 95 1/4/26).
18. See Grandin (2004).
19. See McNeill (1993); Buick & McKay (2000).
20. Caulfield (2007), pp. 278–9.
21. Grandin (2004), p. 130.
22. See Mollison (2006).
23. Len Vine interview, 15 May 2015.
24. McAulay (1986), p. 55.
25. Len Vine interview, 15 May 2015.
26. See McAulay (1986); McNeill (1993).
27. McAulay (1986), p. 55.
28. Geoff Kendall interview, 6 October 2014.

29. See Chamberlain (2011).
30. See Burstall (1990); Chamberlain (2011); Davies (2012).
31. McAulay (1986), p. 56.
32. Geoff Kendall interview, 6 October 2014.
33. Ibid.
34. Mollison (2006), p. 135.
35. See McAulay (1986); Mollison (2006).
36. John Cash interview, 30 March 2015.
37. Burstall (1986), p. 61.
38. John Cash interview, 30 March 2015.
39. Dapin (2014), pp. 137–8.
40. Steinbrook (1995), p. 55.
41. See Breen (2008); Grandin (2004); McAulay (1986); McNeill (1993).
42. McAulay (1986), p. 52.
43. Ibid., p. 53.
44. Ibid., p. 67.
45. See Buick & McKay (2000).

CHAPTER 17

1. See McNeill (1993).
2. Ibid.
3. Ibid.; see also Headquarters 1 ATF Commanding Officer After Action Report Operation Smithfield (AWM 95 1/4/26).
4. Dinh (2005), p. 19.
5. 6 RAR commanders' diaries (AWM 95 7/6/5), 18 August 1966.
6. Ibid.
7. Grandin (2004), p. 140.
8. Parr (2006), p. 47.
9. See Burstall (1986).
10. Ibid., p. 64.
11. See Burstall (1986).
12. John Cash interview, 30 March 2015.
13. Kevin Miller interview, 8 June 2015.
14. See Burstall (1986).
15. See Grandin (2004).
16. Ibid.
17. Graham Smith interview, 26 May 2015.
18. Burstall (1986), p. 62.
19. See Burstall (1986).
20. McAulay (1986), p. 63.
21. See Burstall (1986).
22. Graham Smith interview, 26 May 2015.
23. Bill Akell interview, 7 June 2015; see also McAulay (1986); McNeill (1993).
24. Ibid.
25. Ibid.
26. Ibid.
27. See McNeill (1993).

28. See Burstall (1986).
29. Bill Akell interview, 7 June 2015.
30. Ibid.
31. See McAulay (1986).
32. Ibid., p. 66.
33. See McAulay (1986).
34. Caulfield (2007), p. 274.
35. Geoff Kendall interview, 6 October 2014.
36. See McAulay (1986); Mollison (2006).
37. Tony Stepney interview, 17 April 2015.
38. McAulay (1986), p. 67.
39. Geoff Kendall interview, 6 October 2014.
40. See Buick & McKay (2000); McNeill (1993).
41. See McAulay (1986).
42. See McAulay (1986); McNeill (1993); Mollison (2006).
43. Geoff Kendall interview, 6 October 2014.
44. See Grandin (2004).
45. McAulay (1986), p. 63.
46. John Heslewood interview, 30 September 2014.
47. Caulfield (2007), pp. 274–5.
48. See Grandin (2004); McNeill (1993).
49. Caulfield (2007), p. 275.
50. Buick & McKay (2000), p. 96.
51. See Buick & McKay (2000).
52. McAulay (1986), p. 67.
53. See McNeill (1993).
54. McAulay (1986), p. 67.
55. McFarlane (2000), p. 258.
56. 6 RAR commanders' diaries (AWM 95 7/6/5), 18 August 1966.
57. See Burstall (1986); McAulay (1986); McNeill (1986); Mollison (2006).
58. Mollison (2006), p. 123.
59. Ibid., p. 142.
60. Ibid., p. 123.
61. See McAulay (1986); McNeill (1993); Mollison (2006).
62. See Anderson (2002); Grandin (2004); McNeill (1993).
63. Ibid.
64. See Anderson (2002).
65. See Smith (2015).
66. See McFarlane (2000).
67. Dapin (2014), pp. 130–1; see also McFarlane (2000).
68. See Grandin (2004).
69. McFarlane (2000), p. 262.

CHAPTER 18

1. See McAulay (1986).
2. Quotes 6 RAR commanders' diaries (AWM 95 7/6/5), 18 August 1966.
3. See McNeill (1993).
4. McNeill (1993), p. 322.
5. Ibid.
6. Caulfield (2007), p. 281.
7. See Grandin (2004).
8. Ibid.
9. See McNeill (1993).
10. Grandin (2004), p. 191.
11. Newman (1988), p. 55.
12. Grandin (2010), p. 141.
13. See McNeill (1993).
14. See Anderson (2002).
15. See McNeill (1993).
16. Ibid.
17. See Anderson (2002); Mollison (2006).
18. See McNeill (1993).
19. Captain Charles Mollison After Action Report (AWM 95 7/6/5).

CHAPTER 19

1. McNeill (1993), p. 323.
2. McFarlane (2000), p. 259.
3. Ibid.; see also McGibbon (2010), p. 154.
4. See Davies (2012).
5. See McFarlane (2000).
6. McGibbon (2010), p. 154.
7. See McAulay (1986); McFarlane (2000).
8. Horner (1995), p. 478.
9. See Grandin (2004).
10. See Burstall (1986); McAulay (1986); McNeill (1993).
11. Parr (2006), p. 47.
12. See Burstall (1986).
13. Stan Hodder interview, 8 April 2015.
14. See Buick & McKay (2000); Burstall (1986).
15. Buick & McKay (2000), p. 97.
16. See Grandin (2004).
17. See Burstall (1986).
18. See McNeill (1993).
19. Dapin (2014), p. 133.
20. Dapin 2014, p. 133–4.
21. 6 RAR commanders' diaries (AWM 95 7/6/5), 18 August 1966.
22. Noel Grimes interview, 15 April 2015.
23. See McNeill (1993).
24. 6 RAR commanders' diaries (AWM 95 7/6/5), 18 August 1966; McNeill (1993), p. 325.
25. 6 RAR commanders' diaries (AWM 95 7/6/5), 18 August 1966.

26. See Burstall (1986); McAulay (1986); McNeill (1993).
27. Noel Grimes interview, 15 April 2015.
28. See Burstall (1986).
29. Parr (2006), p. 81.
30. See Burstall (1986).
31. See Grandin (2004).
32. Ibid., p. 162.
33. Parr (2006), p. 48.
34. Dapin (2014), p. 134.
35. Parr (2006), p. 49.
36. Grandin (2004), p. 173.
37. Parr (2006), p. 51.

CHAPTER 20

1. Dapin (2014), p. 141.
2. McFarlane (2000), p. 263.
3. 6 RAR commanders' diaries (AWM 95 7/6/5), 18 August 1966.
4. See McNeill (1993); McAulay (1986); Odgers (1974).
5. See Mollison (2006).
6. See Burstall (1986).
7. Ibid.
8. See Grandin (2004).
9. Ibid.
10. Ibid., p. 169.
11. Ibid.
12. See Grandin (2004); McAulay (1986).
13. Dapin (2014), p. 134.
14. See Burstall (1986); McAulay (1986); McNeill (1993).
15. Ibid.
16. Kevin Miller interview, 8 June 2015.
17. See Burstall (1986); McAulay (1986); McNeill (1993).
18. Ibid.
19. See Grandin (2004).

CHAPTER 21

1. See Anderson (2002); McNeill (1993).
2. Caulfield (2007), p. 287.
3. Burstall (1986), p. 76.
4. See Buick & McKay (2000).
5. Burstall (1986), pp. 84–5.
6. It is not stated whether it was Albert or Denis McCormack, who were unrelated but both serving in 11 Platoon, and who were both killed.
7. See Smith (2015).
8. Burstall (1986), p. 79.
9. Ibid., p. 78.
10. Mollison (2006), p. 151.
11. Ibid., p. 152.
12. Dapin (2014), pp. 131–2; John Robbins

interview, 20 May 2015.

13. See Dapin (2014).
14. See Burstall (1986); McAulay (1986); McNeill (1993).
15. See Burstall (1986).
16. McAulay (1986), p. 90.
17. See Burstall (1986).
18. Ibid.
19. See Mollison (2006); Burstall (1986); McAulay (1986); McNeill (1993).
20. Parr (2006), p. 49.
21. See Burstall (1986).
22. Stan Hodder interview, 8 April 2015.
23. Kevin Miller interview, 8 June 2015.
24. See Burstall (1986).
25. See Buick & McKay (2000).
26. See Grandin (2004).
27. Buick & McKay (2000), p. 102.
28. See Grandin (2004).
29. Burstall (1986), p. 92.
30. Buick & McKay (2000), p. 102.
31. John Heslewood interview, 30 September 2014.
32. See Burstall (1986).
33. Mollison (2006), p. 153.
34. See Burstall (1986).
35. Ibid., p. 91.
36. See Burstall (1986); Grandin (2004).
37. McAulay (1986), p. 92.
38. See Grandin (2004).
39. Stan Hodder interview, 8 April 2015.
40. See Burstall (1986).
41. Stan Hodder interview, 8 April 2015.
42. See Burstall (1986); McAulay (1986); McNeill (1993).
43. See McAulay (1986).

CHAPTER 22

1. McAulay (1986), p. 84.
2. See Grandin (2004).
3. McAulay (1986), p. 84.
4. Ibid., p. 85.
5. Ibid.
6. Ibid., p. 89.
7. Grandin (2004), p. 193; see also McGibbon (2010).
8. Graham Smith interview, 26 May 2015.
9. See McAulay (1986).
10. 105 Field Battery [105 Fd Bty] Enclosure 4–5 (AWM 95 3/5/43), 1–31 August 1966.
11. McAulay (1986), pp. 85–6.
12. Mollison (2006), p. 150.
13. McAulay (1986), p. 86.
14. Graham Smith interview, 26 May 2015.

15. Smith (2015), p. 142.
16. McAulay (1986), p. 87.
17. See McNeill (1993).
18. Grandin (2004), pp. 148–9.
19. See Burstall (1986).
20. Ibid.; see also Grandin (2004); McAulay (1986); McNeill (1993).
21. Geoff Kendall interview, 6 October 2014.
22. See McNeill (1993).
23. Burstall (1986), p. 105.
24. Dapin (2014), p. 138.
25. Ibid.
26. Len Vine interview, 15 May 2015.
27. Graham Smith interview, 26 May 2015.
28. Burstall (1986), p. 94.
29. Grandin (2004), p. 184.
30. See Burstall (1986); Grandin (2004); McAulay (1986); McNeill (1993).
31. Parr (2006), p. 51.
32. See Burstall (1986).
33. Geoff Kendall interview, 6 October 2014.
34. McAulay (1986), p. 77.
35. See McNeill (1993).
36. Grandin (2004), p. 185.
37. See Burstall (1986).
38. McNeill (1993), p. 332.
39. See McNeill (1993).
40. See McAulay (1986).
41. 6 RAR commanders' diaries (AWM 95 7/6/5), 18 August 1966.
42. Buick & McKay (2000), p. 105.
43. John Heslewood interview, 30 September 2014.
44. McAulay (1986), p. 96.
45. Ibid., p. 89.
46. Parr (2006), p. 52.
47. See McNeill (1993).
48. Burstall (1986), p. 93.
49. Ibid., pp. 93–4.
50. See Smith (2015).
51. See Burstall (1986).
52. McAulay (1986), p. 74.
53. See McAulay (1986).
54. See Burstall (1986).
55. See McNeill (1993).
56. See Anderson (2002); McNeill (1993).
57. See Grandin (2004); McNeill (1993).

CHAPTER 23

1. 6 RAR commanders' diaries (AWM 95 7/6/5), 18 August 1966.
2. Ibid.
3. Stan Hodder interview, 8 August 2015.

4. Tony Stepney interview, 17 April 2015.
5. See Grandin (2004).
6. Parr (2006), p. 52.
7. Ham (2007), p. 239.
8. 105 Field Battery [105 Fd Bty]
    Enclosure 4–5 (AWM 95 3/5/43), 1–31
    August 1966.
9. 6 RAR commanders' diaries (AWM 95
    7/6/5), 18 August 1966.
10. McKay (1992), p. 101.
11. Mollison (2006), pp. 175–6.
12. See Burstall (1986).
13. Ibid.
14. See McKay (1992).
15. 6 RAR commanders' diaries (AWM 95
    7/6/5), 18 August 1966.
16. See McAulay (1986).
17. Mollison (2006), p. 174.
18. Steinbrook (1995), p. 56.
19. See Anderson (2002).
20. McAulay (1986), p. 81.
21. Ibid., p. 82.
22. See Mollison (2006).
23. See Anderson (2002); McNeill (1993).
24. Chamberlain (2011), pp. 30–2.
25. Ibid.
26. See Burstall (1986).
27. Geoff Kendall interview, 6 October
    2014.
28. McNeill (1993), p. 328.
29. Noel Grimes interview, 15 August 2015.
30. Graham Smith interview, 26 May 2015.
31. Buick & McKay (2000), p. 106.
32. See Buick & McKay (2000).
33. Caulfield (2007), pp. 297–8.
34. See Burstall (1986).
35. Ibid., pp. 101–2.
36. See Burstall (1986); McAulay (1986).
37. McAulay (1986), p. 98.
38. See Caulfield (2007).
39. Ibid., p. 300.
40. Burstall (1986), p. 101.
41. Bill Akell interview, 7 June 2015.

11. Graham Smith interview, 26 May 2015.
12. Bill Akell interview, 7 June 2015.
13. McAulay (1986), p. 99.
14. Burstall (1986), p. 102.
15. Ibid., p. 106.
16. Tony Stepney interview, 17 April 2015.
17. Burstall (1986), p. 107.
18. McAulay (1986), p. 96.
19. Dapin (2014), p. 138.
20. See McAulay (1986).
21. See Burstall (1986).
22. Ibid., p. 102.
23. See Grandin (2004).
24. See Parr (2006).
25. Dapin (2014), p. 139.
26. See Grandin (2004).
27. John Cash interview, 30 March 2015.
28. McNeill (1993), p. 329.
29. Burstall (1986), p. 102.
30. Ibid., p. 103.
31. Ibid., p. 105.
32. Ibid., p. 104.
33. Caulfield (2007), p. 294.
34. McGibbon (2010), p. 152.
35. See McNeill (1993).
36. Kevin Miller interview, 8 June 2015.
37. McAulay (1986), p. 88.
38. Ibid.
39. Ibid.
40. Tony Stepney interview, 17 April 2015.
41. See Burstall (1986).
42. Ibid.
43. Ibid., p. 108.
44. Ham (2007), p. 237.
45. Bill Akell interview, 7 June 2015.
46. McAulay (1986), p. 101.
47. Caulfield (2007), p. 303.
48. See Burstall (1986).
49. McAulay (1986), p. 102.
50. See McNeill (1993).
51. See Caulfield (2007).
52. See McAulay (1986).

CHAPTER 24

1. McNeill (1993), p. 328.
2. See Grandin (2004).
3. See Caulfield (2007).
4. See Burstall (1986); Grandin (2004).
5. Len Vine interview, 15 May 2015.
6. Tony Stepney interview, 17 April 2015.
7. Bill Akell interview, 7 June 2015.
8. Len Vine interview, 15 May 2015.
9. McNeill (1993), p. 328.
10. See Grandin (2004).

CHAPTER 25

1. 105 Field Battery [105 Fd Bty]
    Enclosure 4–5 (AWM 95 3/5/43), 1–31
    August 1966.
2. Mollison (2006), p. 162.
3. McAulay (1986), p. 82.
4. See Burstall (1986).
5. Ibid.
6. McAulay (1986), pp. 103–4.
7. See Smith (2015).
8. Mollison (2006), p. 167.
9. McAulay (1986), pp. 103–4.

10. Grandin (2004), p. 181.
11. See Mollison (2006).
12. McAulay (1986), p. 104.
13. Ibid., p. 102.
14. See Anderson (2002).
15. Mollison (2006), p. 169.
16. See Caulfield (2007).
17. See McAulay (1986); O'Neill (1993).
18. See McAulay (1986).
19. See Anderson (2002); O'Neill (1993).
20. Ibid.
21. McAulay (1986), p. 105.
22. Ibid.
23. Australian Army commanders' diaries 6 RAR (AWM 95 7/6/5), 17 August 1966.
24. Ibid.
25. McAulay (1986), p. 108.
26. See Grandin (2004); McFarlane (2000).
27. McAulay (1986), p. 196.
28. Mollison (2006), p. 173.
29. See Grandin (2004).
30. McAulay (1986), p. 196.
31. See Anderson (2002); Burstall (1986); McAulay (1986); O'Neill (1993).
32. McFarlane (2000), p. 265.
33. See Anderson (2002); O'Neill (1993).
34. O'Neill (1993), p. 336.
35. See Grandin (2004).
36. McAulay (1986), p. 107.
37. Ibid., pp. 107–8.
38. See McAulay (1986).
39. Ibid., p. 108; see also Smith (2015).
40. Kevin Miller interview, 8 June 2015.
41. O'Neill (1993), p. 338.
42. McGibbon (2010), p. 156.
43. See McAulay (1986).
44. Len Vine interview, 15 May 2015.
45. McAulay (1986), p. 109.
46. John Heslewood interview, 30 September 2014.
47. See Burstall (1986).
48. Grandin (2004), p. 202.
49. Bill Akell interview, 7 June 2015.
50. See Grandin (2004).
51. See Burstall (1986).
52. Mollison (2006), p. 176.
53. See McKay (1992).
54. Mollison (2006), p. 174.
55. See Grandin (2004).
56. Dapin (2014), p. 141.
57. Burstall (1986), pp. 119–20.
58. Mollison (2006), p. 174.
59. See Mollison (2006).
60. See Burstall (1986).
61. Mollison (2006), p. 171.
62. McAulay (1986), p. 111.
63. Burstall (1990), p. 104.
64. Len Vine interview, 15 May 2015.
65. McAulay (1986), p. 110.
66. O'Neill (1993), p. 338.
67. McAulay (1986), p. 112.
68. Ibid., p. 113.
69. Ibid.

CHAPTER 26

1. See Lamensdorf, J. D. (2006) *Write Home for Me: A Red Cross Woman in Vietnam*, Random House Australia, Sydney, p. 96.
2. Ibid.
3. See Burstall (1986).
4. Dapin (2014), p. 141.
5. Ibid., p. 140.
6. Ibid., p. 141.
7. See Buick & McKay (2000).
8. See Burstall (1986).
9. Caulfield (2007), p. 308.
10. See McKay (1992).
11. 6 RAR commanders' diaries (AWM 95 7/6/5), 18 August 1966.
12. See Burstall (1986).
13. Grandin (2004), p. 205.
14. Burstall (1986), p. 118.
15. McAulay (1986); O'Neill (1993); 6 RAR commanders' diaries (AWM 95 7/6/5), 18 August 1966.
16. See Grandin (2004).
17. Ibid., p. 206.
18. See Grandin (2004).
19. Caulfield (2007), p. 308.
20. See McAulay (1986).
21. See Burstall (1986).
22. McAulay (1986), p. 113.
23. See Burke (2005).
24. McGibbon (2010), p. 157.
25. See Burstall (1986).
26. McAulay (1986), p. 114.
27. Burstall (1986), p. 121.
28. Mollison (2006), p. 178.
29. See Burstall (1986).
30. Caulfield (2007), p. 309.
31. Mollison (2006), p. 177.
32. Ibid., p. 178.
33. Ibid.
34. See McAulay (1986).
35. Ham (2007), p. 240.

CHAPTER 27

1. Lamensdorf (2006), p. 97.
2. Ibid.

3. Ibid., p. 98.
4. See McAulay (1986).
5. Ibid., p. 118.
6. Ibid.
7. 6 RAR commanders' diaries (AWM 95 7/6/5), 18 August 1966.
8. See Anderson (2002); McAulay (1986).
9. Burstall (1986), p. 121.
10. See McNeill (1993).
11. 6 RAR commanders' diaries (AWM 95 7/6/5), 18 August 1966.
12. See McNeill (1993).
13. See Caulfield (2007).
14. 6 RAR commanders' diaries (AWM 95 7/6/5), 18 August 1966.
15. See Grandin (2004).
16. Ibid., p. 198.
17. 6 RAR commanders' diaries (AWM 95 7/6/5), 18 August 1966.
18. See McAulay (1986).
19. Ibid., p. 119.
20. See Mollison (2006).
21. McAulay (1986), pp. 119–20.
22. Ibid., p. 119.
23. See Grandin (2004).
24. See McAulay (1986); Grandin (2004).
25. Quote McAulay (1986), p. 118.
26. See Grandin (2004).
27. See Caulfield (2007); McAulay (1986); McNeill (1993).
28. See Mollison (2006).
29. See Anderson (2002); McNeill (1993).
30. Mollison (2006), p. 185.
31. See McNeill (1993).
32. Grandin (2004), p. 214.
33. See Grandin (2004).
34. Mollison (1986), p. 188.
35. Kevin Miller interview, 8 June 2015.
36. See Anderson (2002).
37. Buick & McKay (2000), pp. 108–9.
38. See Burstall (1986).
39. John Robbins interview, 20 May 2014.
40. John Cash interview, 30 March 2015.
41. Grandin (2004), p. 216.
42. Bill Akell interview, 7 June 2015.
43. Steinbrook (1995), pp. 56–7.
44. See Picken (2012).
45. Mollison (2006), p. 184.
46. Smith (2015).

CHAPTER 28

1. McAulay (1986), p. 126.
2. See Grandin (2004).
3. McAulay (1986), p. 126.
4. Ibid.

5. Burstall (1986), p. 130.
6. See Grandin (2004).
7. Caulfield (2007), p. 312.
8. See Grandin (2004).
9. Caulfield (2007), p. 313.
10. Grandin (2004), p. 218; see also McGibbon (2010).
11. Caulfield (2007), pp. 314–15.
12. See Burstall (1986).
13. Burstall (1986), p. 126.
14. John Robbins interview, 20 May 2015.
15. Ibid.
16. Burstall (1986), p. 126.
17. Graham Smith interview, 26 May 2015.
18. See Burstall (1986).
19. See Grandin (2004); McNeill (1993).
20. Graham Smith interview, 26 May 2015.
21. See McAulay (1986).
22. Smith (2015), p. 165.
23. See Grandin (2004); Smith 2015.
24. Mollison (2006), p. 192.
25. See McAulay (1986); McFarlane (2000).
26. See McNeill (1993).

CHAPTER 29

1. Dapin (2014), p. 142.
2. Mollison (2006), p. 193.
3. McAulay (1986), p. 128.
4. Ibid.
5. See Grandin (2004).
6. Ibid.
7. See Grandin (2004); McNeill (1993).
8. McFarlane (2000), pp. 267–8.
9. Dapin (2014), p. 142.
10. Burstall (1986), pp. 131–2.
11. Ibid., p. 132.
12. Graham Smith interview, 26 May 2015.
13. Buick & McKay (2000), p. 116.
14. Ibid.
15. Mollison (2006), p. 194; see also Horner (1995).
16. McNeill (1993), p. 342.
17. See McAulay (1986); McNeill (1993).
18. Steinbrook (1995), p. 57.
19. See Burstall (1986); McAulay (1986); McNeill (1993).
20. See Mollison (2006).
21. Steinbrook (1995), p. 57; see also Mollison (2006).
22. Bill Akell interview, 7 June 2015.
23. Burstall (1986), p. 131.
24. Noel Grimes interview, 15 April 2015.
25. See Grandin (2004).
26. Dapin (2014), p. 142.
27. Stan Hodder interview, 8 August 2015.

28. McAulay (1986), p. 129.
29. Parr (2006), p. 55.
30. See McNeill (1993).
31. Burstall (1986), p. 133.
32. Dapin (2014), p. 143.
33. Ibid., p. 142.
34. Parr (2006), p. 56.
35. McAulay (1986), p. 129.
36. Dapin (2014), p. 143.
37. See Grandin (2004).
38. Caulfield (2007), pp. 316–17.
39. Dapin (2014), p. 144.
40. McAulay (1986), pp. 129–30.
41. See Caulfield (2007).
42. Ibid., pp. 319–20.
43. See McNeill (1993).
44. McAulay (1986), p. 130.
45. Tony Stepney interview, 17 April 2015.
46. Stan Hodder interview, 8 August 2015.
47. Mollison (2006), p. 198.
48. Ibid.

CHAPTER 30

1. McAulay (1986), p. 130.
2. Mollison (2006), p. 197; see also Graham Smith interview, 26 May 2015.
3. McAulay (1986), p. 130.
4. McAulay (1986), pp. 130–1.
5. Grandin (2004), p. 227.
6. Ibid., pp. 230–1.
7. Burstall (1986), pp. 133–4.
8. Parr (2006), p. 56.
9. Buick & McKay (2000), p. 113.
10. Grandin (2004), p. 231.
11. McAulay (1986), p. 131.
12. Ibid.
13. See Ham (2007).
14. Grandin (2004), p. 227.
15. McAulay (1986), p. 132.
16. Parr (2006), p. 57.
17. Buick & McKay (2000), pp. 114–15.
18. Caulfield (2007), p. 322.
19. Graham Smith interview, 26 May 2015.
20. See Burstall (1986).
21. Ibid., p. 135.
22. See Burstall (1986).
23. McAulay (1986), p. 132.
24. Mollison (2006), p. 197.
25. Ibid.
26. Pound (2008), p. 139.
27. John Heslewood interview, 30 September 2014.
28. See McNeill (1993).
29. Burstall (1986), p. 139.
30. McAulay (1986), p. 134.

31. Caulfield (2007), pp. 322–3.
32. Grandin (2004), p. 228.
33. Ibid., p. 229.
34. See Grandin (2004).
35. McAulay (1986), p. 135.
36. See Grandin (2004).
37. Burstall (1986), p. 140.
38. McAulay (1986), pp. 133–4.
39. Ibid., p. 137.
40. See Smith (2015).
41. See Anderson (2002).
42. McAulay (1986), p. 134.
43. See Anderson (2002).
44. Dapin (2014), p. 145.
45. Graham Smith interview, 26 May 2015.
46. Noel Grimes interview, 15 April 2015.

CHAPTER 31

1. See McNeill (1993).
2. Ibid.
3. McAulay (1986), p. 138.
4. McNeill (1993), p. 347.
5. Ibid., p. 348.
6. See Burstall (1986).
7. McAulay (1986), p. 140.
8. Mollison (2006), pp. 199–200.
9. Parr (2006), p. 57.
10. Ham (2007), pp. 244–5.
11. Bill Akell interview, 7 June 2015.
12. Parr (2006), p. 57.
13. Tony Stepney interview, 17 April 2015.
14. Noel Grimes interview, 15 April 2015.
15. Ham (2007), p. 245.
16. McNeill (1993), p. 344.
17. See McNeill (1993); McAulay (1986).
18. See Buick & McKay (2000).
19. Ibid., p. 117.
20. See Grandin (2004).
21. Dapin (2014), p. 146.
22. Ibid., p. 147.
23. See Breen (2008); McNeill (1968, 1993).
24. See Buick & McKay (2000).

CHAPTER 32

1. Dapin (2014), p. 145.
2. Caulfield (2007), p. 325.
3. Parr (2006), p. 57.
4. Caulfield (2007), p. 326.
5. Ibid., pp. 325–6.
6. Dapin (2014), pp. 145–6.
7. McFarlane (2000), p. 269.
8. See McNeill (1993).
9. McAulay (1986), p. 133.
10. See Burstall (1986).
11. Ibid.

12. Burstall (1986), p. 141.
13. Ibid.
14. See Burstall (1986).
15. Grandin (2004), pp. 235–6.
16. See McAulay (1986); Chamberlain (2011, 2015).
17. See Chamberlain (2011); Grandin (2004).
18. See Burstall (1986).
19. See Burstall (1986); McNeill (1993).
20. Ibid.
21. See Mollison (2006).
22. McFarlane (2000), pp. 270–1.
23. See McAulay (1986); McNeill (1993).
24. Ibid.
25. Ibid.
26. See Odgers (1974).
27. See Grandin (2004).
28. See Caulfield (2007).
29. Dapin (2014), pp. 147–8.
30. See Grandin (2004).
31. Parr (2006), p. 57.
32. Kevin Miller interview, 8 June 2015.
33. See Burstall (1986).

CHAPTER 33

1. Burstall (1986), pp. 147–8.
2. See Burstall (1986); Dapin (2014).
3. Dapin (2014), p. 148.
4. Caulfield (2007), p. 327.
5. John Robbins interview, 20 May 2015.
6. Caulfield (2007), p. 314.
7. Lamensdorf (2006), p. 98.
8. Ibid.
9. See Burstall (1986).
10. Ibid., p. 150.
11. Caulfield (2007), p. 328.
12. Lamensdorf (2006), p. 104.
13. Dapin (2014), p. 150.
14. See Burstall (1986).
15. Noel Grimes interview, 15 April 2015.
16. Parr (2006), p. 65.
17. Ibid.
18. Grandin (2004), p. 241.
19. Lamensdorf (2006), p. 102.
20. Ibid.
21. See Caulfield (2007); McAulay (1986).
22. Ham (2007), p. 248.
23. Smith (2015), p. 241.
24. See Smith (2015).
25. See McNeill (1993); Smith 2015.
26. Department of the Prime Minister and Cabinet (2008) *Review of Recognition for the Battle of Long Tan*; Pearce, D. (2009) Australian Government Defence Honours and Awards Tribunal, *Inquiry into Unresolved Recognition Issues for the Battle of Long Tan*.
27. McNeill (1993), p. 357.
28. McAulay (1986), p. 131.
29. Noel Grimes interview, 15 April 2015.
30. See Burstall (1986).
31. Dapin (2014), p. 149.
32. Graham Smith interview, 26 May 2015.
33. Burstall (1986), p. 150.
34. Stan Hodder interview, 8 August 2015.
35. Burstall (1986), p. 151.
36. Graham Smith interview, 26 May 2015.
37. Ibid.
38. Caulfield (2007), p. 333.

EPILOGUE

1. Ekins, A. (2011) 'Unique memorial: the Long Tan Cross', *Wartime: Official Magazine of the Australian War Memorial*, Vol. 55, pp. 39–41.
2. Kevin Miller interview, 8 June 2015.
3. Burstall (1990), pp. 136–7.
4. See Ekins (2011).
5. Bill Akell interview, 7 June 2015.

Bibliography

**TELEPHONE INTERVIEWS –
6 RAR, D COMPANY LONG
TAN, VIETNAM WAR VETERANS**

Akell, Bill, CHQ Platoon (7 June 2015)

Beahan, David, 12 Platoon (30 May 2015)

Cash, John, 10 Platoon (30 March 2015)

Grimes, Noel, 12 Platoon (15 April 2015)

Heslewood, John, 11 Platoon (29 September 2014)

Hodder, Stan, 12 Platoon (8 April 2015)

Kendall, Geoff, 10 Platoon (10 October 2014)

Miller, Kevin, 12 Platoon (8 June 2015)

Robbins, John, 11 Platoon (20 May 2015)

Smith, Graham, CHQ Platoon (27 May 2015)

Stepney, Tony, 10 Platoon (17 April 2014)

Vine, Len, 10 Platoon (15 May 2015)

**AUSTRALIAN WAR MEMORIAL,
CANBERRA**

103 Signal Squadron Duty Officer's Log Annexes (AWM 95 6/1/5), 1–31 August 1966.

103 Signal Squadron Folio 1, Australian Army commanders' diaries (AWM 95 6/1/3), 1–30 June 1966.

105 Field Battery [105 Fd Bty] Enclosure 4–5 (AWM 95 3/5/43), 1–31 August 1966.

105 Field Battery [105 Fd Bty] Narrative, Operations log, Annexes, Summary and Enclosure (AWM 95 3/5/42), 1–31 August 1966.

5th Battalion Royal Australian Regiment, Australian Army commanders' diaries (AWM 95 7/5/6), 1–31 July 1966 Annex.

5th Battalion Royal Australian Regiment, Australian Army commanders' diaries, Annexes Part 1 (AWM 95 7/5/7), 1–31 August 1966.

6th Battalion Royal Australian Regiment Australian Army commanders' diaries (Vietnam) (AWM 95 7/6/4), 1–31 July 1966.

6th Battalion Royal Australian Regiment Australian Army commanders' diaries (Vietnam) (AWM 95 7/6/5), 1–31 August 1966.

ATF After Action Report, Operation Smithfield (AWM 181 1), December 1966.

Bishop letter to father (AWM PR91/18), 18 October 1966.

Headquarters, 1 Australian Task Force Commanding Officer After Action Report Operation Smithfield (AWM 95 1/4/26), 1–31 January 1967.

Headquarters, 1 Australian Task Force Duty Officer's log (AWM 95 1/4/7), 1–31 August 1966.

Headquarters, 1 Australian Task Force Narrative Duty Officer's log, Part 1 & 2 (AWM 95 1/4/6), 1–31 August 1966.

Interview transcript, tapes 17 & 18 with Brigadier O.D. Jackson (AWM 107), 9 March 1973.

OFFICIAL HISTORIES

Coulthard-Clark, C. (1995) *The RAAF in Vietnam: Australian Air Involvement in the Vietnam War 1962–1975*. The Official History of Australia's Involvement in Southeast Asian Conflicts 1948–1975, Allen & Unwin, Sydney.

Dennis, P. & Grey, J. (1996) *Emergency and Confrontation: Australian Military Operations in Malaya and Borneo 1950–1966*, The Official History of Australia's Involvement in Southeast Asian Conflicts 1948–1975, Allen & Unwin, Sydney.

Edwards, P. (1997) *A Nation at War: Politics, Society and Diplomacy During the Vietnam War 1965–1975*, The Official History of Australia's Involvement in Southeast Asian Conflicts 1948–1975, Allen & Unwin, Sydney.

McNeill, I. (1993) *To Long Tan: The Australian Army and the Vietnam War 1950–1966*. The Official History of Australia's Involvement in Southeast Asian Conflicts 1948–1975, Allen & Unwin, Sydney.

O'Keefe, B. (1994) *Medicine at War: Medical Aspects of Australia's Involvement in Southeast Asian Conflicts 1950–1972*. The Official History of Australia's Involvement in Southeast Asian Conflicts 1948–1975, Allen & Unwin, Sydney.

Pribbenow, M.L. (trans.) (2002) *Victory in Vietnam: The Official History of the People's Army of Vietnam, 1954–1975*, Military History Institute of Vietnam, University Press Kansas.

UNIT HISTORIES

Anderson, P. (2002) *When the Scorpion Stings: The History of the 3rd Cavalry Regiment, Vietnam, 1965–1972*, Allen & Unwin, Sydney.

Avery, B. (2001) *Our Secret War: The 4th Battalion the Royal Australian Regiment: Defending Malaysia Against Indonesian Confrontation, 1965–1967*, Slouch Hat Publications, Victoria.

Blaxland, J. (1998) *Signals Swift and Sure: A History of the Royal Australian Corps of Signals 1947–1972*, Royal Australian Corps of Signals Committee, Canberra.

Burke, A. (2005) *105th Battery: Royal Regiment of Australian Artillery: A Concise History*, A. Burke, Queensland.

Chamberlain, E. (2011) *The Viet Cong D445 Battalion: Their Story* (English translation, with significant assessments/comments in footnoting), E. Chamberlain, Victoria.

Chamberlain, E. (2015) *The Viet Cong D445 Battalion: Their Story (And the Battle of Long Tan* (map edition of ibid.), E. Chamberlain, Victoria.

Dinh, P.Q. (2005) *History of the 5th Infantry Division*, People's Army Publication House, Hanoi.

Greville, P.J. (2002) *The Royal Australian Engineers 1945 to 1972: Paving the Way*, Vol. 4, Corps Committee of the Royal Australian Engineers, Sydney.

Horner, D.M. & Bou, J. (2008) *Duty First: A History of the Royal Australian Regiment*, Allen & Unwin, Sydney.

McAulay, L. (1991) *The Fighting First: Combat Operations in Vietnam 1968–69 – the First Battalion, the Royal Australian Regiment*, Allen & Unwin, Sydney.

O'Neill, R.J. (1968) *Vietnam Task: The 5th Battalion, Royal Australian Regiment*, Cassell, Melbourne.

BOOKS/BOOK CHAPTERS

Barclay, G. (1988) *A Very Small Insurance Policy: The Politics of Australian Involvement in Vietnam, 1954–1967*, University of Queensland Press, St Lucia.

Bergerud, E. (1996) *Touched with Fire: The Land War in the South Pacific*, Viking, New York.

Blaxland, J. (2008) 'Consolidation and reorganisation: Australia 1950–65', in Horner, D.M. & Bou, J. (eds) *Duty First: A History of the Royal Australian Regiment*, Allen & Unwin, Sydney, pp. 105–23.

Breen, B. (1988) *First to Fight: Australian Diggers, NZ Kiwis and US Paratroopers in Vietnam, 1965–66*, Allen & Unwin, Sydney.

Breen, B. (2008) 'The build-up: Vietnam, 1965–67', in Horner, D.M. & Bou, J. (eds) *Duty First: A History of the Royal Australian Regiment*, Allen & Unwin, Sydney, pp. 171–95.

Buick, B. & McKay, G. (2000) '*All guts and no glory': The Story of a Long Tan Warrior*, Allen & Unwin, Sydney.

Burstall, T. (1986) *The Soldiers' Story: The Battle at Xa Long Tan Vietnam, 18 August 1966*, University of Queensland Press, St Lucia.

Burstall, T. (1990) *A Soldier Returns: A Long Tan Veteran Discovers the Other Side of Vietnam*, University of Queensland Press, St Lucia.

Buttigieg, P. (1992) 'Phil Buttigieg, Lance Corporal, 6RAR, Long Tan, 1966', in McKay, G. (ed.) *Vietnam Fragments: An Oral History of Australia's War*, Allen & Unwin, Sydney, pp. 99–103.

Caulfield, M. (2007) *The Vietnam Year: From the Jungle to the Australian Suburbs*, Hachette Australia, Sydney.

Dapin, M. (2014) *The Nashos' War: Australia's National Servicemen and Vietnam*, Viking, Melbourne.

Davies, B. (2012) *Vietnam: The Complete Story of the Australian War*, Allen & Unwin, Sydney.

Edwards, P. (1992) 'Some reflections on the Australian government's commitment to the Vietnam War', in Grey, J. & Doyle, J. (eds.) *Vietnam: War, Myth & Memory*, Allen & Unwin, Sydney, pp. 1–13.

Edwards, P. (2014) *Australia and the Vietnam War*, Australian War Memorial, Canberra & New South Books, Sydney.

Fall, B.B. (1966) *Viet-Nam Witness 1953–66*, Frederick A. Praeger, New York.

Fall, B.B. (2002) *Hell in a Very Small Place: The Siege of Dien Bien Phu*, Da Capo Press, New York.

Frost, F. (1987) *Australia's War in Vietnam*, Allen & Unwin, Sydney.

Giap, V.N. (1994) *Dien Bien Phu*, Gioi Publishers, Hanoi.

Grandin, B. (2004) *The Battle of Long Tan: As Told by the Commanders*, Allen & Unwin, Sydney.

Grey, J. & Doyle, J. (1992) *Vietnam: War, Myth & Memory*, Allen & Unwin, Sydney.

Ham, P. (2007) *Vietnam: The Australian War*, HarperCollins, Sydney.

Healy, J. (2008) 'A nine-battalion regiment: Australia, Malaysia and Singapore, 1965–73', in Horner, D.M. & Bou, J. (eds) *Duty First: A History of the Royal Australian Regiment*, Allen & Unwin, Sydney, pp. 149–69.

Horner, D.M. (1989) *SAS: Phantoms of the Jungle – A History of the Australian Special Air Service*, Allen & Unwin, Sydney.

Horner, D.M. (1995) *The Gunners: A History of Australian Artillery*, Allen & Unwin, Sydney.

Horner, D.M. (2000) *Defence Supremo: Frederick Shedden and the Making of Australian Defence Policy*, Allen & Unwin, Sydney.

Horner, D.M. (2005) *Strategic Command: General Sir John Wilton and Australia's Asian Wars*, Oxford University Press, Melbourne.

Horner, D.M. (2008) 'Confrontation: Malaysia and Borneo, 1960–66', in Horner, D.M. & Bou, J. (eds) *Duty First: A History of the Royal Australian Regiment*, Allen & Unwin, Sydney, pp. 124–48.

Horner, D.M. (2009) *In Action with the SAS*, Allen & Unwin, Sydney.

Kolko, G. (1985) *Anatomy of a War: Vietnam, the United States, and the Modern Historical Experience*, Phoenix Press, London.

Krenpinevich, A.F. (1986) *The Army and Vietnam*, Johns Hopkins University Press, Baltimore.

Lamensdorf, J.D. (2006) *Write Home for Me: A Red Cross Woman in Vietnam*, Random House Australia, Sydney.

McAulay, L.F. (1986) *The Battle of Long Tan: The Legend of Anzac Upheld*, Hutchinson, Melbourne.

McAulay, L.F. (2005) *Blue Lanyard, Red Banner: The Capture of a Vietcong Headquarters by 1st Battalion, Royal Australian Regiment, Operation CRIMP 8–14 January 1966*, Banner Books, Queensland.

McFarlane, B. (2000) *We Band of Brothers: A True Australian Adventure Story*, B.W. McFarlane, New South Wales.

McGibbon, I. (2010) *New Zealand's Vietnam War: A History of Combat, Commitment and Controversy*, Exisle Publishing, Auckland.

McKay, G. (1992) *Vietnam Fragments: An Oral History of Australians at War*, Allen & Unwin, Sydney.

Mangold, T. & Penycate, J. (1985) *The Tunnels of Cu Chi: A Remarkable Story of War*, Guild Publishing, London.

Mollison, C. (2006) *Long Tan and Beyond: Alpha Company 6 RAR in Vietnam 1966–67*, Cobbs Crossing Publications, Queensland.

Newman, S.D. (1988) *Vietnam Gunners: 161 Battery RNZA, South Vietnam, 1965–71*, Moana Press, New Zealand.

Nguyen, Lien-Hang (2012) *Hanoi's War: An International History of the War for Peace in Vietnam*, University of North Carolina Press.

Odgers, G. (1974) *Mission Vietnam: Royal Australian Air Force Operations 1964–1972*, Australian Government Publishing Service, Canberra.

'Origins of the insurgency in South Vietnam, 1954–1960' (1971), in *The Pentagon Papers* (Senator Gravel edition), Beacon Press, Boston, Vol. 1, pp. 242–69.

Palazzo, A. (2001) *The Australian Army: A History of Its Organization 1901–2001*, Oxford University Press, Melbourne.

Palazzo, A. (2009) *Australian Military Operations in Vietnam*, Australian Army Campaign Series No. 3 (2nd edn), Australian Army History Unit, Canberra.

Parr, A. (2006) *Memories of Vietnam*, Murray Tucker, Victoria.

Picken, B. (2006) *Viet Nam Diggers' Language: Abbreviations, Acronyms, Terms and Jargon of the Viet Nam War*, Australian Military History Publications, Loftus.

Picken, B. (2012) *Fire Support Bases Vietnam: Australian and Allied Fire Support Base Locations and Main Support Units*, Big Sky Publishing, Sydney.

Pike, D. (1966) *Viet Cong: The Organization and Techniques of the National Liberation Front of South Vietnam*, MIT Press, Massachusetts.

Pound, G. (2008) *What Soldiers Do: An Australian Artilleryman in Vietnam*, Australian Military History Press, Loftus.

Race, J. (1972) *War Comes to Long An: Revolutionary Conflict in a Vietnamese Province*, University of California Press, Berkeley.

Sabben, D. (2005) *Through Enemy Eyes*, Allen & Unwin, Sydney. [Author's note: This is historical fiction – not used as a reference, but well researched and a very good read.]

Schulzinger, R.D. (1997) *A Time for War: The United States and Vietnam 1941–1975*, Oxford University Press, New York.

Sexton, M. (2002) *War for the Asking: How Australia Invited Itself to Vietnam*, New Holland, Sydney.

Smith, A.H. (2008) *Gunners in Borneo: Artillery During Indonesian Confrontation 1962–1966*, Australian Artillery Historical Company, Manly.

Smith, A.H. (2011) *Do Unto Others: Counter Bombardment in Australia's Military Campaigns*, Big Sky Publishing, Sydney.

Smith, H. (2015) *Long Tan: The Start of a Lifelong Battle*, Big Sky Publishing, Sydney.

Smith, N.C. (1999) *Nothing Short of War: With the Australian Army in Borneo 1962–66*, Citadel Press, Victoria.

Steinbrook, G.L. (1995) *Allies and Mates: An American Soldier with the Australians and New Zealanders in Vietnam, 1966–67*, University of Nebraska Press.

Thomson, J. & MacGregor, S. (2011) *Tunnel Rats: The Larrikin Aussie Legends who Discovered the Vietcong's Secret Weapon*, Allen & Unwin, Sydney.

Threlfall, A. (2014) *Jungle Warriors: From Tobruk to Kokoda and Beyond – How the Australian Army Became the World's Most Deadly Jungle Fighting Force*, Allen & Unwin, Sydney.

Truong, N.T. (1985) *A Vietcong Memoir*, Harcourt Brace Jovanovich, New York.

Watt, A. (1968) *Vietnam: An Australian Analysis*, F.W. Cheshire, Melbourne.

Windrow, M. (2004) *The Last Valley: Dien Bien Phu and the French Defeat in Vietnam*, Weidenfeld & Nicolson, London.

JOURNALS/NEWSPAPERS/MISCELLANEOUS

Blaxland, J. (2012) 'Listening to the enemy: signals intelligence played a key role in Malaya, Borneo and Vietnam', *Wartime: Official Magazine of the Australian War Memorial*, Issue 57, pp. 30–35.

Burgess, P. (1966) '6th Battalion in baptism of fire', *Sydney Morning Herald*, 1 August, p. 4.

David Sabben's Home Page (includes an excellent 'Animated Long Tan PowerPoint presentation'). <www.sabben.com/>, accessed 3 November 2015.

Ekins, A. (2003) 'Death due to friendly fire: the life and death of WO Jack Kirby', *Wartime: Official Magazine of the Australian War Memorial*, Issue 21, pp. 36–9.

Ekins, A. (2011) 'A very close thing indeed', *Wartime: Official Magazine of the Australian War Memorial*, Issue 55, pp. 35–8.

Ekins, A. (2011) 'Unique memorial: the Long Tan Cross', *Wartime: Official Magazine of the Australian War Memorial*, Issue 55, pp. 39–41.

Ekins, A. (2011) 'Unravelling the riddles of Long Tan', *Wartime: Official Magazine of the Australian War Memorial*, Issue 55, pp. 42–47.

Hannigan, R.R. (1968) *A Record of the Battle of Long Tan from Task Force HQ log: US Presidential Citation for a Rifle Company.*

'Missing Presumed Dead – A Casualty of the Vietnam War – A gunner lost in the system for 41 years. Gunner Philip Charles Norris, 103 Field Battery RAA, 1st Field Regiment RAA. WIA 17 August 1966, died 3 August 2012' <www.103fieldbatteryraa.net/missing_presumed_dead/missing_presumed_dead.html>, accessed 3 November 2015.

Smith, H. (n.d.) *The Battle of Long Tan, South Vietnam: 18 August 1966, Biography Lieutenant Colonel Harry Smith, MC, SG* <battleoflongtan.reddunefilms.com/wp-content/uploads/2011/03/Long-Tan-Harry-Smith-Biography.pdf>

Smith, H. (n.d.) *The Story Behind the Battle of Long Tan*, Radschool Association Magazine (RAAF) 39.

Smith, H. (2006) 'Eyewitness: Long Tan "No time for fear"', *Wartime: Official Magazine of the Australian War Memorial*, Issue 35, pp. 10–16.

CONFERENCE PAPER

Chamberlain, E. (2014), *The Enemy, and Intelligence in Phuoc Tuy Province: Successes and Failures*, Phillip Island, National Vietnam Veterans' Museum (NVVM), unpublished transcript, 12 April 2014.

INQUIRIES

Department of Prime Minister and Cabinet (2008) *Review of Recognition of Battle of Long Tan.*

Pearce, D. (2009) Australian Government Defence Honours and Awards Tribunal, *Inquiry into Unresolved Recognition Issues for the Battle of Long Tan.*

Index